THE HOLOCAUST'S JEWISH CALENDARS

JEWISH LITERATURE AND CULTURE

Alvin H. Rosenfeld, editor

THE HOLOCAUST'S JEWISH CALENDARS

Keeping Time Sacred,

Making Time Holy

Alan Rosen

Indiana University Press

This book is a publication of

Indiana University Press
Office of Scholarly Publishing
Herman B Wells Library 350
1320 East 10th Street
Bloomington, Indiana 47405 USA

iupress.indiana.edu

Manufactured in the United States of America

Cataloging information is available from the Library of Congress.

ISBN 978-0-253-03826-5 (hardback)
ISBN 978-0-253-03827-2 (paperback)
ISBN 978-0-253-03828-9 (ebook)

1 2 3 4 5   24 23 22 21 20 19

*For my teacher, Eliezer ben Shlomo HaLevi Wiesel,
of righteous blessed memory.*

Contents

Preface

Prosaic during times of peace and tranquility, calendars take on many new dimensions in times of war and crisis. Thus did calendars and calendar making assume a special role during the Holocaust. Holocaust-era calendars were produced in ghettos (both by individuals and, in some cases, by the ghetto authorities), fashioned in labor and concentration camps, crafted in hiding, and, in the case of France, dauntingly circulated while under Nazi occupation. I have reviewed approximately forty examples, obtained largely from diverse archives (including those at Yad Vashem, the United States Holocaust Memorial Museum, and the Ghetto Fighters' Museum) as well as from personal holdings. I have been alerted to other wartime calendars by references in diaries, oral and written memoirs, or historical accounts. A handful of short articles (three authored by one researcher in the 1960s) have sporadically dealt with World War II–era Jewish calendars, though each one in a specialized rather than a general way.[1] Otherwise, the field is wide open.

The three dozen or so wartime calendars that I refer to in my book may seem like a mere ripple in an ocean of inchoate time. Does such a small sample actually document a general effort to track Jewish time during the Holocaust? Doesn't it actually show how rare it was to pursue such a course in times fraught with danger and travail? I will deal with these questions in my remarks that introduce the relevant chapters. But there are several considerations in response to these questions (versions of which have been earnestly asked in forums where I have lectured on the topic).

First, the calendars that survive are only a portion of those produced in the caldron of the Holocaust, a statement that can be made about any of the artifacts that remain from that period. Exactly what portion is, of course, unknown. Yet the very fact that what survived is a remnant of some greater number means that we cannot infer how narrow or wide the phenomenon was. Second, my study includes diaries in order to show that giving attention to the Jewish calendar came through other vehicles than the calendars themselves.[2] Third, in contrast to these diaries, which were generally private compositions not intended to be circulated, calendars were fashioned in order to serve a smaller or larger community. This was obviously true for calendars of which multiple copies were produced. But it was true as well for handwritten calendars of which a single copy was made. So the population of those who benefitted by the wartime calendars was greater than the number of calendars per se.

With no inventory of calendars and almost no reference to them in Holocaust scholarship, I set about combing archives in search of wartime calendars. In a modest way, this book has assembled a collection of calendars where previously there was a spattering here and there (a list appears in appendix 1). A few archives yielded a trove, some museums added to it, books contained leads, and several individuals were kind enough to make connections with family, friends, or teachers who had authored wartime calendars. As often as possible, I have met (or spoken by phone) with the authors, or, if they were no longer alive, with family members. These conversations were precious and informative.

Study of wartime calendars (and diaries that served a calendrical purpose), I believe, can steer the issue of time and the Holocaust in a new direction. Previous study has focused on the disruption of time; since the calendar is associated with normal time—time methodically mapped by day, week, month, and year—calendars have generally received minimal attention. This approach has been so pervasive that even attempts to broaden the analysis of time's diverse roles have still neglected the calendar.

Such neglect, moreover, excludes the important role of the *Jewish calendar*, thereby leaving out almost entirely the multicalendar dimension of European Jewish culture—which means that Europe's Jews experienced the Holocaust by way of the Jewish calendar as well as the Gregorian or Julian (the latter of which was still in use in some countries). Wartime calendars and diaries that served as surrogate calendars help us reclaim the way Jews saw the world that imploded before their eyes.

This book aims to fill a gap in the study of the Jewish victims of the Holocaust. It describes the multifaceted calendar consciousness of these communities, analyzes the significance of the disruption of that consciousness, and recounts the attempt to overcome it. Because calendar consciousness was a basic element of Jewish life, especially in eastern Europe, this inquiry will benefit any study of the Holocaust's Jewish victims. It will extend the recent focus on time and the calendar in Jewish studies to a period that has not been examined in this light. It also offers a case study to those who wish to examine more broadly the relation between persecution and the calendar, particularly in connection to genocide or slavery, where the struggle over control of chronology is always a vital issue.

I come to this project from many years of interdisciplinary research on victim response to the Holocaust. Two of my book projects—one on the problem of English in Holocaust writing (*Sounds of Defiance*, 2005), the other on early postwar victim testimony (*The Wonder of Their Voices*, 2010)—have particularly nurtured my current focus on the calendar. In the first case, I noted that the evolution of English-language Holocaust writing contains many narratives that brood over the calendar's commemorative role. In the second case, I was struck by how the displaced persons interviewed by psychologist David Boder in 1946, having endured the war largely on the margins of civilization, often groped for time coordinates as they recounted their grim wartime tales. In different ways, each project alerted me to the importance of calendar consciousness as a factor in Holocaust-related events and stories. What was a side issue in those books becomes a central one here.

Notes

1. Rabbi Tovia Preschel, "The French Jewish Calendar during the Shoah," *HaDoar* (5723/1962) [Hebrew]; Rabbi Tovia Preschel, "The Jewish Calendar in Belgium during the Shoah," *HaDoar* (5724/1963) [Hebrew]; an English-language article dealing with the wartime Belgium calendar appeared almost four decades later: Pearl Herzog, "Purim Vinz," *Mishpacha* (Kolmus) (March 16, 2011); Rabbi Tovia Preschel, "Calendars in the Theresienstadt Ghetto," *HaDoar* (5726/1966) [Hebrew]; Jacquot Grunewald, "Calendriers de la Resistance," *l'Arche* 498–99 (Sept. 1999); Rabbi Isaac Avigdor, "The Camp Calendar of Buchenwald," in *Faith after the Flames*, New Haven, 2005, pp. 95–106; Bracha Stein, "My Father's Secret Sanctuary," *Mishpacha: Jewish Family Weekly* 313 (5770/2010), pp. 32–40. The latter considers the life and artistry of Rabbi Asher Berlinger, who continued his artistic endeavors—including the crafting of two Jewish calendars—while imprisoned in the Theresienstadt ghetto.

2. I make occasional reference to other forms of writing that use multiple calendars—particularly scholarly chronologies of the Holocaust—but do not consider them systematically. In this respect, the multicalendrical dating of letters written during the Holocaust deserves its own study.

Acknowledgments

Friends have been more than generous: Yisrael Cohen, Martin and Joann Farren, Rabbi Joseph and Reizel Polak, Dr. Jeff Shapiro, Rabbi Avraham Zalman and the late Rochel Weiner, a"h, Rabbi Moshe Weiner, Rabbi Dov Teitz, Rabbi Yeshoshua Looks, Rabbi Moshe Leiner, Rabbi Nehemia Polen, Gershon Greenberg, Adele Reinharz and Barry Walfish, Judy Wilkenfeld, Konrad Kwiet, Herb Levine, Franny Schnall, Don and Dr. Yehudis Mishell, Rabbi Yaakov Feldheim, David Patterson, Lee Monk, Neal Lipsitz, and Avraham Dubosky.

The staff at a number of archives provided indispensable help: at the United States Holocaust Memorial Museum, Susan Snyder, Teresa Pollin, Jane Klinger, Sonya Issaeva, and Judith Cohen; at Yad Vashem, Riki Bodenheimer, Michael Tal, Leah Teichtal, and Emmanuelle Moscovitz; at the Ghetto Fighters' Museum, Noam Rachmilevitch; at Westerbork, Guido Abuys; at the Museum of Jewish Heritage, Esther Brumberg and Jennifer Roberts; and at the Jewish Museum of Prague, Misha Seidenberg, Klára Kinzlerová, and Martin Jelinek.

Many other friends and colleagues have responded with enthusiasm and knowledge: Esther Farbstein, David Roskies, Deborah Dwork, Sacha Stern, Jared Stark, Wolf Gruner, Laurence Roth, Beate Müller, Clare Rosenson, Rabbi Eli Ruben, Uri Kaploun, Michael Chigel, Michael Berenbaum, Simone Gigliotti, Florent Brayard, Dina Goldschmidt, Lisa Peschel, Pavel Sladek, Jory Debenham, Michael Beckerman, Marta Malá, Michal Frankl, Stephanie and Ephraim Kaye, Havi Dreyfus, David Silberklang, Dan Michman, Dalia Ofer, Bella Gutterman, Eliot and Iael Nidam-Orvieto, and Alyson Brown.

The authors of calendars and, importantly, their families and friends were especially generous in sharing with me their insights on wartime calendar making. These include Rabbi Yehoshua Neuwirth, ztz"l, Rebbetzin Neuwirth, and their daughter, Rebbetzin Nechama Shirkin; Yosef Roosen; Yehuda Van Dyck; Bernard Hammelburg (grandson of Rabbi Shimon Hammelburg); Rabbi Yisrael Scheiner; Rabbi Asher Berlinger's daughter Rosie Baum and niece Helen Gross; Ann Goldberg; Rabbi Yisrael Simcha Zelmann's daughter Yehudis Eichenthal and grandchildren Avraham Zelmann, Dovid Zelmann, and Hanni Oppenheim. Others provided resourceful help: a friend, Rabbi Hananya Kahn, was a crucial link in establishing contact with the Zelmann family; Rabbi Moshe Kruskal was more than generous in providing an intact version of Rabbi Zelmann's calendar; Hilda Zimche; Rabbi Yaakov Avigdor's daughter-in-law, grandson Rabbi Mordechai Avigdor, and friend R. Yosef Friedenson, z"l; Tsewie and Annette Herschel;

Rebbetzin Golda Finkler's daughter, Kaja Finkler; and Otto Wolf's nieces Eva and Hanra Garda.

My countless meetings and phone conversations with Sophie Sohlberg over six years have been crucial to writing this book and understanding the profound nature of Jewish calendar making in those difficult years.

I have been fortunate to present versions of this study in nurturing venues, including the University of Maryland (Sheila Jelen); Goucher College (Uta Larkey); Holy Cross College (Tom Landry and Alan Avery-Peck); Vanderbilt University (Leah Marcus); University of Nevada, Las Vegas (Liz Spaulding); Florida Atlantic University (Alan Berger); Chapman University (Marilyn Harran); UCLA 1939 Club (Todd Pressner); Leeds University (Steven Muir); Cornell University (Deborah Starr), Susquehanna University (Lawrence Roth); the Lauder Business School in Vienna (Michael Chigel); Otterbein College (Paul Eisenstein); the Central Synagogue of Sydney, Australia (Rabbi Levi Wolf); University of Sydney (Konrad Kwiet); Western Galilee College (Boaz Cohen); Northwestern University (Phyllis Lassner); Johns Hopkins University (Marc Caplan); Claremont McKenna College (Wendy Lower); University of Michigan (Anita Norich); Michigan State University (Ken Waltzer); and Boston College (Ruth Langer).

Versions of different chapters and sections thereof have appeared in the following publications: "Yiddish and the Holocaust," *In geveb* (August 2015), https://ingeveb.org/articles/yiddish-and-the-holocaust, August 26, 2015; "Tracking Jewish Time in Auschwitz," *Yad Vashem Studies* (fall 2014), pp. 11–46; "Hidden Time: Calendar Consciousness on the Edge of Destruction," in *Hiding, Sheltering, and Borrowed Identities*, ed. Dan Michman (Jerusalem: Yad Vashem, 2018); "The Languages of Time: Translating Calendar Dates in Holocaust Diaries," *Holocaust and Genocide Studies* 26 (2012): pp. 276–93; "Today Is the Day: Reading between the Lines of the Lubavitcher Rebbe's Holocaust-Era Calendar," *Hasidology*/Chabad.org (2012); "On Calendars and the Holocaust," *Jewish Action* (fall 2011).

My wife, Ruth, and our children—Shoshana Leah and her husband Yehuda Bornstein, Tzvia Rachel, Noam Dov, and Rina—have provided unflagging support and care, features that much more important, I believe, when it comes to the study of this difficult period of history. But beyond that, they have been companions and advisers through the course of this study. Their knowledge, depth, and intelligence carried along much of the research and wisely inform a good deal of my commentary. As always, my teacher, Elie Wiesel, of righteous blessed memory, offered important information, wise counsel, and ongoing inspiration.

I think it's fair to say that I would never have been so focused on the Jewish calendar's significance were it not for the Lubavitcher Rebbe's teachings, which constantly give attention to all facets of the calendar's bearing on life and death, learning and commemoration, creation and redemption—and, above all, the special meaning of any given day, week, month, and year. A taste of these teachings can be found in my final chapter, where I discuss his wartime calendar book, *Hayom yom*. But his teachings went on for nearly fifty years, woven into the seams of his great corpus of Torah teaching, analysis, and meditation. Whatever might be worthy of consideration here grows out of my effort to adapt his extraordinary calendar sensitivity to my own purposes.

THE HOLOCAUST'S JEWISH CALENDARS

Introduction

Rabbi Yisrael Simcha Zelmann asked that, when his time came, he be buried with the Jewish calendar he had composed in the Westerbork concentration camp.

I couldn't believe I had heard his grandson correctly. "Do you mean," I queried, "that he asked for it to be put with him in his grave?"

I was dumbfounded. Not because I thought that Rabbi Zelmann's request was absurd or outlandish, or that it expressed an exaggerated sense of the artifact's worth. On the contrary, I was overwhelmed because his desire to be buried with the calendar, his singling out among all others this particular possession to accompany him to his final resting place, corresponded exactly to my estimation of the calendar's importance. To my mind, his calendar was a work of art, a masterpiece, a ledger on which the author had inscribed the lineaments of a Jewish soul. Of this I had no doubt; I myself was sure of its significance. But I had no idea that anyone, least of all the distinguished, learned rabbi who had fashioned the calendar in a place of such travail, shared this view. Now I knew that he did.

The request was unusual in other ways. Traditional Jewish burial practice generally counsels that one not take to the grave any possessions, sacred or otherwise. No keepsakes, mementos, jewelry; not even wedding rings or objects with a similar depth of sentimental value. Not that those items are looked at askance or branded with evil associations. They are considered precious and accorded great value by the family or friends who inherit them. But they are the stuff of life and thus do not accompany the deceased into the grave. To be sure, there are exceptions, prompted by the customs of certain groups or by the individual initiative of a Jew who believes, for example, a specific article will serve as an advocate for him or her in the world to come. But this was the exception to the rule. So for Rabbi Zelmann to make the request to have the calendar—or, indeed, any keepsake—join him in the grave was highly unusual; the object in question had to have had special meaning, had to have been something quite out of the ordinary, for the request to be made in the first place.

There were, moreover, other objects that might have taken priority. Rabbi Zelmann had had with him in the camps a Megilat Esther, a handwritten parchment scroll of the biblical Book of Esther, which is ritually recited on the holiday of Purim. He also had in his possession his own manuscripts, Torah commentaries

Fig. Intro.1: Imprisoned in the Westerbork transit camp in Holland, Rabbi Yisrael Simcha Zelmann composed a typed Jewish calendar for the year 5704 (1943–44). The calendar meant so much to Rabbi Zelmann that, thirty years later, he arranged to have it accompany him to the grave in Jerusalem. Courtesy of Rabbi Moshe Kruskal, who as a young child was deported with parents and siblings to Westerbork.

composed during the war and somehow, miraculously, held on to. But the calendar trumped them all.

One question remained: was his request honored? When his time came in 5734 (1974), at the end of a remarkable life filled with losses, but also with epic scenes of being reunited with wife and children, did the calendar accompany him to the grave? Yes, I was informed by his grandson, the original calendar was buried with him.

This was much more than I had expected. I told the grandson that he had, with immense generosity, just given me the first sentence of my book.

Such devotion to a calendar is clearly exceptional. How could it be that something seemingly so unexceptional could assume monumental significance? How could a run-of-the-mill object of daily life acquire this kind of prestige? Further, calendars are generally a tool we use from year to year and then, without thinking twice, discard. Once the calendar does what it was designed to do, it fulfills its purpose. It is not a book to be reread, or a photograph to be framed. It is rather to be cast off in order to make way for next year's calendar. Why in Rabbi Zelmann's case was it held on to with such reverence and tenacity?

Calendars are usually ordinary, plentiful, taken-for-granted items in daily life, remarkable, if at all, for the pictures or photographs that adorn them. Hung on walls, placed on desks, carried in pockets (and, more recently, read virtually on phones and computers), calendars are rarely surprising. Whether large or small, ornate or plain, they are usually the model of predictability. Days, weeks, and months follow one another, and page after page (or column after column) mirrors the one that came before. Now and then a day is singled out, highlighted or annotated, designating a holiday or anniversary. That too is routine, for calendars generally alternate between the ordinary and the extraordinary, the commonplace and the exceptional, or in a religious idiom, the mundane and the sacred (with more of the former than the latter). And it is exactly this predictability that makes a calendar attractive and that allows us to use it to bring order to our lives.

During the Holocaust, however, all of this predictability fell by the wayside. And the tool by which one normally kept track of time became a rare commodity. "After the everyday Jewish community life came to a halt," writes Osher Lehmann about daily life in wartime Amsterdam circa 1943, "common things such as a *luach* [a Jewish calendar], which most of us take for granted, were no longer available."[1] The calendar wasn't of course the only thing that became scarce. Wartime privation meant that many of the items common to daily life—food, clothes, shelter, jobs, money, and the list goes on—were often difficult if not impossible to come by. But the fact that calendars were "no longer available" is regularly overlooked just because calendars, despite their importance, are usually small and unobtrusive, part of the unremarkable furniture—one of the "common things," as Osher Lehmann so sensibly termed it—of daily life.

Unremarkable though it may have been, the calendar's role had an extra level of significance. For European Jewish culture took as a point of reference *both the Jewish calendar and the civil one*, defining events and experience along two parallel continuums. For the traditional Jewish communities of eastern Europe and elsewhere, moreover, the Jewish calendar was eminently consequential, since the very flow of family and social life depended on the exact marking of the weekly Sabbath, the monthly new moon, and the seasonal holidays. Hence, the Jewish victims also tracked the unfolding of wartime events according to this Sabbath and the festival-oriented Jewish calendar. The Nazi invasion of Poland took place not only on Friday morning, September 1, 1939, but on erev Shabbat (the day before the onset of the Sabbath), Elul 17, 5699, in the month when Jews prepare with special prayers for the onset of the Jewish New Year (5700) and, in this case, a fraught transition to the new fifty-eighth century. As we will see, reckoning the date of wartime events according to this alternative template had a range of practical, cultural, and religious implications.

Described as a lunasolar calendar, the Jewish calendar has some features that overlap with the Gregorian and some that are distinctive.[2] It too is generally divided into twelve months, a year usually numbering 354 days.[3] The months always commence at the new moon (hence the *lunar* designation), last 29 or 30 days, and bear names harking back to ancient Babylonia—the first three, for example, being Tishrei (when Rosh Hashana occurs), Cheshvan, and Kislev (when Chanukah begins). In contrast, the days are known not by names but by ordinal numbers (Sunday is "the first day," Monday is "the second day," etc.). The lone exception is the seventh day, called Shabbat (or, in Ashkenazi pronunciation, Shabbes), the Sabbath day. Notably, Jewish days begin with the onset of night. The year count is traditionally dated from the creation of the world. In the Jewish calendar, then, the Holocaust took place from the end of the year 5699 through the middle of the year 5705.[4] As I write these lines in the year 5777 (2017), we are, according to the Jewish calendar, still in the century of the Holocaust.

Most academic study of the Holocaust simply filters out the Jewish calendar. This omission occurs for several reasons. For one, it presumes the subject can be studied without reference to the Jewish calendar, which is deemed meaningful only for those conversant with it. The Jewish calendar plays an indirect role when the Jewish holidays—Rosh Hashana, Yom Kippur, Passover, and so on—rise to the surface of the historical narrative. But that doesn't have to do with the Jewish calendar per se but rather with the Jewish way of life. Just as one can, in daily life today, honor a holiday without thinking twice about why it seemingly falls on different dates from year to year in the Gregorian calendar, so one can be guided by the same approach in the study of the Holocaust. Another reason may well be that the Jewish calendar is thought to be a body of knowledge too arcane for the non-Jewish scholar or reader, or for the Jewish scholar or reader not schooled in the finer points of Jewish tradition. This rationale, however, makes a basic understanding of the Jewish calendar far more difficult than it needs to be.

In a strange twist, the Jewish calendar most often comes into view in relation to the Holocaust through the perverse use made of it by the perpetrators. In a number of cases, the Nazis methodically carried out murderous actions on days of special sanctity in the Jewish calendar. This form of perversion clearly shows another dimension of the enemy's war against the Jews.[5] Yet to come to know of the Jewish calendar only through such a perspective obscures the role it played for the Jews themselves. Ironically, the student learns more about the significance of the Jewish calendar during the Holocaust—even about the very *existence* of a Jewish calendar—from the enemy's manipulations of it than from the Jews' dedication to it. Attention to the spectrum of Jewish calendars fashioned in ghettos, in camps, and in hiding helps shift the emphasis from the enemy's manipulation to the Jew's dedication.

The upheaval of the Holocaust, which destroyed much of European Jewry over a period of less than six years, also wreaked havoc on Jewish timekeeping. From early on, as we know, the persecutors uprooted Jewish communities and deprived them of basic physical and cultural necessities. This scourge of material resources reached its zenith in the concentration camps, which, according to Yaffa Eliach, "placed men [sic] outside the sphere of societal time and place."[6] Bereft of virtually all personal items, the victims' "time-consciousness" suffered as well. It often became impossible simply to keep track of the day's date.

Losing track of time and thus being at a loss as to just when to observe sacred days was confronted early on in Jewish history. The Talmud speaks of losing one's way in the desert and thereby forgetting which day of the week it is. The most important consideration is the loss of awareness of when Shabbat takes place.

This is no academic question meant to satisfy one's curiosity, nor simply a desire, fulfilled by keeping track of the days of the week, to maintain a sense of cognitive orientation and psychological stability. It rather concerns one's fundamental responsibility to guard the Sabbath day's special sanctity. This is done, on the one hand, by refraining from a formidable array of weekday activities, and, on the other, by performing at the onset and conclusion of the Sabbath special ceremonies that usher the sanctity in and out. If someone becomes lost, disoriented, and unsure of the day of the week, it becomes impossible to know precisely when to refrain from certain activities and when to perform the requisite ceremonies. As a result, every day becomes like the next, no one of them different from the others.

The Talmudic sages believed that this situation was intolerable, even temporarily—that Jewish life was predicated on the observance of a Sabbath day, one day out of seven set off from the rest. They thus debated how to provide a stopgap measure during the period of being lost and disoriented. One sage believes it proper to count six days and then designate the seventh as Shabbat; a second sage believes it best to observe Shabbat on the very first day and then proceed to count six. The first opinion ends up holding sway. But exactly how to observe the Shabbat under conditions of privation is also a matter of discussion and controversy. What is essential is to mark the onset and departure of the designated holy day, so that the idea of a holy day of rest set apart from the other days of the week should remain, even if the actual day is in doubt. No idle speculation, this manner of determining the Shabbat day under such oppressive conditions has thereafter been included in all major guides to observance, medieval and modern alike. It was this body of knowledge that some sages drew on to contend with the wartime upheaval.[7]

Relevant to the upheaval ushered in by the Holocaust, the Talmudic-based teaching was nevertheless addressing a temporary disorientation experienced by an individual. The Holocaust cruelly extended the problem to millions of Jews over the course of months or even years. In the latter case, Jewish calendars of all kinds were fashioned throughout the war, by hook and by crook, to bring a familiar anchor to those who were uprooted from so much.

To a degree, the devastation of time during the Holocaust has come under scrutiny. But, regrettably, scholarly attention to the calendar's role in this period has suffered in the bargain, probably because the calendar suggests normalcy, regularity, and order, while the upheaval of the Holocaust ushered in exactly the reverse. Scholars (and, as we will see, some important creative writers) have maintained that just as wartime Jewry was compelled to deal with oppressive conditions in ghettos, camps, and elsewhere in Nazi-occupied Europe, so did their experience of time become distorted and oppressive. This experience was exacerbated because the resources to manage time were rightly understood to be lacking or proscribed. In the most radical formulation, time was believed to have become a completely different entity than it normally was. In this scholarly view, new terms had to be invented to characterize the passage of time during the Holocaust. Trying to do justice to the scale and ferocity of the Holocaust's carnage, this view, nevertheless, jumps to unwarranted conclusions. What is overlooked is the fact that, even under restrictive conditions, calendars were produced, distributed, and regularly consulted. As we will see, such calendars continued to give the experience of time reason and order.

Sociologist Barbara Engelking is one exponent of the view that the Holocaust distorted the Jew's perception of time.[8] According to Engelking, the Polish Jews' bitter circumstances (in the ghettos and elsewhere) were such as to have brought about the "deformation of time" on three levels. The first level was the exaggerated experience of the "present," which, in view of the complete uncertainty of tomorrow, "dominated" and was "all-embracing." The second level was the exclusion of "the future," since daily encounters with death meant that one could not count on an open-ended horizon. And the third level was the limitation of the past, which was, in Engelking's expression, "foreshortened." Time could extend neither backward nor forward; all that was left was a debilitating present, an overwhelming now.

These deformations, writes Engelking, had the result of nullifying time measured by the calendar: "The irregularity of time is reflected in the fact that it is not continuous, it is measured by events, and not by weeks or months, which are the calendar of peacetime."[9] Engelking here implies that as the experience of time became more irregular and abnormal, the measurement of time was done by means other than a calendar. We will see, however, that many who experienced time's irregularity during the Holocaust chose the calendar as the vehicle by which to remain bound to a tradition-laden past and oriented to a meaningful future.

The belief in the calendar's inadequacy to track time during the Holocaust has been equally dominant in research on the concentration camps. Here scholars highlight the ways in which the perversion of time contributed to the agony of those imprisoned within. Wolfgang Sofsky, a sociologist whose study of the camps is much heralded and whose work I will consider at greater length later on, focuses exclusively on the deformation of time consciousness in the concentration camps, emphasizing again the "absolute primacy of the present" and the consequent destruction of a future.[10] Moreover, he argues that the enemy systematically used time to debilitate the camp prisoners; it was part and parcel of the "order of terror," as Sofsky calls it, unleashed within the camps. Sofsky's focus on the destructive force of time in the concentration camps led him to overlook what was for numbers of prisoners the calendar's immensely sustaining role.

Popular as well as scholarly approaches have wrenched time free of its normal calendar moorings. Indeed, that the Holocaust demands a new countercalendrical mode of measuring time finds one of its most powerful—if problematic—expressions in an influential story, "A Scrap of Time" by Ida Fink, a Polish Jewish survivor who immigrated to Israel in the 1950s but continued to write her finely hewn stories in Polish. From the story's opening sentence, the narrator of "A Scrap of Time" declares the standard calendar obsolete: "I want to talk about a certain time not measured in months and years" but rather "in a word—we no longer said 'in the beautiful month of May,' *im wunderschonen monat mai*, but after the first 'aktzion'"—the word referring to the violent roundup of Jews in a town or ghetto for execution or deportation.[11] The Jews chose the word *aktzion* because these terrifying events became so much a part of the fabric of life that they defined it through and through. These same Jews ostensibly set aside the calendar because its associations with normal life made it irrelevant, an imposition on a reality that had undergone a sea change. Fink draws on the authority of a community of victims—"*we* no longer said"—in order to describe what ostensibly happened to the measurement of time under siege, whereby terms special to the wartime experience replace the calendar. A "scrap of time" (*Skrawek czasu* in the original Polish), a figure of speech that Fink coined, enables one to break free from the calendar's grip.

But there is more. In Fink's formulation, the calendar poses a second problem, since it threatens to obliterate the actual *memory* of wartime experience: "For so long I have wanted to talk about this time, and not in the way I will talk about it now, not just about this one scrap of time. I wanted to, but I couldn't, I didn't know how. I was afraid, too, that this second time, which is measured in months and years, had buried the other time under a layer of years, that this second time had crushed the first and destroyed it within me."[12] The calendar is here the antagonist—"this second [form of measuring] time"—covering over that which cannot "[be] measured in months but in a word." Recovery of the authentic Holocaust-period experience (of time and all else) can only occur if the "layer[s]" of calendar time are circumvented or, in Fink's archaeological metaphor, burrowed through. This the narrator does in order to recount the episode that follows: "But no, today, digging around in the ruins of memory, I found it fresh and untouched by forgetfulness, this time not measured in months but in a word." The story chronicles the ostensible shift of time's measure from the month to the word, from the calendar to the special idiom that came into being during the war.

Though the *Jewish* calendar is never invoked, this shift in time's measurement may also be Fink's version of Jewish time: "We had different measures of time, we different ones, always different, always with that mark of difference that moved some of us to pride and others to humility. We, who because of our difference were condemned once again during this time measured not in months nor by the rising and setting of the sun, but by a word—'action,' a word signifying movement, a word you would use about a novel or a play."[13] The calendar thus does not come off well here. It became obsolete during the war, because the events experienced demanded a novel form of measuring time. Later, in the war's aftermath, it formed a barrier to authentic memory of the period. Only by circumventing the calendar can one reach the true nature of Jewish experience during the Holocaust.[14]

The story's influence has been substantial. Historian Michael Marrus, for example, opens his discussion of Jewish perceptions of time during the Holocaust by quoting from, commenting on, and being guided by the story's notion of time in the Holocaust era. Therefore, while Marrus takes note of a wide array of perspectives, he includes but a single reference to a wartime calendar—and with no information as to who produced the calendar, how or where he or she produced it, or in what way Marrus came to know of it.[15] Another prominent scholar of the Holocaust, Lawrence Langer, reproduces the "scrap of time" passage as the epigraph to his influential book, *Holocaust Testimonies*; perhaps even more telling is the fact that Langer takes the subtitle of his book, *The Ruins of Memory*, directly from the quoted passage. And, true to the title, the study argues that the actual nature of the Holocaust can only be revealed by burrowing beneath the surface of Holocaust survivor testimonies and reaching "the ruins of memory," a level of recall that Langer refers to in a pivotal chapter of the book as "deep memory." As Langer informs us in a related study, when one reaches the substratum of the "ruins of memory," one must relinquish normal notions of time.[16]

Admittedly, the Ida Fink story and the studies that draw on it do not express antagonism toward the idea of the calendar as such; the rejection of the calendar rather comes as a by-product of the required shift of perspective from ordinary to extraordinary time. Since the calendar stands for ordinary time—time measured in months and years, the "rising and setting of the sun"—it is simply squeezed out of the wartime picture, viewed as embodying a form of measurement irrelevant to the circumstances at hand.[17] But not everyone opted out of the calendar as a way of confronting the extraordinary. As we shall see, many opted in.

The obstacles to factoring in the calendar have taken other forms as well. Even when scholars have endeavored to reevaluate the approach to time and the

Holocaust and put "Jewish time" on the map, the calendar has continued to be filtered out. Historian David Engel, for example, attempts to redress the usual focus on "German time" to "measure the Holocaust." What, he asks, "might it mean to measure the Holocaust in Jewish time?" He advocates for this approach to better understand the plight of the victims: "If we follow the path that German perpetrators traveled, we shall see the Holocaust in German time; but if we wish to walk together with the Jewish victims, to understand how they lived in the shadow of death, we can use only Jewish time to mark changes along the way."[18] Engel seems to be heading in a direction similar to my own, calling for a fundamental change in the way of measuring time in the wartime experience of the Jewish victims. By altering our terms of reference, by framing our approach according to the victims' conception and perception of the world, we can "walk together" with them. Yet, surprisingly, Engel's worthy exploration of "Jewish time" in the shadow of death doesn't focus on the Jewish calendar. Indeed, Engel does not refer to the Jewish calendar at all. For him, Jewish time connotes the Jewish perception of the present in relation to the past and future. During the period from 1933 to 1945, Jews at first understood time as going backward, reentering the medieval period. This is how they perceived the Nazis' egregious rescinding of the rights of Germany's Jews. Only gradually was there a perception of the future as something new and unrelated to the past. Eventually, the memory of World War I determined how Jews placed themselves in relation to modes of defiance (these remarks appear in the volume *Daring to Resist*, which explains the emphasis on "defiance"). Assuredly, Engel's remarks here helpfully complicate the usual monolithic approach to periodization of the Holocaust, calling for an appreciation of the *multiple* perceptions of time—Jewish, Polish, German, and others— operating simultaneously. And he forcefully shows how layering in his notion of "Jewish time" will enable us to "walk together with"—that is, understand better and more accurately—the predicament of the Jewish victims during these years.

But what could it mean that Engel fails to invoke the Jewish calendar even once when so powerfully advocating for attention to Jewish time? Can Jewish time be understood without reference to the elements and concepts of Jewish timekeeping—dates, holidays, measurements, memory, and calendar—that informed Jewish perception and action during the Holocaust? For all his advocacy of taking stock of multiple modes of timekeeping, Engel continues to remain within the constraints of standard historiography on the Holocaust. Not only does such historiography generally measure Holocaust time by "German time," but it relies exclusively on a single calendar: the Gregorian. This approach misses what I call the bifocal nature of European Jewish experience and culture. Or, expressed differently, it considers only half of the experience of these communities. Engel rightly believes historiography of the Holocaust must revise its standard approach in order to accurately chronicle the victims' experience. Yet he falls short of what it takes to achieve that understanding.

In contrast, Rabbi Eliezer Berkovits, in his 1979 study *With God in Hell*, joins Jewish time inextricably to the calendar.[19] Rabbi Berkovits agrees that the rigors of the Holocaust, and concentration camp life particularly, removed the usual coordinates of time. What was left was unstructured time, "the complete emptiness of endless duration."[20] This experience of "endless duration," a formulation well-known to students of the Holocaust, will receive more substantial consideration below. But what is of importance here is Rabbi Berkovits' assertion that the Jewish calendar continued to be a point of reference even in the most oppressive circumstances, even (to invoke the sober title of his book) "with God in hell." He pointedly argues that religious Jews refused to submit to the emptying out of time but instead structured time according to the Jewish calendar. For these Jews, "time was not the SS-imposed structureless sameness; their time was structured by the Jewish calendar."[21] He reminds us that, though Europe's Jews were often compelled to live with limited resources, they would go to great lengths to "structure" time, using calendars "handwritten in the ghettos and camps." And when no calendar was in sight, Jews "could calculate and compute the necessary dates on the basis of the scanty information that was available."[22] In Rabbi Berkovits's estimation, calendar consciousness was fully in evidence and remained a, if not *the*, driving force of life-sustaining activity.

Rabbi Berkovits surely provides a healthy corrective to the idea that Jewish time in relation to the Holocaust can be discussed without reference to the Jewish calendar. But his assessment falls short on two counts. First, he makes assumptions about wartime calendars that are not historically borne out. For instance, calendars were not only handwritten but also printed in some ghettos and typewritten in some concentration camps. Resources were more limited and freedom more constricted in some places than in others. And second, he suggests an awareness of calendar dates, and the time-structuring resoluteness that grew out of it, that again don't seem to mesh with the reality of wartime conditions. Many Jews who were eager to know the dates did not have the information at hand; others who knew something were unsure; and still others were too far submerged in the all-consuming struggle of survival to have the knowledge make a difference. What is missing from Rabbi Berkovits's schema is a notion of crisis, of the oppressive conditions being so comprehensively overwhelming as to blunt the reflex to track time. Many who formerly would have aggressively tracked time in order to live according to the calendar were no longer in a position to do so. Moreover, calculating and computing the necessary dates, as Berkowitz phrases it, was a rarer skill than he would allow for, one that often eluded even those, rabbis and laity alike, whose traditional knowledge was substantial. In sum, Rabbi Berkovits gives us half of what we need to know about why calendars were a prized possession, circumventing "the complete emptiness of endless duration" by means of a passionate commitment to the Jewish calendar. But he doesn't give a convincing picture of the "hellish" challenge facing those who endeavored to produce such calendars, to fashion them out of meager material resources, and to live according to them.

In the following pages, through the examination of a number of wartime calendars, I hope to fill in this picture. First of all, this means providing a context for each calendar: where and when was the calendar composed and who was responsible for doing so? Behind every calendar, there is a story that needs to be told in order to appreciate the nature of the accomplishment. From another angle, the story told about a particular calendar can often help convey the nature of life (especially religious life) in a ghetto or concentration camp. The Theresienstadt concentration camp, for example, is renowned for its extensive program of lectures and artistic performance. However, the Jewish calendars fashioned in the camp draw attention to the camp's vibrant religious Jewish life, a lesser known but important dimension of Theresienstadt.

Moreover, whenever possible I sketch the life of the calendar's author. I do this certainly to pay tribute to his or her remarkable achievement. But I also believe such a sketch important for identifying the kind of life experience and knowledge that formed a basis for the calendar-making task. Finally, tracing the outlines of the authors' lives shows the range of men and women who believed that tracking Jewish time was worth making the effort and, in a number of cases, worth taking the risk.

Important as it is to know who composed any given calendar, sometimes authorship can only be surmised. Wartime artifacts that the calendars are, they have in some cases found their way to archives without a clear indication of who authored them. Occasionally I've deemed it worthwhile to share with the reader my effort to establish the identity of the calendar's author; at other times, having no information on which to speculate, I've simply accepted the fact of the absence of identification and gone forward from there.

Composed under trying conditions, the calendars that have been preserved (likely only a portion of the number actually produced) constitute a diverse lot. Some are ornate, others plain; some are intricate in detail, others sketchy, even stark; some calendar authors had access to a range of writing and drawing implements of different colors; others made do with one. Most wartime calendars are small in size, at times diminutive, either because materials were in short supply or because small items were more easily hidden. But a few are surprisingly larger. The majority were penned in notebooks of one kind or another, while a stalwart minority were etched on cruder material, such as paper cement sacks. In one extraordinary case, a Jewish calendar was superimposed on a pocket-size printed Gregorian calendar that was already four years out of date. Under such makeshift circumstances, as the saying goes, beggars could hardly be choosers. A number of calendars bear an official imprimatur of Jewish administrators or organizations, but most display none, since they are simply individual efforts to remain aware of time's sacred dimensions.

The medium in which the calendar's details were set down and their format inscribed varies greatly as well. Official calendars (and some semiofficial ones) continued to be printed; calendars that were privately authored were either typewritten or handwritten. Of the latter, some were rendered in beautiful calligraphy, while others were lettered in a simple hand. Depending on the size and shape of the notebook (or other material) and the calendar's designated purpose, calendars displayed on a page either a single week, a single month, or, in some cases, two months or more. The array of Lodz ghetto calendars covered both ends of the spectrum, with a desk calendar showing a single day and a wall calendar an entire year. Occasionally we see (or hear about) more ambitious, lengthier compilations: for instance, one for ten years (which I will discuss below), a second for fifty.

Not every wartime calendar covers a full year. One lacks a month, another has only a half year, a third includes only four months, and a fourth has two months and twenty-five days. Each omission is curious, unaccounted for, mysterious: was the calendar at first complete and only later fragmented? Or was it that way from the beginning? In one case—the Jewish calendar superimposed on the printed pocket Gregorian—the mystery was solved. I had worked for months with this fascinating calendar, which was missing its cover and, more importantly, about six months of the calendar. I hypothesized as best I could with what remained. Such a superimposed calendar was, after all, a singular example of being resourceful in a way I had not otherwise come across. But even while being resigned to working with fragments, a truncated version of the original, I was puzzled by the description penned by the archivist who had first dealt with this remarkable artifact. These notes indicated aspects of the calendar—for example, the Hebrew or Yiddish word *shechita* (meaning "slaughter" and, in this wartime context, connoting "murder") as well as a list of names—that I saw no evidence of. Had the archivist seen a section of the calendar that included this important material but was now no longer connected to the calendar I was viewing? As it turned out, that was more or less the case. I urged the gracious archivist I was conferring with (alas, the original note-jotting archivist was no longer on the scene) to check again, and, sure enough, the digitized image of the calendar (which I had relied on) had unknowingly excluded almost half of the calendar. Soon thereafter, I was sent the updated digitized image, which included the complete pocket calendar as well as the haunting list of murdered Polish Jews. The omitted sections in the other wartime calendars were not, however, always so successfully recovered.

Nearly all of the wartime calendars complement the dating of the Jewish year with that of the Gregorian (or, in the case of some countries, the Julian), a practice that had been commonplace for centuries. That wartime Jewish calendars continued this practice in kind shows their conservative nature. The authors of these calendars believed that what had been the convention in the past could serve equally well in the present. That said, there are important variations in how the two calendars are paired, and I will regularly draw attention to the significances of these variations.

Combining the two calendars produced a similar interweaving of languages used to designate the names of days, months, holidays, and other features. In eastern Europe, Hebrew, Yiddish, and a vernacular tongue, the lingua franca of the country (Polish or Hungarian, for instance), carried out this task; in western Europe, Hebrew and the lingua franca of the country in question (e.g., Dutch, French, or German) usually performed a similar role. Exceptions to the rule, however, did crop up. Rabbi Zelmann, for instance, whose devotion to his Westerbork calendar led off my discussion, opted for Yiddish, even though he fashioned his calendar in Holland for a community made up mostly of Dutch and German Jews. Across the map of Europe, Hebrew was nearly omnipresent in Jewish calendars, producing a counterpoint of the sacred language in alternation with the secular one. This was only fitting, since this form of presentation mirrored the calendar's mission of organizing the felicitous relationship between sacred and mundane days.

Were the authors of wartime calendars generally able to perform this organizing task competently? Were they able to set down the information accurately? Given the inhospitable circumstances in which the wartime calendars were often brought into being, the question of accuracy might seem to take a back seat. Isn't it enough, one might think, that an effort was made to fashion a calendar, even though the resources that one usually drew on to carry out such a project—pens and paper, guidebooks and charts—were conspicuously lacking? Wasn't it enough that a man or woman ran the risk and produced something? This attitude of "better something than nothing" is indeed how one survivor of a labor camp spoke of a calendar rendered therein: "We had a Rabbi's daughter. She made a luach, a [Jewish] calendar, and she said, even if it's a day ahead or behind, it doesn't matter."[23]

But this view does not take account of why, with the Jewish calendar, the quest for accuracy is so important. I once showed a friend one of the most beautiful of the wartime calendars, praising its many virtues. He replied with a straightforward question: was it accurate? It mostly was, I countered. That "mostly" describes the wartime calendars overall. It also sets the stage for checking the accuracy of the wartime calendars as a worthwhile facet of such an inquiry.

Though comparable in many respects, the Jewish and Gregorian calendars differ in terms of what is at stake in their accuracy. While the Gregorian calendar undoubtedly strives for precision, the Jewish one is under an *obligation* to convey the correct information. This is not simply a pedantic obsession to get the facts right. It is rather because, for observant Jews, the calendar serves as a guide for day-to-day behavior, particularly with regard to the shifting sands of the mundane and the sacred. The latter refers to the Sabbath day and the fixed retinue of holidays, all of which partake of the sacred to a greater or lesser degree. The more the sacred permeates a day, the more rigorous and extensive are the list of restricted and obligatory activities, the goal of which are to create a communal and personal haven of sanctity. The Gregorian calendar also orchestrates the behavior of those who follow it, alternating between weekday work and weekend rest, between a regular pattern of mundane activities and periodic holidays. Specific to the Jewish calendar, however, is the momentous crossing of the border from the mundane to the sacred or vice versa. Once sunset signals that the sacred day has arrived (we recall that the Jewish day begins with the onset of night), all restrictions and obligations are immediately in force. That is why Jewish calendars, including those of the Holocaust era, frequently include the precise time, down to the minute, of when the Sabbath or holiday begins and ends.

As important as this information is for understanding the wartime Jewish calendar, a few qualifications are in order. First, some wartime calendars did not include the time listings, either because, given the shortage of resources at hand, it was impossible to determine the exact moment when sunset would occur or because the calendar's author did not possess the requisite skill to determine it and there was no one readily available to provide assistance, as would be the case in normal settings. Those instances where the Sabbath and holiday times are missing thus reveal something further about the circumstances in which the calendars were composed. Second, not every Jew whose activities were guided by the calendars likely adhered strictly to the time frame set forth. One might think here of the diverse population of religious and secular Jews served by the official calendars produced in the Lodz ghetto, which, despite such diversity even within the upper echelons of the ghetto administration, did list the times.

My interest in the inaccuracy of these calendars is not, of course, intended to find fault with the author or to diminish our appreciation for what was accomplished but rather to read the errors as another revelatory dimension of the calendar-making enterprise during the Holocaust. Some errors were subtle, as with a mistaken calculation of the time of day that Shabbat would enter or exit. More substantial were errors in computing the length of a month and designating the day on which the celebratory first day or days of the month were observed. This oversight could lead to a mismatch between the date of a given month and the day of the week on which it fell—which in turn could (and often did) lead to assigning a holiday to the wrong day of the week. For instance, one of the two surviving Auschwitz calendars got off track two months into the year: the beginning of the month of Kislev (the late fall or early winter month in which the holiday of Chanukah occurs) was placed on a Thursday (November 16) instead of a Friday (November 17). The mistake occurred because the previous month was thought to have twenty-nine days when it actually had thirty (which, in some years, it does). From this point on the Jewish date was out of sync with the day of the week. Thus Chanukah was recorded as taking place on a Sunday when in truth it fell on a Monday. This slight but pivotal error is only a facet of a larger saga regarding this enigmatic calendar, the remainder of which will be told in a later chapter.

But it should be noted that the calendar authors (and the Jews relying on these calendars) were often worried that a mistake had crept in somewhere along the line. One Polish rabbi who fashioned a calendar while in hiding convened an ad hoc rabbinical court to alter the day he had originally set down for the holiday of Yom Kippur; the author of the second surviving Auschwitz calendar, Sophie Sohlberg, having received a postcard inscribed with the Jewish date, saw that she had been mistaken in determining the length of key months and emended her calendar midstream. Another rabbi, who was unsure on which of two days Yom Kippur took place, chose one but fretted about his decision throughout the remainder of the war; the first thing he did when liberated was to search for a calendar to check his decision—which turned out to be correct. So, despite the guesswork that went into the crafting of many wartime calendars, accuracy remained an abiding worry; it was fortunately not so great a concern as to thwart the impulse to bring a calendar into being.

These calendars no doubt present an aspect of what has been referred to as spiritual resistance: a means of countering the enemy's attempt to annihilate the Jewish people, not, in this case, with guns, bombs, and ammunition but rather with weapons of the spirit. That said, I have shied away from using the term for several reasons. First, to view the calendars under this rubric makes them disappear, for they become simply another facet of spiritual resistance rather than being taken on their own terms. Second, other parallel concepts seem to provide a better framework for allowing the calendars to be seen in their proper light. The abovementioned Rabbi Berkovits, for example, refers to the "continuity of existence" and the "continuity of Judaism in the most extreme conditions," terms that relate specifically to one of the essential dimensions of the wartime Jewish calendar: continuity. Throughout my book, I draw attention to aspects of continuity associated with these remarkable calendars; in the epilogue, I comment on the importance of this notion for thinking more generally about the Holocaust.

The calendars are worthy not simply of casual perusal but of focused consideration in their own right. What I try to do here, then, is to describe each calendar and point out what is special about it. I endeavor to pay close attention to its details, how it was conceived and organized, written and ornamented, what it contains and what it leaves out—and, given the fact that I am not looking at any calendar in isolation but rather examining them as part of the collection that I have assembled, I ask what we can learn about it in comparison with the other wartime Jewish calendars? This kind of descriptive enterprise would seem to be par for the course, standard procedure for inventory and analysis of any kind of artifact. But with regard to wartime Jewish calendars, this has not taken place. Certainly, the calendars collected in archives have been recognized as significant, since they, too, like letters and diaries, drawings and photographs, were understood to be strategies by which the Jewish victims of the Nazi onslaught attempted to cope with their predicament. Hence they have been preserved, sometimes even exhibited in museums or reproduced in books. Yet unlike some other forms of response, calendars were presumably thought to yield their significance at a glance, without needing any further investigation. They were what they were. So my attention to a calendar's form and substance attempts to bring out its distinctive manner of organizing Jewish time. They were not only what they were, I want to propose, but were much more than they are usually taken to be.

If Holocaust-era calendars are generally unknown and overlooked, diaries penned during this period are a staple of reading and research. The celebrated diary written by the Dutch teenager Anne Frank, for example, allows us to regularly eavesdrop on how she and her extended family coped with the ordeal of hiding from the enemy in an Amsterdam apartment for months on end. Her remarkable diary is complemented by dozens of others, written in as many languages, under all kinds of forbidding circumstances. Powerful for the insider view they offer, such diaries, structured around a series of dated entries, are especially germane for our purposes because they draw on calendars as well as serve as surrogates for them. Like most calendars, they revolve around the day, week, month, and year—which are often the first things noted at the top of the diarist's page.

Indeed, the date noted was often that of the Jewish calendar. Exactly how the Jewish calendar comes into play in these diaries varies considerably. The diary kept in hiding by the Polish Chasid, Chaim Yitzhok Wolgelernter, was reckoned exclusively by the Jewish calendar; the renowned poet Yitzhak Katzenelson dated his "Vittel Diary" generally according to the Gregorian calendar but switched in key entries to the Jewish one; and Otto Wolf, a teenager who wrote a diary in hiding in Moravia, used the Gregorian for the entry headings while regularly providing Jewish dates (or symbols thereof) in the entries themselves. While virtually all wartime diaries that invoke the Jewish calendar are relevant to my study, most significant are those that shift between dating the entries by the Jewish calendar or by the Gregorian—shifts that, I want to argue, coincide with a transformation of point of view within the diaries. At times, moreover, the wartime diarist's decision to date entries according to the Jewish calendar indicates nothing less than a revolution in perspective.

In some cases, the Holocaust-inspired composition of calendars extended beyond the borders of the European killing fields. And it is here, too, that the notion of a revolution—a full-blown transformation in the understanding of time and in the kind of calendar that would best accommodate it—came to the fore. The unlikely setting was a wartime Jewish pocket calendar produced in America but written exclusively in Hebrew and Yiddish. Incorporating the meaning of the Holocaust into its very essence, this calendar project—based on teachings of Jewish mysticism—revised the conventional Jewish calendar in form and content. It thereby set out to track time not just *during* the Holocaust but according to the *new measure of time* the Holocaust had ushered in

I have organized the book in six parts. Part I, "Time at the End of a Jewish Century," investigates two pivotal calendrical responses to the conflict looming in the summer of 1939 and the beginning of the Second World War. Part II, "Tracking Time in the New Jewish Century: Calendars in Wartime Ghettos," surveys the special nature of the calendars that circulated in Lodz and other wartime ghettos. Part III,': Concentration Camps, Endless Time, and Jewish Time," reviews several previous approaches to what has been considered the oppressive nature of time in the Nazi concentration camps in order to show how close attention to the calendars fashioned in various camps suggests a different view of lived time.

Part IV, "While in Hiding: Calendar Consciousness on the Edge of Destruction," catalogs the Jewish calendars crafted in hiding, often by those who were able to have minimal if any contact with other Jews. In such circumstances, the calendar stood in as a surrogate community. Part V, "At the Top of the Page: Calendar Dates in Holocaust Diaries," considers how wartime diaries regularly served as a sophisticated form of narrative calendars. Part VI, "The Holocaust as a Revolution in Jewish Time: The Lubavitcher Rebbes' Wartime Calendar Book," focuses on a singular wartime calendar that conceived time anew even as it sought to strengthen ties to all facets of Jewish tradition. In an epilogue, I detail the implications that follow from placing the wartime Jewish calendar, perhaps the symbol of continuity par excellence, at the center of the discussion of the experience of time during the Holocaust.

In a number of cases, wartime calendars were not full-blown creations but were rather roughly improvised. Bertha Ferderber-Salz reports her extraordinary meeting in the Bergen-Belsen concentration camp with an old dying women reciting "Gott fun Avraham," a Yiddish prayer traditionally recited by women at the close of Shabbat. Drinking in her words, Ferderber-Salz asked her, "How did you know when it was Shabbes?" The remarkable reply was that the woman had arrived recently from Hungary and since then had made a knot in her dress each day. That is how she knew; that is how others came to know.[24] In this case, no calendar could be found, so one had to be invented. Over the course of the book, I take stock of the more familiar-looking wartime calendars, all of which, nevertheless, came into being with equal ingenuity and with a profound regard for the vital necessity of tracking Jewish time.

Notes

1. Osher M. Lehmann, *Faith at the Brink* (Brooklyn: Lehmann, 1996), p. 71.

2. For overviews of the Jewish calendar, see Rabbi David Feinstein, *The Jewish Calendar: Its Structure and Laws.* Brooklyn: Mesorah: 2003; and Rabbi Nathan Bushwick, *Understanding the Jewish Calendar* (New York: Moznaim, 1989). Classic sources include Talmud Bavli Tractates Rosh Hashana and Sanhedrin; Rambam Mishnah Torah Hilchot Kiddush Hachodesh; Tur Orach Chaim 427–28. A recent in-depth overview appears in the entry, "Luach HaShana," *Encyclopedia Talmudit*, [Hebrew] vol. 36 (Jerusalem: Yad HaRav Herzog, 2016), pp. 75–142 For a historical approach to the evolution of the ancient Jewish calendar, see Sacha Stern, *Calendar and Community: A History of the Jewish Calendar, 2nd Century BCE–10th Century CE.* (Oxford: Oxford University Press, 2001).

3. However, a leap year, which takes place in seven out of nineteen years, adds not a day but a month, an intercalation that allows the holidays to remain fixed in their respective seasons (Passover in the spring, Sukkoth in the fall, etc.).

4. Jewish calendar dating has historically used different (often parallel) systems for determining the year count. See Elisheva Carlebach, *Palaces of Time: Jewish Calendar and Culture in Early Modern Europe* (Cambridge: Harvard University Press, 2011), particularly chapters 1 and 8.

5. For a trenchant analysis of the Nazi assault against Jewish holidays in particular and Jewish sacred time in general, see David Patterson, *Along the Edge of Annihilation: The Collapse and Recovery of Life in the Holocaust Diary* (Seattle: University of Washington Press, 1999). For a recent example that highlights the enemy's perverse manipulation of the Jewish calendar, see David Cesarani, *Final Solution: The Fate of the Jews, 1933–1949* (New York: St. Martins, 2016), pp. 39, 326. On the Nazi attempt to replace the Christian Gregorian calendar with their own, see Michael Burleigh, *The Third Reich: A New History* (New York: Hill and Wang, 2001).

6. Yaffa Eliach, "Jewish Tradition in the Life of the Concentration-Camp Inmate," *The Nazi Concentration Camps*, eds. Y. Guttman and A. Saf (Jerusalem: Yad Vashem, 1984), p. 196.

7. For instance, Rabbi Berish Wiedenfeld of Tzrebinia was asked whether a person could put on tefillin all seven days of the week if he was not certain when Shabbat was. Ordinarily, tefillin are worn only on weekdays; the sanctity of the Sabbath day makes wearing them unnecessary, associates them with the weekdays, and places them out of the sphere of legitimate Sabbath day activity. Hence, might someone be committing a transgression by saying a blessing in vain when he puts on tefillin on Shabbat?

Rabbi Wiedenfeld answered that under the wartime circumstances one could put on tefillin all seven days. In circumstances in which it is not known precisely which day is Shabbat, one bases the decision on the majority of days of the week; therefore the blessing over the tefillin may be recited every day. This explanation followed the guidelines set forth in the Talmud. It should be noted that Rabbi Wiedenfeld went further in addressing the special nature of the wartime persecution, supplying a second reason for why one should follow this approach even if the Shabbat day could be reckoned without doubt. The normal reason for not putting on tefillin on Shabbat is that Shabbat, like tefillin, is considered a *sign* and symbol of the special covenantal relationship with God. Since Shabbat, a day dedicated to spiritual exultation by means of refraining from usual weekday work, is itself a sign of this covenant, the tefillin become unnecessary. But in abnormal times, when the questioner was being forced against his will to work every day of the week, including Shabbat, Shabbat can no longer fulfill its mission as a sign of the covenantal bond. One who is made to work on Shabbat is thus required to put on tefillin every day with a blessing. See *Dovav M'Yedsharim*, siman 18, p. 24.

8. Barbara Engelking-Boni, *History and Memory: The Experience of the Holocaust and Its Consequences, An Investigation Based on Personal Narratives*, trans. G. Paulson (London: Leicester University Press, 2001). In a later publication, Engelking does frame the events of the Holocaust—in this case, as they transpire in the Warsaw ghetto—in an "external chronology" of September 1939 to May 1943 in the Gregorian calendar. Though the chronology and other chapters of the study make occasional (and sometime inaccurate) reference to the Jewish calendar, the victim's perception of time plays at best a minor role. See Barbara Engelking-Boni and Jacek Leociak, *The Warsaw Ghetto: A Guide to the Perished City* (New Haven: Yale University Press, 2009). The chronology runs from pp. 36 to 46. Her characterization of "cursed time" as an extension of the "present" and collapse of past and future echoes research on prisoner perceptions of time. See Alyson Brown, "'Doing Time': The Extended Present of the Long-Term Prisoner," *Time and Society* 7 (1998), pp. 93–103; and Stanley Cohen and Laurie Taylor, *Psychological Survival: The Experience of Long-Term Imprisonment* (Harmondsworth: Penguin, 1972). But Engelking's contrast of wartime with normal time has been challenged as a general premise by Mary Dudziak in *War Time: An Idea, Its History, Its Consequences* (New York: Oxford University Press, 2012) and in "Law, War, and the History of Time," *California Law Review* 98 (2010), pp. 1669–710.

9. Engelking, p. 67.

10. Wolfgang Sofsky, *The Order of Terror: The Concentration Camp*, trans. William Temple (Princeton, NJ: Princeton University Press, 1997). Sofsky nevertheless also emphasizes the "preservation and salvaging of time" as well as its destruction and thus offers a vocabulary for considering the calendar as a way of creating a "fictive future" and an enabling past. I will explore this possibility in the section below devoted to the concentration camps.

11. Ida Fink, "A Scrap of Time," in *A Scrap of Time and Other Stories*, trans. Madeline Levine and Francine Prose (Evanston: Northwestern University Press, 1987), p. 3. The title in the original Polish, *Skrawek czasu*, seems to be Fink's coinage. The English translation of the story also misses several aspects relevant to Fink's formulation of "a scrap of time," including a German-language allusion ("in die wondershonen monat Mai") to a Schuman lied based on a Heine poem. I have thus slightly emended the translation.

12. Ibid.,

13. Ibid., pp. 3–4.

14. As it stands, commentary on the story does not pursue this emphasis on the calendar's antagonistic role. Instead, the story is seen as noteworthy because it investigates the

challenges faced by the survivor in reconstructing his or her wartime experience or giving an account of it. See for example Sara Horowitz, "Ida Fink," in *Holocaust Literature: An Encyclopedia of Writers and Their Work*, ed. S. Lillian Kremer (New York: Routledge, 2002).

15. Michael Marrus, "Killing Time: Jewish Perceptions during the Holocaust," in *The Holocaust: History and Memory—Essays Presented in Honor of Israel Gutman*, ed. S. Almog et al. (Jerusalem: Yad Vashem and Hebrew University, 2001), pp. 10–38. Marrus briefly alludes to "handwritten Jewish calendars that were found in the camps" but does not note the specific camps or calendars and does not cite his source for this information. I thank David Roskies for bringing this article to my attention.

16. Lawrence Langer, "Memory's Time: Chronology and Duration in Holocaust Testimonies," in *Admitting the Holocaust: Collected Essays* (New York, Oxford University Press, 1995). Langer deals with contra-normal time in Holocaust literature in his earliest book-length study, *The Holocaust and the Literary Imagination* (New Haven: Yale University Press, 1975), particularly in the final chapter, "Of Time and Atrocity."

17. A follow-up to the story, appropriately named "A Second Scrap of Time," takes up again the refrain of a new measure of time: "A vast distance separated the old time from the new," begins the story, which eventually chronicles "the second Aktion." It is this word, *Aktion*, referring to the lethal assault by the Nazis upon Jewish communities, that defines the circumstances: "Our vocabulary sprouted new expressions and strange acronyms for long names, but the word Aktion towered above them all. It dominated that time that some people—in their misguided naïveté—continued to call wartime." Taking to task those who continue to call things by outdated expressions, the sequel, "A Second Scrap of Time," is less explicitly pitted against the calendar than its predecessor. This is likely because the memory of this particular "scrap of time" is less difficult to recover and because, despite the lingering habits of misguided naïveté, the new expressions have taken firmer hold. See "A Second Scrap of Time," in *Traces: Stories*, trans. Philip Boehm and Francine Prose (New York: Holt, 1997), pp. 53–58. The final story in the collection, "The Baker's Ongoing Resurrection," though not invoking a "scrap of time" as the standard by which to measure events, also presents the calendar in a compromised fashion.

A "scrap of time" then becomes the name Fink gives to the attempt by certain assimilated Jews to respond to the upheaval they were forced to endure. It provides a language attuned to the special features of the persecution, shows the progressive adjustments made to cope with its intensifying danger, identifies the *Aktion* as the defining element of Jewish wartime existence, and enables a survivor to authentically mine his or her experience.

But it did this for Jews whose bonds to time had already been severed from tradition. This approach was by no means universal. By and large, Polish Jews continued to use the calendar to orient themselves. And this was not, as Fink's depiction would have it, because they were, on the one hand, especially pious or, on the other, significantly inattentive to the specific nature of Nazi persecution. They rather understood that continuing to bind themselves to the calendar would provide the maximum degree of orientation and continuity in a situation where little else could.

18. David Engel, "Resisting in Jewish Time," in *Daring to Resist: Jewish Defiance in the Holocaust*, ed. Yitzchak Mais. (New York: Museum of Jewish Heritage, 2007). I thank Wolf Gruner for bringing this article to my attention in this context.

19. Rabbi Eliezer Berkovits, *With God in Hell: Judaism in the Ghettos and Deathcamps* (New York: Sanhedrin, 1979), pp. 65–71.

In addition to Rabbi Berkovits's commentary and the handful of articles listed in note 1, other studies that have devoted some significant attention to the Jewish calendar during the Holocaust include Yaffa Eliach, "Jewish Tradition in the Life of the Concentration-Camp Inmate," in *The Nazi Concentration Camps*, eds. Y. Gutman and A. Saf. (Jerusalem: Yad Vashem, 1984); Yaffa Eliach, "Popular Jewish Religious Responses during the Holocaust and Its Aftermath," in *Jewish Perspectives on the Experience of Suffering*, ed. Shalom Carmy (Northvale, NJ: Aronson, 1999), pp. 297–329; *Shema Yisrael: Testimonies of Devotion, Courage, and Self-Sacrifice, 1939–1945*, trans. Yaakov Lavon (Bnei Brak: Kaliv World Center / Targum, 2002); Esther Farbstein, *Hidden in Thunder: Law, Reflections, and Customs in the Time of the Holocaust* (Hebrew) (Jerusalem: Mosad HaRav Kook, 2002), pp. 373–91; David G. Roskies, "Landkentenish: Yiddish Belles Lettres in the Warsaw Ghetto," in *Holocaust Chronicles*, ed. Robert Moses Shapiro (Hoboken, NJ: Ktav, 1999), pp. 17–20; Alan Rosen, "The Languages of Time: Translating Calendar Dates in Holocaust Diaries," *Holocaust and Genocide Studies* 26 (2012): pp. 276–93; Alan Rosen, "Hidden Time: Calendar Consciousness on the Edge of Destruction," in *Hiding, Sheltering, and Borrowed Identities*, ed. Dan Michman (Jerusalem: Yad Vashem, 2018); and Avraham Rosen, "On Calendars and the Holocaust," *Jewish Action* 72:1 (2011), pp. 44–47.

20. *With God in Hell*, p. 66.

21. Ibid.

22. Ibid.

23. From the oral testimony of Laura Hollander (née Jacobowicz), *Amcha: An Oral Testament of the Holocaust*, ed. Saul Friedman (University Press of America, 1979), p. 415.

24. Bertha Ferderber-Salz, *Un di zun hot gescheint* (Tel Aviv: Verlag Menorah, 1965), pp. 134–35.

I   Time at the End of a Jewish Century

The Fifty-Seventh Century: Tracking Jewish Time in Prewar Europe

Just as the Gregorian calendar has an almost ubiquitous presence in today's Europe, Jewish calendars in various forms circulated widely across the continent in the first part of the twentieth century (or, in the dating of the Jewish calendar, the fifty-seventh). Not surprisingly, Jewish calendars were commonly published in capital cities with significant Jewish populations and institutions—Berlin, Copenhagen, Paris, Vienna, Budapest, Vilna, Warsaw, and Sofia. But they were so much a part of the fabric of Jewish life that they also originated in regional centers all through Europe: Mainz, Hamburg, Cologne, Breslau, Brno, Bratislava, Tschernovitz, Zhitomir, and Lodz, to name just a few. Because of the built-in obsolescence of most Jewish calendars, they were a favored item for printers in these decades, as they had been for many years before.[1] The *Berliner Volkskalender fur Israeliten*, for example, was published yearly, from the 1860s into the 1930s, by the M. Poppelauer's Buchhandlung. Other publishers, in Germany and elsewhere, were equally committed to annual production of Jewish calendars.[2]

Diverse sources had a hand in the production of Jewish calendars.[3] The city's rabbinate would often circulate a detailed calendar. But they were not alone in doing so. In a manner similar to the customary distributions of calendars in our day and age, schools, special-interest groups, and philanthropic organizations—for example, the Jewish Women's Association, the Jewish National Fund, and even the Jewish Association for the Blind—would also regularly print and make available their own. In the 1920s to 1930s, for instance, the Munich-based family of Sophie Lowenstein (about whom we will hear more later on) kept their Jewish calendar year after year in the kitchen. The calendar was brownish, was printed every year by the same firm, and had a separate page in back which listed times for the entry and exist of Sabbath and holidays. For the young Sophie, this family calendar conveyed the necessary information; she did not possess a calendar of her own, pocket or otherwise. The Orthodox Jewish school she attended followed mainly the general calendar—a fact which did not, as we will see, diminish the importance of the Jewish calendar in the school's curriculum or in the lives of its students.

Though most Jewish calendars printed in this era covered a single year, multiyear calendars, spanning anywhere from ten to one hundred years, were occasionally produced. These lengthier productions were made to give customers more for their money or to offer a long-range view of the future. Though these calendars were meant to bolster confidence in time's unflinching march toward redemption, we will soon see how, with the prospect of war looming over Europe, such a multiyear calendar could be recruited for the arduous task of tracking Jewish time in a period of radically diminishing resources.

The kinds of calendars published in this era were generally those we are familiar with in today's world: pocket, wall, and desk calendars abounded. But the Jewish calendar also found its way into many homes by being published together with other materials—materials sometimes religious in nature, but often having to do with literature or business. These compilations went under the heading of "almanac," "yearbook," or "diary." There was, for instance, the *Yidisher almanach far groise Romanie,* published in Tschernovitz; the *Tagebuch* (diary) *für die Jüdische Jugend,* in Vienna; the *Jüdischer Almanach,* in Prague; and *A Magyar Zsidóság Almanachja* (Almanac for Hungarian Jews), in Budapest.[4] In some cases, the calendar headed the entries, while the supplementary materials played a supporting role; in other cases, the emphasis was reversed, with the Jewish calendar taking a back seat to the writings of celebrated literary figures. Because it was placed in such contexts, the Jewish calendar continued to circulate among those whose focus was no longer on traditional Jewish concerns but rather on the world at large.

With education in mind, publishers of calendars recognized that children, too, formed an important audience for Jewish calendars. A sterling example of such a specialized production was the *Kinder-Kalender des Jüdischen Frauenbundes* (The children's calendar of the Jewish Women's Association), published in Berlin in the 1920s and 1930s, which displayed on its cover vibrant illustrations depicting facets of Jewish life as well as the playful activities of boys and girls.

In one form or another, standard Jewish calendars thus reached communities far and wide. Other clever media for circulating the Jewish calendar included "calendar cards" (*Kalenderblätter*) bearing explanations of festival days and prayers, published in Vienna in the 1930s. In addition to separate cards for each holiday, the series also offered a "booklet card," which combined under one cover cards for Shabbat Shuva and the holidays of Yom Kippur and Sukkoth. An even more unusual item was a copper medal issued in 1938 by the Keren HaYesod (United Israel Appeal). The forty-millimeter medal was just over an inch and a half in diameter, roughly the size of a US silver dollar. It featured a Gregorian calendar, yet it also noted the dates of Jewish holidays. Although designed for an audience that had little or no knowledge of Hebrew, even here the Jewish year, 5697–98, was imprinted on the back of the coin.

The Jewish calendar was thus a taken-for-granted aspect of Jewish life in pre-war Europe, marking Jewish time not only in institutions dedicated to religious Jewish life but also, to one degree or another, in locations secular and unaffiliated. Whether in western, central, or eastern Europe, Jews did not have to look far to check the Jewish date, to calculate the time before an upcoming holiday, or to take note of the anniversary of the death of a relative or friend. Indeed, often one did not need to look farther than a pocket or handbag. But even those who did not make it their business to own a Jewish calendar could, without too much trouble, find one close at hand. Understandably, this does not mean that all European Jews were equally guided in their affairs by the Jewish calendar. Some were, but others surely considered the Jewish calendar a secondary or tertiary reference point. Nevertheless, one could be confident that a Jewish calendar for the current year was nearby when needed. With the onset of World War II, that changed—not all at once, but, like much else that occurred during those years, incrementally, one devastating step at a time. As the availability of Jewish calendars diminished, individuals (and, in certain places, institutions) understood that Jewish life could not persevere without them.

Rabbi Yehoshua Baran's Calendar for a Desolate World

Recognition of the calendar's role as a guide in the face of upheaval came even before war actually broke out. In August 1939 (Elul 5699 in the Jewish calendar), for example, Vilna-based rabbi Yehoshua Baran, acting with a premonition that the looming conflict would go on for years, produced a ten-year Jewish calendar. Recalling the immense difficulty of tracking time during World War I, known then as the Great War or World War, some two decades earlier, he hoped that such a stopgap measure would help maintain some control amid the chaos sure to come.

"The Sages say," writes Rabbi Baran in the calendar's coda, "no one is as wise as one who learns from experience. In the days of the [First] World War, when the world was desolate, there were places where even . . . a calendar to know the dates of the holidays was not to be found."[5] Though in the summer of 5699/1939, Vilna was not yet desolate, he didn't want to wait. To his mind, the signs were there to be seen: "Therefore now, when evil winds hover in the universe, and who knows what the next day will bring, God forbid, I have taken steps to publish a calendar for shabbatot, holidays, the new months, with the times of the onset of Shabbat and holidays, the deadline for saying *Shema Yisrael* on Shabbat and holidays, the moladot, the tekufot, the deadline for saying kiddush levana for every month, for ten years, *from 5701 to the end of 5710*" (emphasis added). For a traditional Jew, keeping track of time in a desolate world meant knowing "the times" down to the smallest detail, so as, in the case of "shabbatot" and "holidays," to preserve the integrity of sacred time. The month-to-month progression would be maintained through special periodic rituals—moladot, the tekufot, and saying kiddush levana—all essential ingredients for following the general sweep of the Jewish year. The amount of detail necessary to provide a decade-long map of Jewish time was such that, even though the calendar was laid out week by week rather than day by day, it still required more than thirty pages to fit everything in.

It was only a matter of days before the evil winds blew the enemy into Poland. Rabbi Baran was on target about what was in the offing, even if Vilna would be spared the worst for the next year and a half. Time and circumstance were here fused to format, the imposing dimensions of Rabbi Baran's calendar conveying a stark message. Made to cover ten years, the scope of the calendar shows he was clearly not optimistic about the carnage the evil winds would bring. He thus learned from the experience of the First World War, and then went a step further, envisioning a conflict twice the length of the previous. Though what became known as the Second World War did not, gratefully, go on for a decade, Rabbi Baran's projection of a ten-year period for the calendar's currency was not far off the mark. The copy of his calendar that I have viewed in the Yad Vashem Archives was given to the donor, Rywka Silberklang (née Senderowska), in the Bad Salzschlirf German DP camp in 1947, intact except for one missing page. She continued to make use of it to track Jewish time in the still-unsettled period after the war and, notably, preserved it as a keepsake when it had outlived its designated purpose.[6]

Another copy of the Baran calendar played a similar role for Rabbi Abba Burstein. Born in Poland and educated in the yeshiva of Bialystok, he fled to Vilna at the time of the German invasion of Poland. Rabbi Abba was able to continue yeshiva study until soon after the Russians took over in 1940. The yeshiva's students and staff were then arrested and deported to Siberia. One of the few possessions Rabbi Abba made sure to bring along was a copy of the Baran calendar: "One vital item that I did bring along was a ten-year Hebrew calendar for the years 5700–10 (1940–50), which I had purchased in Vilna." The difficult circumstances the deportees were likely to encounter made holding on to the calendar, notes Rabbi Abba, a top priority: "Out of concern that we might be taken away to distant lands, the rabbanim [the senior rabbis in charge] recommended that we be equipped with such a calendar." Their advice was on target: "[The calendar] was indeed very helpful in keeping of the dates of Yamim Tovim [high holidays] and other Jewish milestones." And Rabbi Abba's copy of the calendar had an afterlife similar to the one given to Rywka Senderowska: He eventually left Russia in the summer after the war's end and passed his copy of the calendar, with a number of years still to be used, to a Lubavitcher Chasid "who remained there." Though the war was fortunately not as drawn out as Rabbi Baran might have feared, his foresight in extending the calendar to the degree he did was not in the least wasted.[7]

Despite (or because of) the sober appraisal of the circumstances in late summer 5699/1939, Rabbi Baran nonetheless concluded his coda with a prayer for well-being in the year ahead. Beginning with an invocation that "our fears be false fears," he continued, "And may there be in the year to come for us a good year of life and peace, a year of salvation and complete redemption." Certainly, concluding with such a prayer was formulaic, a parting gesture cleaving to the rabbinic dictum to end on an upbeat note. But given the sobriety of the situation, the prayer also sounded an urgent appeal. Coming at the conclusion of this enlarged calendar and its coda, the prayer is almost a prayer that the calendar's special role as an antidote to chaos in a desolate world should not be needed. It thus set forth a prayer against itself.

The Evil Winds and the Messiah's Arrival

True to Rabbi Baran's premonition, the evil winds were not long in coming. They arrived, moreover, at a particularly sensitive period in the Jewish calendar. As mentioned, the Nazi invasion of Poland took place not only on Friday morning, September 1, 1939, but on erev Shabbat (the day before the onset of the Sabbath), 17 Elul, 5699, in the month when Jews prepare with special prayers for the onset of the Jewish New Year and, in this case, to a fraught transition to the new fifty-eighth century.

Though Rabbi Baran's ten-year calendar conveyed the mood of apprehension that lay on the horizon, the Jewish calendar also gave the possibility of solace. This was by way of the "signs of the messiah," the endeavor to find in the Jewish calendar date portent of the Messiah's arrival and an end to the suffering of Europe's Jews. Hence, the dire implications of the conflict were turned inside out. "As soon as the war broke out on the seventeenth of Elul 5699/September 1, 1939," notes Rabbi Shimon Huberband, writing in Warsaw, "all the Jews were confident that the Messiah and his redemption would come in the year 5700." Rabbi Huberband could feel the pulse of Polish Jewry from within. Born in 1909 to the daughter of the rebbe of Chechiny, he was an accomplished student of Torah and was ordained a rabbi by his distinguished grandfather.[8] He also had a gift for writing and historical research as well as a dedication to community activism. When the war broke out, he fled his home in Piotrkow with his wife and child; tragically both were killed in the fierce bombing of the war's early days. Rabbi Huberband soon found his way to Warsaw and, though anguished by the recent tragedy, remarried some months later. In Warsaw he was recruited to serve as a director of the religious section of the Self-Help Agency, and, shortly after, to join the cadre of chroniclers in the group known as the "Oyneg Shabes." Incessantly productive for some two years in documenting both religious and secular topics, he was deported to Treblinka and murdered there at the age of thirty-three.

It was as a member of the Oyneg Shabes group that Rabbi Huberband recorded the widely held belief that "the Messiah and his redemption would come in the year 5700." Confidence in this specific year was inspired, he elaborated, by "a whole slew of allusions to that effect in holy books printed hundreds of years ago,"

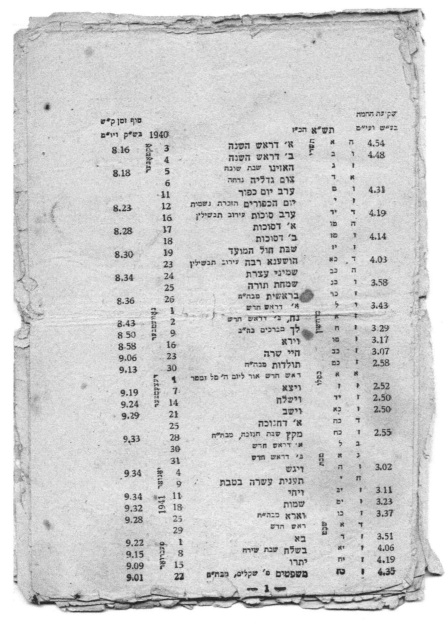

Fig. 1.1: A page from Rabbi Yehoshua Baran's ten-year calendar, printed in Vilna in 1939/5699, just before the German invasion of Poland on Elul 17 (Sept. 1). Courtesy of David Silberklang, Jerusalem.

by other "signs in holy books published decades ago," and by "popularly construed signs that were transmitted orally."[9] Entry into the new century prompted attention to both old and new sources, and those who might not have the means or wherewithal to examine the sources themselves could hear about it from their friend or neighbor. For "all the Jews," the calendar was front and center.

Searching the calendar for clues of the Messiah's yearned-for arrival was not new to the Jewish experience. But past failure had not blunted the hope that this time would be different. Rabbi Huberband thus lists a dozen such speculations, some staying with the number of the centenary year (5700), others believing that it was possible to locate a specific date within the year.

He notes, for example, that in Rabbi Gedalia ibn Yahya's book, *Shalshelet HaKabbalah*, "the following appears: 'My father and teacher in his commentary on the Book of Daniel proves that the end of days will be in the year 5700.'" The authority of a sixteenth-century sage writing of a time four hundred years in the future was a beacon of hope to many. In some cases, the search for the "end of days" tried to zero in on the specific date: "The strongest hint that emerged was that the redemption would be on the day after Passover, 5700." And when the auspicious date and year passed, Rabbi Huberband's compilation showed that the next year too, though seemingly less promising in that it did not provide a gateway into the new century, offered grounds for speculation: "When the year 5700 drew to a close and the Messiah did not come, the search began for signs regarding the year 5701."[10]

A Chasid of distinguished lineage and fiery devotion, Rabbi Huberband would have undoubtedly celebrated the advent of the Messiah with the best of them. Yet he understood his task as setting down the preoccupations of Polish Jewry at the moment. Calculating the "end of days" was one of these. We will see how others, including Torah scholars and leaders of the first rank, continued throughout the war to believe that the monumental upheaval caused by the conflict and the cruelty perpetrated against Europe's Jews had to have a meaning in the larger scope of cosmic events. And, indeed, the meaning construed was often no less than that of marking the "end of days."

A quite different approach to the wartime Jewish calendar surfaces in Rabbi Huberband's collection of wartime jokes. "If we can endure for twenty-one days, then we'll be saved," begins one, giving a sense that redemption will come in a matter of weeks ("twenty-one days"). But the punch line tells a different story. The twenty-one days do not follow one after the next, but rather are spread out through the entire calendar year: they are the "eight days of Passover, eight days of Sukkoth, two days of Rosh Hashanah, two days of Shavuos and one day of Yom Kippur." Spreading the twenty-one days along much of the length of the Jewish calendar year—from Passover in the spring to Sukkoth in the fall—shows the optimism was tentative at best. On top of that there is the inversion of the holidays' connotations, as they quickly shift in the joke from days of joyous celebration and meaningful contemplation to the prolonging of the anguish of the German occupation. (Indeed, R. Huberband elsewhere chronicles the devastating transformation of the holidays' character that took place in 5700.) One wonders, however, if the retinue of the holy days—each of which expressed in its own idiom a message of redemption—itself carried a latent message of hope.

Notes

1. See Carlebach, *Palaces of Time*, ch. 3, for the early modern background to the printing of Jewish calendars in Europe. No comparable study exists, however, for twentieth-century Jewish calendar production. For a country-by-country listing of some calendar publications, see A. Freimann, "Almanac," *Jewish Encyclopedia* (New York, 1906). The *Encyclopedia Judaica*, published some seventy years later, does not seem to have included a similar, updated list.

2. See Max Kreuzberger, "Almanache and Kalander," *Leo Baeck Institute Bibliothek and Archiv, Katalog*, vol. 1 (Tubingen: Mohr Siebeck, 1970).

3. Various collections of Jewish calendars can be found at the websites of Judaica auctions. Though focusing on Israel rather than Europe, "In Pictures: Jewish Calendars Throughout the Ages," by Michal Margalit, contains references to and images of modern European Jewish calendars. http://www.ynetnews.com/articles/0,7340,L-4575042,00.html.

4. See Freimann and Kreuzberger, as well as specific references in Carlebach, *Palaces of Time*, pp. 41–43, 209–211.

5. Yad Vashem Archives. All quotations are my translation from the Hebrew original.

6. My thanks to David Silberklang for bringing the calendar to my attention and providing the postwar anecdote.

7. Rabbi Dov Eliach, *Tales of Devotion: Tales of Triumph III* (Jerusalem: Feldheim, 2016), p. 320.

8. Rabbi Huberband was thus a first cousin of the Piaseczna Rebbe, Rabbi Kalonymous Kalman Shapira, whose important activities in the Warsaw ghetto Rabbi Huberband describes in several writings.

9. Rabbi Shimon Huberband, *Kiddush Hashem: Jewish Religious and Cultural Life in Poland during the Holocaust*, eds. Jeffrey Gurock and Robert Hirt, trans. David Fishman (Hoboken: Ktav, 1987), p. 121. On Rabbi Huberband's life and work, see "Epilogue" (actually a eulogy) by his wartime colleague Menachem Kon, reprinted in *Kiddush Hashem*, pp. 107–112; and several references in Emmanuel Ringelblum, "Oyneg Shabbes," trans. Elinor Robinson, in *Literature of Destruction*, ed. David Roskies (Philadelphia: JPS, 1989), pp. 386–98, penned by the director of the Oyneg Shabes collective in January 1943. For helpful postwar accounts, see Nachman Blumenthal and Joseph Kermish, "On Rabbi Shimon Huberband," in *Kiddush Hashem*, pp. xxi–xxix; and Samuel Kassow, *Who Will Write Our History?: Emanuel Ringelblum, the Warsaw Ghetto, and Oyneg Shabes Archive* (Bloomington: Indiana University Press, 2007), pp. 165–69. A more specialized approach can be found in Lea Prais, "An Unknown Chronicle: From the Literary Legacy of Rabbi Shimon Huberband Warsaw Ghetto, May—June 1942," *Yad Vashem Studies* 38 (2010).

10. Ibid., pp. 122–23.

II Tracking Time in the New Jewish Century

Calendars in Wartime Ghettos

Public and Secret Timekeeping in Lodz and Warsaw

The year of 5700 (1939–40) came and went, however, without witnessing the Messiah's arrival, and the evil winds that, true to Rabbi Baron's auguring, blew into Poland during this period caused immense injury, damage, and death. It was also in the first year of the war that the Nazis began to establish ghettos, a tactic that recast the life and landscape of Polish Jewry.[1]

The first ghetto was established in the fall of 1939 (5700), in Piotyrkow, only months after the German invasion of Poland; over a thousand ghettos eventually imprisoned Jews in eastern Europe. Some ghettos were enclosed behind a wall or a barbed-wire fence; entry and exit were heavily regulated. Others were more open. And still others, such as those established in Hungary late in the war, were temporary transit camps that held Jews already marked for destruction. In most cases, Jews were forced to move to a poor section of the city, were confined to a constricted area, and were crowded into undersized living quarters. Sanitation was often poor, disease common, and rations meager. Though ghettos were usually under the administration of a Jewish council, they were subject to the enemy's reign of terror. In time, this included deportations to labor camps, concentration camps, and death camps.

The World War II ghettos of eastern and central Europe maintained a semblance of Jewish community while creating conditions that often made attention to the calendar difficult and even dangerous. Calendars were at times official publications of ghetto authorities, at other times printed and circulated by the underground press. In some cases, rabbinic figures took it upon themselves to make calendars available to their besieged community, while in other cases laypeople eager to stay in touch with time's passage made their own. Some ghettos brought out an elaborate printed calendar yearly, others were able to publish them only clandestinely, and still others may have had to rely on handwritten calendars. Fashioners of surrogate calendars, ghetto diarists often alternated between Jewish and Gregorian dates, highlighting one or the other as the situation demanded.

The Lodz ghetto was the second largest, the most insular, and the longest surviving in Poland.[2] A cruel temporary home for around two hundred thousand Jews, it was established and sealed off on May 1, 1940; the end came over four years later, in the summer of 1944. In between, starvation, disease, wanton murder, and waves of deportations to the Chelmno death camp thinned out the ghetto population. Forced to live for years on the edge of annihilation, the ghetto administration, dominated by the so-called "eldest of the Jews," Mordechai Chaim Rumkowski, pursued the hope that providing a source of indispensable labor to the enemy's war effort would stave off destruction.

During its precarious existence, the Lodz ghetto administration published official calendars for the years 1941–44, which employed different formats to address a variety of needs and purposes. With a print run of close to six thousand, the calendars were earmarked exclusively for official use; indeed, a stern warning was mailed out to make recipients aware of the fact that the "calendars constitute[d] official inventory and [could] only be used for office purposes."[3] It is not clear, however, how firmly those who "used" the calendars followed the directive or how strictly it was enforced. Be that as it may, a good number of calendars circulated in the ghetto, providing a calendrical guide for those who sought it. To be sure, not everyone did: "In the ghetto," wrote fourteen-year-old Sara Plagier, "we had no need for a calendar. Our lives were divided into periods based on the distribution of food: bread every eighth day, the ration once a month. Each day fell into two parts: before and after we received our soup. In this way the time passed."[4] Hunger was often a preoccupation, sometimes sadly defining life in the ghetto to such a degree that the day had room for little else. But the official calendars undoubtedly helped time pass in other significant ways.

The 1942 printed Lodz ghetto calendar presents one striking version of a thoroughly bifocal calendar. Patterned on the Gregorian, it begins on January 1 (a Thursday that year) and ends on December 31 (also a Thursday). It notes on each page the number of weeks into the Gregorian year: the week of February 22 is the ninth week, of May 17 the twenty-first week, and so on. The Arabic numerals furnishing the day of the month are unusually large and bold, as if they were made to be seen at a distance. The heading also conveys in roman numerals the number of the month (January is I, February II, April IV, October X) and in Arabic numerals the month's allotment of days (February had twenty-eight this time around). The information is uncommonly comprehensive; nothing is left out in providing the data required to locate oneself in time according to Gregorian dating, circa 1942.

Yet the symmetry between the Gregorian and Jewish calendars is equally striking. Gregorian dates occupy boxes on the left, Jewish dates occupy boxes on the right, and, a design touch very much part of ghetto life, a blackened Jewish star, is the symbol stationed between the two. The effect is that of a mirror

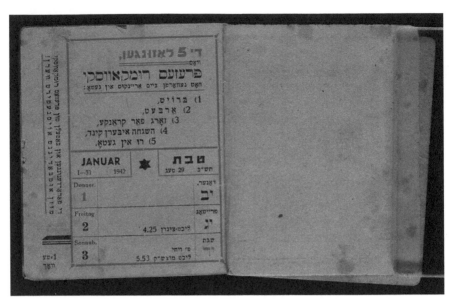

Fig. 2.1: Jewish calendars were issued annually in the Lodz ghetto, the second largest in wartime Poland. Printed in a combination of Hebrew, Yiddish, and German, the calendars commenced with the beginning of the secular year but were oriented around the Sabbath and Jewish holidays. The 1942 calendar also contained didactic maxims authored by Chaim Rumkowski, head of the ghetto. Courtesy of the Yad Vashem Archives.

reflection. The balance notwithstanding, the week is Jewish through and through, beginning on Sunday/Sontag, ending with Sonnabend/Shabbat, and includes the times that Shabbat entered and concluded for that particular week. And as befits a comprehensive Jewish calendar, this one lists the weekly Torah portion (posted at the top of the page), the Omer count in full, the time of the monthly molad, and the seasonal fast days.[5]

The symmetry appears only in the layout and dates of the calendars. As with almost all other bifocal Jewish calendars from this period, the content of the calendars—the holidays, fast days, and other seasonal observances—is exclusively Jewish. There is no reference to the observance of Christian festivals, not even the most conspicuous. The Gregorian calendar laid out here is secular in character; it provides the grid on which the Jewish year can be elaborated. Thus the Lodz ghetto calendar is a sheep in wolf's clothing. It appears to follow the ways of the gentile world but actually uses it to set forth a detailed guide to Jewish observance. In terms of languages, the calendar alternates between German for the Gregorian and Hebrew-Yiddish for the Jewish. This inclusiveness goes far in the calendar's details, especially where it gives the Jewish date in Hebrew script and also, in a smaller font, in Arabic numerals, seemingly for those who couldn't manage the larger Hebrew-scripted date.

Originating in the Lodz ghetto, the calendar is predictably Rumkowski-centered. The title page displays his photo, and his sayings and directives dot each page. A brief outline of the ghetto's five essential concerns prefaces all: (1) work; (2) bread; (3) care for the sick; (4) supervision of children; and (5) maintaining calm in the ghetto—an ensemble of priorities that, as we know, were easier said than done. At the bottom of each page are pithy one-liners culled from his various ceremonial speeches, with information on the occasion provided in parentheses: "For the good of the ghetto," notes the page of 12 Adar / March 1, "you must follow my directives!" (an exclamation mark serves as each directive's ubiquitous concluding punctuation). Or for 6 Tammuz / June 21, "Keep clean your residence, clothing, and furnishings!"—in this case the parental-like counsel is underlined but no source listed, as if this specific guideline were coined fresh and, even though half a year into the calendar, especially urgent to take notice of.

The calendar was also used to track the ghetto's history, as noteworthy events and developments were recorded on the day on which they occurred in the previous years of the ghetto's existence, 1940 or 1941. A year before, on February 1, 1941, for instance, the "culture-house" opened, an occurrence now preserved by the 1942 calendar; or two years earlier, on June 4, 1940, the Reizna branch of the post office was established. Though not every day of the 1942 calendar records an anniversary of a certain feature of Lodz ghetto life, many do. The 1942 edition thus serves as a log of past ghetto events even as it sets forth the coming year.

Such an interior chronicle, as one might call it, demonstrated the multiple achievements of the ghetto's first years and, by means of them, hoped to inspire confidence that the year ahead would be equal to its predecessors. It also gave the ghetto an identity, a history that belonged to it alone. More than many, this calendar envisioned its task as cultivating a common memory among the ghetto's Jews; the recent past had not only been the era of loss and terror but also of building a community day in, day out. Recording such mundane events deflected attention from the bitter privations of ghetto life and focused it on the quiet signs of persisting civilization.

Strikingly, the interior chronicle of significant ghetto events refers exclusively to the Gregorian calendar; the culture house opening occurred in *1941*, not in 5701; the post office branch was established in *1940*, not in 5700. The day-by-day ledger of ghetto events unfolded *according to* secular history; the left side of the calendar weighed in here. Jews may have been the ones to open the culture house, and the anniversary of its opening may have been set down in Yiddish. But the time zone these mundane community events occupied was secular. This approach did not cancel the liturgical, the calendar's right side. It remained just where it was.

In fact, to employ the Gregorian calendar in such a fashion sharpened the character of the traditionally Jewish calendar. For it demonstrated that the Gregorian calendar that stood alongside the Jewish one was patently not Christian, not *theirs*. In a sense, one knew that already, because, as mentioned earlier, the calendar omitted any reference to a Christian holiday. Yet the meaning of that omission was taken another step by using the Gregorian dating as a means to commemorate everyday life in the ghetto. That alone was its role, purpose, and justification. Drained of Christian content, the Gregorian dating could complement the Jewish calendar without posing a threat or challenge to it.

Marking virtually all anniversaries by the Gregorian date, the calendar's only exception may have been Chaim Rumkowski's birthday. Historian Isaiah Trunk has noted that Rumkowski's is the single birthday—and, I would add, the single personal event—noted in the calendar's inventory of community anniversaries.[6] This transformation of the birthday from a personal concern into a community event jibes perfectly with how the calendar is on the whole outfitted to serve Rumkowski's purposes. What Trunk did not mention, however, is that the birthday may also be the only anniversary dated according to the Jewish calendar. Rumkowski's birthday, February 27, 1877, does not appear on this date but rather on the Jewish date of his birth, the holiday of Purim, Adar 14. Opting for the Jewish date is not the surprising element; for eastern European Jews of this period, it was likely more common to mark a birthday according to the Jewish calendar. What is remarkable is how the Jewish calendar dating contrasts with how the other events are listed, setting the marking of Rumkowski's birthday apart from all other commemorations.

Two years on, the Lodz ghetto calendar from 1944 maintains the same design, continues to highlight Rumkowski, and records ghetto events from previous years. But a few changes are noteworthy. First, the Rumkowski-centered approach has been toned down; though this year's version of the calendar again highlights the elder's photograph on the title page, it omits his page-concluding directives. The calendar no longer serves as a vehicle for transmitting his parental voice. But the listing of Rumkowski's birthday remains on the holiday of Purim, its perseverance providing a subtle way to demonstrate his singular prestige in the ghetto. The 1944 calendar continued to record significant community anniversaries. Yet there is a nuanced change here too. For these entries are almost entirely from the year 1943 and thus comprise not so much a comprehensive catalog of ghetto events as an update on developments, acting as a shorthand annual newsletter.

More compact and less editorialized ways of tracking time also existed in the Lodz ghetto. One took the form of a pocket calendar, the other a year-at-a-glance wall or desk calendar. The 1944 pocket calendar follows the design of the larger version but leaves out not only the elder's directives but also any listing of

Fig. 2.2: The first page of a pocket calendar for the year 1944, printed in the Lodz ghetto. The calendar was owned by Bernard Fuchs, head of the employment office of the Lodz ghetto Jewish Council. United States Holocaust Memorial Museum, courtesy of Bert and Irene Fleming.

community achievements or developments. No openings or foundings are thus cataloged, an abridgement that likely came about to conform to the smaller dimensions of this calendar. What does remain is the Purim listing of Rumkowski's birthday: "Geburtstag fun Preses M. H. Rumkowski" is thus the only nonliturgical entry left. In this case, its placement in the Jewish calendar no longer makes it the odd one out but rather of a piece with all the other information about Shabbat, holidays, Rosh Chodesh, and fast days. Indeed, having pruned all secular references, the pocket calendar confers on the elder's birthday a liturgical status of its own.

Appearing by at least 1942, the year-at-a-glance edition maintains virtually all the features of the other versions but compresses them into a single page. The Gregorian calendar orients the January start point and December end point. Otherwise, the calendar, like its more detailed companions, conveys the necessary information for Jewish observance of special days through the year. The mirror effect is here even more intense, the single-page format making it seem as if neither calendar could do without the other. In terms of ghetto life, Rumkowski's picture is still in place. But everything else extraneous to the calendar has gone by the wayside, even the pocket calendar's lingering reference to the elder's birthday. What's left to locate it in time and space is the small right-side heading, positioned fittingly under a Jewish star, written in both German and Yiddish: "Litzmannstadt Getto"—the Germanic name imposed by the enemy.

The Lodz ghetto calendars found in archives enrich our sense of how time was tracked during the Holocaust. But such calendars remain abstracted from the circumstances of their setting and how they were used within them. As with artifacts generally, calendars make demands on our imagination, asking us to create a context for them, or at least to puzzle together the bits and pieces of context that we have.

In some cases, fortunately, there are ways to get a more vivid sense of context. Photographs, although imposing their own conventions, reclaim something of the calendars in situ. Photographs taken in the Lodz ghetto show the honored position given to the calendars in their daily setting. In one instance, the calendar is actually still in formation, and we can see children and adults participating in assembling it. Posed above a table laden with calendar pages and sections—and sheets bearing images of Rumkowski, authoritarian head of the ghetto—each worker sees to his or her own task. Other photographs show the finished calendar in various ghetto offices and businesses, in bakeries, pharmacies, and other locales. Hanging on the wall, standing on a desk, dangling from the pin of a shelf, the calendars, dated from 1941 to 1943, accompanied the activity of daily life, providing the timekeeping service they usually do.

In two instances they do more. The calendars act not simply as background items but rather play a featured role. One photograph, taken inside a pharmacy, displays a desk, a vase with flowers, and a calendar—the type with a window displaying a single day, in this case September 24, 1941. Showing only the Gregorian date, the Jewish one silently hovers in the shadows: it was the third day of the new Jewish year, a fast day in honor of a slain leader of ancient Israel, Gedaliah. On the previous day, Rumkowski, attending New Year's prayer services, "said that menacing clouds were hanging over the ghetto" and asked the assembled to "pray to God that he spare the Jews of the ghetto from any new affliction." He was summoned by the enemy later that day to inform him that thousands of Jews in communities near Lodz would soon be brought into the ghetto.[7]

The second photograph, taken apparently a few months earlier, is special in two respects. First, it shows one of the bifocal weekly calendars we are familiar with, turned to the summer month of Tammuz. And second, in this photograph the calendar is clearly the centerpiece. Standing on a desk, it is positioned directly in the photograph's center. For whatever reason, the calendar was in its own right worth the photograph.

Other Lodz ghetto calendar episodes fall between the cracks. Moshe Prager cites a story told by Yosef Borenstein about his brother Falk. The latter was imprisoned after he and his friends were flushed out of a hideout where they studied Torah. Spiritually focused though the young Chasidim were, the enemy took them for spies or saboteurs. "They were put through all sorts of hellish tortures in order to make them reveal the 'secrets' of their underground. They were beaten bloody. After one beating, the wounded, bleeding lads met for a moment in a corridor. Moshe Liss, who knew the Jewish calendar by heart, quickly called out to my brother Falk, 'Tomorrow night we begin to say "Tal u'matar.""'[8] *Tal u'Matar*, which translates literally as "dew and rain," refers to the blessing for rain invoked in daily prayer during the winter (i.e., rainy) season. Moshe Liss felt that, whatever the ordeal he and his friends were subjected to, this information was what was important to convey. Summarizing the episode in his book *With God in Hell*, Rabbi Eliezer Berkovits distills in sharp terms its significance: "Who cared about the Nazis! In the middle of the inferno, these young Jews, bruised and bleeding from German barbarism, could focus on such a small nuance of their prayers, reflecting the change of season."[9]

But the heroic gesture in the wartime Lodz ghetto took on added depth on my flight from Tel Aviv to New York in fall 2015. In the seat next to me sat a convivial middle-aged Gerrer Chasid, Lazar Borenstein, who, when he heard I was writing a book on wartime Jewish calendars, said, "Do I have a story for you"—and proceeded to tell me the story of his uncle, Rabbi Borenstein, who had told him the above story of Tal u'Matar, which his uncle had lived through. I couldn't help calling out in the middle of Lazar's recounting, "I know that story!" At that moment, however, I heard the story anew, and felt from inside the Lodz ghetto, as it were, the unbending meticulous concern for honoring the precepts of the Jewish calendar.

Lodz's calendars are the most thorough I have found for any wartime ghetto. Exactly how thorough becomes apparent when contrasting Lodz with Warsaw.[10] In the archives of the largest wartime ghetto, no official calendar has surfaced. This may well have been because the printing houses were shut down early on. Indeed, this occurred already in July 1940, months before the ghetto was officially established and sealed off. "This week," lamented Chaim Kaplan on July 8, "another new edict was put into effect. . . . True to their program, the conquerors closed the printing houses owned by Jews, and as if that were not enough, they removed the presses and scattered the type faces."[11]

The edict, however draconian and insolent, did not close off all routes of printing. A vigorous underground press persevered, publishing over the next two years some forty newspapers as well as other forms of vital information. And there is some evidence that calendars were considered vital. In chronicling the sad fate of Jewish holy books in the wake of the prohibition against printing, Rabbi Shimon Huberband singles out the calendar: "No holy books are printed any more. Almost all Jewish printing houses are locked up. Printing materials, such as paper, ink, and other items, are extremely expensive, and there is a general ban on printing, due to reasons of censorship. Only tiny, flawed calendars were secretly printed for the current year, 5702 (1941–42)."[12] Even with the wholesale restrictions, calendars continued to be printed, serving as the exception to the rule. When all else stopped, tracking time in the Warsaw ghetto by way of the "tiny" and the "flawed" had to proceed. Nevertheless, the atypical procedures affected production in three ways, each related to the others. That one could print the calendars only clandestinely meant the preferred format was small in order that it could be less conspicuous and more easily concealed. And the "tiny" format ostensibly made it difficult to compose, leading to "flawed" production or composition. Exactly how tiny and precisely what flaws they contained, we don't know; none of these calendars have turned up. Yet whatever the difficulties besetting their production and shaping the form in which they emerged, calendars remained something essential to life in the Warsaw ghetto.

The secretly printed calendars were apparently no easier to obtain for those in positions of authority. Writing close to when Rabbi Huberband set down his assessment, Adam Czerniakow, head of Warsaw's Jewish council, tells of his fruitless search for a calendar in the Warsaw ghetto in winter 1942 and his prudent response: "It is impossible to buy a calendar either in the ghetto or outside. I have been obliged to make a calendar for myself."[13] A resourceful approach to the lack of what was deemed a basic necessity, Czerniakow's self-made calendar has also yet to appear. But his diary entry itself conveys some important information. First, even with his connections, the head of the Jewish council was unable to obtain a calendar. If he couldn't do it, one surmises, what of others who had less pull? Few statements could show better how elusive tracking time was while imprisoned in the ghetto. Second, several aspects of Czerniakow's comment suggest that the calendar he was seeking as well as the one he made were not primarily Jewish calendars. The unsuccessful attempt to buy a calendar "outside" the ghetto implies trying to obtain a Gregorian calendar from non-Jews. Further, the entry's date, January 7, soon after the onset of the Gregorian calendar year, meant he was active in his search at the time when the Gregorian calendar from 1941 had lapsed and a new calendar would have been required. The calendar he sought, like the Lodz ghetto calendars surveyed above, could have been framed according to the Gregorian year but had joined to it the Jewish calendar. Indeed, knowledge of when the Jewish holidays were slated to occur in the broader context of the Gregorian year may have been important for someone in Czerniakow's position to be aware of. Yet given his modest education in subjects having to do with traditional Jewish observance, the self-made calendar he ended up with probably did not include a Jewish calendar.[14]

Lublin's Rabbinic Chronicler of Jewish Time

Some forty thousand Jews lived in prewar Lublin, a third of the city's overall population. The numerous Jewish institutions of the city included twelve synagogues, many more informal centers of prayer, a hospital, an orphanage, and three cemeteries. Of the many yeshivas, the crown jewel was Yeshiva Chochmei Lublin, renowned throughout the world both for its high standards of Torah study and for its state-of-the-art facilities.

Having entered Poland on September 1, the German army reached Lublin on September 18, 1939, the fifth of Tishrei in the Jewish calendar, a Monday that fell exactly in the middle of the ten days of repentance between Rosh Hashana and Yom Kippur. As with other cities populated by a large Jewish community, the enemy decreed progressively oppressive measures: initially, the forced resettlement of Lublin's Jews and mandatory wearing of the Jewish badge; not long after, in January 1940, the formation of a Jewish council; a year later, in spring 1941 (5701), the establishment of a ghetto; and most devastatingly, in spring 1942, deportations of most of the city's Jews to the Belzec death camp. The final murderous stages occurred when the few thousand surviving Lublin Jews were taken to the Maidanek death camp in fall 1942 or early 1943; a hundred or so remaining souls were killed in summer 1944. In a few short years, Jewish Lublin was made into a ghost of its former self.[15]

Rabbi Tzvi Elimelekh Talmud was one of five city rabbis in Lublin when the war began.[16] Rabbi Talmud was born in 1912 in the Polish town of Glogow to Yisrael Leib and Regina, one of three boys in a family of five children. He had been a prominent student in the Chochmei Lublin yeshiva, where he was already known for his facility in composing calendars.[17] After completing his studies, he had remained in Lublin, becoming in a relatively brief time a major rabbinic voice in the city's Jewish affairs. In the wake of the German invasion and occupation, he continued to play an active role, which included serving on the Jewish council once the ghetto was established in spring 5701 (March 1941). He was thirty years old when, in Elul 5702, he composed a calendar for the year 5703. The previous spring, most of Lublin's Jews had been deported to their deaths. Some four thousand to five thousand Jews remained in what was called the Majdan Tatarski ghetto.

Rabbi Talmud had already published a calendar for 5700 (1939–40), the year the war broke out. This was certainly an accomplishment in its own right. But his calendar for 5703 was a different story, handwritten and composed in the immediate wake of the deportation.[18] The task before him was clearly daunting. The deported had consisted of members of Rabbi Talmud's immediate and extended family, including his wife and son. And he understandably saw the immense difficulty in facing what he described in a letter from this period as a "foreseeable future . . . filled with foreboding."[19] The fact that Rabbi Talmud wrote these words at a particularly auspicious time in the Jewish calendar, 14 Menachem Av—an upswing in the calendar after a three-week period of mourning—intensifies the sense that the future must have appeared especially bleak. Yet such foreboding did not push him off course. For his calendar graphically sketched a future that extended beyond what even in normal times might be termed as "foreseeable." Indeed, to bring forth such a calendar at this juncture not only enabled observance for those who remained in the reconstituted Lublin ghetto but also envisioned—nay, virtually created—a future to be lived. Rabbi Talmud undertook this task as he, in the painful absence of the former *hazanim* (leaders of communal prayer), prepared himself to lead the High Holiday prayers for the first—and, alas, the final—time.

Like most wartime Jewish calendars, Rabbi Talmud's was bifocal, with the days of the Jewish months and those of the Gregorian set down in parallel columns. Yet it is clearly the Jewish dates on the calendar that receive his greatest attention. There he highlights a number of special days, some found in most such wartime productions, others more uncommon. Among the former were Shabbat (marked by a ש, underscored to set off one week from the next and distinguished by candle-lighting times and the name of the week's Torah portion) and holidays; among the latter were a full cycle of fast days, Lag b'Omer, and especially the designation of the four seasonal "tekufot."

Several aspects stand out in Rabbi Talmud's way of presenting tradition. First, his calendar uses only Hebrew letters; no vernacular language or lettering plays anything but a marginal role. Indeed, Yiddish, a vernacular Jewish tongue written in Hebrew letters, appears only sparingly (and even then, only in the headings and not in the calendar per se). It seems the author opted for the Hebrew rather than the Yiddish both as the simplest shorthand abbreviation and also to eschew virtually any vernacular in the main calendar. In this way, sacred time would be given expression through the sacred medium of the Hebrew language. To employ exclusively Hebrew words and Hebrew letters went far to render the calendar itself a sacred object, as close as possible to a sacred book.

Second, setting forth nearly all that an observant Jew requires for fulfillment of his or her religious obligations, Rabbi Talmud's calendar nevertheless often expressed these notations economically, even laconically. The Hebrew letters indicating the days of the week, for instance, fall into this category. But so does the ditto sign (") under the holiday of Purim, on the fourteenth day of the month of Adar, indicating a second day of Purim (called Shushan Purim) celebrated in a small group of ancient cities. Instead of writing out the name fully, Rabbi Talmud added to it the one word *Shushan*. He did not, however, follow this economizing policy in every situation. Special days, whether marking a fast or otherwise, he usually wrote out in full rather than using numerals (e.g., the *seventeenth day* of Tammuz rather than the *17th*). Neither time nor space was saved here. The longer format was a way to honor the occasion, as a name rather than a number would honor a person.

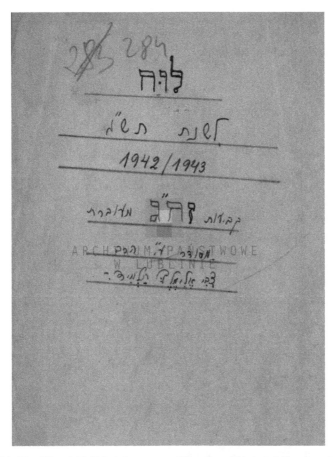

Fig. 2.3: Rabbi Tzvi Elimelekh Talmud was one of five city rabbis in Lublin when the war began and had already published a calendar for 5700 (1939–40). But his calendar for 5703 (1942–43) was a different story, composed in the immediate wake of the deportation of most Lublin's Jews, including Rabbi Talmud's wife and son. To bring forth such a calendar at this juncture not only enabled observance for those who remained in the reconstituted Lublin ghetto but also envisioned a future to be lived. Courtesy of the Polish State Archives.

Third is his special mode of orchestrating the calendar according to the month and week. Each Jewish month of the year 5703 receives its own page, first Tishrei, then Marcheshvan, and so on. The month clearly dominates; it is the pivot of time around which days and weeks, even hours, minutes, and seconds, spin. As we know, this is standard fare. Somewhat less usual are the parallel vertical columns that set out the month's basic coordinates in a rigorously compressed space; the most important data take up a mere fraction of the page. This compression clearly dovetails with Rabbi Talmud's desire for economy of expression; it also enables the eye to take in basic calendrical facts at a glance. But beyond the practical exigencies guiding the calendar's nimble construction, the compression of the columns surrounded by a largesse of uncrowded space also suggests the plight of the ghetto itself. To whatever degree the unfortunate circumstances of the vestige of Lublin's ghetto may have subconsciously influenced the calendar's graphic format, it is equally suggestive that the columns are packed with the fundamental elements of sacred time.

If the month plays the greatest role in shaping the calendar's format, the week nevertheless has its say too. Heavy horizontal lines break the columns into weeks, a steady, predictable unfolding over the course of the month. More than in any comparable month-based wartime calendar, Rabbi Talmud highlighted the week's essential place.

Executed with finesse, learning, and painstaking comprehensiveness, it is no wonder that, under such a weight of loss and foreboding uncertainty, not every detail seems to have been accurate. The calculations for the moladim, for instance—the moment when the new moon first emerges and signals the onset of the new month—are generally on target but occasionally off. Yet the discrepancies are by no means great. And they too show a remarkable dedication to what was deemed an essential aspect of tradition as transmitted by way of the Jewish calendar; it was no accident that, in Rabbi Talmud's 5703 calendar like in many others, the molad was given pride of place at the top of the page of each month. But the conditions of composition at this point in time in the Lublin ghetto must have been such as to make some degree of inaccuracy certain.

Even when conditions worsened, Rabbi Talmud's dedication to calendar making remained firm. When he, together with most of the ghetto's inmates, was transported to the Majdanek death camp in fall 5703 (November 1942), he continued, in a place and time of death and enslavement, to offer religious guidance to the Jews imprisoned there. And to this end, he once again authored a calendar, his trademark way of ensuring that Jewish time would orient Jewish life even in the bleakest circumstances. But this characterization does not do full justice to the degree of his commitment to Jewish time. As reported by another Maidanek prisoner, "[Rabbi Talmud] made calendars and sent them to us in our places of work."[20] Not content to have a single calendar in his own possession, he instead made several that could reach his fellow inmates where they most needed them. In his hands, the Jewish calendar remained a communal artifact, circulating among Jews wherever they might be. Rabbi Talmud was murdered in Maidanek sometime after—the unknown date in 5703 (1943) presumably marked by that year's calendar that he so carefully composed. And yet in the death camp, as in Lublin and the ghetto previously, among Rabbi Talmud's final contributions was to make sure that Jewish time continued to be portable and immediate, a graphic witness to a Jewish past, present, and future.

Making the Past Present: The Midwar Conversion of a Polish Pocket Calendar

Most wartime calendars were built from scratch. The author of the calendar-to-be took a blank sheet of paper and, calling to mind calendars hanging on the wall at home, resting on a desk in the workplace, or carried from one place to another in a pocket, set about fashioning one of his or her own. In a way, the blank sheet of paper was a natural starting point. It allowed the author the freedom to render the calendar as one wished, just like in normal times.

But these were not normal times, and, as with a number of taken-for-granted commodities (what Osher Lehmann in wartime Amsterdam had referred to as "common things"), blank sheets of paper were not always available. In such cases, one made do with what one could. Diarists and other chroniclers, for example, sometimes were compelled to set down their reflections on the margins of printed books or newspapers.

Certainly, a strategy of this sort could also make it easier to hide the evidence of what was seen by the enemy to be subversive activity. For example, Rabbi Shimon Huberband, followed such a procedure in the Warsaw ghetto, even when his friends felt the risk to be minimal.[21] Opting to write in the blank spaces of already printed material could thus conceal what might, if discovered, endanger the author. Reusing printed material could also circumvent the lack of basic materials on which to write or draw.

A remarkable calendar rendered in the midst of wartime Poland shows how far at times one had to go in this direction. In doing so, this rough-hewn calendar for 5704 (1944) testifies uncommonly well to the desperate isolation of the Jews stranded in Holocaust Europe, Jews who were yearning to find a way—any way—to locate themselves in Jewish time. In this case, the technique was to improvise a Jewish calendar within a Polish one (something like the infrequent practice of one kind of bird taking up lodging in the nest of another).[22] At first glance, that one calendar could serve as a sketch board for the other makes good sense; no matter how different they may be, both the Jewish and Gregorian dating share the calendar's basic idiom: days, weeks, and months.

But no calendar is neutral, and this pocket calendar was a case in point. The fit was awkward at best. That this anonymous Jew could in wartime Poland (or Russia or elsewhere) make it serve his ends, using a combination of means one would never have dreamed of in normal circumstances, is nothing short of astonishing.

The basis is all too humble in origin: a Polish pocket calendar for the year 1939, bearing the title *Kieskonowy Kalandarz Podrecznik* ("Pocket Calendar Companion"). The original had a binding, contained an almanac with a vast amount of material, and ran to 157-plus pages. Production was sponsored by the camera-film company Kodak ("Kodak: foto/kino amatora," reads the calendar's subtitle), printed in Warsaw, and distributed by M. Rabinowitz at 8 Wielka Street in Vilna. Other film-developing vendors throughout Poland brought out the same kind of "Kodak" pocket calendar for this year, the only change being the name and address of the shop proprietor printed inside the title page.[23]

It took vision, imagination, and practical acumen to transform this hefty Polish calendar into one that would serve a very different purpose from that for which it was manufactured. Nowhere in the original printed calendar does one see any indication of a Jewish calendar; no days, months, or years are rendered according to its idiom or nomenclature. The "Pocket Calendar Companion" is a Polish-language Gregorian calendar through and through, outfitted with extras. Yet calendar it is. Only this basic, rudimentary, but essential feature—and seemingly this alone—made it attractive enough to serve as a template for a Jewish calendar for the year 5704.[24]

The task of adaptation was formidable. Polish calendars of that era (and many of our time as well) were not neutral timekeepers but rather came equipped with their own local color. This included the red highlighting of not only Sunday but also some fourteen Christian holidays. This was already a substantial dose of Christian-oriented dates. But the Christian influence on the calendar was far more pervasive. Like many Polish calendars from that period, this one lists the name of a Catholic saint canonized on *every date*. Referred to as "Imieniny," the name-date listing made it possible for Catholics to celebrate the occasion, honoring thereby both the saint and those who, having been born on or near this date, were named after him or her.

To have information related to Christian calendar events was not unusual in Jewish calendars from an earlier time.[25] In order to be in sync with market days and other dates pertinent to business dealings, for instance, European Jewish calendars had at times incorporated information about when and where the events would be held. But wartime Jewish calendars, while almost always including a column for the parallel Gregorian calendar dates, studiously avoided any reference to Christian holy days. From the point of view of the Jewish calendar author, such holidays had no currency within the realm of Jewish life and experience and were thus excluded from citation. In the case of the "Pocket Calendar Companion," however, the Jewish calendar author, using the Polish printed calendar as a basis, had to take what came with the territory—including red-highlighted holidays and the daily listing of the relevant saint. The listing of these names in a Polish calendar was such a common convention that it may have made no more impression on the Jewish author than did the Gregorian dates themselves. Nevertheless, in hindsight the name-day custom intensifies our appreciation for how radically the Jewish author had to adapt the printed calendar to a purpose far different than originally intended.

The almanac portion of the calendar must have prompted a separate set of concerns. Though presenting a focus less dissonant than Christian religious observance, the almanac making up most of the calendar's pages brought another side of Polish culture front and center. Indeed, at least every second page of the calendar provided practical or technical information that had nothing to do with the calendar per se; in some cases, the almanac section went on for several pages at a stint. That a pocket calendar should devote so much space to other sorts of information only seems peculiar from today's perspective, where such calendars are usually less encumbered. In former days, however, well-stocked almanacs were as much the rule as the exception.[26]

As one might expect from a publication with a single sponsor, most pages elaborated on aspects of Kodak film production, while others provided tables for measurement conversion and the like; the calendar's closing pages even listed something akin to Kodak's version of the periodic table. In most of the calendar, the author or authors of the improvised Jewish calendar used only the blank spaces opposite the date, leaving the almanac pages free of notes or writing of any kind. The decision not to write on or over the almanac seems first of all an obvious practical step, since most of the almanac was densely packed with printed material. And given the author's focus, there was little or no reason to go beyond the calendar itself and into the adjoining material.

But there is a single deviation. On pages 86–87, the author lists the names of murdered family, friends, or neighbors. In this case, the grim topic at hand carries the author well beyond the border between calendar and almanac; no conventional boundary could constrict the witness's record to a crime of these proportions. The exceptionality of such a gesture shows the stark power of listing the names of the murdered.

For more practical reasons as well, the Polish printed calendar had to have been awkward to use. The "Pocket Calendar Companion" was organized for the year 1939; the Jewish calendar's author arranged it for the year 1944—which was apparently the year he or she was about to enter or already had. For the first two months of the year, the days were thus out of sync: January 1 fell on a Sunday in 1939 but on a Saturday in 1944; February 20 fell on a Monday in 1939 but a Sunday in 1944. However, with 1944 in the Gregorian calendar being a leap year, wherein February gained an extra day, March began in both years on a Wednesday. From that point forward they matched up. The lack of correspondence in the first two months clearly caused some problems: the tenth of Tevet, a fast day, took place in 5704 on Thursday, January 6; on the calendar, it was opposite January 5. Yet this lag of a day did not form an insurmountable barrier. What was of ultimate importance was that the Polish calendar, like many or most, laid out the year in the sequence of days, weeks, and months. And each and every day had blank space where the Jewish date and accompanying information could be set down. This was what mattered most.

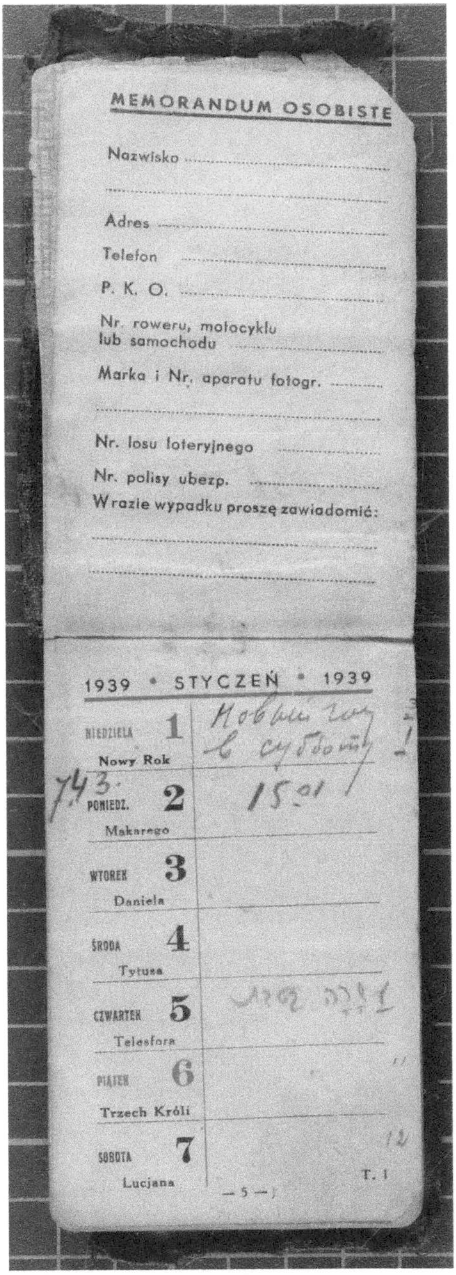

Fig. 2.4: Issued originally in Vilna in 1939 by a photo development shop, the "Kodak Pocket Companion [Gregorian] Calendar" was recycled by an unknown Polish Jew as a Jewish calendar for 5703 (1942–43). It also doubled as a log of the tragic events besetting Polish Jewry. Courtesy of the Ghetto Fighters' Museum Archives.

Exactly how much so is shown by the improvised calendar's starting point: the tenth day of the month of Tevet, written out in full. The date is one of the four traditional fast days, commemorating the onset of the Babylonian siege of ancient Jerusalem, the continuation of which brought about the fall of the city and the destruction of the Temple. The fast day was established to offer the opportunity for repentance for the sins that, according to tradition, played a role in leading to the siege and ensuing destruction. Coming in the middle of the week in the year of 5704, the tenth of Tevet was not a natural point at which to begin the Jewish calendar. It would have made more sense to launch it at the beginning of the week, when the Polish calendar itself commenced on January 1. But the choice to delay the beginning of the Jewish calendar until midweek has at least two implications: (a) By waiting until midweek (Wednesday, January 5, in Gregorian dating), Jewish time unfolds independently of the Gregorian calendar year. January 1 may be the starting point for this Polish Gregorian calendar, but it does not orient the Jewish year. Jewish time marches to a different drummer, and the staggered start to the Jewish dating graphically emphasizes that difference. (b) Bearing associations of travail and repentance, the tenth of Tevet immediately links the start of the improvised Jewish calendar with the commemoration of past Jewish catastrophe as well as with a strategy of responding to it. Hence, the calendar's doorway into Jewish time, a traditional fast day, provided a means to cope with the present catastrophe.

The author perhaps also intuited that the tenth day of Tevet had a particular relevance that would be revealed more fully in the years to come. For, following the war, the day became one of those chosen to publicly honor the memory of the Holocaust's victims. Instead of opting to establish a new day of commemoration, the decision to observe the tenth of Tevet viewed as a virtue the fast day's ties to the Jewish past. The meaning of the past could then be carried over into the future.[27]

The graphic dimension of this calendar's Jewish dating is one of the most complicated of any wartime calendar, no doubt due, at least in part, to the need to adapt the Jewish dating to a non-Jewish calendar. But there are likely other reasons. The Jewish dates are generally written in Arabic numerals. So the improvised dating begins in the month of Tevet (on p. 5 of the calendar) with the handwritten numerals 11, 12, and so on (we recall that the first date, the tenth of Tevet, is written out in script). The dates of the months of Shevat, Nisan, and Iyar are similarly set down in Arabic numerals.

Yet in contrast to all others, the month of Adar (which begins on p. 23, after Shevat and before Nisan) puzzlingly uses not Arabic numerals but Hebrew letters to number the dates, a switch from one method of numbering to another that I haven't found in other Jewish calendars, wartime or otherwise. The change may indicate that multiple authors were, either simultaneously or sequentially, involved in the Jewish calendar's production, and that, for whatever reason, a different hand with a different sensibility took charge in that month. But the explanation may have to do with the nature of the month of Adar itself. One of the main themes associated with the month is the reversal of fortune, the plot of the evil Haman to destroy the Jews being turned on its head, leading to his timely demise and to the Jewish nation's salvation. The month's main theme of reversal may then have spurred the change from the non-Jewish to the Jewish script, and then back again.

The month that follows, Nisan, is notable for a different reason: the number of the date of every day of the month is emended by one. Thus the number 10 is thickly superimposed over the original 9, 11 over the original 10, 12 over 11, and so on. It is likely that the original error in numbering stemmed from attributing to Rosh Chodesh two days rather than one; the emending hand apparently caught the problem and fixed it. Whose hand it was that corrected the mistake is more difficult to know. It could have been the calendar's author who, realizing at some point the mistake, corrected it. But it also could have been someone else, who, when he or she came into possession of the calendar, noticed the error and emended it. Like some of the other improvised wartime calendars, this one went through a process of alteration and adjustment, even during the time period it was reckoning. Nothing was set in stone, simply because much of what was set down was guesswork. It was the labor not of an expert but rather an amateur whose only option to track Jewish time was to take pen in hand.[28]

A Calendar One Could Live By

The author sets forth most of the elements for a Jewish calendar one could live by, designating the holidays, Rosh Chodesh, and some of the Torah portions to be read on the Sabbath. But most of the time the information is basic, without elaboration. In a few cases there is more than one would be led to expect, as with the listing of not only the first days of Passover but also the intermediate, seventh, and last days. The period coming after Passover follows suit, indicating both Pesach sheni (the second Passover) and Lag b'Omer, two days usually reserved for mention in more scholarly and comprehensive calendars.

In this instance, the amount of detail seems almost seasonal, with more in the spring and less in the summer, fall, and winter. Indeed, the summer is virtually blank. Surprisingly, for example, the central fast day, the ninth day of the month of Av, commemorating the destruction of the ancient Jerusalem temples, goes without mention. This omission would be conspicuous under any circumstances. But as I noted, the very launching point of the improvised Jewish calendar was a fast day (the tenth day of the month of Tevet), which I suggested was chosen to link the dire predicament of the Holocaust-era Jews with a similar event in the ancient world. Thus the absence of the central summer fast day is in this case that much more striking. And it seems that that omission is part of a larger pattern in which fast days have generally gone by the wayside. No reference appears to the fast of Esther that precedes Purim, the fast of the firstborn that comes before Passover, or the fall fast day in honor of the assassinated leader in ancient Israel, Gedaliah, that follows Rosh Hashana. Each and every fast day through the year is overlooked—with the exception of the bold reference to the tenth day of the month of Tevet with which the Jewish calendar here begins. (Yom Kippur is marked, but without indication that it is a fast day). It seems that, after making a fast day the rubric under which the calendar unfolds, the author felt that fast days were too onerous to bear under the already oppressive wartime conditions.[29]

Hence, the attention to detail varies, and generally it becomes thinner rather than thicker. But there is one constant: Rosh Chodesh, the entry of the new Jewish month. Over the course of the calendar year, the designation Rosh Chodesh is inscribed in the calendar, from the beginning of the month of Shevat, written in pale blue pencil in the blank space to the right of Wednesday, January 25, until the beginning of the month of Tevet, nearly a year later, written in the same pale blue pencil opposite Saturday, December 16. It was the regularity of the Jewish months, coming at intervals of twenty-nine or thirty days, that extracted from the blank spaces of the Polish calendar a rhythm of Jewish time and destiny. The author must have sensed the pivotal significance of this monthly rhythm. So while some facets of Jewish time could, due to compassion, forgetfulness, haste, or ignorance, not be set down, the beginning of the new Jewish month *always* had to be. Otherwise the Jewish calendar would have been swallowed up by the Polish one.

This unswerving discipline came even though the author often got it wrong, presuming that Rosh Chodesh, the beginning of the Jewish month at the time of the new moon, was celebrated, unvaryingly, for two days. In actuality, the months alternate in the observance of one or two days. Based on this mistaken assumption, the computations were off track and then back on. In contrast to what one might think, improvising a Jewish calendar in the blank spaces of the Kodak pocket companion was not a task taken up by someone with a special aptitude or expertise. The calendar's author was evidently someone without a deep knowledge of the Jewish calendar. He or she knew enough to place the festivals on the correct dates. But the finer points of calendar composition went awry. Yet weak facility did not stop the author from taking what steps he or she could to track Jewish time. Nor did the fact that the only calendar he could lay his hands on was outdated, indeed from the period before the war even broke out.

Why would the author of the Jewish calendar have resorted to using this obsolete text? It may have been that no later calendar was available. Clearly, nothing better was. We shouldn't be surprised by the dearth of calendars—even Gregorian calendars—by this date. As mentioned earlier, already in early 1942 the well-placed Adam Czerniakow, head of the Warsaw Jewish Council, noted in his diary how difficult it was to obtain a calendar for the new year ("It is impossible to buy a calendar either in the ghetto or outside. I have been obliged to make a calendar for myself"). Some two years later it was likely that fewer were available and that one would have had to make do with what was at hand. The Polish "Pocket Calendar Companion" could have been in the author's possession since 1939 and thereafter held on to because, for some unknown reason, it was deemed worth saving. Another possibility is that the author came upon it either in flight or in hiding. Out of date though it may have been, it afforded enough of a scaffold on which to sketch in the Jewish dates for the present year.

Whatever the reason, the decision to use the obsolete calendar demonstrates how essential it was to live in Jewish time. Indeed, the greater the mismatch—the more jarring the juxtaposition of one set of dates (5704/1944 in the superimposed Jewish calendar) with the other (1939 in the original printed version)—the greater the accomplishment. Jewish time had to be given its due, even using unconventional means.

Moreover, layering the current Jewish calendar onto the outdated Gregorian one must have created for the author, and for anyone else that made use of the calendar, a unique, and certainly wrenching, template of time. The interwoven calendars meant living in two time zones simultaneously: before the war and during it, a time when Polish Jewry was still more or less intact and a time when it was in the very midst of its murderous undoing. The two frames of reference nearly, though not completely, span Polish Jewry's devastating ordeal. That said, that the *Jewish* calendar section is the one to form the later reckoning goes against the grain of what one might expect. Jewish time would seem to belong with the 1939 prewar world, giving graphic expression to that year's holiday cycle when there were Jews and Jewish communities en masse to celebrate them. Instead, Jewish time in the form of the improvised, layered-in Jewish calendar somehow kept ticking in the year 5704/1944, when the number of Polish Jews remaining to honor those holidays had diminished profoundly. Yet the inverse logic is compelling. The fewer and thus more isolated the Jews were, the more desperate the desire to use whatever means at one's disposal, no matter how imperfect, to have at hand a Jewish calendar.

Likely composed at the end of 1943, the calendar came into being at a terrible low in the fortunes of Polish Jewry. Much of the sad destruction of thousands of communities had already taken place in 5702/1942 and continued at a murderous pace the following year. After October 1943, only Lodz among the major Polish ghettos had avoided wholesale destruction. A staggering two million Polish Jews in other major ghettos—Warsaw, Kracow, Lublin—and in smaller ghettos and towns outside them had been deported to death camps. The brutal decimation of the Kracow ghetto (eerily restaged in the film version of *Schindler's List*) occurred in March 1943. In April 1943, on the eve of Passover, a remnant of Warsaw Jewry,

the largest and the most famous of the Polish Jewish communities, offered tenacious resistance to the enemy's entry into the ghetto, in what came to be called
the "uprising." They and most of the ghetto's other prisoners were nonetheless
systematically annihilated over the next six weeks. Later that summer, on August
16, the Jews in the Bialystok ghetto, who had hoped against hope that their forced
labor would be viewed as indispensable to the war effort and thereby keep them
afloat until the war's end, were rounded up and deported to their death. To compose a Jewish calendar at this point in time, in the aftermath of such carnage and
when few Jews were left to benefit from it, was in some sense tilting at windmills.
But this clearly was not as it was seen by the Jewish calendar's author, whose conduct the penciled-in Jewish calendar presumably continued to guide.

The improvised calendar was meant, like others of its kind generally, to make
Jewish time visible and graphic, so that one could live in sacred time according to
tradition and in concert with Jews the world over. This particular calendar also
played another role, serving as a memorial for the murdered. To help memorial-
ize the dead was not a new role for a Jewish calendar to play; keeping track of the
days and dates enabled the observance of a yahrzeit, the anniversary of the date
when someone passed away. Being aware of the date made it possible to carry out
the array of rituals that honored the memory of the deceased and aided his or her
spiritual passage in the next world.

But this calendar added another dimension. After the almanac entry listing
"English Measures," on the calendar date of the ninth of Tevet / December 24 is
the word *shechita*, meaning "slaughter." Something terrible had to have happened
to move the author to use such a stark expression. Moreover, the clarity with
which the word is written is striking. Penned in ink rather than pencil, each letter
is fully distinct and recognizable. Both the Gregorian and Jewish dates are evocative as well, though naturally for different reasons. December 24, the onset of the
year-end Christian festival, was understood to be a dangerous occasion for Jews,
a time when anti-Semitism often intensified. From a different vantage point, the
ninth day of the month of Tevet brought the Jewish calendar full circle, marking
the final day of a year begun twelve months before on the tenth day of Tevet, 5704.
I argued that the author chose the tenth of Tevet as the initial day of the improvised calendar year in order to stake a claim to Jewish time and to link the wartime calendar to a Jewish past fraught with upheaval. That said, the ninth of Tevet
of the following year, bearing a coded signature of death, is much more ominous.

For all of the tragic connotations, what follows in the calendar makes it less
certain that the word *slaughter* was actually associated with these two dates.
Written *beneath* the word *shechita* are an indecipherable word and then "erev
Rosh Hashana 1942," designating a time—the day before the onset of the Jewish
New Year holiday that took place more than two years earlier—when the rapa-
cious slaughter of Jews in Poland was unfortunately an all too regular occurrence.

It is not clear what had the earlier 1942 date surface at this point, whether it is meant to commemorate an earlier massacre or to indicate one that had just occurred. If the latter, it is not clear whether the sad episode was recorded in 1942 or, in keeping with the flow of the adapted calendar, inscribed later in 1944. In any case, the 1939 Polish "Pocket Calendar Companion" served as a point of convergence, allowing for documentation *and* commemoration of times and events that needed a calendar to enter them into the ledger of reality.

As with other wartime calendars, the graphic dimension of this one—even more multileveled and complex than most—can be read as an allegory of the fate of Polish Jewry. For the Jewish calendar takes refuge, as it were, in the Polish calendar's open spaces, not so much a stable entity as a kind of interloper, establishing a home where there isn't really room for one. In truth, there is no room for Jews or what is Jewish, no room for a Jewish language or for Jewish time. Most of the calendar qua almanac is given over to two sides of Polish life, religious and technological. Amid these, Jewish time carves out an iota of space. In this respect, it is telling that the majority of the Polish printed calendar is devoted to the prewar year of 1939, when Polish Jewry could still find a habitable zone. Symbolically, then, the mismatched years make sense: in 1939 (the year of the printed "Pocket Calendar Companion"), the Jewish calendar could still be publicly honored and lived; in 1944 (the year of the improvised Jewish one), it could be no longer. In that year, Jewish time was salvaged only by the extraordinary will to make it live, even in a place where it was not permitted to dwell or exist. It is said that the Rebbe of Kotzk's answer to the question "Where can God be found?" was "Wherever you let Him in." So it was with this Jewish calendar, wedged into a dated map of foreign time. It was truly a calendar of exile; it was also truly a calendar of redemption.

Filling the Blank Spaces of Jewish Time: Theresienstadt

Calendars produced in the Theresienstadt ghetto brought the wartime crafting of Jewish time to a new level. Dedicated to plotting the coordinates of traditional Jewish observance, the calendars forged in this singular ghetto/camp nevertheless innovated strikingly, both in content and composition. In doing so, they contended forcefully with the bitter circumstances of Jewish life in Theresienstadt, fashioning a calendrical deposition that was anything but oblivious to the camp's onerous conditions. Yet they also seized the opportunity at hand, making the calendar a vehicle for envisioning—sometimes explicitly, sometimes between the lines—a different sort of future. Each Theresienstadt calendar rendered the year in its own distinctive idiom. But all of them together undoubtedly nurtured both the camp's significant community of committed Jewish celebrants and also those who discovered, perhaps for the first time, the Jewish calendar's carefully orchestrated interplay of sacred and mundane time.

Established by the enemy in a northwestern Czechoslovakian town in 1941, Theresienstadt (Czech: Terezin) combined features of both ghettos and camps. From its founding until the war's end, the camp interned Jews of Bohemia and Moravia, elderly Jews and persons of "special merit" in the Reich, and several thousand Jews from the Netherlands and Denmark. Although it served as a transit camp en route to extermination camps, it was also presented as a "model Jewish settlement" for propaganda purposes.

A Jewish council, headed at first by the Czech Zionist leader Jacob Edelstein, administered Theresienstadt's internal affairs. But overcrowding, poor sanitation, and malnourishment spread disease so vehemently that, in 1942, nearly 15,900 people, half the population, died in the camp. These unfavorable conditions, together with a staggered schedule of lethal transports, destroyed most of those who entered its gates. Altogether, more than 155,000 Jews passed through Theresienstadt; 35,440 perished in the ghetto itself, and 88,000 were deported to be murdered in the killing centers of eastern Europe.[30]

Despite these dire conditions and the tragic fate they most often led to, Theresienstadt's prisoners were eminently resourceful in organizing extensive educational and cultural activities. Indeed, the camp has become renowned for having produced original orchestral works and giving notable renditions of classic ones, staging theatrical performances, offering a plethora of lectures, and teaching classes in schoolrooms that helped children not only cope with imprisonment but also nurture creative talent.

Less well-known is the prisoners' intense cultivation of Jewish observance and learning.[31] Theresienstadt's Jewish calendars emerged from an active culture of Jewish religious observance. The two-sided character of the oppression in the camp made such activity possible. Similar to Holland's Westerbork transit camp, Jews in Theresienstadt could give open expression to religious life and practice. To what degree is not precisely clear. One source states that observance was not expressly *permitted* but nonetheless *allowed*.[32] A second contrasts the camp's permissiveness with that of the region in general: whereas Bohemia and Moravia *forbid* Jewish religious practice, Theresienstadt, located within the same restrictive domain, *permitted* it.[33] A third, more popular source implies that religious observance could only take place in a manner hidden and covert, as if the draconian strictures of Birkenau had been imposed on the significantly different form of oppression in this camp.[34] Finally, a fourth source, this one academic, goes to the opposite extreme, claiming that Theresienstadt was the only concentration camp where religious life was practiced *undisturbed*—a flattering if seemingly unwitting tribute, one might hope, not to the largesse of the authorities but rather to the composure of Theresienstadt's Jewish prisoners.[35]

Though all accounts of Theresienstadt justly laud the cultural achievements, virtually none of the recent studies refer to the religious ones. This was not always the case. For example, an important 1965 anthology on Terezin includes a substantial chapter on "religious life in Terezin," authored by Dr. Richard Feder, one of those who played a role in furthering it.[36] But in the decades since, as the attention given to Theresienstadt's remarkable cadre of composers of classical music has increased, the information about religious ritual has decreased. It is as if the aesthetic and religious realms, both of which nourished what has come to be called spiritual resistance, inhabited two separate camps. In truth, however, just as the crowded conditions offered little space in which to seal oneself off from the common woe, so did the aesthetic and religious activity share common space. At times this was literally the case, as when the same room might be used for prayer in the morning and lectures later in the day.[37]

The oversight in scholarship on Theresienstadt regarding religious activity has come about even though Jewish religious observance was given a prominent position in art from the camp. Numerous prisoner renderings (by Haas, Nagl, Ullmann, and Fleischmann) show synagogue services, the congregation in attendance often outfitted with prayer shawls and tefillin.[38] Aiming to document camp events, the artists likely found morning prayer services an especially attractive compositional subject because of the flowing robed effect created by the shawls. The services as depicted are unfailingly packed with worshippers, possibly because the rooms available were too small to accommodate even a modest congregation. In this vein, Jan Ullmann's drawing of prayer services highlights those worshippers spilling over outside a makeshift synagogue in a converted garage, a seated group that includes a number of women. Space was clearly at a premium. And the crowds suggest that synagogue attendance was not an arcane activity limited to a few particularly devout souls. That numbers of artists took the trouble to depict scenes of public prayer intimates that such scenes were part and parcel of Theresienstadt life.[39]

That said, it is clear that the artists did not always have an easy time construing the exact nature of the religious activity he or she depicted. For instance, a drawing by Karel Fleischmann, entitled "The Torah Reading on the Sabbath," highlights several men around a platform with an open Torah scroll.[40] The rendering certainly pays tribute to the perseverance of this central rite of Jewish observance under difficult circumstances. But the drawing is also an indication of the confused perception of religious activity, since it portrays the men wearing tefillin, something that is not done on Shabbat. The artist must have gotten his signals crossed (if he is the one who gave the drawing its title); a Torah scroll is read publically not only on Shabbat but also on a number of occasions when one is obliged to wear tefillin, including Monday, Thursday, Rosh Chodesh, and fast days. Works of art (and the titles or captions joined to them) can't always be taken at face value as documenting events as they occurred in Theresienstadt (or anywhere else, for that matter). But neither can what they convey about the high level of communal prayer be unduly ignored.

Whatever the degree to which open observance was countenanced, there existed daily, weekly, and seasonal religious activity. Eight synagogues, each with their own rabbi and cantor, operated in standard rooms of a number of camp barracks, whereas those short on space resorted to using attics and garages. Attendees donned tefillin and talesim and read from Torah scrolls. More generally there was ritual circumcision, Jewish education of both children and adults, bar mitzvahs, about five hundred ritual weddings (and a number of divorces), and, largely as an outcome of disease and malnutrition, many thousands of funerals—which, given the enemy's insistence on cremating bodies, tried in a fashion to incorporate traditional Jewish rites.[41]

Mapped on multiple camp calendars, Jewish holidays were observed by a significant swath of the prisoner population. Indeed, at times the sizable numbers made formidable the task of providing basic materials. In preparation for Passover, for instance, religious leaders baked ten thousand kilograms of matzah to fill the needs of most of Theresienstadt's Jewish prisoners.[42] Yet even under these bleak conditions there was allowance for different levels of observance. A group that held to a higher standard of supervision baked separate batches of matzahs using specially guarded wheat.[43] Ritual objects brought from home communities were put to good and regular use, seemingly without risk (as in many camps) of confiscation or desecration.[44] Indeed, one witness notes that the silver kiddish cup filled not with wine but rather bitter black coffee could serve as a symbol of Theresienstadt's manner of maintaining observance in the breach.[45]

The range of observance was great. At one end of the spectrum was a group of fifteen young men who endeavored to maintain in the camp the much stricter standards of observance they were brought up with. To this end, they obtained their own accommodations, consisting not only of a separate living space but also a kosher kitchen and synagogue, and held regular Torah classes and social activities.[46] It was as close as one could get to a yeshiva in Theresienstadt's particular fabrication of hell. At the opposite end of the spectrum were those who distanced themselves from religious observance, at least in one case jeering at and insulting those who attended services at a nearby synagogue. Yet the diarist who records the incident counters, "I regret it thoroughly—I feel more of a Jew than almost ever before."[47] By and large, a modicum of religious observance seems to have carried the day among the Jews of Theresienstadt.

The four Jewish calendars to emerge from Theresienstadt reflect this desire to maintain traditional practices. Understandably, the camp's Janus-faced character gave rise to innovations, for instance a multicolored illustrated Gregorian calendar showing various work details. The Jewish calendars, for their part, also varied considerably, ranging from the simple to the ornate, the basic to the elaborate, the abbreviated to the full-blown. But each one distinctively mapped Jewish time as lived and envisioned within the camp. The earliest was an extraordinary "small calendar" from the pivotal year 5703 (1942–43), the author of which remains unknown, and which fused detailed traditional practice with subtle yet startling innovation. The second was an evocative 1943 painting by Hilde Zadikow of the names of the Jewish months, behind each of which a stirring drama of tradition coping with adversity was played out. It conveyed the power of the Jewish calendar without actually being one per se.[48] And the final two calendars from the years 5704 and 5705 (1943–44 and 1944–45) were crafted by a learned, artistic rabbi, Asher Berlinger, who blended a resolute focus on day-to-day observance with graphic creativity.

All in all, Theresienstadt, the camp known for its courageous pursuit of secular arts and university-like study, nurtured the calendrical mapping of Jewish time in ways that one might expect, harnessing the artistic skills so widely evident among the camp's cultured Czech and German Jews. More surprisingly, it also gave rise to intricately learned Jewish calendars, fashioned to guide the adept and, as we will see, to use tradition to contend with the camp's fearful symmetry of death.

Terezin's "Small Calendar"

An anonymous 5703 German-Hebrew calendar from Theresienstadt is less elaborate than many wartime calendars but singly powerful in its focus on the sacred and in its stark simplicity. The calendar is all of five pages. The title page attractively proclaims *Luach Katan: Verzeichnis der Sabbathe, Feste and Fasttage* ("A Small Calendar: A Listing of Sabbaths, Festivals, and Fast Days"). The title is handwritten (or drawn), while the calendar per se is typewritten. And since the keypad used exclusively Latin letters, no Hebrew script appears within.[49]

The *small* in the title no doubt accords with the calendar's compact "postcard" size (roughly ten by fifteen centimeters, or what is referred to as A6). But it also likely refers to the selective nature of the calendar's contents, since it sets down not every day of the year but rather only the "Sabbaths, festivals, and fast days"—the days that call for special prayers and observances. The calendar's selective nature calls attention to what is left out; in general, one must when reviewing the contents of wartime calendars take account of what is omitted as well as what is included. In the case of this extraordinary calendar, as we will see, what is excluded is surprising, even mystifying—yet in the final analysis evocative to the highest degree.

Two prominent Jewish symbols distinguish the cover page of the *Luach Katan*: a Jewish star flanked by flowers and a drawing of Rachel's Tomb, the burial site of the biblical matriarch outside of the town of Bethlehem. The Jewish star served widely as a wartime emblem of Jewish pride, turning inside out the enemy's use of it to mark and stigmatize Jews and Jewish-owned property.[50] A symbol less circulated, Rachel's Tomb—and, by extension, the famous nineteenth-century drawing of it reproduced at the calendar's head—carried associations of the exile of the Jewish people and their eventual return to the land of Israel, associations overtly expressed by Zionist activists in the camp but transmitted by others in a more traditional idiom. The sentiments found classic formulation in the prophet Jeremiah: "Thus said Hashem: A voice is heard in Ramah, lamentation, and bitter weeping, Rachel weeping for her children; she refuses to be comforted for her children, because they are not. Thus said Hashem: Refrain thy voice from weeping, and thy eyes from tears; for thy work shall be rewarded, said Hashem; and they shall come back from the land of the enemy. And there is hope for thy future, said Hashem; and thy children shall return to their own border."[51]

Located off the beaten track, Rachel's burial site nevertheless allowed her crying to escort the exiled Jews en route to ancient Babylon. In her role as a comforter, she beseeched God for mercy on their behalf and was granted the promise that they would "come back from the land of the enemy" to once again dwell in the land of Israel. Rabbinic sources elaborate that, of all the worthy forebears who petitioned for the exiles, it is Rachel's intercession that aroused God's compassion for his exiled people and, on account of her merit, will eventually lead them back to the land of Israel.[52]

The drawing of Rachel's Tomb fronting the calendar would certainly recall God's pledge of mercy for his exiled people; indeed, the bitterness of exile, intensified by recent uprooting and transport, had to have been felt keenly in the oppressive conditions Theresienstadt foisted on its unfortunate inmates. Strikingly, the matriarch Rachel's pleas were again brought to bear on the inmates' plight by another Theresienstadt prisoner, the composer Viktor Ullman, whose 1944 sonata refers to "Rachel, the mother of mothers," whose "blood flows in my blood" and "voice croons in me."[53] The author of the *Luach Katan* was thus not alone in recalling in symbolic form Rachel's role as comforter of the Jewish people and the promise that exile—in this case the privation experienced in Theresienstadt—would one day come to an end. A fitting embellishment in its own right, the drawing may have also deputized the calendar as a kind of proxy for the comforter Rachel, enabling the Sabbaths, holidays, and fast days listed therein to instill a comfort of their own. In essence, the drawing joined to the "Small Calendar" implied that, by sanctifying time, the duress of exile could be tempered even if not yet done away with entirely.

Most of the Jewish calendars to emerge from the period of the Holocaust date from 5704 or 5705, the last two years of the war. The *Luach Katan* is thus unusual in the time frame it covers: the year 5703 (September 1942–September 1943). This year was pivotal in the Terezin ghetto. First, the already crowded conditions peaked just prior to the onset of the new Jewish year (September 1942)—quite possibly when the *Luach Katan* was being produced—with some sixty thousand souls incarcerated in an area that had formerly housed seven thousand. Second,

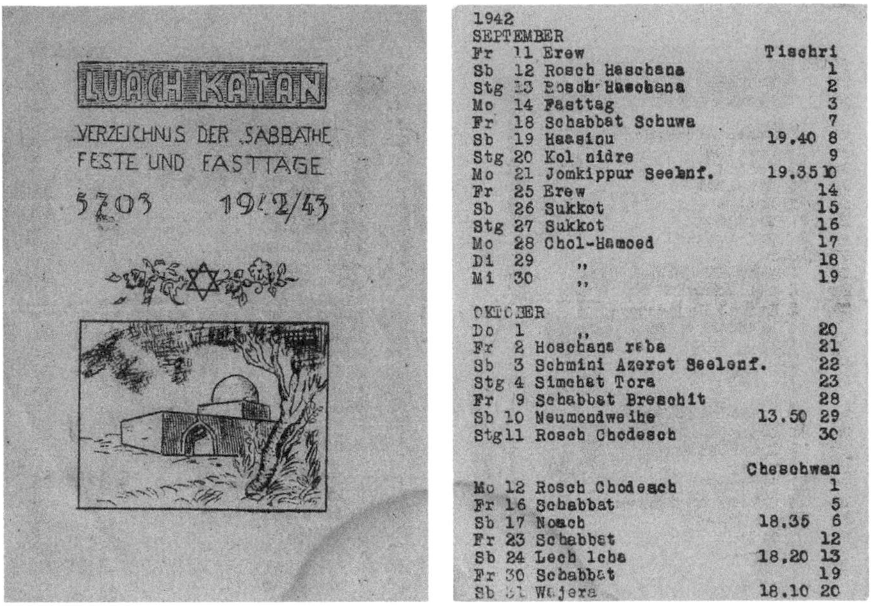
LUACH KATAN
VERZEICHNIS DER SABBATHE
FESTE UND FASTTAGE
5703 1942/43

1942
SEPTEMBER

Fr	11 Erew		Tischri
Sb	12 Rosch Haschana		1
Stg	13 Rosch Haschana		2
Mo	14 Fasttag		3
Fr	18 Schabbat Schuwa		7
Sb	19 Haasinu	19.40	8
Stg	20 Kol nidre		9
Mo	21 Jomkippur Seelenf.	19.35	10
Fr	25 Erew		14
Sb	26 Sukkot		15
Stg	27 Sukkot		16
Mo	28 Chol-Hamoed		17
Di	29 "		18
Mi	30 "		19

OKTOBER

Do	1 "		20
Fr	2 Hoschana raba		21
Sb	3 Schmini Azeret Seelenf.		22
Stg	4 Simchat Tora		23
Fr	9 Schabbat Breschit		28
Sb	10 Neumondweihe	13.50	29
Stg	11 Rosch Chodesch		30
			Cheschwan
Mo	12 Rosch Chodesch		1
Fr	16 Schabbat		5
Sb	17 Noach	18.35	6
Fr	23 Schabbat		12
Sb	24 Lech lcha	18.20	13
Fr	30 Schabbat		19
Sb	31 Wajera	18.10	20

Fig. 2.5: The Theresienstadt ghetto outside of Prague had an openly vibrant religious Jewish community. The *Luach Katan* ("Little Calendar") for 5703 (1942–43) was one of the Jewish calendars composed therein, special in the frontispiece drawing of the Tomb of Rachel, the typed or printed format, and the exclusively German language of its composition. Courtesy of the Jewish Museum in Prague.

the tragic fate that awaited most of Terezin's Jewish prisoners became eminently clear. Deportations directly to killing centers were initiated during this period and punctuated it at regular intervals. Indeed, ten deportations to Treblinka began the year, the first taking place on Friday, September 18, erev *Schabbat Schuwa* (in the German spelling of the *Luach Katan*), the eve of the Sabbath that falls between the fall holidays of Rosh Hashana and Yom Kippur, less than a week after the new Jewish year commenced. After these ten murderous Treblinka-destined convoys had run their course, deportations to Auschwitz-Birkenau took over—the first on the fifteenth of Cheshvan (Oct. 26, 1942), initiating over forty-five thousand souls being sent in twenty-seven transports during the next two years.[54]

Hence, the calendar tells its dated story against the immediate background of the volatile shifts and sad decimation of the Theresienstadt community. But it almost never lets on about these conditions. Instead, it sets down each Shabbat through the year, giving the name of the Torah portion a separate entry, abbreviating the day not with its secular initials but rather the letters *Sb* (a designation that sets the Sabbath apart from the weekdays), and recording the time the holy day

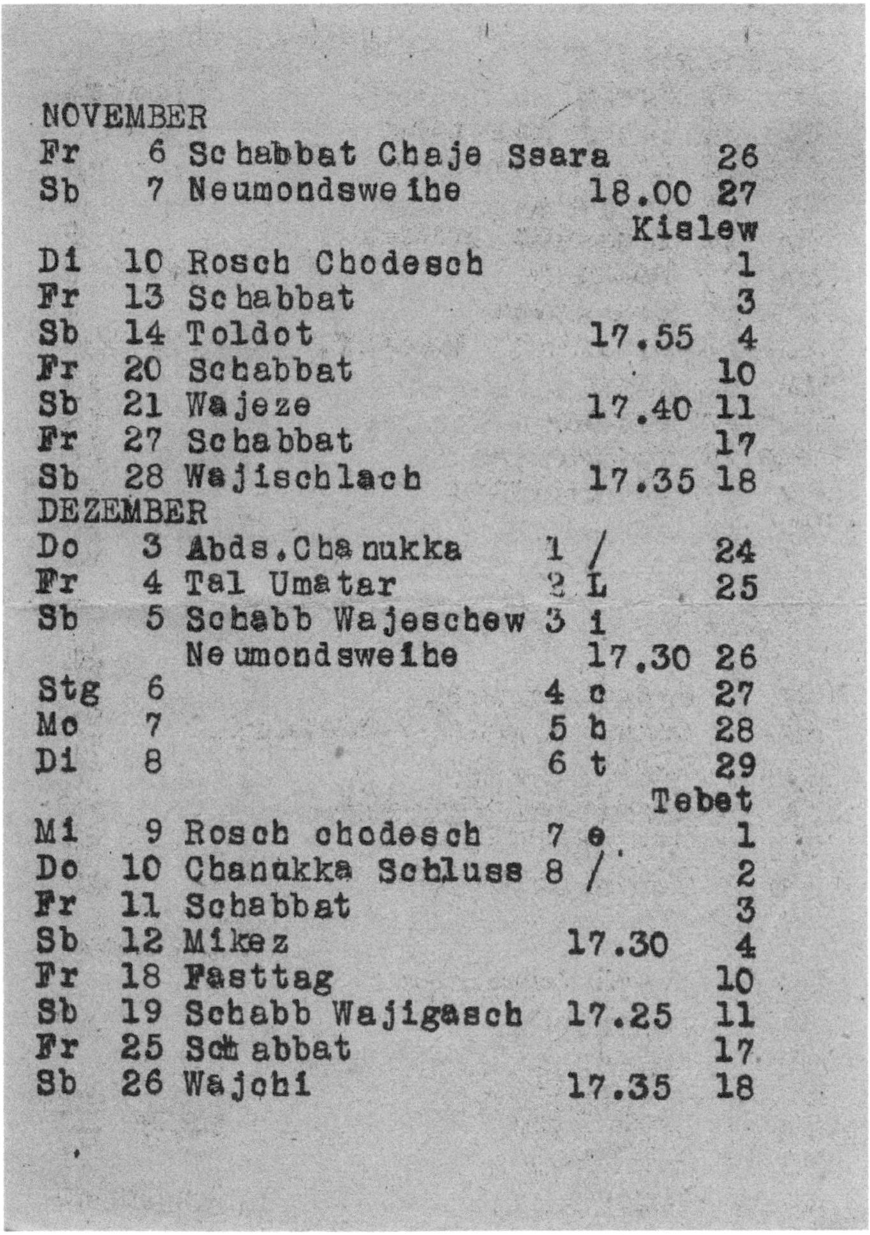

```
NOVEMBER
Fr    6 Schabbat Chaje Ssara        26
Sb    7 Neumondsweihe      18.00 27
                              Kislew
Di   10 Rosch Chodesch                1
Fr   13 Schabbat                      3
Sb   14 Toldot            17.55  4
Fr   20 Schabbat                     10
Sb   21 Wajeze            17.40 11
Fr   27 Schabbat                    17
Sb   28 Wajischlach       17.35 18
DEZEMBER
Do    3 Abds.Chanukka    1 /      24
Fr    4 Tal Umatar       2 L      25
Sb    5 Schabb Wajeschew 3 i
        Neumondsweihe       17.30 26
Stg   6                  4 c      27
Mo    7                  5 h      28
Di    8                  6 t      29
                              Tebet
Mi    9 Rosch chodesch   7 e      1
Do   10 Chanukka Schluss 8 /      2
Fr   11 Schabbat                   3
Sb   12 Mikez            17.30  4
Fr   18 Fasttag                  10
Sb   19 Schabb Wajigasch  17.25 11
Fr   25 Schabbat                 17
Sb   26 Wajchi           17.35 18
```

Fig. 2.5: (Continued)

```
JANUAR 1943                     Tebet      Stg  7 Rosch Chodesch              30
Fr  1 Schabbat Schmot             24                                      Weadar
Sb  2 Neumondsweihe     17.50     25        Mo  8 Rosch Chodesch            1
                               Schwat       Fr 12 Schabbat                  5
Do  7 Rosch Chodesch               1        Sb 13 Pkude            19.40    6
Fr  8 Schabbat                     2        Stg 14 Geburts/Todestag Moses   7
Sb  9 Waera             17.55      3        Do 18 Fasten Esther            11
Fr 15 Schabbat                     9        Fr 19 Schabbat                 12
Sb 16 Bo               18.00      10        Sb 20 Wajikra Sachor   19.50   13
Do 21 Chamischa assar             15        Stg 21 Purim                   14
Fr 22 Schabbat schira             16        Mo 22 Schuschan Purim          15
Sb 23 Beschallach      18.10      17        Fr 26 Schabbat                 19
Fr 29 Schabbat                    23        Sb 27 Zaw Para         20.00
Sb 30 Jitro            18.20      24        APRIL
                                            Fr  2 Schabbat                 26
FEBRUAR                                     Sb  3 Hachodesch Schmin'
Fr  5 Rosch Chodesch Schabb.      30          Neumondsweihe        20.15   27
                                Adar                                    Nissan
Sb  6 Rosch chodesch   18.35      1         Di  6 Rosch Chodesch            1
Fr 12 Schabbat                    7         Fr  9 Schabbat                  4
Sb 13 Mischpatim       18.45      8         Sb 10 Tasria           20.20    5
Fr 19 Schabbat /Kl.Purim         14         Fr 16 Schabbat                 11
Sb 20 Trumah           19.00     15         Sb 17 Hagadol Mzora    20.35   12
Fr 26 Schabbat                   21         Mo 19 Erew Pessach Seder       14
Sb 27 Tzawe            19.10     22         Di 20 Pessach 1.Tag Seder 1.Omer 15
                                            Mi 21 Pessach 2.Tag       2.Omer 16
MARZ                                        Do 22 Pessach Chol Hamoed 3.Omer 17
Fr  5 Schabbat                   28         Fr 23 Schabbat   ,,    ,,  4.Omer 18
Sb  6 Wajakhel Schkalim                     Sb 24 Chol Hamoed  20.50  5.Omer 19
      Neumondsweihe    19.25     29         Stg 25   ,,     ,,        6.Omer 20
```

Fig. 2.5: (Continued)

concludes. It does the same for holidays and Rosh Chodesh. This form of dedication to marking the special days, as we have seen, was almost par for the course in wartime calendars, even under fraught conditions. The Terezin calendar thus follows suit.

But there are extras, such as listing "tal u'matar" (December 4), the day when the prayers turn during the winter months to beseeching God for rain rather than dew. Even more exceptional is its recalling of the seventh of Adar as the "Geburts/Todestag Moses" (the birthday and deathday of Moshe, the leader of the Jewish nation)—a notation I have not found in a single other wartime calendar. Moreover, some fast on the day, a custom followed with particular devotion by local burial societies. Highlighting the seventh of Adar reinforces the special connotations of fast days in this calendar (even though the day is not explicitly tagged as such). The practical and memorial elements of tradition wove their way into the typed Terezin calendar in a remarkably uninhibited way.

None of this prepares one, however, for the saga associated with the Terezin calendar's overtly designated fast days—a facet already announced on the title page with the seemingly prosaic subtitle "Feste and Fasttage" (Festivals and Fast Days). As we've already pointed out, for Jewish calendars fashioned during the Holocaust to indicate obligatory fast days, at a time when rations were generally

APRIL			Nissan
Mo	26	Pessach	7.Omer 21
Di	27	Pessach Schlusstag	
		Seelenfeier 8...	22
Fr	30	Schabbat Achare 11.,,	25

MAI			
Sb	1	Neum.Weibe 21.10 12.,,	26
Mi	5	Rosch Chodesch 16.,,	30
			Ijar
Do	6	Rosch Chodesch 17.,,	1
Fr	7	Schabbat 18.,,	2
Sb	8	Kdoschim 21.25 19.,,	3
Fr.	14	Schabbat 25.,,	9
Sb	15	Emor 21.40 26.,,	10
Fr	21	Schabbat 32.,,	16
Sb	22	Bhar 21.55 33.,,	17
Stg	23	Lagbaomer 34.,,	18
Fr	28	Schabbat 39.,,	23
Sb	29	Bchukottaj 22.00 40.,,	24
		Neumondsweibe	

JUNI			Siwan
Fr	4	Schabbat 46.Omer	1
Sb	5	Bmi^bar 22.15 47. ,,	2
Mi	9	Schawuot	6
Do	10	Schawuot Seelenfeier	7
Fr	11	Schabbat	8
Sb	12	Nasso 22.20	9
Fr	18	Schabbat	15
Sb	19	Bhaalot'cha 22.25	16
Fr	25	Schabbat	22
Sb	26	Schlach lcha	
		Neumondzweihe 22.25	23

JULI			
Fr	2	Schabbat	29
Sb	3	Korach 22.20	30
			Tammus
Stg	4	Rosch Chodesch	1
Fr	9	Schabbat	6
Sb	10	Chukkat 22.15	7
Fr	16	Schabbat	13
Sb	17	Balak 22.10	14
Fr	23	Schabbat	20
Sb	24	Pinchas 22.00	21
Fr	30	Schabbat	27
Sb	31	Mattot Masse	
		Neumondsweibe 21.50	28

Fig. 2.5: (Continued)

meager and starvation all too common, demonstrated a profound commitment to tradition and a studied indifference to the terms of privation dictated by the enemy. Indeed, the calendar's listing of fasts honored the special character of the day even though most would not be able (nor obliged, given the oppressive conditions) to undertake the fast. In the wise words of literary scholar Marc Caplan, in such circumstances the calendar would observe the fast even when the Jews themselves would not be able to.

So the fact that the Terezin calendar, true to its title, lists the fast days is in keeping with wartime Jewish calendars generally. As one would expect, the listing begins with the third day of the Jewish year (the third of Tishrei), called Tzom Gedaliah (the fast in honor of Gedaliah), which is marked on the *Luach Katan* calendar simply as *Fasttag* (fast day). That year it fell on a Monday. A few months later, the tenth day of the month of Tevet followed in the same vein, marked again simply as *Fasttag*. It took place on a Friday.[55] Three months down the road, before the holiday of Purim, "Fasten Esther" (the Fast of Esther) took place, named after the biblical heroine who first proclaimed the fast in order to solicit divine favor to defend her people against an enemy set on annihilating the Jews in ancient Persia. So far everything on this calendar has come at the time it is expected to and, germane to our purposes, has been given the name that it normally goes by. Up

```
AUGUST                                          Ab
Mo    2  Rosch Chodesch                          1
Fr    6  Schabbat                                5
Sb    7  Dwarim                         21.35    6
Di   10                                          9
Fr   13  Schabbat                               12
Sb   14  Waet'chanan                    21.10   13
Mo   16  Freudentag                             15
Fr   20  Schabbat                               19
Sb   21  Ekew                           20.55   20
Fr   27  Schabbat                               26
Sb   28  R'e Neum.Weihe                 20.40   27
Di   31  Rosch chodesch                         30

SEPT.                                          Ellul
Mi    1  Rosch Chodesch                          1
Fr    3  Schabbat                                3
Sb    4  Schoftim                       20.25    4
Fr   10  Schabbat                               10
Sb   11  Ki teze                        20.10   11
Fr   17  Schabbat                               17
Sb   18  Ki tawo                        20.00   18
Fr   24  Schabbat                               24
Sb   25  Nizawim Wajelech               19.45   25
Stg  26  1.Salichot                             26
Mo   27  2.   ,,                                27
Di   28  3.   "                                 28
Mi   29  4.   "
         Erew Rosch Haschana                    29
Do   30  Rosch Haschana 5704
         Haba alenu ltowa
```

Fig. 2.5: (Continued)

to this point, little has distinguished this calendar from many that came before and many that would come after.

When it comes to the next scheduled fast, however, that remarkable—one might say heroic—conformity disappears. Slated to occur in the early summer, the fast of the seventeenth of Tammuz does double duty. First, it commemorates no less than five tragedies in ancient Jewish history, and second, it initiates three weeks of communal mourning. Known as *Bein Hametzarim*, this period culminates and concludes with the next—and the most important—fast day, Tisha b'Av (the ninth day of the month of Av). These two fast days—and the three-week period they bracket—serve to bring the memory of ancient tragedy into the present.

But for all of its methodical orchestration of tradition, for all of its registering fast days in the order they come in the year, the Terezin *Luach Katan* calendar skips over the two summer fast days. Not a word, not an indication. The seventeenth of Tammuz simply does not receive mention. It is as if the day dropped off the calendar. The situation with the ninth of Av is more complex. The calendar does include it in the listing of significant days—a kind of table of contents, as it were, that precedes the dates in the calendar per se; conformity seems to have returned. But the space next to the date, where one usually finds the designation or title of the day, is, in this single case, left blank. Nowhere is *Fasttag* (fast day) written—or anything else that would offer a clue to its observance or character.

How does one account for these unexpected deviations? The calendar's meticulous character makes it unlikely that the complete omission of one fast day and the vacant space of the other can be explained as an oversight. Nor might it be explained, coming toward the calendar's end, merely as a result of fatigue. And if the reason was that the privation in Theresienstadt made undertaking such a fast unthinkable because it posed a threat to one's life, which would in effect cancel the fast—a reasonable surmise, under the circumstances—than why were the earlier fasts included and set down in such a matter-of-fact fashion?

One possibility is that these two fasts were slated to take place during the summer, when the days were longer and warmer. On the seventeenth of Tammuz, the fast was scheduled to begin at 2:45 a.m. and not conclude until 9:43 p.m.—a challenging number of hours even for those in the best of health. How much more difficult and debilitating such a fast would be for those whose nourishment was substandard. The strictures of the ninth of Av are even more demanding, necessitating a round-the-clock, dusk-to-dusk fast. To undertake these fasts could have been understood to pose a threat to the well-being of already weakened prisoners. Under such circumstances, the calendar's author may well have received rabbinical permission to omit the word *Fasttag* in the case of these two summer days. In this case, neither the Jews themselves nor the calendar they hoped to adhere to would be expected to keep a fast, which had been, for all intents and purposes, temporarily erased from the traditional itinerary of observance.

This explanation leaves unresolved, however, the meaning of the vacant space: why is the ninth of Av listed as a special day but left without a designation as to its special character, *Fasttag* or otherwise? It is tempting to think that the vacant space was meant to evoke the ambivalent character of the day. On the one hand, the ninth of Av also commemorates five catastrophes, including the destruction of the temples in ancient Jerusalem. On this day, mourning reaches its highest pitch and most intense expression. On the other hand, it is the day on which the Messiah was to be born. Moreover, at the time of the Messiah's arrival and the onset of the era of redemption, the fast day would be turned into a feast day (in the idiom of the calendar's title page, the *Fasttag* would become a *Festtag*) and the day celebrated as a holiday. The space might have been left blank so that, rather than being prematurely designated as a fast day, changed circumstances—especially but not only in the Terezin ghetto itself—would warrant filling the space with a different, hopefully joyous designation.[56]

This speculative reading of the vacant space is given more weight by the even more astonishing entry that follows soon after. Coming six days later, the fifteenth of Av traditionally carries upbeat connotations, which are mainly registered in tradition-bound circles by an abatement of the day's penitential prayers. These connotations derive from various affirmative events that took place in ancient times on the fifteenth day of Av, among which were the end of a harsh decree against the Jewish nation, the final celebratory day of a festive temple rite, and the performing of a chaste courtship ritual. While thematically significant and mystically charged, the day's virtues are subtle and rarefied. Thus most Jewish calendars simply pass over the fifteenth of Av or at best draw rudimentary attention to it. This circumspection is not so much a reflection on the merits of the day as it is a feature of the popular idiom calendars generally adopt, even those calendars composed by a sage and featuring what seems to be a welter of detail and minutiae. This was also the case with wartime calendars. They too either refer to the fifteenth of Av prosaically or not at all.

The only one to go a step further is this particular *Luach Katan*, the small abbreviated Terezin calendar. It dubs the fifteenth of Av a *Freudentag*, a day of joy. There is nothing circumspect about this description; it pulls out all the stops. To be sure, this designation accords with the day's deeper nature, which the Talmud describes as one of the two most joyous in the year.[57] But such sentiments do not usually find their way into the fine print, as it were, of calendars. Yet in the Terezin calendar it did; the author simply, we have to say, ignored the conventions.

To proclaim the day's joy, moreover, flew in the face of the circumstances at hand. This 5702–3 calendar had to have been composed in the period when the Jews of Europe were weathering the most intense oppression to date. In the late summer of 5702 (1942), the Great Deportation of Warsaw Jewry was raging full force, with a quarter of a million Jews being sent to the Treblinka death camp;

additional death camps were simultaneously destroying community after community of both eastern and western European Jewry. The calendar's author did not likely know in any detail what was transpiring outside the camp; what was more or less vaguely known, together with the conditions in the camp itself, must have nevertheless made the future look anything but promising. Yet this foreboding sense of what lay ahead did not work its way into or constrain the captioning of the fifteenth of Av. To the contrary, the designation of the day as "joyous" went in the other direction, showing how the calendar would continue to rise above the distressing events unfolding at the time.

The inexplicable vacant space of the ninth of Av—the day commemorating the beginning of exile and the day marking a harbinger of its end—found its fitting complement, then, in the audacious designation of the fifteenth of Av as a *Freudentag*, a day of joy. The two days played off one another, working as partners in conveying the astonishing message of the moment. Using the momentum of prophetic tradition, they together staged a startling reversal, whereby the commemoration of tragedy would lead to an upsurge of joy where and when one would least expect it. The *Luach Katan* thereby showed the nature of time traditionally rendered as being supple, elastic, malleable, equally responsive to the needs of a besieged community as it was to the needs of custom and convention.[58]

Painting Jewish Time in Theresienstadt

The *Luach Katan* made sure the Jewish calendar was available in Theresienstadt, and it pitted against the year's devastation of transport and privation an extraordinary inventory of traditional Jewish time. It even crescendoed to an ode to joy. Other calendars came in its wake and were likely guided by it. One rendered during that murderous year came from an unexpected source. Hilde Zadikow, by all accounts an assimilated central European Jewish artist, was an unlikely figure to compose a Jewish calendar in Theresienstadt. The fact that she did—at least to the degree that the remarkable painting she composed can be said to be a Jewish calendar—helps to show that the robust secular culture the camp gave rise to had a parallel Jewish culture, similarly robust in nature and inspiration. Indeed, the almost ubiquitous vitality of the camp's Jewish life was such that an artist in search of a subject would be guided to something as traditional and unassuming as the Jewish calendar. As it turned out, her Jewish calendar painting may have been the most Jewish piece of artwork Zadikow ever made.

Born in 1890 in Prague to Samuel and Ernestine Lohsing, Hilde and her husband, sculptor Arnold Zadikow, set up residence in Munich and together pursued art careers.[59] They also raised a daughter, Marianne. While not conventionally traditional, the family observed Jewish holidays in some fashion and maintained ties with Arnold's father, who was born and bred in eastern Europe and whose love of music—he was said to be a cantor—influenced all members of the family. While their work was mainly geared to a general European audience, they also produced pieces with Jewish themes, including a menorah and a challah cover. Having a sense in the mid-1930s that life for Jews in Germany would soon enough no longer be viable, the Zadikows relocated to Prague.[60]

It was from there that they were deported to Theresienstadt in May 1942. Hilde and her nineteen-year-old daughter were able to persevere until liberation in April 1945; Arnold was not so fortunate, succumbing in March 1943 to delayed treatment of a ruptured appendix. After the war, Hilde spent time in Italy and Israel before joining her daughter in the United States. Hilde passed away in 1974, some three decades before Marianne's Theresienstadt book, an idiosyncratic collection of sayings solicited from fellow prisoners during and soon after the war, became a modest critical and popular success. The first entry in the book was Hilde's.

Once imprisoned in Theresienstadt, the Zadikows had to adapt their talents to the wishes of the enemy. Hilde worked in the so-called Lautschwerkstette, a German enterprise producing official kitsch: covers for such everyday items as glove boxes, telephone books, and bookmarks. She also had to paint on demand for those in positions of power and authority, in some cases being summoned in the middle of the night. But like other Terezin artists, she made time and found the gumption to draw and paint what she felt needed to be made, including the Jewish calendar.

As it stands, the calendar is not actually a calendar but rather a china ink and watercolor painting of Jewish calendar themes.[61] Produced in 1943—the year that, as we recall, witnessed the tragic deportation of thousands of Theresienstadt's Jews to the murderous East—the author's name and the Gregorian year are inscribed at the image's lower right edge. A substantial canvas measuring 475 by 645 millimeters (18.7 by 25.39 inches), the Hebrew-lettered twelve months of the Jewish year are presented in two columns of six each. Behind each month are nestled symbols and scenes prominent in that season.

The letters of Tishrei, for example, overlay a shofar and etrog, with the first letter, *Taf*, deftly forming the roof and walls of a sukkah, and the bottom of the final letter, *yud*, extending into the shape of a shofar. In the month of Kislev, the branches of the Chanukah menorah grow out of the letter *Lamed* and join it to the letter *Samech*; for the month of Tevet, snow covers the tops of the letters, dramatizing the dip in temperature during the winter season; for the month of Nisan, a plate of matzos lies before haggadah-reading celebrants; for the month of Av, mourners sit on the ground intoning kinot; and, finally, for Elul, the shofar reappears, this time in the mouth of a blower rather than simply as an appendage to one of the letters. The elegant Hebrew letters of the monthly names thus do double duty. They guide the steady progression through the holidays of the year,

Fig. 2.6: Hilde Zadikow was a respected artist who was forced while imprisoned in the Theresienstadt ghetto to paint decorative objects and portraiture for the Nazis. She nevertheless produced a number of works of her own devising, including the 1943 calendar, which features names of the Jewish months overlaid on scenes of rituals associated with the month and season. Courtesy of the Jewish Museum in Prague.

while also contributing their very substance and design to the thematic action taking place in the background.

They also camouflage activity too provocative to put out in the open. The month of Adar, with scenes from the Scroll of Esther read communally on the holiday of Purim, brings such provocation to its highest pitch. It shows the triumphant Mordechai, having foiled Haman's plot to annihilate the Jews, being paraded by the humiliated villain through the city on a horse. Faithful to the ancient storyline, Zadikow nevertheless catapults the scene into the brutal present by sketching Mordechai wearing a Jewish star and emblazoning the villains with swastikas.

Two points follow. First, for those who knew it, the Purim story and its diabolical antagonist easily lent themselves to analogy with the current threat to Jewish life and limb. No addition was really needed to see its relevance and to hope for a similar reversal of fortunes. A more recent anecdote demonstrates how easy it can be to apply the lesson of Purim to modern circumstances. Shortly before the onset of the Purim holiday in the 1990s, a terrorist bombing killed numbers in the streets of Tel Aviv. The loss was devastating. For some communities, the loss was so searing that it inhibited the joy of Purim and dampened all thought of celebration. After all, how could one rejoice in the face of such devastation? Wouldn't the joy desecrate the memory of the murdered? But other communities in Israel responded differently, celebrating without the slightest trace of inhibition. Indeed, celebrating Purim was for them the most fitting response. In one community, the climax came when an effigy of the evil Haman was hung from the uppermost part of the Torah ark. Under siege in contemporary as well as ancient times, every Jew present knew who really had come out on top

But Zadikow did not want her viewers to have to make any leaps of imagination. So she dressed the story up in modern garb. To add the up-to-the-minute symbols, the Jewish star and, in contrast, the Nazi swastika, meant that the painter felt some viewers may have required guidance in adapting the ancient story's message to Theresienstadt's particular form of oppression. But the star and swastika also proclaim boldly that what is at stake in Purim is the eventual overthrow of the tyrant. By sticking to one's guns, as it were, by holding fast to one's Jewish identity, the oppressor would be undone. The message likely lies within every holiday nestled in the curves and spaces of the calendar's letters. Undoubtedly, Purim's images state the case most brazenly. But sounding the shofar, eating matzahs, mourning the loss of the ancient Temple—every traditional practice carried a similar theme.

The Hebrew letters in the foreground assuredly camouflaged the provocative messages lurking beneath the surface. But the foreground/background design of Zadikow's calendar painting also sets forth an aesthetic principle fitting for the evil particular to Theresienstadt. The camp itself, after all, was conceived to present one reality on the surface, another beneath it. On the surface, the construction of Theresienstadt as a model ghetto/camp attempted to mislead the world at large about the enemy's murderous intentions. Admittedly, the Nazis practiced deception widely, trying to make sure that the malevolent nature of the camps, in Poland, Austria, and Germany, was hidden from public view. But Theresienstadt went further, creating the fiction of a spa in which even the elderly could find shelter and benefit by recreational activities. The fiction was bolstered by setting up (in 1943) cafés, a bank, a post office, and a petty-crimes court. Even the flourishing culture of music and lectures that helped prisoners persevere contributed to the spa-like picture of Theresienstadt displayed to the outside world. Eventually, in preparation for the Red Cross delegation's visit in June 1944, buildings were freshly painted and gardens planted.[62] Everything was made to seem hospitable. Beneath the surface, however, Theresienstadt imperiled Jewish life, either by transporting its prisoners to be murdered in camps in Poland or by creating conditions within the camp unfavorable to maintaining basic health and well-being.

The two levels of reality stood in direct contrast to one another. The surface level told one story, the subterranean level a different one. Indeed, the stories were so discordant that what one saw on the surface could not be used to construe what went on beneath it. Among other things, this rift between levels of reality explains the failure of the Red Cross to understand Theresienstadt's true purpose and nature. Its delegation was so taken in by the deception that they seemed to have no idea there was anything behind the placid scenes.

The two levels in Zadikow's painting operate in a completely different manner. The lettered months of the surface relate directly to the scenes below. Indeed, the months guide the content of the scenes, serving as a kind of title or heading. Even more than that, Zadikow often used the forms of the month's letters to render the scenes and symbols. The connection between surface and depth was both thematic and substantial. No doubt, the letters did act as a screen, diverting attention from the provocative background scenes. Only those who chose to look closely could see how the symbols challenged the tyrant's rule. But Zadikow aimed to join foreground and background, surface and depth, what could be seen at a glance and what demanded excavation and study. Her calendar painting thus ran counter to the nature of the camp itself, the purpose of which was to create a veneer that had little if anything to do with the reality beneath. In Zadikow's deft hands, the calendar painting turned the tables, harmonizing the foreground and background through and through.

This may also be why Zadikow's painting defines time exclusively in a Jewish idiom. Unlike any other wartime Jewish calendar fashioned in or around the killing fields of Europe, this one has no Gregorian counterpart. The composition forcefully brings out this omission. Most Jewish calendars weave in the Gregorian with a mirror effect: the Jewish dates appear on one side, the non-Jewish directly across on the other. Zadikow's painting also uses the mirror effect. But in this case the parallel columns contain only the names of Jewish months. One looks in vain for their Gregorian equivalent. Such a strategy emphasizes the strictly uniform nature of time in this special calendar, where Jewish time is not (or is barely) interwoven with non-Jewish; instead the Jewish calendar stands fully, ornately, on its own.

But not quite on its own. The year inscribed at the calendar's lower edge brings into play (almost imperceptibly) another time measure: 1943. The Gregorian dating is both expected and surprising—expected because the art world the author moved in no doubt primarily dated according to this time frame; surprising because the painted Jewish calendar, with its facing columns of Jewish months, made such a resounding declaration that its Jewish time reckoning stood alone. In this respect, one can't help but compare Zadikow's painting with the wartime calendar of Rabbi Menachem Schneersohn, which also dates time exclusively by the Jewish calendar. Certainly, differences outweigh and overwhelm the similarity, a fact that will become clearer in the discussion of Rabbi

Schneersohn's calendar below. Yet it is the case that both came into being in the same year, a year of unprecedented devastation, but one in which, according to the calculus that animated each project, the Jewish calendar could, and should, track time unburdened by any other point of reference.

Despite—or, as we will see, because of—the 1943 dating, Zadikow's Jewish calendar painting is actually abstracted from any specific year. Much like the pelican that adorns it, the twin columns of twelve months soar above the particulars of observed time. The holiday cycle shrouded among the letters is also untouched by time's flow. One way this abstraction from lived time comes across is through the omission of a second month of Adar, the thirteenth month of the leap year added to the calendar seven times in a nineteen-year cycle. Thirteen months make up the Jewish calendar about 35 percent of the time. Symmetrical and balanced though Zadikow's composition may be, the twelve months do not do complete justice to the Jewish calendar's variable size, since they fail to take account of the fluid expansion and contraction necessary for the lunar calendar to stay seasonally on track.

The 1943 dating shows that such considerations were not irrelevant to the circumstances at hand, given that the corresponding Jewish year of 5703 contained an added thirteenth month of Adar. Zadikow's painting thus heroically presented the Jewish lunar year, in what one may call a stylized version, but overlooked the special character of the specific Jewish year in which she carried out her project. The elastic nature of the Jewish calendar is not merely a technical matter but rather reflects a deeper spiritual reality:

> One of the lessons we can derive from [the periodic addition of a thirteenth month] is that God always affords us an opportunity to catch up, as it were: to complete whatever was left undone for whatever reason, and even to counteract the effects of not having utilized our time to the fullest extent possible.
>
> Remarkably, this integral feature of the Jewish calendar implies that we are given the ability not only to change the future, but the past, as well. Furthermore, the fact that we intercalate a full month, thereby "correcting" the accumulated discrepancy of several years at once, indicates that we can change the remote as well as the recent past.
>
> If we look even deeper, we note that the commandment to intercalate the year invests us with the power to overcome the Divinely-instituted laws of nature. God decreed that the lunar year be shorter than the solar year, in response to the moon's complaint about having to share dominion with the sun. Nevertheless, through this commandment, God empowers us to not only neutralize this inequality but even make the lunar year *longer* than the solar year. This is clearly an example of how God intends us to be His "partner in creation," that is, in bringing the world to its true fulfillment.[63]

The thirteenth month not only guarantees the calendar year's stability, ensuring that holidays remain anchored in the biblically mandated season. From a spiritual vantage point, what is also crucial is the interplay between the expanded and contracted calendar year, the thirteenth month periodically providing the opportunity to go beyond the fixed limitations and boundaries of time.

Zadikow's *Terezine* is thus out of sync with the year in which it was fashioned. This does not mean that the calendar painting wouldn't have had its purpose, perhaps serving as an educational tool in clandestine teaching for children.[64] Besides the letters and monthly scenes, the calendar's main decoration pictures a pelican nurturing her brood of four children. Traditional sources praise the pelican's love for its children, and hence the image, prevalent in Ashkenazi Jewish ritual art, came to represent a mother devoted unconditionally to the well-being of her young. Borrowed from ancient iconography and texts, the image usually included the macabre twist of the mother ripping open her breast to feed her young with her own blood.[65] Zadikow's depiction, faithful in most respects to the convention, omits the bloodletting. The camp setting was likely too macabre in its own right to see in the spilling of blood anything but evil. Hilde's daughter Marianne has commented on the fittingness of the (bloodless) pelican image, noting that nothing could be more important to a mother during wartime than to help her children.[66] Close by her mother's side for the war's duration, the daughter's words give an insider's appreciation of the image's pertinence. Such indefatigable care may also speak directly to the calendar's pedagogic role, whereby the letters, symbols, and holiday scenes could school children in the basic idiom of Jewish observance. From this vantage point, the nurturing mother was the calendar painting itself, and the children were the young of Theresienstadt charmed and buoyed up by its inspired medium and message.

Indeed, for either children or adults Zadikow's calendar painting conveyed in clever fashion some basics about Jewish history, calendars, customs, and holidays. Yet for all of its eloquence and creativity in bringing to visual life many of the essential elements of the Jewish year, Zadikow's painting nonetheless remains a painting, hovering slightly above or beneath the actual year of 5703 being contended with in Theresienstadt.

That said, the full story may be different. Some speculate that what is left of the painting is only a vestige of a larger production—which may have included an actual calendar. Indeed, before the war, Hilde had apparently painted background displays especially designed for a packet of calendar days.[67] One can certainly envision her *Terezine* as featuring, between the columns of letters and beneath the nurturing pelican, a year's bundle of days. Such a calendar would no doubt have been different in kind from that of the *Luach Katan*, boasting a less austere, more visualized Jewish calendar year, with each month again displaying symbols and scenes appropriate to season and circumstance. Like the *Luach Katan*, however, Zadikow's calendar would have to have had a thirteenth month— undoubtedly drawn with mesmerizing symbols and scenes of its own. But even as it stands, *Terezine* testifies to the extent to which the Jewish calendar served as a sophisticated idiom of Jewish timekeeping, even among the camp's cultural elite.

Illustrating Time in Theresienstadt

Painting gave Hilda Zadikow a medium to enter the world of Jewish time and share it graphically with her fellow prisoners. Her painting—black fire written, as it were, on orange and yellow fire—distilled the idea of Jewish time to its core. Certainly, no one could hope to use the painting to track time on a day-to-day basis. Rather, at least in the artifactual form we have before us, the painting forsook the day-to-day and week-to-week movement of the year in order to present it as a solid whole. Not numbered dates and days but pictures were the keys that unlocked the Jewish calendar's symbolic essence.

Rabbi Asher Berlinger, a fellow prisoner in Theresienstadt, shared Zadikow's passion and respect for the eloquence of the pictorial image. Yet he came to the idea of a Jewish calendar from the opposite end of the spectrum. A rabbi who was also a gifted artist, the fifty-three-year-old native of Germany produced, while in the camp, Jewish calendars for two successive years (5704 and 5705). In his case, the day-to-day progression of Jewish life stood above all. Fast days, festivals, Sabbaths, monthly beginnings, seasonal variations—he meticulously set down the glory of the Jewish year's special days and occasions. And this exalted content, what the *Luach Katan* had distilled in a highlighted and austere format, was embellished, fore and aft, by illustrations, pictures directly linked to the movement of the year and others more obliquely commenting on it. In each case, the images declared that the calendar, an ode to time's sacred character, not only had to be functional but also beautiful.

This was all well and good. But the bedrock of the calendar was the day-to-day. Every day's inflection, every nuance mattered. An observant Jew's commitment was day in, day out. This prosaic insistence on each day's mindful journey is what the format and focus of Rabbi Berlinger's calendars reflected, setting forth the message in an altogether understated but visually compelling way.

Asher Berlinger was born on December 30, 1889 (the seventh of Teves, 5650) to Yaakov Gavriel and Rivka Berlinger.[68] His father was a businessman; the son chose a different path by becoming an artist and teacher. Trained at the Würzburg Jewish Teacher's Seminary, Asher first taught in Burgpreppach, a small Bavarian town with a Jewish population of one hundred. He and his wife, Breindel, relocated to the somewhat larger nearby town of Schweinfurt, where he served as the cantor of the synagogue as well as a teacher of the Jewish community, in subjects ranging from Hebrew language to music. Accomplished in fine and graphic arts and sculpture, he also taught these subjects at the local girls' high school.

The town of Schweinfurt is situated in Bavaria, not far from the regional hub of Frankfurt am Main. The Jewish community dates back to the 1200s, when reference to a Jew by the name of Abraham of Schweinfurt appears in a Würzburg document. The town counted a hundred Jews in 1553 but expelled them two years later. No Jewish presence resided in Schweinfurt for the next three hundred years. The community was reestablished in the 1860s and eventually achieved enough prominence to serve as the seat of the *landes-rabbiner*, the chief rabbi of the district. The Jewish population grew to 490 in 1880 but diminished thereafter, numbering 415 in 1905, 363 in 1933, and 120 in 1939 in a general population of 49,000 (neighboring Würzburg, in contrast, had just over 1,000 Jewish residents). In recent times, Schweinfurt had become a center of a flourishing metal industry and by the late 1930s produced most of Nazi Germany's ball bearings. During World War II, strategic Allied bombing thus targeted its factories in order to cripple tank and aircraft production.

Pillars of the small Jewish community, the Berlingers had two young girls of their own, Senta and Rosa. The family lived in the two-story building of the Schweinfurt Jewish Community Council, occupying half of the upper floor; the local rabbi and his family resided in the other half. The children attended public school for a few grades but were then expelled for being Jewish and subsequently studied in a one-room school operated by the Jewish community. During the Kristallnacht pogrom, the synagogue adjacent to their home was looted and set on fire. The Berlingers' family home was ransacked and damaged, and a fire was started on the lower level of their building. However, it was extinguished when a local citizen observing the mayhem objected on the basis that there were people upstairs. Rabbi Berlinger was arrested and sent to the Dachau concentration camp. He was released after more than a month, probably because of his military service as a frontline soldier during World War I.

After Kristallnacht, the girls were sent to England on a Kindertransport, but Asher and Bertha's efforts to leave Germany were unsuccessful. They were deported from Schweinfurt to Theresienstadt on Yom Kippur, 5703 (September 21, 1942).[69] They spent almost exactly two years in the camp, during which time Asher continued using his artistic gifts to great effect and with remarkable results. He was unfortunately deported to Auschwitz the day after Yom Kippur, 5705 (September, 28, 1944); Bertha met the same fate a week later, the nineteenth of Tisrei, in the middle of the Sukkoth holiday (October 6, 1944). He was fifty-four, and she was fifty-three.

The subject of magazine articles and research institute websites, Rabbi Berlinger's remarkable calendars have received the greatest notoriety to date of any to emerge from the cauldron of the Holocaust. But the description has made it seem as if Rabbi Berlinger fashioned them in a vacuum, circumventing the authorities' decrees at every turn of the road and fighting single-handedly a battle to preserve Jewish religious life and culture—which, had he not persevered as he did, would have disappeared from the scene.[70] The same holds true for the Theresienstadt synagogue Rabbi Berlinger lovingly decorated with image and verse. Beautiful and moving, the synagogue is nevertheless set forth as the sole place of prayer in the camp and, as such, fashioned in defiance of outright prohibition. But as we have learned, such a description does not do justice to the circumstances of Jewish religious life in Theresienstadt, where the practice of Jewish precepts was tolerated and, to the degree that the meager provisions of the camp allowed, actively pursued. Heroic though they may have been, Rabbi Berlinger's calendars were not the result of an isolated gesture but rather part of the camp's larger tapestry of religious observance. Indeed, the widespread religious activity may have been the prod that moved him to fashion the calendars.

Resourceful though he was, he did not have to reinvent the wheel. As we know, at least one detailed (if "small") Theresienstadt Jewish calendar preceded Rabbi Berlinger's own. And importantly, that calendar, the *Luach Katan*, commenced precisely at the period of time when he arrived in Theresienstadt, in Tishrei 5703 (September 1942); if the *Luach Katan* had any circulation to speak of, Rabbi Berlinger would have made himself familiar with it. More than that, it would have been on hand to help him adapt to the difficult circumstances of camp life, to orient his own religious practice, and, most fundamentally, to declare in its understated fashion that a Jewish calendar year also existed in a place such as Theresienstadt.

That said, while Rabbi Berlinger must have undoubtedly appreciated the *Luach Katan*'s deft presentation of the key coordinates of traditional Jewish life, his calendars were guided by a different concept of production. As we recall, the *Luach Katan* presented the year in a highlighted format, listing only special days. Moreover, though traditionally Jewish in every respect, the *Luach Katan* used only Latin letters, a limitation seemingly imposed by the typewriter keypad available to the calendar's author. Finally, the *Luach Katan* was austere in appearance, with ornamentation limited to two images on the title page. As we will see, Rabbi Berlinger's calendars differ in many key features: they were committed to record each and every day, were handwritten and drawn, used German but also Hebrew lettering—and included a generous allotment of illustration and ornamentation. What the *Luach Katan* sketched and condensed, one might say, Rabbi Berlinger chose to fill in and fill out.

Having arrived in Theresienstadt in Tishrei 5703 (September 1942), there is no evidence that Rabbi Berlinger produced a calendar for his first year in the camp. The Jewish year was already in progress; he and his wife, we may recall, were deported to the camp on Yom Kippur, ten days into the new year. It may be that he brought with him a printed calendar for that year and thus was in no need of producing his own; it may be that the *Luach Katan* provided what was essential. In any case, the task of composing a Jewish calendar from scratch was not simple under the best of conditions. The upheaval that came with deportation from home and the surely arduous adjustment to his largely inhospitable surroundings may have caused his energies to be directed to meeting a formidable range of other tasks.

The next two years tell a different story. During his sojourn in Theresienstadt, Rabbi Berlinger sketched full-blown Jewish calendars for 5704 and 5705.[71] They share most features. Scripting the month's Jewish name in bold, both calendars note the time at which Shabbat begins, holidays, fast days (the first year includes the special Monday/Thursday/Monday cycle), and Yom Kippur Katan. The Jewish day of the month is numbered in ascending Hebrew script. The secular calendar, for its part, refers only to the month, year, and, in Arabic numerals, day. No holidays, whether religious, national, or civic, receive mention. Longer month names in the Gregorian calendar (e.g., September and November) are always abbreviated; Jewish month names (even the longest, Marcheshvan) never are.

The alternating role of the Latin and Hebrew scripts is especially telling when it comes to Rabbi Berlinger's notation for the days of the week and, by extension, the special notation for the Sabbath day. All the weekdays are abbreviated in German (So, Mo, Di, Mi, Do, Fr), using Latin script. But the Sabbath day deviates from the norm and uses the Hebrew letter *shin*, ש, the initial letter of the word *Shabbat*. The change in script powerfully conveys the distinction of the Sabbath day, separated as it is in character from the other days. The less-than-optimal conditions under which the calendar was forged may be signaled by the lone instance in which Latin script appears and the Hebrew letter *shin* is replaced by the *Sa* (an abbreviation of the German *Samstag*—i.e., Saturday). That such a slip occurs only once, however, testifies to Rabbi Berlinger's careful industry, even in the Theresienstadt ghetto.

He produced, moreover, truly bifocal calendars. At pains in one arena to mark the Sabbath's special distinction, he nevertheless consistently uses its secular name in another. On the few occasions when the onset of the new moon (referred to as the "molad") took place on Shabbat, Rabbi Berlinger would refer to the day as "*Samstag*/Saturday," seemingly unperturbed by the fact that, week in, week out, he identified the Sabbath by its Hebrew name and Jewish character. But perhaps in the apparent contradiction lies its resolution. The Sabbath's special character comes to the fore in the context of the week, where it serves as the seventh and culminating day. Hence Rabbi Berlinger's choice of the Jewish name in the column of weekdays. The onset of the new moon, in contrast, steps outside of the context of the week; the Sabbath day is, as it were, a day like any other. In this case, Rabbi Berlinger's choice of nomenclature implies that the German name in Latin script is sufficient and proper.

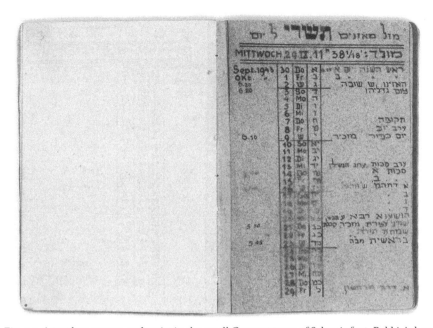

Fig. 2.7: A teacher, cantor, and artist in the small German town of Schweinfurt, Rabbi Asher Berlinger composed Jewish calendars for the years 5704 (1943–44) and 5705 (1944–45) while imprisoned in the Theresienstadt ghetto. Illustrated with pastoral as well as ghetto scenes, the calendars display an unusual blend of rabbinic expertise with artistic craft. Like many Theresienstadt prisoners, he and his wife, Breindel, were tragically deported to and murdered in Auschwitz. Courtesy of the Yad Vashem Museum.

That Rabbi Berlinger had the wherewithal to compose calendars for two successive years was unusual; that both calendars emerged from the war may be unique. From one angle, the decision to compose a calendar for the succeeding year makes good sense. He had already fashioned a design for the first calendar. The second year's design followed it closely: three middle columns for the dates and days; the Jewish holiday notation to the right, the Gregorian to the left; the name of the month and the time of its "birth" at the top of the page; and every last word and number handwritten and drawn. In 5705, Rabbi Berlinger adhered so closely to the previous year's model that he must have felt that the calendar for 5704 had accomplished much of what it set out to do.

Other calendar-savvy Jews in hiding and in ghettos and camps acted on a similar impulse. To compose a second year's calendar in hiding, while no mean feat, was both less difficult and less risky. In Amsterdam, making a calendar was a way for the young Yehoshua Neuwirth to keep himself busy and to keep the holed-up family abreast of the Sabbath and holiday times.

Nothing had greatly changed in the second year that would have made the task any less important. The same was true for the middle-aged rabbi Shlomo Scheiner in Debowka, Poland. Living in the home of the Christian family that had taken them in and thus being at their mercy, the awareness of anything Jewish could come only by means of the Scheiners' own efforts. As time passed and as fewer Jews remained alive on Polish soil from one year to the next, the experience of isolation grew only greater. The family became more dependent on the self-made calendars. Materials were increasingly hard to come by as the war went on. But the momentum was in favor of continuing what had been started the year before.

This was also the case with the Lodz ghetto, where official *Litzmannstadt* calendars were brought out year by year from 1941–44. The format of the calendars stayed the same, with minor shifts of emphasis. But the content evolved, allowing the calendar to also serve as a ledger for the previous year's events. Publishing in successive years conveyed a sense of stability, despite the hazardous fluctuations of ghetto life.

The overwhelming privation, draconian edicts, and minimal protection of personal effects in the concentration camps—Auschwitz, Bergen-Belsen, Buchenwald, and others—was something altogether different. In Auschwitz, as we will see, Sophie Solberg did compose calendars for successive years (5704 and 5705). But only the latter calendar survived, watched over as it was by her with infinite care in the aftermath of the disappearance of the first. In Buchenwald, Rabbi Avigdor set about composing a calendar for 5705, just as he seemingly had at the other way stations and camps where he had been interned. But while the Buchenwald calendar was, as it were, liberated with him, the previous calendars had all been destroyed.

That these second (and presumably third) year calendars most often did not survive does not diminish the heroic impulse that had some prisoners, in whom the reflex was especially well-honed, produce calendars on a yearly basis. But with such individually composed calendars, only in the case of Rabbi Berlinger can we see the evolution over the course of time and circumstance.

In terms of the essential aspects of the Jewish calendar, the transition from the year 5704 to 5705 was not as drastic as in some years. Neither had the extra month of Adar, and the latter year, 5705, had only a single day more than the previous. Otherwise, all the key components remained the same. Jewish holidays and fast days always fall on the same date and last the same number of days, and most months have the same number of days from year to year.

While continuities outweigh differences, the changes in the 5705 calendar are nonetheless striking. First, Rabbi Berlinger introduced some minor revisions in format, making the frame thicker, the script neater, and the abbreviations less frequent. Second, in the content, not everything carried over to the next year:

the post-holiday fasts known as Behab were dropped, as was any special notation for the fifteenth day of the month of Av—the day the *Luach Katan* had so audaciously called a *Freudentag*, a day of joy. By the summer of 1944, after almost two years of contending with the camp's special forms of duplicity and adversity, proclamations of joy may have been that much more difficult to utter.

The most conspicuous change came in the illustrations. The first year 5704 version opens with a counterclockwise series of images of the constellations for each month: scale (Tishrei), crab (Cheshvan), archer (Kislev), and so on. It is not unusual for calendars to picture or refer to the cycle of constellations, with the convention dating back hundreds of years. Rabbi Berlinger clearly had a special sensitivity, having studied astronomy and paid particular attention to the constellations in the night sky. In the first calendar, the heading of each month notes the constellation associated with it, but that is as far as it goes; images are relegated to the beginning and end of the calendar but did not appear within.

The second-year calendar reproduces the constellation-adorned title page and then takes the association a step further: the page heading of each month includes a smaller drawing of the constellation icon (scale, crab, archer, and so on) but features a larger one dramatizing some pastoral scene, presumably tied to the constellation. Exactly how the image corresponds to the constellation (or some other aspect of the month in question) is not altogether clear. The larger drawings do not, for instance, contain the easily discernible holiday symbols and scenes found in Zadikow's painting. Though the specific message may be difficult to tease out, a broader inference can be gleaned from Rabbi Berlinger's desire to add to what he did the previous year. The more time he spent in Theresienstadt, the greater the sophistication he introduced into his calendar making. We might have expected the unsettling events he witnessed over the course of two years to have the opposite effect, eliminating what was deemed superfluous and paring the calendar down to bare essentials. He did not follow this course of action, did not opt to prune or diminish, but instead chose to add to the decorative beauty.

These constellation-based images Rabbi Berlinger wove into the fabric of his calendar. But a few others, different in kind yet intriguing in their own right, he appended to each year. One appears in both calendars: a rearview self-portrait, which shows him standing before a synagogue lectern attired in the formal dress of a *chazzan*, a leader of prayer. The drawing displays at the bottom right his full signature; indeed, the portrait itself serves as a kind of extended symbolic signature to the calendar, linking it to liturgy. Like the prayers he led, the calendar he composed guided the congregation, both within and outside of the synagogue. This message concluded the calendar so appropriately that the portrait appears again in the back pages of the 5705 calendar.

A second drawing, different for each year, accompanies the portrait. For 5704, it pictures an open Torah scroll on the synagogue lectern, a starred ceiling arching above, and an empty bench positioned below or beneath. The items rendered in the synagogue setting complement the self-portrait, showing another facet of worship, this time with the Torah rather than the worshipper at the center. The Torah focus may be as straightforward as the fact that the calendar marks the occasions on which the Torah is publically read; the calendar is a means to a greater end, an instrument through which the regular recitation of God's word can be counted on. Regularity is crucial, the calendar the key to maintaining it. The calendar is only worthy, Rabbi Berlinger's drawings imply, if it serves as a stepping-stone to prayer and Torah.

The second calendar closed with a much bolder statement: a drawing of a lit menorah resting on a lion's head. The flames ascend against a circular backdrop of light (whether it represents the moon or the sun is not clear), which in turn emits rays of light that extend beyond the picture frame. Everything—within the frame, beyond the frame—is illuminated by the menorah's light. The menorah, symbol of the miraculous triumph of the Jews over the pagan enemy of old, projects strength; the lions on which it stands intensifies it; the all-surrounding light dramatizes it. The calendar's final gesture is its most forceful, unyielding, and resolute.

To be sure, this drawing, like the others, is dated 1943; unlike the calendar itself, the assertive image of the menorah was fashioned at an earlier juncture. Rabbi Berlinger penned its unbending stance at the same time as he did the quiet serenity of the Torah waiting to be read. Both flow from the same source. And it may have been that other hands than his placed the images in their respective positions in the calendars. But as it stands, the closing image sent an unmistakable message, wherein the calendar served in its own right as a source of miraculous light that refused to be intimidated by the darkness at hand.

Indeed, each of the three Theresienstadt calendar projects served in their own way as a source of spiritual light and guidance for the camp's prisoners. Composed at different stages under increasingly difficult conditions, the calendars reflect the Jewish religious culture actively pursued and practiced. In this respect, they help us appreciate this generally overlooked facet of Theresienstadt. But their role goes deeper than that. Two of the three nurtured religious observance, mapping holy days and fast days alike, while the third fashioned the calendar into a symbol that could inspire and educate. Each one, moreover, used the calendar to convey a message special to the circumstances of Theresienstadt: in the case of the *Luach Katan*, it intimated the joy that would surely emerge from sadness; in the case of the Zadikow painting, it taught one how to see beneath the surface and know who the true victors would be; and in the case of Rabbi Berlinger, it presented the fusion of subtly rendered artistic images with meticulous attention to daily ritual. Individual projects though they were, each seized the opportunity provided by the camp's provisional religious freedom to render Jewish time sacred—and more.

The Promise of New Beginnings: French Jewry

French Jewry was not confined to ghettos. But the life of a Jew in wartime France was nevertheless subject to hardship and the threat of deportation. And sadly, this was no idle threat. Thousands of Jews were arrested and incarcerated in French concentration camps, fifteen of which were operated by the French Vichy government in the south, twenty-six in the German-occupied north. Conditions in the camps were generally poor, hundreds perished from disease and malnutrition, and men were recruited for forced labor brigades. A number of the French camps also served as way stations to death camps in Poland, where, in the wake of a series of deportations that took place from 1942–44, close to seventy-five thousand Jews were murdered.

The upheaval of French Jewish life made tracking time difficult yet essential. But another obstacle entered into the equation. After the occupation of France in spring of 1940, official Jewish publication was subject to draconian censorship. Considered texts like any other, Jewish calendars were also reviewed by the censor. Duly scrutinized, the Jewish calendar fashioned by the rabbinical council of Paris for the year 5701 was approved for publication, reportedly the only Jewish publication to be thus authorized in the months following the fall of France. Issued it was, and one of the copies that remains is that which belonged to Rabbi Menachem Schneersohn, who, having taken refuge in the south of France and making several notations on the calendar, took his copy with him to the United States the following summer (1941). As we will see, his interest in the French calendar found more extensive expression in New World. In France, however, the censors were turning the screw tighter; their demands for omitting materials from the 5702 calendar composed by the Parisian rabbinate were so extensive that it was deemed better not to issue the calendar at all rather than do so in a truncated fashion.[72]

But the wartime censors wielded an uneven, if often harsh, hand. For some did make it through. Nephtali Grunewald, a Jewish publisher from Strasbourg who, like many Alsatian Jews, was evacuated to the city of Limoges in west central France at the time of the German invasion, published a Jewish calendar every year of the war.[73] This was done, moreover, with review by the censor of each year's edition. An accomplishment in their own right, the calendars featured the text of a defiant psalm, a list of rabbis to whom one could turn for council, and prefaces that lyrically extolled the virtues of a calendar published in times of cruelty and misfortune.

As with many wartime calendars, these also offered a comprehensive guide to ritual observance, indicating holidays, Rosh Chodesh, fast days, and the weekly Torah reading, but also the special reading for the Sabbath during the holiday of Sukkoth—the biblical book of Kohelet—and the arrival of the fall "Tikufah."

More prominent than these nuances, however, were the transliterations that fill the calendar's left column. Virtually every Hebrew detail in the right column appears again in French in the left. "Roche-hachanah," "Jeune de Guerdalyah" (the fast in memory of Gedalya), the Torah portion "Ha'azinou" and the accompanying designation that this Sabbath was that of "Choubhah [Teshuvah]," the Sabbath of repentance falling during the Days of Awe—each and every item finds its transliterated complement. The calendar was thus meant to reach every Jew, those who had facility in Hebrew and those who did not. The transliterations into French, moreover, made the calendar transparent to any who would care to look, including the French authorities. Nothing was hidden; everything was there on the surface.

Like many wartime calendars, Grunewald's contained times for concluding Sabbaths, holidays, and fast days. In this case, however, it listed these times (and their nuanced variations) not only for the city of publication, Limoges, but also for a wide range of outlying communities, including Périgueux, Lyon, Marseille, Ensuite, Paris, Toulouse, Vichy, Clermont-Ferrand, and even places as far-flung as Algiers and Oran. Going to the trouble of setting down a plethora of communities in France and beyond suggests the calendar was meant to find its way, by land and by sea, to the various locations.

The broad geographic reach was matched by a striking expansiveness in dating Jewish history. Most Jewish calendars, as we recall, number the year according to the traditional reckoning of the world's beginnings—which, in this case, was 5703 "of the era of creation," as the calendar's title page lyrically proclaims. Unlike most, however, the dating doesn't stop here but rather draws on two other systems of computing the number: (a) the year "2253 in the era of Contracts of the Seleucids" and (b) the year "1874 of the destruction of the Temple." At earlier stages of Jewish history, these alternative computations were the preferred method of chronology (i.e., of dating the number of the current year); they continue to be used in more technical aspects of Jewish legal documents. But almost all Jewish calendars opt to date the year according to the traditional reckoning of the creation of the world, and since the "era of creation" has been so widely accepted, the authors or publishers of calendars have not felt obliged to allude to, much less to incorporate, other systems of calculation.

The Grunewald 5703 calendar is thus exceptional in its decision to refer to these alternative systems. Why exactly Nephtali Grunewald might have included them and placed them front and center on the calendar's title page is not known. But their inclusion shows an admirable sensitivity to the way in which Jewish history can find its expression in a calendar, not only as an item of the past but also as providing for multiple points of new beginnings. The points at which these calculations begin, moreover, stem from unfavorable moments in the Jewish past. In the first instance ("2253 in the era of Contracts of the Seleucids"), the date refers to the subjection to the rule of a foreign power; in the second instance ("1874 of the destruction of the Temple"), it corresponds to the pivotal loss of the ancient Jerusalem sanctuary and the exile that followed. Endeavoring to cope with the occupation of France by an enemy bent on tormenting the Jews, Grunewald may have added these computations to convey that, whatever the misfortune that might befall the people of Israel, it, too, could be seen as another new beginning.

Written by two notable leaders of French Jewry, the prefaces served not only as approbation for the publication of the respective wartime calendars. They also interpreted the calendar's mission in the specific context. For the 5704 calendar, Rabbi Rene Hirschler articulated the role of the Jewish calendar in a time of "many miseries": "For four years, the order of the day has been a succession of many miseries, large and small, collective and individual. The past year may have been the cruelest and most severe of them all. But take note! This [cruel] rhythm is interrupted by a different cadence: Regardless of our daily sufferings, the Sabbath days and holidays, like the stars of heaven which guide their work, still continue their tireless march . . . . Israel continues! Israel lives!" The author of the preface, Rabbi Rene Hirschler, was born in Marseilles, France, in 1905, served for a time as the chief rabbi of Strasbourg, and, in his role as chaplain general of the inmates of camps in southern France, must have known well cruelties and severities perpetrated therein.[74] The preface was likely written not long before he and his wife were arrested in December 1943. They were imprisoned in St. Pierre, taken from there to Drancy, and deported to Auschwitz, where Mrs. Hirschler was murdered. Rabbi Hirschler ended up in the Ebensee concentration camp in Austria, where he was beaten to death shortly before the camp's liberation in May, 1945. His all too short life snuffed out by one of the succession of miseries afflicting France's Jews, he nevertheless left in his calendar preface an understanding of the rhythm of Jewish time that showed it breaking free from the ongoing welter of daily suffering.

The calendar for the following year, 5705, saw the light of day under changed circumstances, as the Allied Normandy invasion took place in June 1944 and the liberation of Paris (and Limoges as well) some ten weeks later. Not all of France had been set free by the time of the Jewish New Year; indeed, Strasbourg remained under German control until late November. But Rabbi Avraham Deutsch's lyrical preface noted that a line between one era and another had been crossed: "The publication of this calendar—a veritable tour de force," wrote Rabbi Deutsch.

> Its "gestation" came at a somber time, a period when violence and crime seem to have become state law [. . .] The editor himself has not escaped arrest and forced labor [. . .] Once again, optimism was proved right. Prepared in the shadows, this calendar, with the bold tenacity of the family of the editor, was born at the dawn of the new times. [. . .]

Calendar 5705! Like the dove [sent] from the ark after the cataclysm revolutionized the world of yesteryear, be the messenger of peace with our brothers released! Bring the salvation of brotherhood and happiness in the coming days![75]

Previously based in an Alsace community, Rabbi Deutsch (1902–1992) had moved to Limoges to assist the large influx of Jewish refugees.[76] He did this by helping to maintain not only an active synagogue and kosher butcher but also a Jewish high school, an institute for technical training, and various aid organizations. He, too, was arrested in a roundup in November 1943 but was fortunately released. He knew well what French Jewry had endured over the past four years and what it meant to experience the liberation in Elul 5704 (summer 1944), the concluding month of the Jewish year. The calendar for the new Jewish year of 5705 must have appeared on the heels of the celebration. Thus, in his approbation, the calendar plays a role similar to that of the dove sent by the biblical Noach after the flood, marking the start of a new era. The earlier 5704 calendar indirectly played such a role by listing the multiple dates by which Jewish time and history can be counted; this later 5705 calendar, issued as the war turned a pivotal corner, could directly assume that role.

Rabbi Deutsch was nonetheless under no illusions. No matter how welcome, liberation did not efface the suffering, the extent of which, he soberly notes, was, in late summer of 1944, "still unknown." Through it all, Nephtali Grunewald's wartime calendars kept a Jewish presence intact, circumventing deportation, destruction, and the paralyzing edicts of the censors. They gave France's Jews the information they needed to know about how and when to celebrate what they could. They went a step further in integrating rabbinical approbations that conveyed the inner meaning of the calendar's outward details and facts. Published annually, they were a guide that could be counted on by the French Jewish community year after year. French Jewry was spared the humiliation and privation that came with life in a ghetto. But they had to contend with ruthless enemies, many of whom arose from within the ranks of France's native-born sons and daughters. In spite of grappling with the legacy of collaboration and mourning the losses, some things, as Rabbi Hirschler noted, had remained constant, "like the stars of heaven." The Grunewald calendars made clear just what those things were.

Notes

1. The number of studies on wartime ghettos is vast. I cite here and below a short selected list: Geoffrey Megargee, et al., *Encyclopedia of Camps and Ghettos, 1933–1945*, vols. 1–3 (Bloomington: Indiana University Press , 2009–2018); Dan Michman, *The Emergence of Jewish Ghettos during the Holocaust* (New York: Cambridge University Press, 2011); Guy

Miron, ed. *Encyclopedia of the Ghettos during the Holocaust* (Jerusalem: Yad Vashem, 2009); Isaiah Trunk, *Judenrat: The Jewish Councils in Eastern Europe under Nazi Occupation* (Lincoln: University of Nebraska Press 1996); for religious response within the ghettos, see *Shema Yisrael*, pp. 49–116 and the other studies on the topic of religious response listed above.

2. Michal Unger, ed., *The Last Ghetto: Life in the Lodz Ghetto, 1940–44* (Jerusalem: Yad Vashem, 1995); Lucjan Dobroszycki, ed., *The Chronicle of the Lodz Ghetto, 1941–1944*, ed. (New Haven: Yale University Press, 1984); Isaiah Trunk, *Lodz Ghetto: A History*, trans. Robert Moses Shapiro, intro. Israel Gutman (Bloomington: Indiana University Press, 2006). For religious response, see Farbstein, *Hidden in Thunder*, esp. pp. 166–83; Moshe Prager, *Those Who Never Yielded*; and other sources referred to above.

3. *Chronicle of the Lodz Ghetto*, ed. L. Dobroszycki (New Haven: Yale University Press, 1984).

4. Sara Zyskind (née Plagier), *Stolen Years* (Minneapolis: Lemer, 1981), p. 67. For a more thoroughgoing account of how time was cruelly taken over by hunger (in this case, in the Warsaw ghetto), see Leyb Goldin, "Chronicle of a Single Day (1941)," in *Literature of Destruction*, ed. David Roskies (Philadelphia: JPS, 1989), pp. 424–34.

5. The forty-nine-day Omer count from the holiday of Passover to that of Shavuot has stimulated the making of specialized calendars in order to maintain the daily obligation. For a sample of such calendars, see the holdings of the Israel Museum's permanent collection: http://museum.imj.org.il/imagine/galleries/viewRoomE.asp?case=36&rm=Counting%20the%20Omer.

6. Isaiah Trunk, *Lodz Ghetto: A History*, , p. 316.

7. *Chronicle of the Lodz Ghetto*, p. 76.

8. Moshe Prager, *Those Who Never Yielded*, p. 111.

9. Rabbi Eliezer Berkovits, *With God in Hell*, p. 70.

10. Israel Gutman, *The Jews of Warsaw, 1939–1943: Ghetto, Underground, Revolt*, trans. Ina Friedman (Bloomington: Indiana University Press, 1989); Samuel Kassow, *Who Will Write Our History?: Emanuel Ringelblum, the Warsaw Ghetto, and Oyneg Shabes Archive* (Bloomington: Indiana UP, 2007); for religious response, see in addition to sources cited above, see Havi Dreyfus, "'The Work of My Hands is Drowning in the Sea, and You Would Offer Me Song?!': Orthodox Behaviour and Leadership in Warsaw during the Holocaust," in *Warsaw, the Jewish Metropolis*, eds. Glenn Dynner and François Guesnet (Leiden: Brill, 2015), pp. 467–95.

11. Chaim Kaplan, *Scroll of Agony*, pp. 171–72.

12. Rabbi Huberband, *Kiddush Hashem*, p. 216.

13. *The Warsaw Diary of Adam Czerniakow*, eds. Raul Hilberg, et al. (New York: Stein and Day, 1979).

14. It is important to note that Czerniakow often knew more than he wrote; he was careful, for instance, not to write about any activities that the Nazis deemed illegal. I am indebted for this helpful caution to Havi Dreyfus, via email, March 26, 2014.

15. David Silberklang, *Gates of Tears: The Holocaust in the Lublin District* (Jerusalem: Yad Vashem, 2014).

16. Gershon Greenberg, "The Theological Letters of Rabbi Talmud of Lublin (Summer–Fall 1942)," *Ghettos 1939–1945: New Research and Perspectives on Definition, Daily Life, and Survival* (Washington, DC: USHMM, 2005), pp. 113–27.

17. David Silberklang, personal communication, 2015.

18. Rabbi Talmud's calendar for 5703 survives in two versions, one handwritten, the other typewritten. They can be viewed in the Rada Zydowska w Lublinie section of the Polish State Archives, http://www.szukajwarchiwach.pl/35/891/0/1/32/str/1/9/15#tabSkany. I first viewed and obtained copies of the calendars while at the United States Holocaust Memorial Museum Archives, RG 15.101M, ACC.2003.102. The calendars are in file 32, microfilm reel 6. I am indebted to David Silberklang for information regarding Rabbi Talmud's calendars.

19. Greenberg, p. 114 (trans. Greenberg). The letter was written to his friend and colleague Rabbi Chaim Aryeh Berglas.

20. Shimon Turkltoyb, "Maidanek," in *Encyclopedia shel Galuyot*, vol. 5, *Lublin*, eds. Nahman Blumental and Meir Kuzhin (Jerusalem: Hevrat Encyclopedia, 1953), p. 737.

21. In the words of Emanuel Ringelblum, head of the Oyneg Shabes collective to which Rabbi Huberband belonged, "Rabbi Huberband kept his records in the form of marginal notations inside various religious books so that they should pass for textual emendations. Not until later did he let himself be convinced that no danger accrued in his recording everything rather than using the cryptic method he had first employed." Emanuel Ringelblum, "Oyneg Shabbes," trans. Elinor Robinson, in *Literature of Destruction*, ed. David Roskies (Philadelphia: JPS, 1989), p. 387.

22. Archive Ghetto Fighters' Museum, Holdings Registry 11900.

23. See for example the Kodak calendar from the city of Lask, distributed by K. Dabrowski: http://lask.archiwa.org/zasoby.php?id=15540.

24. The fifteen-year-old Zvi Liberman, born in Stryj, Poland, but based in the town of Zurowna, performed a similarly stunning feat of adaptation. He too used an older Polish calendar, correcting the Gregorian dates and adding the Jewish ones. He and his family gratefully escaped the 1943 deportation and were liberated in July of 1944. See Yad Vashem Archives, id. 3727969.

25. See for example Carlebach, *Palaces of Time*, ch. 5 and 6; Elisheva Baumgarten, "Shared and Contested Time: Jews and Christian Ritual Calendar in the Late Thirteenth Century," *Viator* 46 (2015), pp. 253–76; C. Philipp E. Nothaft and Justine Isserles, "Calendars beyond Borders: Exchange of Calendrical Knowledge between Jews and Christians in Medieval Europe (12th–15th Century)," *Medieval Encounters* 20 (2014): 1–37; Sacha Stern, "Christian Calendars in Hebrew Medieval Manuscripts," *Medieval Encounters* 22 (2016): 236–65.

26. On the background of almanacs, see Bernard Capp, *Astrology and the Popular Press: English Almanacs, 1500–1800* (London: Faber, 1979); Molly A. McCarthy, *The Accidental Diarist: A History of the Daily Planner in America* (Chicago: U of Chicago P, 2013), particularly chapter 1; Stuart Sherman, *Telling Time: Clocks, Diaries, and English Diurnal Form, 1660–1785* (Chicago: University of Chicago Press, 1996); Paul Glennie and Nigel Thrift, *Shaping the Day: A History of Timekeeping in England and Wales 1300–1800* (London: Oxford University Press, 2009); J. A. Baggerman, R. Dekker, and M. Mascuch, *Controlling Time and Shaping the Self: Developments in Autobiographical Writing since the Sixteenth Century* (Leiden: Brill, 2011).

27. On the tenth of Tevet, 5709 (1949), the Israeli chief rabbi Isser Yehuda Untermann declared that "the day on which the first *hurban* (destruction) commenced should become a memorial day also for the last hurban," and two years later (1951) the rabbinate decided officially to turn this day into a memorial day for Shoah victims whose date of death is unknown. On the role of the tenth of Tevet in commemorating the Holocaust, see J. J. Schachter, "Holocaust Commemoration and Tisha B'Av: The Debate over 'Yom

HaSho'a'," *Tradition* 41 (2008), pp. 171, 191; Yom Tov Levinsky, ed., *Sefer ha-Moadim*, vol. 8 (Tel Aviv: Dvir, 1962), 93–95; Rabbi K. P. Tkhursh, "Hiyyuv ha-Kadish ha-Kelali le-Zekher ha-Nispim ba-Shoa," *Shana be-Shana* (5729), 131–40; Irving Greenberg, *The Jewish Way: Living the Holidays* (New York and London: Summit Books, 1988), 329–30; Rabbi Yeshayah A. Steinberger, "Asara be-Tevet, Yom ha-Shoa she-Hafakh le-Yom ha-Kadish ha-Kelali," *Shana be-Shana* (5751), 378–85; Rabbi Yeshayah A. Steinberger, "Asara be-Tevet ke-Yom ha-Shoa," *Shana be-Shana* (5752), 311–20; Yehudit Tydor Baumel, "Zikhron Olam: Tefilot ve-Yemei Evel le-Ahar ha-Sho'a le-Zekher Korbanot ha-Shoa," *Sinai* 101 (1988), 172.

28. There is the possibility that the author had already fled from Poland and composed the Jewish calendar while out of harm's way in the Russian interior. Handwritten in Russian on the blank page following the calendar's title are two names and addresses. The first could have been that of the sender, Sim[cha] Abramovich Rerkov, based near a military post office in Belarus; the recipient was a woman, Hava Finkelshtein, who had been evacuated from Russia in 1942 to southeastern area of the USSR, the Baltasi District in the Tatar Republic. Out of immediate danger, the author, like a number of other Jews, could have felt it imperative to fashion some kind of artifactual guide for holiday observance. These would likely have been in short supply in this austere setting. I comment further on tracking Jewish time in this setting in my discussion below of Rabbi Chaim Stein's wartime diary. I thank Yisrael Cohen for his help in deciphering some of the fragments of Russian.

29. This is not the only wartime calendar with significant omissions of fast days. I discuss below the selective omissions in other wartime calendars, including the *Luach Katan* fashioned in Theresienstadt and the calendar of Rabbi Avigdor rendered in Buchenwald. Most wartime calendars do, remarkably, designate a full retinue of fast days.

30. See Ruth Bondy, *"Elder of the Jews": Jakob Edelstein of Theresienstadt* (New York: Grove, 1989); Zdenek Lederer, *Ghetto Theresienstadt* (London: Edward Goldston and Son, 1953); H. G. Adler, *Theresienstadt, 1941–1945* (Tubingen: Mohr, 1960); and Miroslav Karny et al., *Theresienstadt in der "Endlosung der Judenfrage* (Prague, 1992).

31. Marte Marlá, "Judaism in the Terezin Ghetto," diss. [Czech] (Prague, 2013); *Misaviv l'Kikar: A Virtual Tour of Theresienstadt*, disc and pamphlet (Jerusalem: Michlala Yerushaliym, n.d.); Rabbi Sinai Adler, *Your Rod and Your Staff: A Young Man's Chronicle of Survival* (Jerusalem: Feldheim, 1996).

32. Michlala; Yad Vashem's website overview, though bringing a different emphasis, comes close to this evaluation: "Religious observance had to contend with difficult conditions, but it was not officially banned." http://www.yadvashem.org/yv/en/exhibitions /this_month/resources/theresienstadt.asp.

33. Mala, diss. abstract [English].

34. Bracha Stein, "My Father's Secret Sanctuary," *Mishpacha: Jewish Family Weekly* 313 (5770/2010), pp. 32–40.

35. Livia Rothkirchen, *The Jews of Bohemia and Moravia: Facing the Holocaust* (Jerusalem: Yad Vashem, 2005), p. 266.

36. Richard Feder, "Religious Life in Terezin," in *Terezin* (Prague: Council of Jewish Communities in the Czech Lands, 1965). pp. 53 -71.

37. Feder, "Religious Life in Terezin, p. 53.

38. Janet Blatter and Sybil Milton, *Art of the Holocaust* (New York: Routledge, 1981), pp. 84, 89, 94; Ziva Amishai-Maisels, *Depiction and Interpretation: The Influence of the Holocaust of the Visual Arts* (Oxford: Pegamon, 1993).

39. "Prayers in a Garage," p. 162. For other Theresienstadt examples as well as a broader context, see Yehudit Shendar, "Brethren in Misery and Endurance: Religious Life Reflected in Holocaust Art," *Yad Vashem Magazine* 28 (2002), pp. 10–11, http://www.yadvashem.org/yv/en/pressroom/magazine/pdf/yv_magazine28.pdf.

40. Fleischmann's drawing is reproduced in Gerald Green, *The Artists of Terezin* (New York: Hawthorn, 1969). Green does not call attention to the inconsistency.

41. See sources cited in note 31, and Feder, "Religious Life in Terezin.".

42. Feder, "Religious Life in Terezin," p. 57.

43. Ibid.; Rabbi Moshe Nosson Notta Lemberger, "In the Merit of Our Holy Forefathers," in *The Forgotten Memoirs*, ed. Esther Farbstein (Brooklyn: Shaar, 2011), pp. 229–31.

44. Rothkirchen, *The Jews of Bohemia and Moravia: Facing the Holocaust*, p. 266.

45. Feder, "Religious Life in Terezin," p. 57.

46. Rabbi Sinai Adler, *Your Rod and Your Staff*, p. 20.

47. Eva Ginzová, in *Salvaged Pages: Young Writers' Diaries of the Holocaust*, ed. Alexandra Zapruder (New Haven: Yale University Press, 2002), p. 178. Notably, Eva recorded the entry on September 16, 1944, the eve of Rosh Hashana, 5705—the same day I comment on in my discussion of the Auschwitz calendars.

48. Zadikow also produced a calendar for Terezin having a miniature image for each month that captured scenes from within and around the barracks (Pařík, 1991, p. 54).

49. I have viewed a scanned copy of the *Luach Katan* calendar archived in the Jewish Museum in Prague. I received my copy from Dr. Marte Malá, and am indebted to her.

50. For example, writing in response to a forthcoming decree to fix the star on clothing and businesses, Warsaw ghetto diarist Chaim Kaplan confers on the star a different meaning than the enemy intended: "Today [November 30, 1939] two harsh decrees reached us. First, the Star of David decree"; soon, he conjectures, "everywhere we turn we shall feel as if we were in a Jewish kingdom."

51. Jeremiah 31: 14–16.

52. Midrash Bereshith Rabbah 82:10.

53. Musicologist Jory Debenham brought Ullman's composition to my attention and writes the following about its context:

> The poet Rachel and the musician Yehuda Sharett/Shertok teamed up and wrote a number of populist Zionist songs in the 1920's, some of which were published in the 1930's German Jewish songbooks. . . .
> As far as Ullmann's use of it goes, it forms the basis of the variations and fugue I discussed from his seventh piano sonata. He identifies it only as "Hebraisches Volkslied." Some people have suggested that he chose it because of its similarity to the banned Slovak national anthem, although no one knows exactly his intention or its meaning to him. The sonata was never performed in Terezin as far as I know, so there are no survivor accounts or records of responses that might give us further clues about his choice. (via email, July 15, 2014)

The English translation of the song lyrics is by Robert Friend and appears in the collection entitled *Flowers of Perhaps: Selected Poems of Ra'hel* (London: Menard, 1994).

54. See Sybil Milton, "Chronology," in *Art, Music and Education as Strategies for Survival: Theresienstadt 1941–1945*, ed. Anne Dutlinger (New York: Herodias, 2001); Milton's helpful year-by-year summary must be supplemented with other chronologies of events gleaned from overviews, including those of the websites of the United States Holocaust Memorial Council and Yad Vashem.

55. It is unusual for a fast day to be commemorated on a Friday, the day before, and leading into, Shabbat. But it happens occasionally (only, it is important to note, with this particular fast day), for reasons that have nothing to do with the war.

56. Though the *Luach Katan* draws our attention to the ninth of Av, the most severe and fraught of the fast days, the slated transformation of the fast days into feasts in the Messianic era pertain to all such days, as the prophet Zechariah first spells out, the Talmud then amplifies, and the Rambam later codifies: "All these [commemorative] fasts will be nullified in the Messianic era and, indeed ultimately, they will be transformed into holidays and days of rejoicing and celebration, as [Zechariah 8:19] states: "Thus declares the Lord of Hosts, 'The fast of the fourth [month], the fast of the fifth [month], the fast of the seventh [month], and the fast of the tenth [month] will be [times of] happiness and celebration and festivals for the House of Judah. And they shall love truth and peace'" (Rambam Hilchot Taanit 5:19).

57. B. Talmud Taanit 26b, 30b; Baba Batra 121a. Strikingly, the other joyous day the Sages paired with the fifteenth of Av is Yom Kippur.

58. After completion of my manuscript I came across a Theresienstadt Jewish calendar for 5705. (1944–45) in the style of the Luach Katan but called simply "Juedischer Kalender" (Jewish Calendar). I plan to discuss the two calendars in another venue.

59. See Deborah Dwork, intro., *The Terezin Album of Marianka Zadikow*, Marianne Zadikow May, ed. Deborah Dwork (Chicago: University of Chicago Press, 2008), pp. 1–18; Sara Meli, "Art from Within: An Encounter with Holocaust Art from the Terezin Ghetto," MA thesis (University of British Columbia), p. 24. Ilka Wonschik, *Es war wohl ein anderer Stern, auf wir lebten . . . : Kuensterinnen in Theresienstadt* (Berlin: Heintrich and Heintrich, 2014), pp. 81–102, 214; phone interview with Marianne Zadikow May (daughter of Hilde), Sept. 7, 2014 (Elul 12, 5774). Hilde's maiden name, Lohsing, had at some point been changed from Loewy.

60. For professional reasons, Arnold Zadikow spent some time in Paris before making his way to Prague.

61. A black-and-white reproduction can be found in Janet Blatter and Sybil Milton, *Art of the Holocaust*, p. 95. I am grateful to have received a color scan from the Jewish Museum in Prague and wish to thank Michela Sidenburg and Martin Jellinek for their help in obtaining it.

62. Gerald Steinacher, *Humanitarians at War: The Red Cross in the Shadow of the Holocaust* (Oxford: Oxford University Press, 2017); François Bugnion, *The International Committee of the Red Cross and the Protection of War Victims* (Oxford: Macmillan, 2003); Jean-Claude Favez, *The Red Cross and the Holocaust*, eds. and tr. John and Beryl Fletcher (Cambridge: Cambridge University Press, 1999).

63. Rabbi Menachem Mendel Schneersohn, *Likutei Sichot*, vol. 34, pp. 338–41; *Igrot Melech*, vol. 1, pp. 428–33.

64. Michaela Sidenburg thoughtfully speculates along these lines. Email, Aug. 15, 2014.

65. See Michael Studemund-Halévy, "The Persistence of Images: Reproductive Success in the History of Sephardi Sepulchral Art," in *The Dutch Intersection: The Jews and the Netherlands in Modern History*, ed. Yosef Kaplan (Leiden: Brill, 2008), citing Bauche and Wischnitzer-Bernstein.

66. Phone interview with Marianne Zadikow May, summer 2014.

67. Ibid.

68. Sources for Rabbi Berlinger's biography include his daughter, Rosie Baum, phone interview and email correspondence, Feb. 2012 and Dec. 23, 2012; his niece, Helen Gross,

phone interview, Jan. 2012; "'Despite All This . . .'—Observing the Jewish Calendar in Theresienstadt," Yad Vashem website on Rabbi Berlinger: http://www.yadvashem.org/yv/en/exhibitions/bearing_witness/life_ghettos_berlinger.asp; and Bracha Stein, "My Father's Secret Sanctuary," *Mishpacha: Jewish Family Weekly* 313 (5770/2010), pp. 32–40.

69. An alternative source lists the date of deportation to Theresienstadt as September 23; see the list of Theresienstadt camp inmates found in *Terezinska Pametni Kniha / Theresienstaedter Gedenkbuch, Terezinska Iniciativa*, vol. I–II (Melantrich: Prague, 1995), vol. III (Academia Verlag: Prague, 2000).

70. See especially the article by Bracha Stein.

71. One copy of the Berlinger calendar for 5704 was donated to Yad Vashem by the wife of a fellow Theresienstadt cantor, Avraham Hellman. Rabbis Berlinger and Hellman apparently ended up on the same Auschwitz-bound transport—and presumably met the same fate. For more information on Rabbi Hellmann's contributions to religious life in Theresienstadt, see the Yad Vashem website devoted to his legacy: http://www.yadvashem.org/yv/en/exhibitions/bearing_witness/life_ghettos_hellman.asp.

72. Renee Poznanski, *The Jews in France during World War II*, trans. Nathan Brachner (Waltham: Brandeis University Press, 2001). Poznanski summarizes the set of events:

> And while the chief rabbi was flatly denied permission to publish a weekly newsletter, he was allowed to put out a Jewish calendar. This calendar was a most valuable reference work that allowed practicing Jews to celebrate holy days at the appropriate time; the Hebraic lunar calendar would make the date of any particular celebration vary from year to year on the French calendar. Duly inspected by the censor, it was the only Jewish publication to be approved since the Armistice. It was in the fall of 1940; a year later [1941], after the censor's cuts had affected more than half of the texts inserted into the calendar, the rabbi's office discontinued its publication." (p. 144)

73. Rabbi Tovia Preschel, "The French Jewish Calendar during the Shoah," *HaDoar* (5723/1962) [Hebrew]; Jacquot Grunewald, "Calendriers de la Resistance," *l'Arche* 498–99 (Sept. 1999; the article can be accessed on the website of the Jews of Alsace and Lorraine: http://judaisme.sdv.fr/histoire/shh/calendr/calendr.htm); Alexander Kline and Chaim Shalem, *Spiritual Resistance in France During the Holocaust* [Hebrew] (Jerusalem: Michlala, 5772/2012), pp. 48–49.

74. On Rabbi Hirschler's wartime activities and contributions, see Donna Ryan, *The Jews of Marseilles: The Enforcement of Anti-Semitic Policies in Vichy France* (Urbana: University of Illinois Press, 1996); Zosa Szajkowski, *Analytical Franco-Jewish Gazetteer, 1939–1945* (New York: Ktav, 1966); Susan Zuccotti, *The Holocaust, the French, and the Jews* (New York: Basic Books, 1993); Michael Curtis, *Verdict on Vichy: Power and Prejudice in the Vichy France Regime* (London: Weidenfeld and Nicholsen, 2002); Paula Hyman, *The Jews of Modern France* (Berkeley: University of California Press, 1998).

75. I am indebted to my colleague Yoni Berrous for his help with the translation of these two lyrical prefaces as well as his thoughtful comments on them.

76. Shannon Fogg, *The Politics of Everyday Life in Vichy France* (Cambridge: Cambridge University Press, 2009), pp. 81, 121; Pascal Plas and Simon Schwartzfuchs, eds. *Mémoires du grand rabbin Deutsch: Limoges 1939–1945* (Saint-Paul: L. Souny, 2007).

III Concentration Camps, Endless Time, and Jewish Time

As we have seen, Jews in Holocaust Europe tenaciously clung to the calendar. They had undergone periods of foment and chaos in history when time's coordinates became next to impossible to know. Chastened by past experience, they strove to do better, to have at the ready the tools to chart Jewish time even when the going got difficult. And this they did. Rabbi Baron's ten-year calendar, composed and printed as the signs of war grew unmistakable, led the pack. Others soon followed. In the ghettos that came to dot the eastern European landscape, Jews made it their business to produce calendars, sometimes individually and clandestinely, other times officially and out in the open; sometimes calendars circulated year in, year out, while other times they surfaced only in the last throes of a ghetto's tentative existence. Finally, in those occupied regions of Europe in which Jewish publishing had been outlawed or heavily censored, Jewish calendars smuggled Jewish time to the many that cared.

So it went in places where one could wrangle materials to write out (and in some situations, even put in print) columns of days, weeks, and years, not to speak of having the knowledge to do so accurately. But the Holocaust-era concentration camps: surely these infamous, and all too frequently lethal, prisons operated according to a regimen that made it impossible to track Jewish time? Compelled by torturous conditions to fight for survival, how could one even think of something so abstract and arcane as the orchestration of a Jewish year, of plotting in an ordered format the alternation of the sacred and mundane in a place where the profane ruled over all? According to some, the conditions in the concentration camps were so extreme as to render them a world unto themselves, a different planet, with rules and features found nowhere else on earth. Hence time, too, could not be measured or experienced in familiar ways. "Time there," as the well-known survivor and author Yechiel Dinur (a.k.a. Ka-tzetnik) put it categorically, "is not like time here."[1]

The view that time was so out of joint within concentration camps that the calendar could have no currency comes across in other important sources as well, such as the classic literary memoir by a member of the French resistance and former Auschwitz prisoner Charlotte Delbo, entitled *None of Us Will Return*.[2] Both the content and style of Delbo's poignant chronicle go far to drain the memoir of calendar references. Instead, the sections are pointedly general: "One Day," "The Next Day," "The Same Day," "Morning," "Evening," and, finally, "Sunday"—"was the worst day of all." No date is ever singled out. Even when at the conclusion of the "Sunday" section the memoir comes closest to zeroing in on a date, it chooses to remain vague: "The sky was blue, the sun was out again. It was a Sunday in March."[3]

According to Delbo's reckoning, time was flattened out, uniform, without the kind of distinction that a calendar gives. Moreover, the specific form in which Delbo chose to relate her Auschwitz experience, that of the prose poem, is meant to cultivate simultaneity. It makes everything the "same day," viewed from various angles. In a place where everything is made the "same," the calendar can play little or no role. Like the life left behind outside the confines of the camp, the calendar too, differentiating between one day and the next, between one week and that which follows, could not have importance.

Others have analyzed what made "time there" not only different but oppressive, a potent agent used by the enemy to debilitate prisoners. In this view, time could not be measured in the camps both because one did not have the means to do so and also because it was turned against the uprooted souls confined there.

We will soon look at several important attempts to analyze the disjointed nature of time in the concentration camps. But, following suit with what I have argued above, this approach, to my mind, comes at the topic from the wrong side. From the outset, it presumes an unbridgeable gulf between Jewish life outside the camp and that within ("time there is not like time here") and thereby overlooks the fact that there were dedicated efforts to track Jewish time in the camps—and to fashion calendars that would enable the prisoners to do so. Indeed, calendar making took place in concentration camps, even in some of the most severe. True, the obstacles that loomed before the camp prisoner were often more formidable, the risks greater than in other locales. Yet obstacles and risks did not in the end hold sway.

From the start, the Nazis erected special prisons—concentration camps—to deal with those perceived as enemies and to terrorize the population at large.[4] As the German empire grew, these arenas of terror came to dot the European landscape. Special camps exploited the labor of millions of prisoners, treating them, in Benjamin Ferenz's phrase, as "less than slaves." From late 1941 to 1945, death camps operating in German-occupied Poland murdered millions of Jews. A few nefarious sites joined the exploitation of labor with systematic murder. Other so-called transit camps served as way stations to sites of labor or, more often, factories of death.

From a practical standpoint, the camps made keeping track of time difficult, since personal possessions were few, watches and calendars generally outlawed, and writing often forbidden. The practical problems were compounded by the psychological and institutional ones, whereby the experience of time underwent a process of distortion. It is to two influential discussions of the nature of time in concentration camps that I now turn, considering also the implications for thinking about calendars and calendar making in these brutal locales.

Influential both as a concentration camp deposition and as setting forth the psychological implications to be drawn from the experience, psychologist Victor Frankl's memoir, first published in 1946 as *Ein Psycholog erlebt des Konzentrationslager* (translated into English in 1959 with the title *From Death-Camp to Existentialism* and shortly thereafter retitled *Man's Search for Meaning*), has also furnished the basic idiom for the pathology of time experienced in the camps.[5] Like so many others, historian and Auschwitz survivor Yisrael Gutman draws on Frankl's formulation to describe the oppressive routine prisoners were forced to endure, noting that "the prisoner's physical and mental capacities are unceasingly employed in a never-ending effort to get through all the tortuous stages that constitute an ordinary day . . ." He then invokes Frankl's authoritative summary: "In a camp, a small time unit, a day for example—filled with hourly tortures and fatigue, appeared endless."[6]

Incisive on how in the concentration camp routine time underwent massive distortion, Frankl emphasizes this "endlessness," the breakdown of a normal future-oriented life. He encapsulates this breakdown with the phrase "provisional existence of unknown limit" (*privisorische Existenz ohne Termin*).[7] Most concentration camp inmates were imprisoned without a fixed sentence. This indeterminacy—the "unknown limit"—of just how long one's incarceration would be led to a life lived "without future and without goal." To be imprisoned in a camp without a known limit not only brought about a "peculiar sort of deformed time" but also gave a sense that there was nothing to live for. Thus, according to this view, time played a key role in creating the debilitating conditions found within the camps. As we will see, this characterization of the pathology of concentration camp time is not Frankl's final word; strategies could be found to overcome the deformity. But he clearly considered the futureless condition a fundamental aspect of concentration camp life and hence worthy of explication.

Importantly, he brings three anecdotes to support the characterization, two of which implicate the calendar. The first recounts Frankl being told by a fellow prisoner that his march to work felt as if he were marching at his own funeral. It seemed to him that he was "absolutely without future." The collapse of a sense of future prompts the idea that life as such has come to an end.[8] Demonstrating vividly how time was perceived as deformed, this anecdote leaves the calendar per se out of the picture.

The second anecdote puts it well within the frame. It tells of a prisoner who dreamed of his release on March 30, 1945. As the date approached without sign of liberation, the prisoner grew ill. When the date passed without the prisoner being set free, he broke down and passed away the following day. Here the calendar plays a pivotal role, establishing a provisional existence, one might say, with a known limit. But the limit is actually false, the calendar date deceptive. In Frankl's words, the prisoner's "faith in the future became paralyzed" when the prisoner, lured by his dream, fixed on the date. This paralysis brought about the prisoner's demise. Though in Frankl's recounting of the anecdote the calendar serves merely as a stage prop in the sad drama acted out in the prisoner's psyche, the calendar and its potentially treacherous dates play a vital yet damaging role. At least in this case, to be without a future was better than to be locked into one from which there was no escape.[9]

In this way, the tragic anecdote expresses in a secular form the harsh censure with which many rabbis of stature discouraged attempts to calculate the date of the coming of the Messiah. The rabbis, too, understood that such speculation could paralyze faith in the future.[10] They exhorted those who might be tempted to locate their faith in a specific date based on clues in passages of the Torah to direct their efforts to less dangerous study. But that advice was not always taken to heart. Indeed, some of those who threw caution to the wind and speculated broadly were preeminent Torah sages and leaders of communities. This intrepid readiness to fix on a date for redemption—the cosmic version of the individual prisoner's embrace of a fixed date for liberation from the evils of the camps—has been explained as one of the means Torah sages adapted to elevate the depressed spirits of a community at times of particularly intense travail. In such cases, the suffering threatened to overwhelm any notion of well-being that might lie on the horizon, beyond the immediate disaster. Fixing on a date of redemption was deemed an acceptable, if irregular, remedy to carry a community forward.[11] In Frankl's example, however, the prisoner's decision to fix on a date carried only negative associations.

Another instance discussed by Frankl in which the calendar played a destructive role reinforces this negative verdict. In this case, significant dates in the Gregorian calendar framed a particularly lethal stretch of time: "The death rate in the week between Christmas, 1944 and New Year's, 1945," notes Frankl, drawing on an authoritative source, "increased in camp beyond all previous experience." This unprecedented vulnerability occurred because the prisoners believed that, come this holiday period, they would already be home. When liberation did not arrive at the appointed time, they lost hope. This crushing disappointment in turn weakened their resistance, thereby causing the increase in fatalities. In Frankl's concluding elegiac phrase, he says simply, "A great number of them died."[12]

This situation is similar to the previous one. In both instances a specific date held out the promise of liberation from the hell of the camp, and in both the settled calendar date failed to deliver the longed-for redemption. But the difference is also telling. In this instance it was not just one prisoner that suffered from a somewhat freakish, dream-inspired devotion to the calendar. Many prisoners soberly put their faith in a calendar date that served as a marker for all concerned. No dreams, no idiosyncratic conviction, no manipulations of the calendar to suit one's fancy. Here the calendar was common property. And yet in this case, too, the calendar was viewed as having summoned forth hope only to betray it.

Presumably, Frankl does not intend for the calendar to be viewed in this light. His emphasis is rather on the way the "provisional existence of unknown limit," tragically highlighted in this episode by the false hope, could imperil the prisoner. The calendar is simply a tool, a prop, an accessory to the crime of deception. But from the angle I am pursuing, the calendar's contribution comes across as more than that, playing a hostile or antagonistic role. This likely explains the manner in which Frankl reports the episode, whereby the unprecedented death rate took place "between" *two* significant calendar dates. He could just as well have referred to a single date, could have indicated that the increase took place in the aftermath of the first date or in the week following it. One date is clearly enough to bring home the point. Instead, the two significant dates frame the episode, implicating the calendar fore and aft.

All of this leaves aside, of course, the fact that it is the Gregorian calendar Frankl invokes here and elsewhere in his memoir; he presumes it to be that which all prisoners, Christian and Jewish alike, would use as their single point of reference for marking time—even when the point in question had to do with Jews. On the other hand, the Jewish calendar is simply absent. This omission is not unusual, especially among those who, like Frankl, were assimilated Jews of western European origin and background. Yet at times Frankl casts a wider net than one might expect. The moving closing words of his memoir, for instance, acknowledge the special Jewish response at the moment of the ultimate test: "Our generation is realistic for we have come to know man as he really is. After all, man is that being who has invented the gas chambers of Auschwitz; however, he is also that being who has entered those gas chambers upright, with the Lord's Prayer or the *Shema Yisrael* on his lips."[13] Earlier in his account, Frankl tells how the same Shema Yisrael prayer had played a central role in "that which was perhaps the deepest experience [he] had in the concentration camp."[14] The manuscript of his first book, which was hidden in his coat when he arrived at Auschwitz, disappeared as he, like all others, was forced to surrender his clothing. The loss was profound: "It now seemed as if nothing and no one would survive [him]." He felt confronted by the basic question of "whether under such circumstances [his] life was void of meaning." But an answer to the question soon appeared in the "worn-out rags" he was given in exchange for his own clothing: "Instead of the many pages of my manuscript, I found in a pocket of the newly acquired coat one single page torn out of a Hebrew prayer book, containing the main Jewish prayer, *Shema*

Yisrael." The discovery moved him to make a fundamental shift in perspective: "How should I have interpreted such a 'coincidence' other than as a challenge to *live* my thoughts instead of merely putting them on paper?"[15] The exchange of the secular psychological treatise for the Shema Yisrael prayer thus transformed his life in the camp and brought forth the vocation that emerged from it.

When it came to prayer, Frankl recognizes that the Christian idiom did not and could not serve as the idiom for Jews (himself included) and for Jewish prayer. When it came to time and tracking its import in the concentration camp, however, he thought along the lines of a universal idiom that would serve all equally well. This is the role played in his memoir by the Gregorian calendar.

As we can see, Frankl's calendar examples drive home the point that a futureless existence was not only debilitating but also could be lethal. And it is the idea that the concentration camp cruelly revolved around a futureless existence—a "provisional existence of unknown limit"—that other important critics have drawn on. But eking out a life confined to the present was not, according to Frankl, the only option. Both the future and the past were available in at least three respects: (a) what had been lost could someday be restored; (b) a sudden change of circumstance could open up a future that had seemed closed; and (c) the past was full of meaning. Without a doubt, such a vantage point could be achieved only with uncommon effort. But the fact of an unknown limit did not necessarily cut off the future or drain the past of its meaning. The "absolute primacy of the present" was not absolute.

And indeed the calendar makes one final appearance in Frankl's comments, in this instance referring not to an actual experience from the period of the war but rather to a general psychological theme. In the section entitled "Life Transitoriness," Frankl brings two opposite approaches to dealing with a calendar. The pessimist "resembles a man who observes with fear and sadness that his wall calendar, from which he daily tears a sheet, grows thinner with each passing day."[16] Up to this point, the calendar again serves as an antagonist, underscoring with its diminishing size the diminishing future. In this case, not only the date but the calendar itself, in its very way of marking time, seems the culprit. But unlike with the earlier examples, Frankl does not stop here with the calendar as simply providing evidence of a shrinking future. Surprisingly, he reverses himself—and reverses as well the ominous role the calendar was made to play: "On the other hand, the person who attacks the problems of life actively is like a man who removes each successive leaf from his calendar and files it neatly and carefully away with its predecessors, after first having jotted down a few diary notes on the back. He can reflect with pride and joy on all the richness set down in these notes, on all the life he has already lived to the full."[17] Inverting the previous example, this one shows the calendar breaking free of its negative associations. Not confined to demonstrating the emptiness of time, it here dramatizes time's fullness. It can, of course, only do this by becoming more than a simple calendar, doubling as a kind of diary. The pride and joy emanate from the "richness set down in these notes" rather than from the calendar's marking of days, weeks, months, or years. Indeed, this improvised diaristic facet suggests why the positive connotations of the calendar derive from the past, "the life he has already lived to the full." The calendar's meaningful aspect lies in "each successive leaf" carefully filed away, a trove of indisputable events that have already occurred. In contrast, the calendar's setting forth of a day-by-day unfolding of a future does not figure. In a curious sense, the concentration camp's futureless existence continues to obtain here even under normal conditions. In this case, however, it is not the person but the calendar that lacks a future. Be that as it may, this final nod to the calendar transforms it from an opponent into an ally in marking time.

Such a step is also taken, if in a roundabout way, in one of the most important studies of time in the concentration camps. Two chapters of Wolfgang Sofsky's *The Order of Terror: The Concentration Camp*, first published in German in 1993, deal with the nature of time from different angles: "camp time" and "prisoner's time."[18]

Placing time front and center in the discussion was itself an advance. Earlier studies of Nazi concentration camps, such as that of Eugen Kogon's influential book *The Theory and Practice of Hell,* originally published in 1946, detailed one or another version of the torturous camp regimen, which included the daily schedule. "The camp was awakened by whistles, in the summer between four and five o'clock, in the winter between six and seven o'clock," begins the chapter entitled "Daily Routine."[19] He then proceeds step by step through the day's "routine," noting the time of day but focusing on the distinguishing punishing activity (roll calls, labor details) or the parsimonious meals that took place at that hour. He concludes with a brief evocation of the day's end: "For a few short hours each night sleep spread its balm over the misery. Only the aged, the fretful, the sick, the sleepless, lay awake in a torment of worry, awaiting the ordeal of another day."[20]

Time thus frames Kogon's account as he moves from morning to afternoon to evening to night. That said, two points stand out. First, time as he implicitly depicts it is familiar, matching what we know of it outside the concentration camps. Time proceeds in a normal fashion and can be described as such; what is abnormal is the perpetrators' diabolic use of it. The second point is related to the first. At no juncture does Kogon explicitly reflect on the nature of time in the camps. And this is no surprise given the normalcy of time as Kogon characterizes it. It follows that none of Kogon's twenty-four chapters highlight the nature of time; by contrast, at least one considers "special *places*."

Kogon's approach was typical of decades of research on the concentration camps. Introducing a different vantage point, Sofsky's revolutionizing study gave attention to time because it was understood to serve as a tool of absolute power, which aimed to destroy personality by extinguishing time consciousness. To a large extent, the camps achieved this cruel goal. But the elimination of time consciousness and particularly consciousness of a past and future was neither complete nor inevitable.

Sofsky argues that the "order of terror" in the camps deformed normal time consciousness in three ways. The first is by means of an indefinite duration of confinement. No one knew if or when they would emerge from the camp. He quotes Frankl's well-known formulation: "Existence in the camp was a 'provisional existence without final date.'"[21] The second and third ways are an omnipresence of death and an absolute primacy of the present, of the here and now. Concerned exclusively with the concentration camp, Sofsky's model overlaps with that of Barbara Engelking, whose highlighting of the perverse "absolute primacy of the present" and the consequent destruction of a future I referred to in the introduction. Like Engelking in another respect, Sofsky only minimally invokes the calendar, and the single reference casts it in a negative light. And since his discussion of time moves at a universal level, he doesn't refer to the particular fate of the Jews or to any aspect of Jewish culture. As Omer Bartov has tellingly noted, two factors in Sofsky's account filter out Jewish experience: first, the prisoners are generally "weirdly faceless"[22]; and second and most important, he bases his analysis on camps where Jews were the minority.

But the calendar enters through the back door, since Sofsky also factors in the prisoner's "time strategies," the possibility of responding to and resisting the deformation of time. "Prisoners reacted in diverse ways to the destruction of time. . . However, survival always demanded a specific temporal strategy. Self-preservation in the camp [sic] inevitably necessitated the preservation and salvaging of time, a restitution of time-consciousness."[23] For some, then, the "absolute primacy of the present" wasn't the only possibility. Indeed, "a successful time strategy resembled a tightrope walk" between accepting the dominance of the present while also distancing oneself from it.

Moreover, one could walk the tightrope with the help of a religious community or at least a religious outlook. Such a perspective "counterposed a higher temporal plane to the all-powerful time of the camp" and was one means to create what Sofsky refers to as a "fictive future," a region of time that enabled some prisoners to break free from the tyranny of the present.[24] While his discussion of the camps does not factor in the Jewish calendar per se, Sofsky does offer a basis for considering the calendar as a way of creating a "fictive future" and an enabling past. Admittedly, Sofsky presents this possibility almost between the lines. Omer Bartov, for example, misses it, suggesting that, according to Sofsky's view, "nothing [the concentration camp prisoners] might do could conceivably change the reality of their present condition."[25] But to my mind, Sofsky implies that a different mode of envisioning time could "change the reality."

That Sofsky divides his discussion of time into *two* chapters reinforces the possibility of this change. The first chapter, "Camp Time," shows how time served in the camps as a tool of power and terror; the second chapter, "Prisoner's Time," explains how the goal of using time as a tool of power was to ravage individuality. Indeed, much of the second chapter does not refer to "time" per se but rather to the rituals the individual was forced to undergo that ruptured time and undermined the sense of continuity that issued from it. In one respect, then, the second chapter follows directly from the first, arguing that the destructive force of camp time was made to extinguish the individual personality. But the end of the second chapter reverses the flow. For it concludes by briefly elaborating how religious belief could "salvag[e] in this way the prisoner's personal time."[26] In the final analysis, absolute power cannot subdue belief in the Absolute. This ending leads suggestively to the role of the Jewish calendar in the camps. For by way of the Sabbath, holidays, and much else, the Jewish calendar graphically articulated the "a higher temporal plane" that Sofsky referred to.

Sofsky's analysis is uneven, at times off base, and questionable in the theory that he draws on. But for our purposes, he does make concentration camp time an entity and enemy against which one could battle. In his formulation, time was not "empty" but rather full of menace. Those who fashioned Jewish calendars and those who lived by them did not simply fill an empty container with sacred content. They used the sacred content to contend with a diabolic force. In taking inventory of the remarkably diverse calendars forged in transit camps, labor camps, and concentration camps, we will see the tactics used to ascend to that "higher temporal plane."

Nine concentration camp Jewish calendars are known to have survived: one from Buchenwald, two from Bergen-Belsen, three from Terezin, one from Westerbork, and two from Auschwitz; there are references to four others produced in camps (two in Leipzig labor camps, one in Maidanek and, as we will see below, one in Auschwitz that did not survive the war). Calendar making was clearly an uncommon, complex, and dangerous activity. But the complexity and danger was greater in some places than others. Transit camps (such as Terezin and Westerbork) offered conditions where some Jewish religious activities could take place without threat of reprisal. Further, while Jewish religious activity was outlawed in both Auschwitz and Birkenau, there was greater opportunity for clandestine expression in the former than in the latter.

Though the number of known calendars produced in concentration camps is admittedly small, it is difficult to gauge exactly how uncommon this achievement was. Most artifacts produced (or, for that matter, possessed) in the concentration camps did not survive the war; and, even more tragically of course, most of those to whom these artifacts belonged did not survive either. As I noted earlier, wartime calendars in general have not been a sought-after item, calls for artifacts have not specified them, and scholarly and popular attention has not gravitated toward them. This has been equally true of calendars associated with concentration camps. Indeed, though I have gratefully found examples archived in general collections of Holocaust artifacts, and have benefited significantly from those calendars owned by individuals, my inquiries to on-site concentration camp archives have turned up nothing. My impression was that they had never been asked before about calendars composed or used by those imprisoned within the camp.

Yahrzeits in Westerbork

The opening sentence of my book told of Rabbi Yisrael Simcha Zelmann's moving decision to be buried with his Westerbork-composed calendar—a decision presumably made because his calendar had the merit of guiding numbers of imprisoned Jews in Sabbath and holiday observance as well as in the daily regimen of prayer. The calendar would serve as his advocate in the hereafter, a ledger of good deeds rendered under fearful circumstances in the world left behind. It clearly had played a serviceable role in an inhospitable corner of Holland in the year 5704 (1943–44). Like Theresienstadt, the Westerbork transit camp permitted religious practice to an extent that such a calendar would aid daily observance. The policy also enabled such a calendar, produced on a Hebrew-lettered typewriter in multiple copies, to circulate at all.

Rabbi Zelmann's Westerbork calendar contains several features nearly unique to surviving wartime Jewish calendars, including a prologue outlining the challenges faced by the observant Jew in Westerbork and a listing of the memorial days on which to honor the memory of three prominent Chasidic masters. These two features, each in their own way, aimed to provide his fellow prisoners with a spiritual foothold in a time of unrelenting hardship.

Anne Frank succinctly characterized the fortunes of Jews sent to "the big Jewish camp in Drenthe": "Our many Jewish friends are being taken away by the dozen. These people are treated by the Gestapo without a shred of decency, being loaded into cattle trucks and sent to Westerbork, the big camp in Drenthe."[27] The province of Drenthe lies in the northeastern part of the Netherlands, near the town of Assen. In October 1939, the Dutch government established a camp at Westerbork, one of a number of facilities used to intern Jewish refugees who had entered the Netherlands illegally.[28] The camp continued to function after the German invasion of the Netherlands in May 1940, with a population in 1941 of 1,100 Jewish refugees, most of whom hailed from Germany.

In early 1942, the Germans enlarged the camp, and in July the German Security Police, assisted by an SS company and Dutch military police, took over control. Erich Deppner was appointed commandant, and Westerbork's role as a transit camp for deportations to the East began. Nearly 107,000 people were deported from Westerbork on ninety-seven transports. The first transport was dispatched to Auschwitz-Birkenau on July 15, 1942. From March 2 to November 16, 1943, a train would depart every Tuesday with between 1,000 and 3,000 people. A total of 54,930 were sent to Auschwitz in sixty-eight transports, 34,313 to the Sobibor death camp in nineteen transports, 4,771 to the Theresienstadt ghetto in seven transports, and 3,762 to the Bergen-Belsen concentration camp in nine transports. Most of those deported to Auschwitz and virtually all of those shipped to Sobibor were killed upon arrival.

The Westerbork camp had two distinct prisoner groups. While most inmates stayed in the camp for only short periods of time before being deported, a camp population of two thousand, made up mostly of German Jews, Jewish council members, camp employees, and certain other categories of persons were exempt from deportation.

Rabbi Yisrael Simcha Zelmann arrived at Westerbork, middle-aged and apparently alone, on February 27, 1940, just about six months after the camp had been established; he was forty-five years old when he crafted his Westerbork calendar. Born on May 30, 1897 (Iyar 28, 5657), in the Polish shtetl of Skierniewice to Berel and Ester (née Grünberg) Zelmann, Yisrael Simcha, while still a young man, was directed to leave Poland by the leader of the Ger Chasidim, Rabbi Avraham Mordechai Alter (known as the Imrei Emes), and to resettle in Germany. He was initially based in Breslau and then moved to Dusseldorf, where he married in 1926 to the twenty-year-old Bajla (Beila) Eimer. Over the next decade, they raised a family of four children, remaining in Dusseldorf until it was not possible to remain any longer.

On November 11, 1938, the day after the Kristalnacht pogrom, Yisrael Simcha arrived in a refugee center in Holland, having fled Germany at the eleventh hour with his wife and children. The family was able to stay more or less together until the occupation of Holland in spring 1940, at which time Beila and the children negotiated their way aboard an England-bound ship. They spent the war years in Manchester, knowing their husband and father was alive but not much more. Rabbi Yisrael Simcha was himself not so fortunate, imprisoned as he was for the duration of the war in a series of refugee centers and concentration camps, including Westerbork.

The Dutch transit camp served as his residence for the next four years, during which time he avoided the lethal deportations to Auschwitz and Sobibor. It is likely that his having obtained (through the good offices of Swiss activist Chaim Eis) a Paraguayan passport helped him remain in Westerbork and eventually aided him in his transport to the lesser evil of Bergen-Belsen in January 1944. At the time of his departure from Westerbork on January 11, "Herrn Rabbiner" Yisrael Simcha received a Chumash (the Five Books of Moses) with commentaries as a token of appreciation ("in Dankbarkeit") for his great service on behalf of Westerbork's Jewish community.[29]

He survived the fifteen-month ordeal in Bergen-Belsen and was reunited in Manchester, England, with his wife and four children at the end of 1945. Wartime privation had made him nearly unrecognizable. He had nevertheless brought with him powdered milk and other supplies, concerned as he was for his family's well-being and, given the postwar scarcity of food, unsure what nourishment they had available. Back under his wife's watchful eye, he soon regained strength and continued where he had left off, learning Torah, teaching a class, and helping his wife run the factory she had established. After the Israeli War of Independence in 1948, he traveled to Israel to visit his elderly mother, who had settled there already in the 1930s. Yet Manchester remained home for the next two decades. In 5728 (1967), he and his wife immigrated to Israel, where they resided in the religious enclave of Bnei Brak until his passing in 1974. As we heard, the Westerbork calendar followed him to the grave, a link between worlds and a ledger of good deeds rendered in a place of cruelty, hardship, and loss.

Rabbi Zelmann's calendar is as detailed and learned as any; indeed it contains much information lacking in calendars produced in far more nurturing environments.[30] Such specificity speaks to the possibilities of religious observance in the Westerbork transit camp. His prologue tells the other side of the story, referring to the onerous work conditions that forced prayer and ritual observance to take place at abnormal times under more than trying conditions. Yet, as we will see, even under such harsh conditions, Rabbi Zelmann was resolute in his belief that one could aim at carrying out religious precepts to the letter of the law. The calendar's detailed specificity could only have helped the Westerbork Jews to go as far as they possibly could in this regard.

But the calendar's unique feature is the listing of yahrzeits of three Chasidic masters, adding a special commemorative dimension that I have not found in any other calendar. Certainly, calendars fashioned during the war made it possible for Jews to observe the anniversary of the passing of a family member or friend, which is observed on the Jewish date. For example, in the luggage of another Westerbork prisoner, Louis Asscher, "was a list in which he had inserted a calendar and dates of death of members of his family before he was deported from Westerbork to Bergen-Belsen so that precisely on the according day [i.e., the anniversary of the date] of death he could say Kaddish for his deceased relatives."[31] Asscher, a diamond merchant and artist who perished days before the war's end, was likely one of any number of Jewish prisoners that endeavored to keep track of the yahrzeits of family and friends and thereby honor their memory with whatever prayers or rituals were available to them. Behind such care and calculation lies a belief that the soul of the deceased proceeds on a journey of ascent in the hereafter, with the anniversary of the day of passing affording special opportunities for greater progress. Moreover, these opportunities can be aided by the family member or friend on this day invoking relevant prayers (including the mourner's Kaddish) and conducting a regimen of Torah learning. Having a Jewish calendar at hand can thus ensure the prayers and learning occur on the precise and proper date.

Rabbi Zelmann's calendar would have been useful in this regard; it might well have been the case that, given its inclusion in the archive of Asscher's wartime possessions, this was the very calendar Louis Asscher carried with him in his luggage. But Rabbi Zelmann also went a step beyond, singling out the anniversaries not only of family members but also of righteous leaders, individuals whose date of passing would have *communal* importance. The calendar thus served as the means to communicate the information about these dates to a wider community—even though not all or even most of the Westerbork community would, like Rabbi Zelmann, have felt equally obliged to commemorate them.

Giving special attention to the yahrzeit of a righteous person has its origins in Jewish tradition, both as a way to honor the memory of the deceased and to proclaim his or her ongoing significance to Jewish life in the present. Hence, the seventh of Adar, the anniversary of passing of Moses, the righteous figure par excellence, is widely noted and commemorated by some communities as a fast day; we saw how recognition of the day found its way into the selected entries of the *Luach Katan* composed in Theresienstadt. These considerations would have played a significant role in moving Rabbi Zelmann to list the three yahrzeits that he did, honoring the three founders of the Chasidic group of which he—and tens if not hundreds of thousands of eastern European Jews—was a member. His affiliation was thus very much in tune with the evolution of Jewish life in Poland, where the Ger Chasidim had since the mid-nineteenth century come to dominate Chasidic life in particular and Orthodox Jewish life in general. In less than a hundred years, the three leaders had guided their growing contingent of followers and thereby altered the landscape of eastern European Jewry.[32]

The effects in western Europe were less conspicuous and the number of adherents tiny in comparison. But though the total of Ger Chasidim in the Dutch camp was clearly small, there was a contingent of some five hundred to eight hundred Polish-born Jews in Westerbork.[33] Not every one, of course, was a Gerer Chasid. But, in addition to Rabbi Zelmann, some likely were, an affiliation conveyed by the telltale name that one bore, which was chosen to honor the leaders' memory. Among those listed as having originally come from Lodz, there was for instance Ichek Meier Mlynek, a clothing salesman in Amsterdam. His first and middle names (the Yiddish form of the Hebrew names Yitzchak Meir) were those of the founder of Ger Chasidism (known as the *Chidushe HaRim*). Moreover, Ichek Meier Mlynek's father had the first and middle names of Abraham Mordke, which also reflected the names of a venerable personage in the Ger Chassidic line. So together with the broader Jewish community of Westerbork that would have benefitted from the calendar but would not have felt a special bond to the memorialized Chasidic leaders, there would also have been a small informed readership who would have joined with the calendar's author in commemorating these days with special ardor.

The three masters whose dates are singled out were themselves intimately related. The first, Rabbi Menachem Mendel of Kotzk (1787–1859), did not actually hail from the town of Gur (whence the group derives its name), nor is he associated exclusively with the group that claims him as their founder. He rather comes to be honored for having served as the teacher and master of the first leader to base his Chasidic court in Gur, Rabbi Yitzhak Meir Rothenberg Alter (1789–1866). His is the second anniversary. The third figure, Rabbi Yehuda Aryeh Leib Alter (1847–1905), the grandson and disciple of Rabbi Yitzhak Meir, took over the leadership from his grandfather. It was his son, Rabbi Avraham Mordechai Alter (1866–1948), who served as the head of the Ger Chasidism from the time of his father's passing in 1905 through the trials of wartime Europe. It was also he who had counseled a younger Rabbi Zelmann to leave Poland in order to avoid conscription into the army and to make his way to Germany. The listing of the three yahrzeits paid homage to those who were Torah scholars of the first rank, deft interpreters of the Chasidic legacy, and leaders of the movement to which Rabbi Zelmann belonged. To place the three in the calendar's foreground at precisely the time when their followers were being subjected to the full wrath of the enemy's evil designs was undoubtedly a statement of loyalty and perseverance.

It was also likely more than that. The mystical tradition to which Chasidism belongs adds a further instruction regarding the righteous person's demise: he or she is actually, if paradoxically, more present in this world after his or her passing. The limitations that time, space, and a physical body imposed no longer play a role; the righteous person's influence can be felt that much more directly and pervasively once he or she has shed the constraints of a this-world existence and passed on to the realm of the afterlife. As he is more accessible to disciples after his demise than before, the master's influence can be experienced most intensely on his yahrzeit.[34] Hence the added importance of listing the three yahrzeits in the calendar. A reminder about the dates of the yahrzeits would be especially welcome to Ger Chasidim—and to those who were not formally followers but who nevertheless recognized the three leaders as righteous persons and might turn to them with their own petitions—at a time of crisis when the influence the righteous might wield to solicit God's mercy could be pivotal.

Such a mandate would seem to rule out any possibility of error. But the fact that Rabbi Zelmann erred in two out of the three yahrzeits demonstrates how difficult the task of exactitude was in Westerbork in 1943. He accurately notes the yahrzeit of the *Sefas Emes*, Rabbi Yehuda Aryeh Leib (the third in the dynastic line) on the fifth day of the month of Shevat. But he seems to confuse the yahrzeits of the first two masters: he assigns the yahrzeit of the founder, Rabbi Menachem Mendel of Kotsk, to the twenty-third day of the month of Adar—which is actually the yahrzeit of his successor, Rabbi Yitzhak Meir Alter (known as the Chadushei Harim). Rabbi Alter's yahrzeit is designated as the eighteenth day of Adar, five days before its proper date. And Rabbi Menachem Mendel's yahrzeit, the twenty-second day of the month of Shevat—falling almost exactly a month before the date assigned on the calendar—receives no special designation or mention. Undoubtedly, the errors are not great; in least in one case, it is easy to see how the mistake could occur. Yet that the error crept in at all in a matter where the desire to honor the deceased was clearly so great goes to show the disruptive force of the camp's isolation, of being uprooted from family and community, of the punishing work schedule, and of the ever-looming threat of deportation to the East.

Though clearly the work of a Gerer Chasid, the calendar composed by Rabbi Zelmann circulated to a wider contingent of Westerbork Jews. Exactly how wide is not known; we have no record of the number of calendar copies produced. But the two surviving copies I have reviewed give some indication of who made use of the extraordinary artifact. The first belonged to the abovementioned Yehuda (Louis) Asscher, a Dutch diamond merchant whose luggage, as we previously heard, bore the dedicated list of family members' yahrzeits. Born in 1885 to Eliezer and Rozalie (née van Gelder), Asscher was one of twelve children. His father was a ritual scribe, the family was devout, and Louis himself became a well-known supporter of Torah learning and institutions, particularly associated with the Zionist-oriented Mizrachi movement. From an early age he also developed a high level of proficiency in art.[35]

He and his family were deported to Westerbork in May 1943 and shunted to Bergen-Belsen in January 1945. While there he made some thirty-five sketches, reproducing with a delicate hand many features of the camp. He survived to the last weeks of the war, when he was transported on the last train to leave Bergen-Belsen—the so-called Lost Transport. Together with hundreds of other deportees, he perished at the train's aborted destination in Tröbitz, Germany. His children, however, donated a number of war-related artifacts, including a copy of the calendar composed by Rabbi Zelmann, to the Ghetto Fighters' Museum in Israel.

Most of the artifacts are of a personal nature, such as letters and a diary. The calendar is nonetheless listed among them, its placement among the personal items giving a sense of the importance it was deemed to have; Asscher must have hung on to it as something of a keepsake, even once the year that the calendar tabulated had run its course. He held on to it, moreover, despite the difficult conditions he undoubtedly faced after he was compelled to leave Westerbork. Noteworthy is the fact that, in the archive listing, the calendar's contents are not described altogether accurately; moreover, it lacks an attribution to Rabbi Zelmann, likely because missing from this copy is the calendar's first page, at the bottom of which Rabbi Zelmann identifies himself as the author. Though Asscher's copy was somewhat damaged and rendered anonymous, it is no small wonder that, given what he was compelled to endure in Westerbork, Bergen-Belsen, and the final deathly ordeal of the Lost Transport train, the calendar in the GFM archive remained nearly complete.

A second copy of the calendar has its own saga. The wartime fate of Herbert (Chaim Noach) Kruskal paralleled that of Asscher in a number of respects; indeed, he, too, held on to his outdated copy of the Westerbork calendar. Imprisoned from September 1942 on in Westerbork and Bergen-Belsen with his wife and three young children, he fortunately was one of the members of Transport 222, the group of 222 Jews who in the summer 1944 were freed and provided with passage to Palestine in exchange for an equal number of Palestine-based German Templars.[36] In contrast to Asscher, Kruskal, and his family, beneficiaries of this extraordinary prisoner swap survived the war.[37]

Determined to keep a careful artifactual record of his experience, Kruskal filed his copy of Rabbi Zelmann's Westerbork calendar in his private wartime archive together with three other calendars: one from Frankfurt, 5699, a last compilation of normality before the deluge; one from occupied Amsterdam, 5701, in the year before the printing of Jewish calendars was outlawed; and one produced in Paris, for the year 5705, seemingly the fruit of the newly wrested freedom for Jewish publishing in the aftermath of the liberation of the city the preceding summer. How he came to own copies of these calendars is not clear. But the fact that the calendars earned a place in his archive shows that he himself had more than an inkling that wartime calendars were artifacts worth preserving. They are in turn part of an impressive collection of documents and memorabilia chronicling the family's extraordinary good fortune.[38]

Carefully placed within the greater whole of the accordion file book, the Kruskal copy of the Zelmann Westerbork calendar remains whole, bound within its maroon paperboard covers. It also includes the tile page missing from Louis Asscher's copy, on which we find two vital pieces of information: first, it specifies Drenthe—the region of Holland in which Westerbork was situated—as the place where the time listings incorporated into the calendar were being calculated. This detail confirms that the calendar was produced at Westerbork; while circumstantial evidence had led the Ghetto Fighters' Museum archivists to indicate that it had emerged from the infamous Dutch transit camp, there was nothing in the calendar itself to link it to Westerbork. The recovered title page made the connection crystal clear. And second, the very bottom of the page contains the author's name: "Yisrael Simcha son of the righteous Rabbi Dov Zelmann, of blessed and righteous memory." What had existed anonymously in one copy had recovered its identity in the second. The Kruskal family's survival allowed them to oversee the preservation of the calendar in a manner that the guardians of Asscher's posthumous file could not.

Beyond providing the factual details that identify where the calendar was authored and who composed it, the Kruskal copy's title page also sets forth a remarkable prologue, forthright in laying out the religious obligations implied by the calendar's dates and information. Within the prologue, Rabbi Zelmann issues an uncompromising plea for the Jews imprisoned in Westerbork to observe fundamental commandments, even if they must be carried out in a compromised manner: "I hereby request," implores the rabbi, "that my brethren of Israel presently in freedom [a euphemism for interment], and for whom it is impossible to pray the morning prayers [in the proper and standard manner] after dawn, and [equally impossible] to don the prayer shawl and to put on tefillin at sunrise, that you should get an early start to the day—which means two hours before sunrise according to an opinion brought by the Rambam, of blessed memory—and that you pray with true intention, and put on tefillin and don a prayer shawl."[39] In Jewish ritual observance, certain precepts can be carried out only by day or only by night. Donning prayer shawl and tefillin and praying the morning service can usually be performed only after sunrise. But compulsory attendance at early morning work squads made it impossible to do so. Rabbi Zelmann counseled how to get around the dilemma, invoking a leniency in the performance of such commandments when dictated by the circumstances. The calendar's author had resided in the camp for over three years when he composed this prologue; he knew from the inside that one had to join the work squad to which he or she had been assigned; that was a foregone conclusion. What was possible was to summon forth the effort to rise while it was still dark and, because no other option existed, carry out the commandments. That strategy was less than optimal. But it still had considerable merit. We know that numbers of Westerbork inmates (and those in other camps, where similar conditions were in force) did rise early and carry out these precepts; Rabbi Zelmann was not trying to invoke an unobtainable goal but was rather encouraging his fellow prisoners to take advantage of the room they had, as it were, to maneuver.

The leniency that allows prayer before the day begins must not be interpreted, as the prologue's continued exhortation made resoundingly clear, as an excuse to perform the precepts in a casual manner: "And don't skip, God forbid, even a single letter from the prayers, and if at all possible remain in [wearing] the prayer shawl and tefillin until sunrise [the beginning of the normal time for praying], when you would touch [the tefillin] with full intention [and thereby fulfill in the proper manner the commandment to wear tefillin only during the light of day]." When all is said and done, it would be best to carry out the precepts in the normal daytime hours. Of course, one may not have the opportunity to do so, and Rabbi Zelmann's phrase "if at all possible" left open the prospect that irregular observance of the precepts might be the best that one could hope for.

But his closing directive shows with what bold inclusivity he understood the obligation of observing commandments for every Jew: "And don't exclude, God forbid, a single Jew from performing the commandment of counting the omer [which, in the case of this precept, is normally to be done only *after* nightfall], even when one needs to count *before* nightfall" (italics added). Again and again Rabbi Zelmann joins leniency with rigor. The oppressive circumstances in Westerbork require flexibility and compromise in terms of *when* the precepts can be carried out. Yet there is no question that they must be done—and must be done by every "single Jew." Casting such a wide net to include every Jew may have been inspired by the relative ease of performing this commandment. Counting the Omer is essentially just that: counting. Unlike morning prayer, it doesn't demand special equipment or gear; because night is the optimal time for counting, it does not require the strenuous effort of rising before dawn; and it can be enacted in a matter of seconds. All of these considerations made it something every Jew, no matter what his or her level of devotion, could carry out. On top of that, the abnormal schedule Westerbork imposed on prisoners allowed for a greater latitude than usual in the hours when one could count. Hence Rabbi Zelmann's concluding phrase, "even when one needs to count before nightfall," indicated a leniency that extended the hours when one could count for those whose compulsory early rising brought in turn an early, pre-nightfall bedtime.

Rabbi Zelmann's passion for including everyone found meticulous expression in the very format of his calendar. For it not only specifies the forty-nine days of the Omer count (from the second day of the holiday of Passover to the day before the holiday of Shavuot) but, unique among wartime calendars, it creates for the days of the count a column of their own. This went beyond what most felt they could or needed to do. Many wartime calendars make no mention of the Omer count; some refer to it in passing at the point when it begins, on the second night of Passover; a few even list on the side or in the margins the specific number of the count. But no other calendar earmarks a separate space where the sequence unfolds day by day. Such clarity in the calendar's format undoubtedly served as an aid to performing the commandment, simply because the separate column could let one know the day of the count that much more easily. In that practical respect, the calendar guided performance in a hands-on manner.

It also maintained the same exacting standard in the calendar's layout and execution as the author had set forth, compassionately yet scrupulously, in the calendar's prologue. Rabbi Zelmann's followed what is one of the standard formats dating back hundreds of years. The compact size of the calendar (a third of A1) is built around three vertical columns, with the Jewish date on the right (in Hebrew letters), the day of the week (abbreviated in Yiddish) in the middle, and the Gregorian date on the left (in Arabic numerals). The space on the right of the columns is reserved for designating special days (holidays, fast days, etc.),

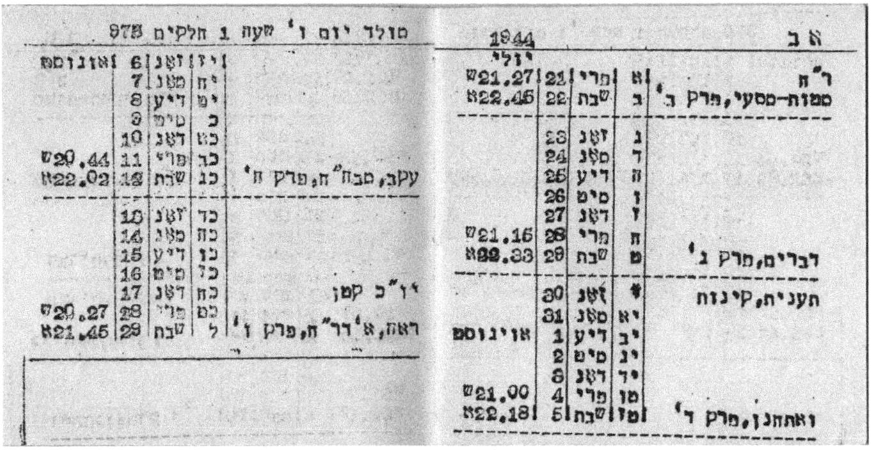

מולד יום ו' מעה 1 חלקים 975   1944   א ב

Fig. 3.1: Calendar, 5704 (1943–44), Rabbi Yisrael Simcha Zelmann, Westerbork concentration camp.

while the space on the left specifies the times at which the Sabbath day enters and exits and, in a different vein, the name of the Gregorian calendar month. The top tells the year, the Jewish month, and the molad (i.e., the precise time at which the month begins). Facing pages split the month approximately in half.

Though the format is standard, there are several unusual features. First are the footnotes, annotations at the page bottom that give information about special dates. Second is the meticulous attention to both law and custom: all fast days are designated, including the post-holiday Monday-Thursday-Monday cycle of fasts. Unlike the progressive attrition of fast days in the Theresienstadt *Luach Katan* and other calendars, in the case of this Westerbork calendar fast days are firmly entrenched. This may be because basic availability of food does not seem to have been as much of a concern in Westerbork as in many other camps. But the difficult manual work conditions must have made such fasts an added burden. Nevertheless, Rabbi Zelmann clearly saw them as part and parcel of any calendar, a feature of what must be included in order to be considered a viable Jewish digest of important dates. Third, several customs appear uniquely here among wartime calendars. This calendar, observes one rabbinic authority, is composed for the *talmid hacham*, for one versed in the intricacies of law and custom.[40]

Fourth, while the name of the weekdays is always abbreviated (in Yiddish: *Son, Mon, Dien, Mit, Don,* and *Fri*), Shabbat, the name for the seventh day, is always written out in full. The contrast is telling. The distinction between the mundane character of the weekdays and the holiness of the Sabbath day is a fundamental element of Jewish belief. Rabbi Zelmann's choice of idiom thus reflects that belief and gives it cyclical expression. His decision went beyond practical considerations. Writing *Shab* would have indicated to the user of the calendar the day that was being referred to; it would not, however, have graphically conveyed the religious principle that underlies the very notion of a Jewish week. This is what writing (or typing!) out the word *Shabbat* did week in and week out.

The gesture no doubt took on special import in the camp context. The compulsory camp routine made it difficult if not impossible to follow the usual steps of making the distinction between weekday and Sabbath, such as partaking of wine and challah, donning special clothing, and, most of all, desisting from weekday work and activity. Instead, inmates were required to work a full day while wearing the camp uniform, degrading Shabbat to the same level as any other day of the week. All kinds of strategies were sought to insinuate into Shabbat an iota of difference. Yona Emanuel, a teenage inmate of Westerbork, recounts how they attempted to honor the special character of Shabbat and why the strategy was at best half-successful: "For the sake of honoring the Shabbat, we changed our underclothing on Friday afternoon. It felt strange to wear our work clothes over a clean set of underclothing, and to set out to work on Shabbat; the dichotomy of simultaneously honoring and desecrating the Shabbat disturbed us to the depths of our souls."[41] The measure taken was resourceful, even ingenious. At one and the same time they could honor Shabbat yet conform to the requirements of camp attire. By doing so, they continued to observe the age-old tradition of changing into fresh clothing in preparation for the onset of the holy day, a custom that, prior to imprisonment, had been kept week in, week out, as far back as they could remember. Despite the camp's onerous conditions, they found a way to maintain continuity with the past.

But the most dedicated efforts could only produce partial, dichotomized results; Shabbat observance remained fractured, split in two. Though the fresh clothing honored the day's special character, compulsory work assignments violated the very essence of the day of rest. Struggling to cope with the profound spiritual disturbance, symbolic gestures must have carried that much more weight.

Rabbi Zelmann's choice to preserve the whole word—*Shabbat* instead of the abbreviation *Sh*—was one of those. An abbreviation would have abbreviated, as it were, the day's sanctity. It, too, would have honored and not honored, would have put the veneer of weekday work over the cleanliness of Shabbat. Typing out *Shabbat* removed the dichotomy, not just once but every week. This is what, Rabbi Zelmann intuited, the calendar could do in Westerbork: it could keep the Shabbat whole, unabbreviated, undisturbed. It could do what the prisoners could not.

Fig. 3.2: A Dutch-language Gregorian calendar for the year 1945, *Lager Westerbork*, ostensibly composed and used in the Westerbork transit camp in Holland, contains simply the months, weeks, and days in a checkerboard pattern. In contrast to most calendars, it lacks explicit reference to holidays, religious or secular. It can thus be called a calendar without memory. Courtesy of the Ghetto Fighters' Museum.

Calendar without Memory: A Second Westerbork Calendar

In contrast to Rabbi Zelmann's calendar, resolutely committed to orchestrating Jewish ritual life, stands what seems to be the official Westerbork calendar for 1945.[42] It differs from Rabbi Zelmann's in almost every respect. First, it records only the Gregorian dates, with each page presenting (in German) a month (*Januar, Februar, Marz*). The days of the week (again written in German: *SONNTAG, MONTAG*, and so on) move vertically down the left side of the page, while the number of each day is set out horizontally in one of five columns. Together they form a neat rectangular (almost square) grid.

Second, in addition to the German name of the month and the Gregorian calendar year, the top of every page bears the words *Lager Westerbork* (Camp Westerbork) enclosed in a banner and written in a flowing script. One doesn't, in other words, need to search in order to discover the locale the calendar was meant to serve. Third, this straightforward calendar is carefully hand-drawn, without embellishment but with an artist's eye for balance, variety, and clarity of presentation. And fourth, and likely most significant, no day is regarded as different from any other: no holidays, no memorials, no associations are recorded. It is a calendar without memory.

This last point has to be qualified in a small but important way. Two dates are marked. They do not, however, annotate a past event or anniversary but rather simply single out the date by marking the corner of the box in pencil. The first date of the two is April 12, 1945, the day on which Canadian army forces liberated the camp. The special character of the day is registered by having not one but four Xs inscribed, one in each corner.

The Xs heralded not something from the past but rather indicated a watershed in the history of the camp itself, the day when the camp no longer functioned as a way station to death. When exactly the Westerbork prisoners were set free and the backdrop to the camp's liberation is actually a matter of dispute. Some claim the German guards fled already on April 10, while others say it was only on April 11. One version has it that the advancing Canadians were unaware that the Germans had absconded and were planning to shell the camp, a disaster averted only because an intrepid inmate left the camp, journeyed to where the Canadians were stationed, and informed them that there were no longer German forces in Westerbork. A second version claims that, even after the guards fled, the prisoners feared that the Germans would return to destroy the camp; once the Canadians, for their part, had arrived in the vicinity of the camp, it was discovered that the troops had no idea of the camp's existence. All versions seem to concur that the date the Canadians entered Westerbork was April 12.[43]

However, the Xs spell out none of this, say nothing concrete or even vague about the liberation and its implications. Unforthcoming though they were, the four Xs nevertheless established a before and after, with the day (and the four Xs themselves) dividing one era from the other. In a calendar designed to omit the conventional markers of memory, ritual or otherwise; designed to keep the flow of the past from streaming into the present; designed to filter out any oscillation, any movement back and forth, between the mundane and the sacred; in the midst of such stark uniformity, this day refuses to conform, breaks the undifferentiated pattern, and returns the calendar to its moral mission, one might say, of differentiating between the ordinary and the extraordinary, and, in this case, from the time lived as a prisoner and that of a free human being.

The second date singled out is October 26, marked in this instance with only one X. It comes some six months after the first marked date, and more than five months after the war's end on May 8. During this period, Westerbork changed from a camp imprisoning and transporting Jews to their death in the East to one confining wartime collaborators. Chaotic throughout the summer following the liberation, camp conditions stabilized in the fall, at which time the remaining Jewish inmates also left.[44] Whether October 26 is linked to this phase of the camp's postwar transformation (perhaps indicating the day of departure from the site of the camp) is not clear; the date is opaque, inviting attention but yielding little in the way of known significance. But it, too, perforates the calendar's unvarying surface, hinting at events, dramatic or quiet, that made it special. Neither set of Xs truly recasts the calendar, allowing the memories of a people, a nation, or a world to pulse through. Yet they do intimate that the job of a calendar is not only to convey larger and smaller units of time in a conveniently human idiom but also to be an ever-absorptive vehicle for sifting the varying meaning of the past, present, and future.

Clearly, the *Lager Westerbork* calendar continues to occupy a corner diametrically opposite Rabbi Zelman's, which revealed on a daily, weekly, and monthly basis the comprehensive presence of Jewish tradition. While the *Lager Westerbork* calendar floated above almost all particulars of memory, Rabbi Zelmann's was obsessed with them; while the former presented a Gregorian calendar aloof from the past, the latter endeavored to make room on its pages and dates, in the name of tradition, for whatever it could. Both were faithful to the basic task of a calendar, exhaustively listing each and every day. But one, *Lager Westerbork*, chose uniformity, evenness, a virtually undifferentiated stream of dated days; the other, Rabbi Zelmann's, had as its purpose to differentiate, to highlight the distinctive, the unordinary, to specify days filled with special sanctity or given over to carrying out special commandments. Blank spaces served only as steppingstones to those filled with annotation and instruction. The only uniformity it countenanced were those activities tradition understood as a daily occurrence or obligation.

Rabbi Zelmann's calendar showed the time he and his fellow prisoners were living through to be as consequential as ever. The calendar's prologue made clear that the regimen in Westerbork might well demand compromise, attenuation, and adjustment in observing fundamental religious precepts. The calendar itself, however, created a zone of Jewish time freed from the constraints that Westerbork imposed. Rabbi Zelmann, true to traditional practice, calculated the times to be listed according to the region where the camp was located; Jewish time always takes its cue from the place and setting in which the precepts are to be lived out. But the times etched onto the calendar's sacred days became associated not with the camp and the cruelties it perpetrated but rather with the holy days and the spiritual domain they ushered in. Moreover, everything listed on the pages of Rabbi Zelmann's calendar underwent a similar transfiguration. Even death, thickly present in the routine of Westerbork's Tuesday deportations to the murder factories in the East, found its altered way into the calendar, meaningfully transformed as the yahrzeits of luminous leaders whose care for their followers existed beyond the grave. Indeed, Rabbi Zelmann's request to be buried with the calendar—to take it with him to the world beyond the grave—demonstrated that, of the precious items he was miraculously able to salvage from the war's inferno, the calendar was the most precious of them all.

The Month of Redemption: Bergen-Belsen

On January 11, 1944, Rabbi Zelmann was on the first transport from Westerbork to the Bergen-Belsen concentration camp near Hannover, Germany;[45] eight more transports would follow the same route over the course of the next ten months, conveying a total of 3,700 Westerbork prisoners. Most of these prisoners—which in addition to Rabbi Zelmann included those carrying a copy of his calendar, Louis Asscher and the Kruskal family (who arrived in the camp on April 5)—had a special status of "exchange prisoners" and were therefore housed in the so-called Star Camp.

The Star Camp was both representative of and exceptional among the Bergen-Belsen subcamps. From 1940 to 1943, Bergen-Belsen had served as a prisoner-of-war camp.[46] But in 1943 it became part of the concentration camp system, particularly as a holding tank for prisoners deemed suitable to be exchanged. And indeed, to a limited degree, such exchanges were carried out, including that which brought the Kruskal family their freedom in Palestine. Yet as the fortunes of war turned against the Axis powers, Bergen-Belsen took in thousands of prisoners evacuated from camps outside of Germany. Hence the number of prisoners jumped from seven thousand in July 1944 to fifteen thousand in December and then increased to twenty-two thousand in February 1945. In the next month the leap was even greater, with the incoming torrent of evacuees spiraling the camp population to some sixty thousand. Food and water were scarce, hygiene dismal, and disease rampant, and many prisoners died as a result of these atrocious conditions.

Up until the last grueling months of the war, the Star Camp provided better conditions for its four thousand prisoners, most of whom hailed from the Netherlands.[47] Among other privileges, these prisoners were able to dress in their own clothes rather than wear a camp uniform. It is thus likely that the first of the two Bergen-Belsen calendars, which used Dutch to render the names of the Gregorian calendar months, was composed in 1944 in the enclave of the Star Camp.

Wartime calendars differ significantly in their presentation but less often in their manner of framing a Jewish year. Almost all Jewish calendars take as their starting point the holiday of Rosh Hashana, the first day of the month of Tishrei, commonly understood to be the beginning of the Jewish year. Indeed, many customs associated with the holiday commemorate the new year, including that of wishing a good New Year to family and friends. Also, the year's new number—5705, the final year of the war, commences at this point in time.

An exception to this rule of beginning the calendar with Rosh Hashana can be found in this Dutch/Hebrew calendar, fashioned in Bergen-Belsen late in the war. Instead of commencing with the Jewish New Year in the fall, this calendar begins with the Jewish month of Nisan 5704 (March/April 1944) and continues over the course of twelve months (a full Jewish year), ending with the month of Adar 5705 (February/March 1945). In a sense, this is truly beginning in medias res, since the year 5704 thus actually begins not with the spring month of Nisan but rather back in the fall with the month of Tishrei.

To start the calendar with the month of Nisan was then itself a bold stroke. No doubt, the Nisan starting point has a logic behind it: this month has the legal status of a New Year. But such a status does not usually translate into the beginning of a calendar. The anonymous author may have chosen the unusual starting point simply because that was when he or she scripted it; beginning with the present set the future out and gave the greatest span of time. To begin the calendar where most did, with the fall holiday of Rosh Hashana, would have had little practical value under such conditions.

Yet the choice of the month of Nisan, unconventional though it was, could also have had behind it symbolic reasons. The spring month of Nisan carries many associations of beginning, since the Jewish people first became a nation at this time and in this season and first received the command to make a calendar. Perhaps most important under the circumstances of imprisonment in Bergen-Belsen was the fact that Nisan is the month when the Jews broke the bonds of slavery in ancient Egypt, a deliverance ritually recalled every year (even under the atrocious conditions in Bergen-Belsen circa 1944) in the Passover seder held in the middle of the month. Moreover, the Pesach seder's drama of liberation is understood to permeate the entire month and to show its special redemptive powers. Hence, not only in the month of Nisan were the Jews of ancient Egypt freed from slavery and delivered from despotic rule, but so is the final redemption slated to occur in the month of Nisan. Liberation in the ancient past and an even greater liberation in the future are thus tied inextricably together. The Bergen-Belsen calendar thus begins with that season of the Jewish year most auspicious for envisioning an end to the terrible ordeal of the moment.

In many other respects, however, this Bergen-Belsen calendar follows wartime conventions. Likely constrained by the shortage of paper, it consigns not one but two months to every page (with Dutch spelling): Nisan/Iyar, Siewan/Tamos, Aw/Elloel, Tishrie/Marchesvan, Kislev/Teiwes, Shevat/Adar. But not every decision was dictated by economy. For instance, it spells out the name of the month in both Hebrew and Latin scripts, the wish to include the broadest audience trumping the need to be frugal. The desire to honor both the Jewish and the secular does not, however, apply across the board: guided by the directional movement of the Hebrew script (written and read from right to left), the months move in sequence from right to left.

Like most Jewish calendars of this period, this one is outfitted with information that would guide religious observance: candle-lighting times for Sabbath and holiday (within two to four minutes of the most precise calculations available), the Torah portion for the given week, and fast days (an always remarkable notation in the midst of such wholesale deprivation, such as that which afflicted the inmates of Bergen-Belsen in 1944–45). It also contains several special features—for instance, Yom Kippur Katan, the special day of repentance at the end of the month. Strikingly, Yom Kippur Katan for the month of Nisan 5705 concludes the calendar, bringing the year full circle.

One peculiar omission is worth noting: nothing appears for Chanukah until the last of the eight nights, which is called by one of its names, חנוכה מזבח. This contrasts, for example, with Adela Levisson's meticulous identification of every night of the eight-day festival. The explanation may be straightforward. Perhaps she could observe more—or could imagine observing more--while hiding in northern Holland rather than those who were compelled to endure imprisonment in Bergen-Belsen.

A Kasztner Transport Calendar

The second Bergen-Belsen calendar was authored in the so-called Hungarian camp, a section of Belsen that granted more privileges than any other. The story of this camp is linked to a larger saga of rescue, that of the Kasztner transport, which was played out as one of the last murderous chapters of the Holocaust. relentlessly unfolded. The calendar in question, colorful and ornate, testifying to youth and impetuosity as well as to learning and diligence, conveys it own story. It had to serve as a bulwark of Jewish sensibility against a backdrop almost unrelieved torture and murder. In some ways like the Kasztner transport itself, the calendar created an ordered vision of time aloof, untrammeled, and undamaged by the real-time conflagration as it was lived out and witnessed.

The backdrop was indeed full of anguish. Spring 1944 witnessed the tragic annihilation of most of Hungarian Jewry, the last surviving community of Jews in central Europe. Even so, the tragedy was played out at first only gradually. Though Hungary was an ally of Germany, it had refused to yield up the Jews that resided within its domain. To be sure, there had been some egregious compromises when it came to the so-called "foreign Jews," those that had been born outside of Hungary and had not become Hungarian citizens. Already in 1941 thousands of foreign Jews had been deported and murdered. But Hungary remained adamant regarding those defined as Hungarian Jews. Only when Germany occupied Hungary late in the war were the majority of its Jews, some six hundred thousand strong, subjected to wholesale restrictions, internment in ghettos, and, at a lightning pace, deportation and annihilation.[48]

There were desperate attempts to rescue or ransom the Hungarian Jews slated for deportation and death. One successful (if controversial) effort was the Kasztner transport.[49] This was a trainload of more than a thousand Jews who, through negotiations led by a committee of Budapest Jews, including Rudolf Kasztner, were ferried out of the lion's den. In the end, thirty-five train cars of 1,680 Jews departed from Budapest on June 30, 1944 (Tammuz 9, 5704), ostensibly en route to freedom in a neutral country. But the trip did not proceed as planned. After a stop in Linz, Austria, the train was diverted, for seemingly unknown reasons, to Bergen-Belsen. The "Hungarian subcamp" in Belsen was created to house the members of the transport. It would serve as a temporary home for a smaller contingent of the group, numbering over 300, for about a month; they were then sent to Switzerland, apparently as a goodwill gesture tendered by high-ranking Germans to the Allies. But for the majority of the group, the tenure in Bergen-Belsen ended up being just over five months, a period of time that, significantly for the calendar in question, included the high holidays and the months that followed.

The Kasztner group was made up of a cross section of Jews—young and old, wealthy and less well-off, influential and unknown, and including a minority of Orthodox Jews. Among them were a family named Neumann, who hailed originally from Poland but had relocated in the 1930s to Budapest. The father, Israel Baruch, was born in Tarnow, the mother, Rachel, in Galicia, and one son, Menachem Emil, in Poland in 1927. Two other children, Sonia, age seven, and Erwin David, age five, had been born after the move to Budapest. Somehow, the Neumanns, young children and all, were able to gain passage on the train. And though its route was anything but smooth and direct, the transport did eventually convey the family to freedom in neutral Switzerland. Like many of their fellow passengers, the Neumanns continued on to Israel after the war, arriving in 1945 and settling in Tel Aviv. The oldest son, Menachem, the calendar's youthful author, became active in the Tze'irai Hamizrachi movement. He later married a woman named Devora and moved to Bnei Brak, the religious suburb of Tel Aviv where, some twenty years later, Rabbi Yisrael Simcha Zelmann came to spend his last years. Menachem Neumann passed away in 2002, at the age of seventy-five.[50]

But the Kasztner transport on which the Neumanns had secured passage first had to go through hell and high water. Along with the other Jews on board the train, the Neumanns arrived at Bergen-Belsen on July 9, which in the Jewish calendar marked the deferred observance of one of the summer fast days, the seventeenth day of Tammuz, and the onset of the traditional three-week mourning period. While the passengers were compelled to cope with a welter of practical concerns on arrival, the fact that entry to the camp coincided with such a fraught date in the Jewish calendar was, at least for the traditionally minded, not overlooked.[51]

Imprisonment in a concentration camp in wartime Germany was a far cry from the promised freedom in a neutral country. Yet the conditions in the Hungarian camp, albeit crowded and restrictive, were tolerable, both materially and spiritually; the prisoners held within were deemed the privileged among the already privileged exchange prisoners (such as those Dutch Jews confined to the Star Camp). This was the case even for the Orthodox Jews, whose needs for religious expression were usually viewed with intolerance. In this instance, however, the enhancements given to prisoners generally were extended to them as well. They were apparently able to receive kosher food, were not compelled to work on Shabbat, were permitted to have and use ritual articles and religious books, and were allowed to perform basic religious ceremonies, such as circumcision, bar mitzvahs, and, at the other end of the spectrum, funerals.

It was as a member of this special cadre of concentration camp prisoners that Menachem Emil Neumann, who arrived in Bergen-Belsen some three weeks shy of his seventeenth birthday, composed his Jewish calendar for the year 5705. Indeed, the calendar was one of a number of religious texts he fashioned during this period, the others that survived being handwritten copies of Rosh Hashana and Yom Kippur prayers.[52] All of these efforts—certainly the high holiday prayers but also the calendar—indicate that Menachem had his eye toward the beginning of the New Year, some ten weeks away. His work on the calendar and prayers not only occupied the time but also gave substance to a future that, like for the members of the transport, had been diverted from its course.

Menachem's writing down the high holiday prayers may have been part of a group effort to make up for the shortage of high holiday prayer books.[53] Given that the passengers on the transport believed it would travel directly to freedom and be situated in Jewish communities by the time Rosh Hashana rolled around, no

Fig. 3.3: Emil Menachem Neumann traveled by train from wartime Budapest with his family on the Kasztner Transport, which was compelled to stop at the Bergen-Belsen concentration camp in Germany in the summer of 5704 (1944). It was during what turned out to be a five-month layover that Neumann, fifteen years old at the time, composed a Jewish calendar for 5705 (1944–45) in Hebrew and Hungarian. Courtesy of the Yad Vashem Archives.

one thought to bring along on the improvised journey high holiday prayer books. As the holiday approached, a handful of copies were located in other sections of Belsen. This would of course hardly suffice for the numbers eager to join in the holiday prayers. To make up for the lack, copyists were recruited to set down on paper fundamental holiday prayers such as *U'natane Tokef* and *Kol Nidre*. Menachem's preserved copies may well have stemmed from this joint enterprise.

In contrast, his calendar seems to have come out of individual initiative, witnessing dedication both to the future that lay just out of reach and the present predicament that kept the fate of the Kasztner group in abeyance. On the one hand, the format of the calendar points to the future, overflowing as it is with detail, color, shading. Every element of the religious year to come—and more—finds articulate expression: holidays, Rosh Chodesh, and Sabbaths. And this time around, there is no scrimping on fast days. Every one of them—whether taking place in the fall, winter, spring, or summer—is present and accounted for, marked, recognized, ready for observance in conditions that, with the final leg of the journey to a place of freedom hovering before their eyes, would make it easy

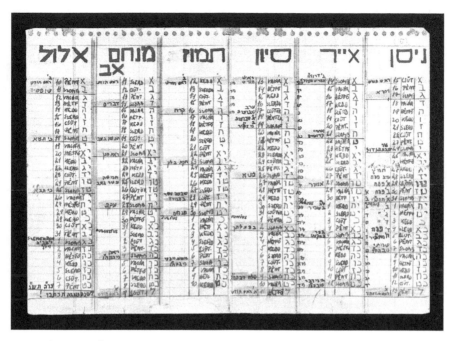

Fig. 3.3: (Continued)

enough to carry out the precepts—big and small, major and minor. The calendar joins the future to the imminent prospect of freedom.

On the other hand, the present bears down as well, a fact communicated by nothing so much as the Hungarian language that Menachem uses to refer to the days of the week—*hétfő* (Sunday), *kedd* (Monday), *szerda* (Tuesday), and so on—and to the names of the months (*január, február, március, április,* etc.). The calendar's audience was the one with whom he was transported from Budapest on the train and imprisoned in the "Hungarian camp" while in Belsen. Polish-born though he may have been, Menachem's allegiance was to his adopted Hungarian home. The calendar's language was in sync with the camp setting in which he was domiciled in the present.

Privileged as far as Bergen-Belsen prisoners went, Menachem still had to improvise when it came to finding something to write on. He resorted to lined paper with cardboard backing arranged lengthwise, which worked well enough to get the job done. His script was singular. Seventeen years old when he crafted the calendar, Neumann wrote the Jewish calendar section using block Hebrew letters. Since such letters are most often the handiwork of children, who learn to write with this script but shift to a more fluid one at a later stage, the calendar, for all of its sophistication, has a childlike character and charm.

The overall color-embellished design adds to this feeling. The names of the months, for instance, are boldly inscribed high up on the page at the top of the column, six months per page. Each month is made up of four columns, and each column is separated by a red boundary. In contrast, all Jewish holidays are shaded blue. Together, the boundaries and holidays form an almost gay checkerboard pattern of red, blue, and off-white.

The detail recorded on the checkerboard is truly astonishing. Not only are all holidays set down, but, as mentioned all fast days are as well (summer included). There is also the Omer count, the seventh day of Adar commemoration of Moses's birthday/yahrzeit, erev (eve of) Rosh Chodesh as well as Rosh Chodesh itself, and every day of the eight days of Chanukah. There are no omissions; the calendar is chock-full of significant dates and sacred times. Perhaps Menachem's industry was encouraged by the hope of full-scale observance under hospitable circumstances in whatever neutral hosting country the Kasztner group would end up in; perhaps, more soberly, it was preparing for any eventuality, for whatever might come, or not come, during the year before them. The calendar would have done its work no matter what new twist arrived on the scene.

As it turned out, the Neumann calendar partly guided observance in Bergen-Belsen, partly in conditions far more agreeable. Negotiations for release took not only the remainder of the summer but continued through the fall and into the winter. The prisoners' spirits rose and sagged in turn. News of the slated release from the camp was met with skepticism that yielded to frenetic preparations for departure. The passengers arrived in Switzerland on the twenty-first of Kislev (December 7), four days before the festival of Chanukah. Once across the border, those aboard the transport, writes Ladislaus Lob, "were received by friendly Swiss soldiers, members of the Women's Auxillary Corps and Red Cross personnel."[54] Sima Halberstam's version of events was more dramatic: "It was as if we had gone from Hell to Heaven in minutes."[55] But the calendar date of arrival in the land of freedom, the twenty-first of Kislev, continues to reverberate for many; for the Satmar Chasidim, it became a date of yearly celebration, a time of rejoicing and thanksgiving that their leader, Rabbi Yoel Teitelbaum, one of the most renowned members of the Kasztner transport, had been delivered to safety. So not only was Menachem Emil Neumann's calendar able to track time within the confines of Bergen-Belsen, but it could also mark the date of deliverance for the author, his family, and all those members of the transport whose lives had been uncannily and miraculously spared.

Surviving along with Him: Rabbi Yaakov Avigdor's Buchenwald Calendar

Wartime calendars have experienced little notoriety. Like similar artifacts, they have sometimes found their way into archives, and occasionally into museum exhibitions, but have most often remained with the authors' families. They are considered interesting as relics of the past but thought to shed little light on the circumstances of those who made or used them.

In rare instances, someone has been moved to tell their story. That is the case with Rabbi Yaakov Avigdor's Buchenwald calendar for the year 5705 (1944–45), where the history of his calendar's making has already been penned in a moving chapter written by the author's son some years after the war.[56] If any wartime Jewish calendar has been seen or heard about, Rabbi Avigdor's may be the one. But in spite of its modest fame and the story that celebrates its gestation, the calendar, like its wartime counterparts, remains a closed book, unexamined in any detail or depth. Yet when the calendar is looked at closely and viewed in relation to other wartime Jewish calendars, it reveals a special attempt to map Jewish time in a concentration camp.

Rabbi Avigdor was born in 1896 in the Galician village of Tyrawa Woloska and named after his paternal grandfather.[57] His father, Rabbi Avraham Yissachar Ber, was the town rabbi and also headed the rabbinic court. Sixty-five years old at the time of Yaakov's birth, Rabbi Avraham had already had six children from a previous marriage; Yaakov was one of three from his second wife, Rachel (née Galler).

Yaakov was educated in cheder until the age of eleven, at which point he began to study on his own. At the age of thirteen he started to compose essays for Torah journals, and, having reached a degree of maturity in his self-study, he began to travel throughout Galicia in order to listen to lectures by various renowned Torah scholars and teachers. He married at the age of eighteen and was appointed rabbi of Drohobycz at the age of twenty-four. He wrote several books and, already well-versed in secular studies, went on to obtain a doctorate. During the upheaval of World War II, he was imprisoned in the Drohobycz ghetto, and deported to concentration camps in Plaschow and Gross-Rosen and then, in late 1944, to the Buchenwald concentration camp outside of Weimar, Germany. He arrived there a "very sick man."[58]

By the time Rabbi Avigdor came to Buchenwald, the camp had already gone through a number of cruel phases. It was established in 1937, just north of the city of Weimar, in the central German region of Thuringia, some eighty kilometers southwest of Leipzig. At first, the camp incarcerated political opponents of the Nazi regime. But in 1938, some two thousand Jews were brought to Buchenwald from Austria. Following the Kristallnacht pogrom in fall 1938, another ten thousand German Jews were imprisoned in the camp, of whom six hundred were murdered; the others were released after they agreed to leave Germany.

During the war years the camp held many political prisoners, and the population grew to thirty-seven thousand in 1943 and sixty-three thousand in the beginning of 1944. The Communist prisoners formed an underground movement, which managed to sabotage work in the ammunition factories and smuggle weapons into the camp. Indeed, the Communists played a significant role in shaping prisoner life in general in Buchenwald . Yet the final phase of the camp added another wrinkle. In January 1945, in the face of the advancing Red Army, the Germans began to evacuate Auschwitz and other camps in the East. Thousands of inmates herded in death marches toward Germany ended up in Buchenwald, causing the number of inmates to swell to one hundred thousand or more. The many Jewish inmates in this group were put in the so-called small camp and in a tent camp where conditions were terrible. In early April 1945, as the American forces were close by, the Germans began to evacuate the camp, bringing about the death of between fifteen and twenty-five thousand inmates. The camp resistance managed to slow down the evacuation, and when Buchenwald was liberated on April 11, 1945, there were twenty-one thousand survivors, including four thousand Jews and one thousand children. Overall, two hundred fifty thousand prisoners passed through the camp, some fifty-six thousand of whom—including eleven thousand Jews—were murdered.

Though Rabbi Avigdor does not specify a date, he must have arrived in Buchenwald in the fall of 1944. He was imprisoned in the Plaschow labor camp in Kracow until August 1944, transferred to the Gross-Rosen camp in Germany for "a few weeks," and then shipped to Buchenwald. He was there assigned to block sixty-three. The years of imprisonment, labor, and flight had weakened him greatly, yet his well-honed disposition to carry out religious precepts to the maximum kept him moving forward. He quickly formed a Sabbath prayer quorum, at which he would lead the prayers and recite the week's Torah portion, all from memory. Composing a Jewish calendar must have been carried out in the same spirit.[59]

Even after liberation he remained in "terrible physical condition" until the task of serving as "acting chaplain" helped lead to his recovery. He thereafter assisted with the rehabilitation of former prisoners. In 1946, he immigrated to the United States, where he served as a congregational rabbi and head of a yeshiva. After a short stint in Buenos Aires, he was appointed chief rabbi of the Ashkenazi Jewish community of Mexico in 1952 and held that position until he passed away in 1967.

While Rabbi Isaac Avigdor, author of the chronicle on his father's Buchenwald calendar, was himself a survivor and thus can speak by way of experience to wartime deprivation and the spiritual responses thereto, he was not with his father in Buchenwald and hence was not a witness to the fashioning of his father's calendar. That said, Rabbi Isaac's account is still worth summarizing. The calendar making of Rabbi Yaakov Avigdor came in response to the war's devastating effect on tracking time: once the Nazis occupied Poland, writes his son, "one of the greatest ordeals was not having a luach [a calendar]. . . . In the concentration camps no one knew the day of the week except for Sunday, because there was no work then." He adds, "after 1940, no new calendars were printed."[60] Though the latter claim is inaccurate and the former needs to be qualified, what is important is that Rabbi Isaac articulates a context—a vacuum in tracking time—that his father's efforts hoped to address.

To fill the vacuum, Rav Yaakov Avigdor "took upon himself the task of creating from memory a Hebrew luach, synchronized with the dates of the general calendar. He considered this a holy duty, a mission in his role as a rabbi."[61] This role was largely pastoral. Having a calendar at the ready would allow Rabbi Avigdor to answer correctly a question about when a holiday or a fast day would occur. Even the muselman, those prisoners who were at the end of their tether, "collected strength to continue life, when told in a whisper of a forthcoming holiday, like 'tonight is Purim or Kol Nidre.'"[62] Although the information came at the eleventh hour, communicating a significant date enabled even some of the weakest prisoners to go forward. Calendar knowledge played a role in nothing less than preserving life.

One detail in particular stands out in Rabbi Isaac's account. His father did not compose a calendar a single time only. Rather, at every locale he "reconstructed" a new calendar. These repeatedly improvised calendars were confiscated and destroyed along the way. Nothing of them remains. The calendar fashioned in Buchehenwald "survived" since this camp was the final one Rabbi Yaakov was interned in before the war's end. As Rabbi Isaac evocatively puts it, when his father "became a free man, in the Spring of 1945[,] the calendar survived along with him."[63] For Rabbi Yaakov, keeping a community informed of sacred time was an ongoing necessity; fashioning a calendar to do so was a regular wartime occupation.

The features of the Buchenwald calendar's composition tell a more complicated but equally remarkable story. Using lined yellow paper—said to have been salvaged in the camp from "yellow cement sacks"—the Buchenwald calendar spans the months Tishrei to Av of the year 5705 in two pages of eight columns. The last part of the month of Av, and the final month of the year, Elul, were either not included in the original or were tabulated on a separate, now lost page (an astonishing aspect of the calendar that I comment on below). The clarity of the lettering is stunning, especially given the conditions under which it was fashioned. But despite the clarity of the script, the calendar is not designed to be read casually.

Like most, Rabbi Avigdor's calendar lists holidays, Shabbat, and the weekly Torah portion, some fast days, some Rosh Chodesh holidays, and even the special eighth day of Chanukah. The calendar is also bifocal. The Gregorian calendar date is scripted in Arabic numerals, the Jewish calendar date in Hebrew letters, and the day of the week also in Hebrew letters (aleph to zion). Two exceptional features can be noted here. First, Rabbi Avigdor referred to the days of the week

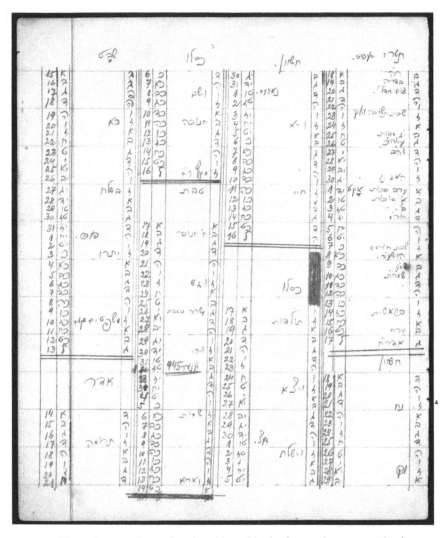

Fig. 3.4: Rabbi Yaakov Avigdor, a Chasidic rabbi and leader from Galicia, was said to have composed a Jewish calendar in every camp in which he was imprisoned, but they were all destroyed. The only one that survived was the one he fashioned for 5705 (1944–45) in the Buchenwald concentration camp. Written entirely in an elegant, clear Hebrew script, the calendar is mysteriously missing the month of Elul, the last one of the year. Courtesy of the Yad Vashem Archives.

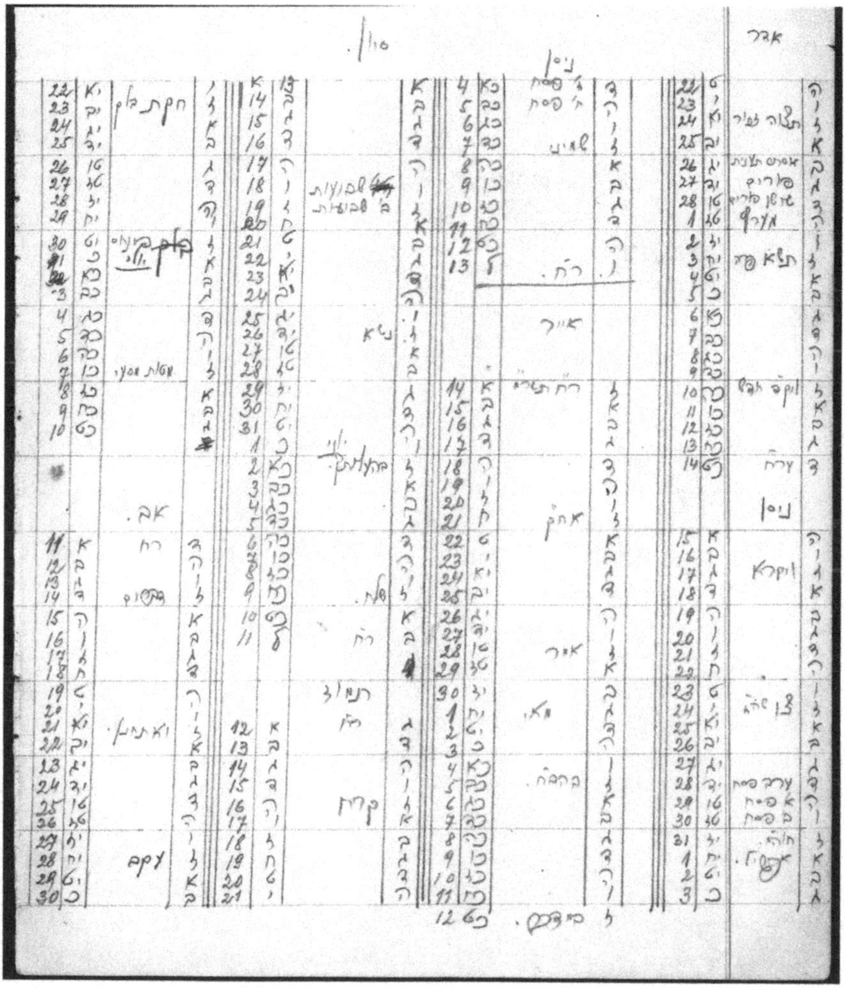

Fig. 3.4: (Continued)

only in a Jewish idiom; there is no corresponding indication of the names of the Gregorian days of the week: no Sunday, Monday, Tuesday, and so on (or, in German, no *Sontag, Montag, Dienstag*). In the Buchenwald concentration camp, ruled by forces anything but sympathetic to Jewish life and practice, the rabbi viewed the calendar as the means by which to transform the week into a Jewish nomenclature. The second point is related to the first. Unlike many, Rabbi Avigdor does not explicitly list the seventh day by its name. Rather he simply indicates it by the Hebrew letter zion, the seventh letter. In this respect, he maintains continuity with other days of the week, which are also referred to by a Hebrew letter.

This does not mean that he did not recognize the special nature of the seventh day. He likely assumed that the Shabbat Torah portion, diligently set down every seventh day, would communicate on its own the Sabbath day's special nature.

Four other distinguishing features of Rabbi Avigdor's Buchenwald calendar stand out: (1) it is written completely in Hebrew script; (2) over the course of the two-page calendar, he introduced changes in content and format; (3) inconsistencies regularly crop up; and (4) the final month and half of the year 5705 do not appear on the calendar.

(1) Most wartime Jewish calendars record the Gregorian calendar dates in the script native to the country and language. For example, most use Latin letters to write the name of the month of *Mai* (May in English); the bifocal identity thus extends to the lettering itself. Rabbi Avigdor does not proceed in this fashion. Instead, he pens virtually all elements of the calendar in Hebrew script. This uniscript approach did not issue from Rabbi Avigdor's linguistic shortcomings. He had written sophisticated articles in German and Polish and had facility in writing other languages as well. His decision must have been based on the notion that the integrity of a Jewish calendar included its being fashioned only in a Jewish script.

(2) Most wartime calendars choose a certain content and format in the first month or two and remain loyal to it throughout the remainder of the year. For example, if the calendar indicates the Sabbath Torah portion, it will continue to adhere to this pattern in the months that follow. Moreover, if in the month of Tishrei (the first month of the Jewish year) the author lists the name of the Torah portion on a Friday (rather than on a Saturday), so will the ensuing months list it the same way (no way is necessarily better; either gets the message across). Indeed, rules of consistency, parallelism, and symmetry generally guide the production of wartime calendars (and much else); the basic structural units remain regular and constant. Again, if the name of the first month of the year, Tishrei, is positioned at the top of the page, so are the names of the months that follow: Marcheshvan, Kislev, and Tevet. This way of listing the Jewish months was standard operating procedure, even for the highly irregular conditions under which wartime calendars were composed.

But Rabbi Avigdor improvised more than most. For instance, in the Buchenwald calendar he places the name of the Jewish month at the top of every column—except for the final one, the last one of the second page. It would be hard to tease out a reason for making a change at this point in the calendar. More likely, the pace at which Rabbi Avigdor was compelled to complete it made him not take notice of certain irregularities—the number of which became greater in the later part of the calendar. A more dramatic variation appears with the marking of Rosh Chodesh, the holiday-like day or days that celebrate the beginning of the new Jewish month. Sometimes it is flagged, sometimes it is forgotten, and sometimes the day before is indicated ("erev Rosh Chodesh") but not Rosh Chodesh itself! For their part, fast days are duly noted—until the summer, that is, when two of the most important are left blank. It is an omission uncannily similar to that in the anonymous *Luach Katan* calendar made in Theresienstadt. It may be that observing a fast during the long summer days was more than could legitimately be imposed upon a community suffering such privation day in, day out. As it turned out, in the case of the *Luach Katan*, covering the year 5703, the summer fast days had to be confronted, either in the Terezin camp or somewhere else at least equally arduous; in the case of Rabbi Avigdor's 5705 calendar, the European war ended a few months before the summer fast days would have arrived on the scene.

Finally, another omission in Rabbi Avigdor's calendar is more comprehensive. Not only is there no special indication of La'g B'Omer, the thirty-third day of the Omer count, on which are celebrated the cessation of a number of tragedies that afflicted ancient Jewry. But the Omer count itself, extending from the holiday of Passover until the holiday of Shavuot, receives no mention whatsoever. Its absence is curious, in that most wartime Jewish calendars referred to it and some Jews even dated events during the war according to the Omer count. For example, Rabbi Yehoshua Grünwald, in his memoir describing the final moments before liberation of the Ebensee labor camp in Austria, writes that "on the thirty-sixth day of the Omer, early in the morning, at the fifth hour, they called us to an Appel."[64] And we recall Rabbi Zelmann's adjuration to his fellow inmates to maintain the Omer count in the Westerbork camp in Holland.

But Rabbi Avigdor's calendar bears no trace of it. Perhaps its omission, along with the erratic tracking of Rosh Chodesh, conveys the difficulty in fashioning a calendar under such conditions. Clearly, Rabbi Avigdor put great effort into forging the calendar accurately; his pages of computations testify to his determination to arrange the calendar meticulously. Yet the variations, omissions, and gaps present the kind of calendar, blemishes and all, Rabbi Avigdor was compelled to fashion in Buchenwald.

This is the case even with the change in the layout of the calendar's first page as opposed to the second. On the first page, Rabbi Avigdor was careful to signal the shift to a new Jewish month (Tishrei to Cheshvan, Cheshvan to Kislev, etc.) by inserting a double-lined boundary to separate one month from the next. The thickly drawn horizontal lines stand out on the page, defining the month as the key unit. Not every month is exactly the same. The amount of space between the lines varies, and in one case the space is blackened. But while the details fluctuate, the pattern is fixed; the boundary is secure.

The double-lined boundary honors the Jewish month and is generally reserved for it alone. But in a single exception to the rule, Rabbi Avigdor uses the double-lined boundary to announce the transition to the Gregorian year of 1945. In this case, too, these year-defining lines assuredly form a boundary. But they are nonetheless drawn lighter and narrower. They also contrast with the others by not quite stretching across the column. In this way, Rabbi Avigdor has his cake and eats it too. He indeed adapts his special "underscoring" idiom to mark the transition between the Gregorian calendar years of 1944 and 1945. But the less impressive boundary makes clear that the transition from Jewish month to Jewish month is more significant than the entry of a new Gregorian calendar year.

On the calendar's second page, all of this goes by the wayside; no such boundary exists. The Jewish months follow one another in a nearly seamless flow of unbounded time. In the first column of the second page, the month of Adar modulates to the month of Nisan barely distinguished by a space; from the month of Sivan to the month of Tammuz, a line from the yellow paper (not from Rabbi Avigdor's underscoring) forms a thin boundary; in the calendar's final transition, ample space but no line separates the last day of the month of Tammuz from the first day of the month of Av. At least in terms of visually construing time's passage, the difference between the calendar's first and second pages is thus substantial. While on the surface the two pages appear to share an essential design, on another level they diverge; the special punctuation and the lines, spaces, and shading serving as visual cues are all but missing from the second page.

Certainly, the calendar's second page still tracks time much like the first does; Hebrew script still reigns, right-to-left columns still mark the succession of days, Torah portions and holidays still orchestrate the calendar's Jewish year. The appearance is not altogether deceptive. But for whatever reason— haste, the increasing pressure of obligations amid trying to survive the ordeal of Buchenwald, or, perhaps subconsciously, a change in the conception of time's movement—Rabbi Avigdor revised his calendar craft midway through his careful composition.

Another variation is more pointed in its meaning. As mentioned above, Rabbi Avigdor underscored the new Gregorian year. But the manner in which he penned the numerals of the year may have greater significance. Just over the border (which sits atop one of the horizontal paper lines), he writes "ינואר945" (945January). Missing the number "1" from "1945," the date seems to be an abbreviated form of the actual Gregorian year. The provisional quality of the calendar does not rule out that the absent "1" is simply an error, an oversight that would have been corrected if it had been noticed. Mistakes are infrequent but present. There are, for example, dates or names of weekly Torah portions entered and then etched out or written over. And at least in one case, the dates of the Jewish and Gregorian years, in side-by-side columns, were wrongly exchanged. So it may well be that the "945" is the result of a similar slip, a small and atypical lapse in an otherwise magisterial work composed with minimal resources under brutal conditions.

But that conjecture may not be on target. Rather than having committed an oversight, Rabbi Avigdor may have deliberately left out the "1," and the "945" may have never been meant to have been written "1945." He may have wanted to refrain from writing it out in full, since the number 1945 calibrates the year according to a Christian frame of reference. By abbreviating the year count as "945," the author could display the transition to the new Gregorian year while at the same time avoiding honoring its full scope and dimension. It would be a shorthand way to recognize its place on the calendar without validating the theology that underpins it.[65]

It is hard to gauge Rabbi Avigdor's specific sentiments in this regard. At no other point in the Buchenwald calendar does he invoke the Gregorian year. This restraint is not in itself conclusive. But it does suggest that he was chary in his use of the Gregorian calendar. At the very beginning of the calendar, for instance, he notes that the Gregorian month is September but does not indicate the year. Most other wartime Jewish calendars do. A memoir chronicling his wartime ordeal, which serves as the preface to his book *Chelek Yaakov* (1950), does not invoke the Gregorian calendar at all but rather dates his experiences solely by the Jewish year. Nevertheless, his writing out the Gregorian year in full is not unheard of; in the pages of computations that he used to figure out the dating of the Buchenwald calendar, there is one place (but only one) where he does cite the complete year, including the "1." That said, Rabbi Avigdor may have distinguished between a worksheet and the calendar per se; the latter would be the place where withholding the "1" would carry visible symbolic weight.[66]

It is tempting to interpret another, far more conspicuous omission in a similarly symbolic fashion. The Buchenwald calendar does not span a full year but rather ends just over a month before, on the twentieth day of the month of Av. The final ten days of this month simply don't appear on the calendar, and the whole month of Elul, the final month of the Jewish year, is absent and unaccounted for. It is as if a piece of the calendar were chipped off; the greater part remained with the author, while the broken fragment remained behind.

How can it be, one wonders, that Rabbi Yaakov took such pains with his calendar, fashioning it so scrupulously in the midst of such travail, only to run out of steam at the end? Surely there must be more to it than that. Perhaps the calendar did continue, did include the final forty days of the year, on a third page—a page which somehow became separated from the others. If this is the case, Rabbi Yaakov did not flag in his efforts to compose a calendar for the year 5705 but rather finished the job he set out to do. This is the simplest, most direct explanation to account for the missing forty days.[67]

Strangely, the calendar's assiduous chronicler, Rabbi Isaac Avigdor, makes no mention of the missing month or a lost page.[68] He presents the Buchenwald calendar as if it were whole. In truth, the oversight is not so strange, since the calendar is celebrated as an artifact that demonstrates a special form of spiritual resistance. In Rabbi Isaac's words, the Buchenwald calendar is a "historical document and spiritual testament to my father's unique resistance to the evils of that period."[69] In other words, the calendar speaks for itself; it doesn't require any special tools of investigation to unearth what it reveals about the courage and determination of a rabbi to carry on with Jewish life and observance in circumstances completely opposed and inhospitable to them. Hence, the calendar doesn't need to be looked at in detail. Such an investigation of the kind I have initiated here only makes sense once the calendar is thought of as having something specific to teach in its own right.

Seen in this light, it is possible to toy with the idea that Rabbi Yaakov *purposely* concluded the Buchenwald calendar *before the end of the year*, leaving off the end of the month of Av and the whole of the month of Elul. Two especially intriguing interpretations have been proposed to account for this unconventional strategy. The first one suggests that he didn't want to project that the plight of the Jews would continue for another full year, so by leaving out Elul, the final month of the Jewish year, he also hints that salvation—or at least the end of the war— would come before then.[70] Liberated from Buchenwald on the twenty-eighth of Nisan (April 11), the time of imprisonment turned out to be even shorter than the period he had proposed. The second interpretation is linked more directly to the themes of the month of Elul. In the lead-up to the Jewish New Year on Rosh Hashana, also referred to as the Day of Judgment, Jews are summoned to the task of introspection, a labor of self-judgment and evaluation that are intended to temper the severity of the Divine judgment. By leaving out the month of Elul, Rabbi Avigdor implied that the ordeal the Jews were being made to endure had already occasioned the kind of self-judgment that would make the month of Elul superfluous.[71]

In the final analysis, however, the Buchenwald calendar is remarkable not so much for what it leaves out as for what it includes and how it presents it. In Rabbi Avigdor's brave conception, the Hebrew script is not simply useful but central, sweeping every element into its holy grip. Even the Gregorian calendar days, months, and year are made to follow in kind, becoming players in a larger Jewish production. Fashioned in Buchenwald, Rabbi Avigdor's calendar showed that, despite or because of the conditions in which it was forged, the Jewish idiom was not to be reduced but expanded. Time would not be drained of its Jewish look, feel, and texture. It would rather be rendered more emphatically Jewish. In the end, what is left out of the Buchenwald calendar testifies to hardship; what is included intimates a world, and all calendars within that world, redeemed by Jewish time.

Tracking Jewish Time in Auschwitz

As Joseph Czarnecki's volume *Last Traces: The Lost Art of Auschwitz* shows, Auschwitz concentration camp prisoners were staunchly dedicated to composing calendars and were uncommonly resourceful in the means and materials they used to achieve that end.[72] In a section entitled "Marking Time," Czarnecki notes that "keeping track of time is a way of keeping one's sanity, one's dignity and one's sense of connectedness to the world."[73] Under this sensitive rubric, photographs then display the remnants of various sorts of calendars carved or sketched on prison block walls. Some Auschwitz prisoners carefully drew days, weeks, months, and years, while others simply used columns of dots or slashes.

But for all that *Last Traces* serves as a tribute to the unswerving determination to track time in Auschwitz, it offers no trace of *Jewish* time, either in providing examples of Jewish calendar composition in Auschwitz or in reporting on the plentiful efforts to honor Jewish time by way of observing Jewish holidays and the Sabbath, even though one may have been compelled to do so in an abridged and concealed manner. If we only had Czarnecki's volume, we would be left with the idea that Jewish calendars in particular and Jewish time in general had no currency in Auschwitz (or anywhere else, for that matter)—an oversight made more curious by the fact that the volume's introduction was penned by the celebrated Jewish author Chaim Potok.[74]

But in concept and composition, the Jewish calendar was present in Auschwitz. In this respect, Auschwitz was similar to the other camps previously discussed and, more generally, to the other wartime settings in which, as we have seen, Jews endeavored to live according to Jewish time and to fashion the means to track its progress.

Sophie Sohlberg's Jewish Calendar

Yet Auschwitz presented its own particular challenges. The largest of the concentration camps, Auschwitz was said to have been cut off from the rest of the world. Located outside of Cracow in the southwestern corner of Silesian Poland, the notorious Auschwitz complex actually consisted of three main camps. Auschwitz I (1940) incarcerated ostensible enemies of Nazi Germany; Auschwitz II, also known as Birkenau (1942), served as a site of forced labor and systematic murder; and Auschwitz III, referred to as Buna-Monowitz (fall 1942), functioned as a massive industrial complex of slave labor. Non-Jews as well as Jews were imprisoned in the camp. But the largest number who entered, and by far the highest percentage of those who perished there, were Jews.[75]

If the camp and especially its prisoners were generally cut off from the rest of the world, so were they cut off with respect to time. Prisoners were not allowed to possess the basic tools to track time, such as calendars or watches. A rigid work routine, moreover, which was in place six days a week, kept time largely undifferentiated. There was no change of routine generally or on holidays. While most work squads did not operate on Sunday, a different fixed routine took its place. All in all, the Auschwitz prisoner's day, comments one observer, was "hollow, empty, and mirthless, lacking any novelty and enveloped in everlasting gloom."[76]

Yet amid the enveloping gloom, Jewish holidays were known about, at least by a number of prisoners, and, in a fashion, observed. Indeed, some have claimed that the awareness of major Jewish holidays permeated the "hollow" atmosphere of Auschwitz, though exactly how the information about the holidays was obtained remains unclear. "Even though we [prisoners of Auschwitz] were cut off from the world," notes Rabbi Sinai Adler, "we knew the Jewish calendar."[77] More specifically, Zahava Szász Stessel recalls that Rosh Hashana was "a date that somehow all of us knew even without a calendar."[78] This knowing "even without a calendar" may have had to do with the particular inmate's religious devotion, since others report they were less cued in. "We had lost track of time," reports Anna Ornstein, "soon after we arrived in Auschwitz."[79] Yet even those who were devout often had to rely on exceptional channels of information. In rare cases, these channels included prisoners who possessed a mental command of the Jewish calendar so sweeping that they were able to alert other inmates about the onset of the Sabbath and holidays. One of these prisoners, Rabbi Itzik Mottel from the Mlawa ghetto in Poland, "had the entire Jewish calendar in his memory. Every month, if Rosh Chodesh [the beginning of the new Jewish month] was one or two days, every fast day, every festival—he had all of it in his head. How did he manage it?"[80] Though the question of how such a feat was managed goes unanswered, the writer, a former prisoner in block fourteen, not only admires Rabbi Mottel's virtuosity but also celebrates the influence such knowledge exerted on the other prisoners in his block. Other strategies for maintaining an awareness of Jewish time likely included drawing on the knowledge of recent Auschwitz arrivals, who days before had had available the means to consult a calendar, or receiving information from members of the Sonderkommandos, whose ghastly assignment gave them access to the abandoned possessions of the condemned, including calendars.[81]

Yet a few prisoners took steps to fashion a more systematic guide to counter the feeling of being cut off from Jewish time. The Jewish calendar of Sophie Sohlberg (née Loewenstein) for the year of 5705 (1944–45), written in a neat hand in what could pass for a simple school copybook, is one of two to emerge from Auschwitz. To put together such a calendar is no mean feat under the best of circumstances. To do so in Auschwitz was remarkable. That she was able to accomplish the task attests to the force of tradition, to the merits of a rigorous education and an inspired educator, and to the will to bring one to bear on the other, even or especially in the radically inhospitable circumstances of Auschwitz.

The challenge of safeguarding personal possessions made the task of fashioning and living by a calendar that much more difficult. Precious keepsakes and sacred items were constantly confiscated, lost, or stolen; as we know—and as we will pointedly see—Jewish calendars were among them. Thus, to hold on to the calendar through the ordeal of the concentration camp, the ambulatory chaos of the death march, the numerous uncertainties of postwar wandering, and the immigration to Israel proclaims the value of the calendar, the author's reliance on it, and her steadfast determination to preserve it.[82]

Biography and early education played a crucial role in providing Sophie with the requisite calendar-making skills and aptitude. Born in Munich in 1923 to Victor and Erna Loewenstein, Sophie's father worked as a head clerk in a bank and was active in Jewish community affairs. Her mother was a housewife. She had one sister, Rosa, who had married at a young age. (Eventually, Rosa and her husband, Ernst Nordheimer, were deported to Auschwitz, and she was murdered there a few weeks before Sophie arrived.)[83]

For eight years (from the age of six to fourteen), Sophie attended a Jewish primary school in Munich, where the teachers were excellent and where, as we will see, she took the lessons to heart. After her father's forced retirement from his position in 1938, the family moved to Berlin, and in the wake of Kristallnacht, the November pogrom that ravaged German Jewry, Sophie was forced to leave school. The next few years she gave over to helping her mother.

From 1941–43, she found her way to a *hachshara*, a preparatory training camp for immigration to Palestine. Located in Neuendorf im Sande, in the Brandenburg region of Germany some fifty kilometers from Berlin, the training camp proved to be an "island," in Sophie's words, strangely remote from the war, where work was mixed with the study of Jewish subjects. Originating in the 1920s, thirty-five hachsharot were distributed throughout Germany, thirteen in the area of Berlin. They initially catered to devoted Zionists but eventually broadened their membership to include those who, like Sophie, were in need of refuge. When emigration from Germany was banned in October 1941, the hachsharot were turned into forced labor camps. During 1942, the six training centers still active in the Berlin area, with some 290 residents, were gradually closed down. Neuendorf remained the last active hachshara. It served as an oasis for some eighty Jews, twenty-eight of whom formed a religious community to which Sophie belonged.[84] She worked in the kosher kitchen, slept with the three other religious girls in the main house, and enjoyed the comfort of not having to work on the Sabbath. Indeed, it was for this reason that she chose to go there.

But the oasis of Jewish life and study in wartime Germany ended with deportation to Auschwitz on the eve of Passover 5703 (April 19, 1943)—the same day that, 550 kilometers to the east, the Warsaw ghetto uprising had commenced. Some ten days earlier, the Neuendorf camp had been closed down and its residents qua prisoners shuttled to a Jewish school in Berlin. The Germans timed the actual deportation to Auschwitz to coincide with their leader's birthday on April 20. But Sophie and the other deportees, who had baked matzah while still in Neuendorf, lived according to a different calendar, conducting a Passover seder in the railway car—"an animal wagon," as she called it, "without windows."

The women's camp in Auschwitz had come into being just over a year before and was moved to Birkenau in the summer of 1942, where grueling outside labor details, abject living conditions, interminable roll calls, and selections for murder were already the common lot. Subjected on arrival on the first day of Passover to the usual initiation rites, Sophie endured several months in Birkenau battling typhus before she was transferred to the so-called Stabsgebäude laundry detail in the Auschwitz camp proper.[85] A collection of indoor prisoner details meant to provide basic services for camp administration and guards, the Stabsgebäude was a "paradise" compared with the deprivation of Birkenau. The Stabsgebäude offered not only a more or less sheltered environment with no selections and no interminable roll calls but also more food, daily washing, and other life-preserving benefits.

It was here sometime around Rosh Hashana 5704 (September 1943) that Sophie made her first calendar, according to which Jewish holidays were known and observed by the Auschwitz women with whom she lived.[86] She also composed a second calendar for the following year, 5705 (1944–45), which as it turned out tracked time in Auschwitz for only four months before Sophie, the other women in the Stabsgebäude, and most of the prisoners of Auschwitz-Birkenau were forced to leave the camp and march toward Germany. Sometime in the fall of 5705, the first calendar disappeared. Sophie had stored it in a bag that also contained some bread, and the parcel was stolen. It was never recovered. From that time forward, she kept the remaining calendar on her person at all times, including during the compulsory flight from Auschwitz in January 1945.

The "march of death" from Auschwitz was clearly a watershed. In the copy of the calendar that I was given by the author, Sophie has added a marginal note, positioned between the eighteenth and nineteenth of January, which was the night of the fifth of Tevet in the Jewish calendar, designating the time of "leaving [Auschwitz] for the march of death." Those who survived the march ended up in the Ravensbruck concentration camp for women; after a month they were taken by train to one of Ravensbruck's satellite labor camps, Neustadt-Glewe, in the north of Germany.

Inscripted Time

Today, Sophie keeps the calendar in a small box, on one side of which is nestled a small prayer book she received in Auschwitz, on the other side the calendar. The third set of items is small French flags she and her friends wore on their dresses after the war to let the Russian soldiers know they were not Germans and should be left alone.

Set down in a small ledger book, the calendar for the year 5705 moves from page to page in a left-to-right sequence, with each week occupying a single page. Three columns orchestrate the flow of the week: the first column lists the name

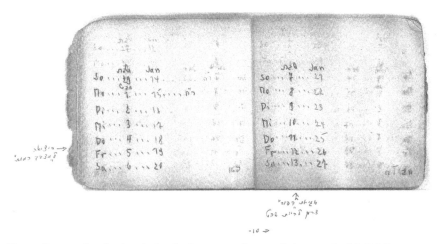

Fig. 3.5: Deported to the Auschwitz death camp at the age of nineteen, Sophie Sohlberg was assigned to one of the work details catering to the needs of the SS. Having been schooled by a master teacher in Munich in making a Jewish calendar, she composed one for 5704 (1943–44) and one for 5705 (1944–45). She was willing to run the risk of possessing a forbidden religious article so that the women she worked with would be able by consulting the calendars to observe the Jewish holidays. Courtesy of Sophie Sohlberg.

of the day (in German), the second column the Jewish date, and the third the civil date (both the Jewish and civil dates are written in Arabic numerals). Three orderly dots embellish the space between each column. The right side of the page plays its own special role. It is reserved for annotation of special days (holidays, Rosh Chodesh, fast days), always written in Hebrew lettering and sometimes also preceded by a series of carefully spaced dots. Smudge marks, the residue of computations or the blotting out of errors, form a kind of patterned background to this side of the calendar. Finally, the notation closest to the bottom of the page is the Torah portion read for every Sabbath, signifying that even in Auschwitz the cycle of the Torah should be kept in mind as faithfully as the days of the week.

A striking anecdote bears out this commitment. Sohlberg had been given a Chumash, the core of the Jewish Bible containing the Five Books of Moses, which she studied with a fellow prisoner, Irene Kunstler. Once when Kunstler was studying alone during a break in the night shift, an SS man saw her and took away the Bible. Irene was in tears when she told Sohlberg of the loss—and also related to her that she was more afraid of Sophie's reaction than of what the SS man might do to her. Sohlberg's ongoing recording of the week's Torah portion in her calendar displays the calendar's link to the Torah and to the sacred in Jewish life and experience, no matter where or when it occurs.

The Torah portion notation is also one of the few places where the calendar, composed in near isolation in Auschwitz, makes a mistake.[87] In the winter month of Adar (February in the Gregorian calendar of that year), Sohlberg joined two portions that are not among those that are combined (Terumah and Tetzave). She herself discovered this deviation only when, after the war, she attended a Sabbath synagogue service and found that according to her calendar "they [the synagogue community] were late" by one portion. However, it was not they but Sophie who, isolated in Auschwitz from a universe of Jewish time, was in error. Devoted student that she was, the faulty impulse to combine the two came, she recollects today, because her class had studied them in the same unit. Brought under a shared rubric for reasons of pedagogy, the portions of Terumah and Tetzave, Sophie cleverly but wrongly surmised, belonged together ritually as well.[88] She again added an annotation pointing out the slip on the copy that I received.

The error not only affected that specific week but threw the sequence of portions off kilter for some four months. In the late spring, just after the holiday of Shavuoth, the name of the weekly portion got back on track. By that time (May 19, 1945), the war had gratefully come to an end. In its immediate aftermath, Sophie and her companions were endeavoring to stay out of harm's way, warding off the unwanted advances of Russian soldiers while trying to reach the more benign Americans. The calendar and its resolute listing of the week's Torah portion thus continued to be of use even after the European war was over and imprisonment per se came to an end.

Once she arrived in Israel at the beginning of 5706 (fall 1945), Sophie kept the calendar with some letters and other old things. Some years later she was asked to loan the calendar to be put on exhibit at Hechal Shlomo, a Jerusalem synagogue museum that displays religious artifacts from Jewish history. She consented, on the condition that they return the calendar to her after a year—a provision which, despite friends' skepticism, the museum fulfilled. Although the exhibit curators insisted on displaying the original, they inadvertently protected the calendar from deterioration by placing it in an out-of-the-way corner, where few who viewed the exhibit likely noticed it. While some other religious institutions devoted to memorializing the Holocaust have expressed interest in obtaining the calendar or a reproduction, no copy presently exists in their archives or in that of the major Holocaust museums and repositories in the world, including in Israel.

In many respects, the Sophie Sohlberg Auschwitz calendar resembles those composed under less formidable conditions in that it contains the Jewish and Gregorian dates, records the Jewish holidays and other momentous occasions punctuating the year with meticulous, careful script, and integrates the weekly Torah portion as a crucial dimension. However, what this calendar is missing also tells a story. Almost all other Jewish wartime calendars endeavor to list the times at which the sacred days begin and end, information that is essential to proper observance of the day's protocol. The official Lodz ghetto calendar, for instance, lists the conclusion of Shabbat as 4:44 p.m. on the sixteenth of Kislev, 5705; in the Theresienstadt ghetto, Rabbi Asher Berlinger lists the time for the conclusion of Shabbat on this date as 5:00 p.m.; the anonymous child author of a Bergen-Belsen calendar notes the concluding time for this Shabbat as 5:17 p.m.

Sophie Solberg's calendar does not however include this information, both because she was unfamiliar with the technique of calculation and because, given the camp's unbending work routine, it did not even occur to her to list the times. In a comment rich in implications for reading properly wartime calendars, Solberg has thoughtfully added that since her family's Jewish calendar (some details about which I referred to in an earlier chapter) did not list the times for Shabbat and holidays *within the calendar itself* but only on a separate page, she wouldn't have been moved to record the times within the calendar. In other words, if the circumstances had encouraged setting down the times, and if she had had the requisite skill to compute them, she too would have followed suit and fashioned a separate page. Hence, the prewar conventions with which one was familiar (and, in this case, grew up with) guided wartime calendar composition. The calendar fashioned in wartime adversity not only represented an abstract set of rules but also might well have replicated prewar calendars with which the author had particular associations and attachments.[89] In any case, the fact that most other wartime Jewish calendars I have seen—whether composed in hiding or in a ghetto or camp—record these details while Solberg's does not might well also intimate the far-reaching degree of oppression met with in Auschwitz.

The Legacy of Würzburg: Teacher Julius Kissinger

Serving a community of women laboring in Auschwitz, Sophie Loewenstein's calendar also testifies to the extraordinary bond between teacher and student, without which it never would have existed. For eight years—from the age of six to fourteen—Sophie had attended the Judische Volkschule in Munich, a Jewish primary school established in 1924; it was associated with and adjacent to the Ohel Yaakov Orthodox Synagogue on the upper floors of Herzog-Rudolf Strasse 5.[90] She was one of forty children in her classroom. Among the excellent teachers, Julius Kissinger stood out. Born in Urspringen to Shimon and Babette (née Frankel), Julius had been trained at the highly regarded Jewish Teachers Seminary (Israelitische Lehrerbildunganstalt) in Würzburg and had moved to Munich in 1927 at the age of thirty-four.[91] His older brother, Ferdinand, had pursued a similar course, arriving in Munich three years earlier and also teaching at the Judische Volkschule. Teaching was in their blood, their father having pursued the same vocation. Both brothers belonged to the Agudas Israel Orthodox Jewish organization.

Julius taught Sophie in four different grades: first, second, fifth, and sixth. At some point during the fifth and sixth grades, he schooled his young students in the rules of composing a Jewish calendar. The teaching was done with depth and rigor. At no point did the students actually compose a calendar from scratch, yet it was these rules that Sophie drew on some ten years later in order to compose her two Auschwitz calendars.[92] To apply these rules under such conditions took the dedication of a superb teacher *and* the aptitude of a gifted student. Another student remembers Julius Kissinger as a fine teacher, noteworthy in terms of his ability, integrity, and fairness—showing no favoritism based on parental standing in the community—and exceptional in his understanding of the minds of his pupils during increasingly stressful times. But he does not recall the lessons in how to compose a Jewish calendar.[93]

While the Loewensteins moved to Berlin in 1938, the Kissingers—Julius, his wife, Jenny, his two sons, Albert and Manfred, and his brother, Ferdinand—remained in Munich. Both brothers had in 1940 made efforts to immigrate to the United States but were unsuccessful. Their failure left them stranded. Together with nearly a thousand other Jews from Munich, they were deported on November 20, 1941, on a train bound for Riga but diverted to Kovno, where they were murdered at the infamous Ninth Fort on November 25, 1941 (the fifth of Kislev, 5702). The Kissingers were thus no longer alive when Sophie made her calendars. Yet, in their way, the Auschwitz calendars composed by Sophie in 5704 and 5705 were the joint project of student and teacher, the vehicle through which Julius Kissinger continued to live and by which he gave others the possibility of reclaiming sacred time—even as his own time among the living had several years before been put to a cruel end.

Postwar Considerations

Sophie added another note later, this time affixed to the special day known as Lag b'Omer, the thirty-third day of the Omer count, the eighteenth day of the month of Iyar. Traditionally, the day has festive associations, either marking the end to a period of devastating plague in ancient Israel that targeted the students of Rabbi Akiva or commemorating the anniversary of the passing of the great Talmudic sage and author of the Zohar, Rabbi Shimon bar Yohai. The tie to Rabbi Shimon also links the celebration of the day to the Jewish mystical tradition

For Sophie, the date earned a special annotation because it was the day when, in late spring 1945, she and her friends heard they were free, that the Germans had retreated and left them on their own. But the end did not come easily:

> On May 1, 1945—Lag B'Omer—there was no roll call. We got nothing to eat. We heard no shooting, saw no airplanes. It was very quiet outside. We heard from somewhere that the Russians were very close. We were sitting in our barracks very hungry. All of a sudden many girls started running to the kitchen

and taking all they could find there. The SS-men on the watch started to shoot at them. It was a terrible turmoil. Ruth Carliner got a bullet in her foot. All of a sudden the shooting stopped. Our SS-men, as well as the soldiers of the camp nearby, had run away. We were free![94]

A story and then some, the understated note added to the 5705 calendar reads simply "Day of liberation." But for all the significance the moment of liberation had for Sophie and her friends (and the others who enjoyed the same on that day)—whether "We were free!" with the shout of the exclamation mark or the prosaic "Day of liberation"—the date, Lag b'Omer, had for her a special meaning that continued to unfold in the future and was already etched into the past. After the war, having immigrated to Israel, established a life as a teacher, and worked in that capacity in Jerusalem for more than a decade, she became engaged—on Lag b'Omer.

The wartime and postwar significance of the day—liberation and engagement—loops back to the prewar period: it was on this same date, Lag b'Omer, that she left her parents' house to go to the Zionist training center in Neuendorf. And, finally, it was at Neuendorf a year later, on Lag b'Omer, that her childhood braids were ceremonially cut off. The latter incident may seem much less consequential than the others. Yet it is connected for two reasons. First, the festive spirit that, in the midst of a period of sobriety and restriction, pervades the day of Lag b'Omer also makes it known as an occasion for haircutting, both ceremonial and otherwise. And second, the cutting off of her childhood braids clearly marked the occasion as an important rite of passage into adulthood—into a kind of maturity that would be an aid to cope with the ordeals she was forced to endure, including Auschwitz, in the next phase of her life.

Deft in making a wartime calendar, Sophie is similarly deft at seeing the thread tying together pivotal occasions in her life that, over and over again, took place on this date. For Sophie, the Jewish calendar was a means to track Jewish time—but also a means to view through the calendar the hand of Divine Providence at work in her life. It was no accident that a number of pivotal events should occur on the same date—and on such an auspicious date at that. It sent a message that her life was not a random string of days but rather that the days were organized by a guiding hand. That the date was already charged with auspicious associations was important as well. What had been meaningful for the Jewish people collectively was equally meaningful for her personally. One fed into the other. Having been born in an especially tumultuous time and place, her fate was bound by the calendar to that of the Jewish people at large over the course of a long history.

A Second Auschwitz Calendar

A second preserved Auschwitz calendar, remarkable in its own right for its size, its quotation of sacred passages, and the sheer audacity of its concept and execution, is more difficult to account for. Presented some years ago to the Yad

Vashem Museum Archives, the calendar is listed as having been in the possession of (and possibly composed by) the prestigious Zionist German youth leader, Ora Aloni, who (under her European name, Anneliese Borinski) endured nearly the same fate as Sophie Sohlberg: sanctuary in the Neuendorf hachshara, deportation to Birkenau/Auschwitz at Passover 5703/1943, a death march to Germany in the winter of 5705/1945, survival in postwar-ravaged Europe, and immigration to Israel. And, as might be surmised from the parallel fates they endured, the two young women knew one another, even though they hailed from different backgrounds and milieus. In this respect as well as others, the crisis into which German Jewry was plunged brought together—in Neuendorf, Auschwitz, and elsewhere—those who, had life continued as normal, would not have frequented the same social circles. But times being as they were, Sophie and Anneliese both ended up in Auschwitz's Stabsgebäude, the former laundering and the latter (who at thirty years old was some ten years older than her colleague) mending.[95] It was in this sanctuary of sorts from the cruelty and privation of Birkenau that both young women composed Jewish calendars.

That is at least as it appears on the surface. However, it seems unlikely that Anneliese composed the calendar that is listed under her name. There are several reasons to be skeptical. First, she herself was not the one to present the calendar to Yad Vashem; it was rather donated by her friend, Hilde Zimche (née Grunbaum), about whom we will hear more.[96] The museum therefore has no firsthand information from the author about the circumstances that gave rise to its composition. Moreover, Anneliese makes no mention of the calendar in her memoirs, even though she details with care the events she witnessed while in Auschwitz and the Stabsgebäude.[97] Again, a son who is familiar with the artifacts that Anneliese/Ora Aloni possessed says that he knows nothing about such a calendar.[98]

Finally, Anneliese's background and schooling do not seem to tally with the devout perspective that, as we shall see, pervasively informs the calendar. She grew up in a secular German environment where, as she candidly writes, she fraternized more with Christians than with Jews. Her Jewish education only began in the 1930s when, in the intensifying exclusion from German society that she and her fellow Jews were forced to endure, she turned to Zionism. Her about-face clearly provided her with a remedial Jewish education and a strong Jewish identity. Yet her affiliation remained secular. In contrast, the quotations cited in the calendar, while focused largely on Israel and thus bearing an affinity with the land of Israel in Zionist ideology of Israel as home for the Jewish people, are culled exclusively from religious literature. It seems unlikely that a secular Zionist would confine herself to these traditional texts. While these texts are almost all among the most popular, and thus would be easily accessible under normal conditions (though not so easily in the wholesale privation of Auschwitz), they nevertheless would be not be so well-known or seen to be pivotal to any but a religious Jew. Those who brought the calendar to Yad Vashem tried to account for this discrepancy by surmising that Borinski was aided in obtaining these quotations from religious literature by more devout colleagues. This kind of collaboration remains a possibility. But to a certain degree it begs the question, since the very project of crafting a Jewish calendar, even one as spare as the example before us, and as beset with important errors in computation and some serious shortcomings in the use of the Hebrew language—to undertake such a project in Auschwitz required a technical religious knowledge seemingly greater than that possessed by someone with Anneliese's upbringing and education. As far as we know, she did not have the privilege of studying with a Würzberg-trained master of religious precepts such as Julius Kissinger.

That said, Borinski's role may not have been negligible. Her memoir does mention her pre-Auschwitz participation in fashioning a Jewish calendar, a project undertaken together with a cadre of Zionist activists in the Neuendorf training camp: "During the night, we still worked on our calendar, which we had put together in a tiny format, with German-Hebrew dates, all major holidays, and also all of the days that were important to the [Zionist] fellowship."[99] She describes that this remarkable calendar collaboration took place just before the Neuendorf group was deported on Thursday, April 8, 1943 (Nisan 3, 5703), to Berlin, the first stage of their perilous journey. As we will see, this "tiny" calendar seems a prototype of the Auschwitz calendar in format and content. But besides the obvious fact that it comprised dates a year or two earlier, it also differs from the one composed in Auschwitz in one important respect: the Auschwitz calendar makes no reference to the "days important to the fellowship (allen Tagen, die der Chewrah wichtig sind)."[100] Unlike the Neuendorf calendar, the Auschwitz one includes no reference to anything outside of the traditional Jewish orbit. Were Borinski the author of such a calendar, it would have likely followed in the footsteps of its Neuendorf predecessor, referring not only to traditional Jewish holidays but highlighting "also all of the days that were important to the [Zionist] fellowship."

In a later, shorter Auschwitz-related memoir, Borinski does write of her participation in various religious observances en route to and once incarcerated in Auschwitz: celebrating a seder on the train on the night of deportation; joining an occasional Friday night Oneg Shabbat gathering, where songs were "softly hummed"; praying "some solemn words" in a secret Yom Kippur ceremony; and kindling a festive light in honor of Chanukah. Living within the Jewish calendar cycle was thus part and parcel of her experience in Auschwitz, even though conditions were hardly optimal and were attended by some degree of risk. But again in this later memoir she does not refer to composing or possessing a calendar.[101]

Of all the considerations, Borinski's connection to the Auschwitz calendars surfaces most clearly in two respects. First, in what might be called a symbolic bond to the Jewish calendars of Auschwitz, Borinski is curiously linked to Sophie

Sohlberg's Auschwitz calendars. For she gave Sohlberg an embroidered ledger book that was used by Sohlberg to compose her first Auschwitz calendar. The gift was presented in honor of Sohlberg's twentieth birthday, which took place just after Rosh Hashana 5704 (September 1943, some five months after their arrival in Auschwitz). Importantly, the connection here came by way of association rather than design: as far as we know (and as far as Sohlberg's tenacious memory recollects), Borinski did not specifically have in mind that the ledger book be rendered into a calendar. Nor do we know Borinski's reaction when she found out (as she must have) that this was the use to which it was put by her fellow deportee.

And second, the strongest affirmation of Borinski's authorship of the calendar comes by way of her friend, Hilde Zimche (née Grynbaum), who herself played the central role in preserving the second Auschwitz calendar. Born in Berlin in 1923, Zimche had been with Borinski first in a hachshara based near the German town of Ahrensdorf, and then afterward in Neuendorf.[102] Like the others, she was deported first to Berlin and then, on April 19, 1943, to Auschwitz. But while Borinski and Sohlberg found their way to the main Auschwitz camp and the indoor work details that kept them alive, Zimche remained in Birkenau.

Yet she too was recruited for work that helped her remain alive. Just before her arrival in April 1943, the camp administration formed a women's orchestra. Zimche joined the orchestra as a copyist. Over the next months, the orchestra's prestige grew, especially after appointing violin virtuoso Alma Rose as its director. Even after Rose's mysterious death in April 1944, the orchestra stayed together, though its prominence was diminished. At the end of October 1944, the orchestra's Jewish prisoners, including Hilde Zimche, were transported in cattle cars to Bergen-Belsen. Despite the increasingly difficult conditions they faced in Bergen-Belsen during the final phases of the war, Zimche and a number of her fellow orchestra members survived.[103]

Sometime in the fall of 5705/1944, Borinski, via a courier, was able to convey the tiny calendar (with some other special items) to her friend Hilde in Birkenau. It seems that, employing the services of male kapos, Borinski and her Stabsgebäude chaverot (i.e., her friends dating back to her Zionist youth group) tried to make it a regular practice to communicate with the other chaverot from whom each had become separated. Sending such letters or small parcels thus may have been not so unusual. But it is not clear why she sent the calendar at this time, especially when barely a month had passed of the time frame, the year 5705, that the calendar was made to cover. In any case, Zimche kept the calendar with her, secreted in a shirt pocket, through the migrations that followed to Bergen-Belsen and then, in the war's aftermath, to Israel. The question of how her friend with little religious training could compose a calendar featuring classical religious teachings occurred to Zimche as well; though she never asked her directly, she believes that Borinski was aided in this task by religious Agudah Yisrael girls.[104]

A Broken Trail of Jewish Time

The calendar resembles Sophie Sohlberg's in a number of ways. First, it too covers the Jewish year 5705 (several months into which the notorious death march took place and shortly thereafter the remaining Auschwitz prisoners were liberated). Indeed, the year is written out in Hebrew letters, ה"תשה, on the calendar's attractive cover. This, and the fact that it begins with the Jewish New Year (actually the day before, a wonderfully sensitive addition the virtue of which I will say more about below), identifies it clearly as first and foremost a *Jewish* calendar.

As with Sophie Sohlberg's calendar, Borinski's also charts the secular year, presented in German. The format in this respect is again quite similar: at the top left stands the name of the Gregorian month (beginning with *September, Oktober, November*—written out in full on virtually every page). Underneath comes a two-letter abbreviated day of the week (*So, Mo, Di, Mi, Do, Fr*); the Sabbath day earns three letters, *Sch*—and the distinction of being written according to Jewish nomenclature: *Schabbat* rather than *Samstag* (or *Sa*). To their right is the Gregorian date, written in Arabic numerals.

The name of the Jewish month, for its part, is inscribed on the top-right side of the page, and underneath it the date is written in Hebrew letters. Holidays are also designated in Hebrew script, written to the right of the dates.

Two features are notable, interdependent, and consistent with Sohlberg's. One is the calendar's very small size: two and a half by five and a half centimeters, roughly the length of an index finger to the first knuckle by the length to the second knuckle. As with many artifacts produced by Jewish camp inmates, the calendar's tiny dimensions were presumably chosen (if choice were at all available) in order to make it easier to conceal.[105] Such a strategy already guided clandestine calendar production in the somewhat less severe conditions of the Warsaw ghetto. "No holy books are printed any more," notes ghetto chronicler Rabbi Shimon Huberband. "Almost all Jewish printing houses are locked up. Printing materials, such as paper, ink, and other items, are extremely expensive, and there is a general ban on printing, due to reasons of censorship. *Only tiny, flawed calendars were secretly printed for the current year, 5702 (1941–42)*" (emphasis added).[106] What was crafted small would seemingly have a better chance of going undetected, both in the ghetto and also in Auschwitz.

The second feature follows from the first: each page presents a week, Sunday through Shabbat (*Sonntag* through *Schabbat* in the German). Given the necessarily small size of the rectangular page, a week is what could fit. (As Sophie Sohlberg has recounted in relation to fashioning her own calendars, the week format is what she could manage given what she had to work with.) That said, both authors maintain the integrity of the week even while presenting the month in installments. The week's presentation always in full ensures that Jewish time,

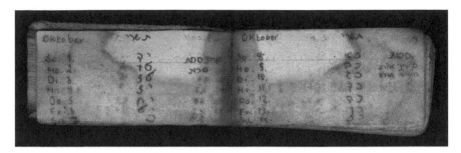

Fig. 3.6: German-born Anneliese Borinski (a.k.a. Ora Aloni) was assigned to a similar Auschwitz work detail as that of Sophie Sohlberg. She too produced a unique Hebrew/German Jewish calendar for the year 5705 (1944–45), embellished with psalms and excerpts from Pirkei Avot (Ethics of the Fathers). While the Jewish calendar enigmatically breaks off midstream, the teachings continue to set forth the vision of a redeemed Jerusalem. Courtesy of Yad Vashem Museum.

fundamentally oriented by the weekly Sabbath, remains intact, visualizing wholeness even while those prisoners observing it in the breach were forced to suffer its abridgment.

Several points are relevant to the Borinski calendar's designation of the holidays. First, as mentioned above, the calendar begins not with Rosh Hashana, the Jewish New Year, 5705, but with the day before, a Sunday. It is described simply but honorifically as "Erev Rosh Hashana," the eve of the holiday. Indeed, as with most other festivals, the day that precedes the Jewish New Year has its own significance and a retinue of customs to give it expression. Honoring the day preceding Rosh Hashana with its own designation thus has a firm basis in the Jewish liturgical calendar. In this case, however, not only does the eve of the holiday serve as a lead-in to the festival, but it also (in contrast for example to the opening days in the Sohlberg calendar) allows for the first day of the first week—a Sunday or Sonntag—to merit a purposeful place in the scheme of the calendar. From the outset, then, Borinski's calendar resourcefully maintained the integrity of the Jewish week.

Moreover, that specific "eve of Rosh Hashana" of 5705 had a particularly fraught context. It is not known when the Borinski calendar was actually composed and thus when the first day, the eve of Rosh Hashanah, was set down: before, after, or on the day itself? But Auschwitz memoirs depict the charged atmosphere that surrounded the day: "The summer was coming to an end," writes Elie Wiesel in a well-known set of recollections. "The Jewish year was almost over. On the eve of Rosh Hashana, the last day of that cursed year, the entire camp was agitated and every one of us felt the tension. After all, this was a day unlike all others. The last day of the year. The word 'last' had an odd ring to it. What if it really were the last day?"[107] Wiesel's remarkable homage to the "eve of Rosh Hashana" (5705/1944) actually complements its role as set forth in the Borinski Auschwitz calendar. For Wiesel, the focus is on the end, the "last day of the cursed year." For the calendar, the focus is on the beginning: last though the day may have been, it here launches the year to come—a year that indeed witnessed the liberation of Auschwitz but also the terrible loss of life in the final months of the camp's existence.[108]

Given this sensitive designation of the "eve of Rosh Hashana," it is striking that, in Borinski's tiny calendar, few holidays (or the special days associated with them) receive the explicit mention they do in most of the other wartime calendars, including that of Sophie Sohlberg. Borinski's calendar refers neither to "Hoshana Raba," the seventh day of the festival of Sukkoth, which is distinguished by its own array of practices and customs, nor to "Rosh Chodesh," the festive day or days that inaugurate every new month. This is a calendar with no frills. The reasons behind such an approach are likely multiple. One is reminded of Emanuel Ringelblum's description of the kind of spare writing that set the standard in the Warsaw ghetto: "Every redundant word, every literary gilding or ornamentation grated upon our ears and provoked our anger. Jewish life in wartime is so full of tragedy that it is unnecessary to embellish it with one superfluous line."[109] If such a response to tragedy was the case in the Warsaw ghetto, how much more so in the Auschwitz concentration camp.

Yet what may have been a stylistic preference in ghetto chronicles was presumably close to a necessity when composing a calendar in Auschwitz, where the materials that could help guide the proper form and substance of a Jewish calendar were in the main nonexistent. A number of errors in the calendar's composition bring home this point forcefully. First, two months into the year the calendar gets off track: the beginning of the month of Kislev (the month in which the holiday of Chanukah occurs) is placed on a Thursday (November 16) instead of a Friday (November 17). The mistake occurred because the previous month was thought to have twenty-nine days when it actually had 30. From this point on, the Jewish date is out of sync with the day of the week. Thus Chanukah is recorded as beginning place on a Sunday when in truth it commenced on a Monday.

The Borinski calendar authors thus erred when dealing with one of the crucial aspects of Jewish calendar composition. The regular Jewish (lunar-based) year has 354 days. In certain years, however, the count may be one day less or one day more. The year 5705 (1944–45)—the year of the Sohlberg and Borinski Auschwitz calendars—contained one day more, added to the second month of the year, Marcheshvan, for a total of 355 days. The author of the Borinski Auschwitz calendar was not aware of the added day. To lack such knowledge in the midst of Auschwitz is not surprising; though Sophie Sohlberg got it right in her first Auschwitz calendar, she says she does not recall how she knew. She too erred in the second, throwing the count off by a day until a "postcard from somebody 'outside'" bearing both dates somehow found its way into the Stabsgebäude, revealing Sophie's error and prompting her to redo the month in question.[110]

In hindsight, Borinski's error may be symbolically revealing. Thrown off track, the Borinski calendar captures a sense of the warping power of Auschwitz, where, as depicted in this calendar, Jewish time was a day out of sync. From this vantage point, the isolation and deprivation of Auschwitz—the experience of being "cut off from the world"—could not stop the effort to chart Jewish time. But it could deflect it off course.

Other inconsistencies also reflect the difficult conditions under which the Borinski calendar was composed. Both the Jewish and Gregorian dating does not proceed in a normal fashion. The Jewish calendar's aberration is much more conspicuous and radical: the dating ends a quarter of the way in, with the first day of Chanukah, on page 17. From that point forward, over the course of the remaining fifty-four pages, the column listing the Jewish calendar dates, written in Hebrew script, disappears. So does the name of the Jewish month, likewise scripted in Hebrew, under which on each page the column was written. Hence any trace of the Jewish calendar strangely evaporates. The calendar per se continues, registering column after column, month after month of Gregorian dates, the progression seemingly unfazed by the disappearance of its Jewish counterpart. In hindsight, the calendar's breakdown might be read as an unnerving parable of the events unfolding across Europe: like the Hebrew-scripted dates in the column of the calendar, the Jews, too, increasingly disappear from the European landscape. In this respect, it parallels Moshe Flinker's wartime diary entry allegorically describing the disappearance of Jews from Europe's cities and towns: "It is like being in a great hall where many people are joyful and dancing and also where there are a few people who are not happy and who are not dancing. And from time to time a few people of this latter kind are taken away, led to another room, and strangled. The happy dancing people in the hall do not feel this at all. Rather, it seems as if this adds to their joy and doubles their happiness."[111] Like many of the Jews who disappeared, Flinker himself was eventually deported to Auschwitz and perished there, not long before this calendar and its vanishing column of Jewish dates were scripted.

But the author's decision to leave off with the Jewish dating (or her inability to continue it) likely came from other considerations. It may have been that, despite the fact that the calendar is oriented by the beginning of the Jewish year, the author actually wrote out the Gregorian calendar first and only later began to fill in the Jewish dates. One might be tempted to think that these dates were entered day by day or week by week. But Borinski sent the calendar to her friend Hilde Zimche in Birkenau sometime before the latter's deportation to Bergen-Belsen on November 1, 1944—which falls in the middle of the month of Marcheshvan, some six weeks before Chanukah. So the hypothesis that the Jewish calendar was filled in on a daily or weekly basis doesn't stand up. The author either chose or was compelled to make the first day of Chanukah the final one in the calendar's Jewish dating. Such a date carries of course its own symbolic force. The holiday of Chanukah commemorates the victory of the weaker Jewish army over the mighty Syrian one in ancient Israel and the miraculous triumph of Jewish spirituality in the face of the corrosive power of ancient Greek culture.[112] And in this vein, testimony tells about the moving observance of Chanukah in the concentration camps, including in Auschwitz/Birkenau, which often was inspired by the ancient example.[113] That said, we are left uncertain whether the breaking off with the Jewish dating was a gesture meant to invoke these associations, especially since the calendar acknowledges only a single day of the eight-day festival. Whatever symbolic power resided in reference to a single day would have been intensified by specifying all eight.[114]

If the Jewish dating ends prematurely, the Gregorian dating continues beyond what one might expect. We recall that the calendar was framed according to the Jewish year and thus began the day before Rosh Hashana 5705. We would then presume that the calendar would end at the same point a year later—which corresponded to September 7, 1945. But the Gregorian dating does not stop at the point one might expect. Rather, it concludes only on September 29, 1945 (p. 68), some three weeks after the start of the new Jewish year. So despite the fact that the Jewish dating guided the calendar at the outset, and despite the fact that the passages in Hebrew from Jewish religious literature continued to proclaim its Jewish character, Jewish time no longer defined the calendar's conception of a year.

Indeed, the tracking of Jewish time in the case of this calendar is two sided. On the one hand, we see a profound effort to produce a Jewish calendar by means of a Jewish idiom. But the artifact that remains reveals a lack of resources to carry out the task fully. This lack of resources comes again to the fore in the inaccurate Hebrew spelling of key expressions. This is the case from the outset: the first recorded day in the Jewish calendar is penned as ארב רוש השנה instead of ערב ראש. The spelling inaccuracies continue: קול נידרי instead of כל נדרי; סכות instead of סוכות; שמיני אצרת instead of עצרת; סמחת תורה instead of שמחת; and, finally, the third month of the year is written as כסלב instead of כסלו. The errors show an author with a rudimentary knowledge of Hebrew trying to cope, seemingly unaided, with penning the basic terms for the holidays. For our purposes, such consistent spelling mistakes suggest that the author was someone relatively unschooled in Hebrew.

The errors also stand out in two other respects. First, none of the other wartime Jewish calendars that I have reviewed are beset by spelling errors of this kind. As one might suspect, those who took up the challenge of composing Jewish calendars under these conditions were literate in the language and terminology of Jewish tradition. This calendar is the exception to the rule. And second, the passages culled from the traditional religious literature regularly interspersed in the calendar, as we shall soon see, do not suffer from the same spate of inaccurate spellings. This discrepancy can lead us to think in two directions. In the case of the religious passages, this author with weak spelling ability may have had the sources at hand (by way of a prayer book, for example) so that she could have copied the text. Spelling would then have been a negligible issue. Another possibility is that the passages were the work of an author different from that of the Jewish calendar per se. The calendar would then be a collaborative product (a view set forth by the calendar's recipient, Hilde Zimche). If so, an obvious question would be why the partner would not have looked at and corrected the spate of misspellings?

Fashioning a Future

Although the exact relation between the composition of the calendar and the text that complements it remains unclear, the religious passages offer a distinctive, even singular, contribution. When viewed as a whole, moreover, they together make this calendar the most thematically centered of any of the wartime calendars that I have reviewed, ardently bringing forth the message of the Jews' return to Jerusalem and the land of Israel. And even though it is one of the smallest of the wartime calendars, it develops the theme of return to the Holy Land by way of a generous allotment of quoted text: fifteen passages from the prayer book, the Torah, and rabbinic literature. Each passage is given its own page; the concluding one, which includes most of Psalm 126, is spread out over three pages. The first page sounds this note of return by invoking one of the theme's most famous passages: "l'shana haba'a b'yerushalayim" (next year in Jerusalem), a sentiment that would have had particular force when voiced in Auschwitz in 5705/1944. The final lyrical statement of Psalm 126 provides the calendar's closing words: "those who sow in tears will reap with songs of joy / He goes along weeping, carrying the bag of seed; he will surely return with songs of joy, carrying his sheaves."[115]

In between, the theme of return to the Holy Land unfolds step by step. From the morning prayer, the words of the prophet Tzefaniah declaim the promise, "At that time I will bring you and at that time I will gather you in" (p. 6 and again in a German translation on p. 11; Tzefaniah 3:20). The "bring[ing]" and "gather[ing]" will come at the appropriate moment, surmounting the struggles of exile and oppression. The latter is the message of the theme's next installment: "Oh, sanctuary of the king, royal city / Arise and depart from amid the upheaval, / Too long have you dwelled in the valley of weeping. / He will shower compassion upon you" (p. 31).[116] Culled from the sixteenth-century poem celebrating the onset of Shabbat on Friday night, the encouraging stanza calls on the "royal city" of Jerusalem (and, by extension, the people Israel) to get ready to leave exile, attended by God's interest and solace. Further passages convey that the temporary hardship of exile will surely give way to an eternal sojourn in the Holy Land: "And I will give to you and to your offspring after you the land of your sojourns—the whole of the land of Canaan—as an everlasting possession" (p. 36; Bereshit/Genesis 17:8). God's undisputed dominion provides the basis for an enduring home: "And the land shall not be sold for ever, for the land is Mine" (p. 46; Vayikrah/Leviticus 25:23).

Traditional teachings that articulate the miraculous nature of Jerusalem complement the promise of return: "Neither serpent nor scorpion ever caused injury in Jerusalem" (p. 51; Pirkei Avot 5:7). Protection from evil creatures is followed by reference to the unwavering policy of hospitable shelter: "Nor did any man say to his fellow, 'the space is insufficient for me to stay overnight in Jerusalem'" (p. 56; Pirkei Avot 5:7). Such a vision of civility must have run directly counter to the wartime conditions in which the author found herself. In this sense, ancient Jerusalem's beneficence stands as the antithesis to Auschwitz's violation of all codes of protection and hospitality. The vision of once again dwelling in a beneficent Jewish homeland climaxes in the calendar's closing words: "he will surely return with songs of joy" (p. 71; Psalm 126:6).

The focus on Zion was not a necessary outcome of trying to cope with wartime travail. For some who were confronting the mayhem head-on, the psalm bore within it a message consonant with times of upheaval. In the summer, Tammuz 5703 (1943), Elchanan Emanuel, a teenager writing from occupied Holland days before his family's arrest and imprisonment in Westerbork, gave a stirring interpretation of Psalm 126:

> It is written, "Those who sow in tears will reap in joyous song." (Tehillim 126:5). One does not sow seeds during the summer months, but rather in the season of rain and storm . Indeed, it is impossible to conceive of a fruitful harvest where there had been no rain and wind. A farmer must venture forth into the fields during the height of the storm season and endure the rain in order to sow his seeds. He knows that he must do so in order to reap a bountiful crop.
>
> So too, our nation's most opportune time to sow its seeds has been in the midst of dreadful persecution. Let us remember the great sages of Israel who lived in the very generation that saw the destruction of the Second Temple—Torah luminaries such as Rabbi Yochanan ben Zakkai and Rabbi Akiva, who made Judaism blossom by risking their own lives. Let us remember Rashi and his disciples, who succeeded in their most crucial contributions in the dark shadows of the Crusades.

He had been teaching the Psalms as understood by the classic Jewish commentators to the children of the family of another Dutch Jewish family by the name of Kaiser. Emanuel apparently hoped to continue the lessons by correspondence. The unfinished letter somehow reached the Kaisers, who were in hiding.[117]

For the authors of the Borinski calendar, the psalm gives the closing words to a series of inspired verses promising return to the homeland. Yet the sowing of seeds in times of dreadful persecution may well have characterized the present reality for those in Auschwitz no less than those biding their time in occupied Holland. In such a light, the return to the homeland and the redemption it bespoke could only have been that much more yearned for.

This enigmatic calendar—crafted in Auschwitz, conveyed to Birkenau, secreted in Bergen-Belsen—thus pulls in two opposite directions. On the one hand, it breaks off suddenly, precipitously, bringing to an unnerving end its goal of fashioning a day-by-day record of Jewish time in Auschwitz. What was begun so emphatically leaves off mysteriously, at precisely the moment—the first day of Chanukah—when sanctity was, by way of rededication of the Jerusalem Temple, miraculously restored to the ancient Jewish world. All that is left on the calendar is the emptiness of the column meant for the Hebrew-lettered scripting of Jewish dates and the festivals they periodically refer to.

Yet there is another side. From this vantage point, Jewish time does not dissolve but rather takes on a symbolic shape. The evocative religious passages filled with yearning gather momentum as the calendar unfolds, articulating a message of return to an eternal homeland. These passages not only continue at regular intervals. Undeterred by the breakdown of time and future in the recorded dates, they fashion a future of their own, projecting a time to come when exile will end and the return home will begin. The past, too, plays a vital role in scripting a future, since the passages hail from the ancient world and, drawing on the words of the prophet Tzefaniah and others, bring forth a promise of what will be—what will be when the cruel confines of the Auschwitz concentration camp in 1944–45 will be replaced by the welcoming song of a redeemed Jerusalem.[118]

Clearly, we can in this case only conjecture. This approach, however necessary in order to tease out the many rich threads of meaning latent in the Borinski calendar, stands in sharp contrast to Sohlberg's, where the abiding presence of the author guides and disciplines any and all speculation. In the latter case, the calendar not only tracks time but also reveals the process of transmission from teacher to student, answering by means of it the question of how such a calendar could have come into being in the first place.

Notes

1. The statement derives from Dinur's testimony at the Eichmann trial (June 7, 1961 / Sivan 23, 5721). It is part of a somewhat longer reflection on his experience of time in Auschwitz: "This is a chronicle of the planet of Auschwitz. I was there for about two years. Time there was not like it is here on earth. Every fraction of a minute there passed

on a different scale of time." *The Nizkor Project: The Trial of Adolf Eichmann*, session sixty-eight. http://www.nizkor.org/hweb/people/e/eichmann-adolf/transcripts/Sessions /Session-068-01.html.

2. Charlotte Delbo, *None of Us Will Return*, trans. John Githens (Boston: Beacon, 1968). Delbo wrote the memoir shortly after the war's end and published an excerpt. But she waited some two decades before publishing the remainder of the memoir. Her final book, *Days and Memory* (2001), similarly omits almost all reference to specific calendar dates.

3. Delbo, *None of Us Will Return*, p. 105. I am indebted to David Roskies for his comments on Delbo's manner of dealing with time and calendar.

4. Overviews include Yisrael Gutman and Adi Saf, eds., *The Nazi Concentration Camp* (Jerusalem: Yad Vashem, 1984); and, more recently, Nikolaus Wachsmann, *KL: A History of the Nazi Concentration Camps* (London: Little, Brown, 2015); Kim Wünschmann, *Before Auschwitz: Jewish Prisoners in the Prewar Concentration Camps* (Cambridge, Mass: Harvard University Press, 2015).

5. Viktor Frankl, *Ein Psycholog erlebt des Konzentrationslager* (Vienna: Verlag für Jugend und Volk, 1946); *From Death-Camp to Existentialism: A Psychiatrist's Path to a New Therapy*, trans. Ilse Lasch, preface Gordon W. Allport (Boston: Beacon, 1959), *Man's Search for Meaning: An Introduction to Logotherapy*, trans. Ilse Lasch, preface Gordon W. Allport (Boston: Beacon, 1963).

6. Yisrael Gutman, "Social Stratification in the Concentration Camps," in *The Nazi Concentration Camps*, eds. Yisrael Gutman and Avital Saf (Jerusalem: Yad Vashem, 1984), p. 155.

7. *Man's Search for Meaning* (New York: Simon and Schuster, 1977), p. 70.

8. Ibid, p. 71.

9. Ibid, pp. 74–75.

10. One classic formulation: "Rabbi Shmuel bar Nachmani said in the name of Rabbi Yonaton, 'May the bones of those who calculate the end be blasted away. People will say, "Since the fixed time for his coming has arrived, and yet he has not come, he will never come." But we must wait for him, as it is written [in Habakkuk 2:3], "Though he tarries, wait for him; [for he will certainly come, he will not delay]"'" (Talmud Bavli, *Sanhedrin* 97b).

11. Rabbi Yissachar Frand, "Determining the Date of the Messiah's Arrival," Yad Yechiel, audiotape 487.

12. Frankl, p. 76.

13. Ibid., p. 134.

14. Ibid., p. 114–15.

15. Ibid., pp. 114–15.

16. Ibid., p. 121.

17. Ibid.

18. Wolfgang Sofsky, *The Order of Terror: The Concentration Camp*, trans. William Templar (Princeton: Princeton University Press, 1997).

19. Eugen Kogon, *The Theory and Practice of Hell* (New York: Berkeley, 1980), p. 77.

20. Ibid., p. 84.

21. Sofsky, pp. 86–87.

22. Omer Bartov, *Germany's War and the Holocaust: Disputed Histories* (Ithaca: Cornell University Press, 2003), pp, 109–110.

23. Sofsky, p. 89

24. Ibid., p. 93.

25. Ibid., p. 109.

26. Ibid., p. 93.

27. Anne Frank, *The Diary of a Young Girl*, trans. B. M. Mooyaart-Doubleday (New York: Pocket, 1965), p. 34. The entry is dated October 9, 1942.

28. Jacob Presser, *Ashes in the Wind: The Destruction of Dutch Jewry*, trans. Arnold Pomerans (Detroit: Wayne State, 1988); Jacob Boas, *Boulevard des Miseres: The Story of Transit Camp Westerbork* (Hamden, CT: Archon Books, 1985); *Pinkas ha-kehilot: Holland*, eds. Yosef Mikhman, Hartokh Bim, and Dan Mikhman (Jerusalem: Yad Vashem, 1985); and more recently, Bernard Wasserstein, *The Ambiguity of Virtue* (Cambridge, MA: Harvard University Press, 2014). Important memoirs include Philip Mechanicus, *Year of Fear*, trans. Irene S. Gibbons (New York: Hawthorne, 1968), and, from a Jewish religious vantage point, Yona Emanuel, *Dignity to Survive: One Family's Story of Faith in the Holocaust* (Southfield, MI: Targum, 1998). For wartime witnesses, see Mirjam Bolle, *Letters Never Sent: Amsterdam, Westerbork, Bergen-Belsen* (Jerusalem: Yad Vashem, 2014). On the uneven historiography concerning Dutch Jewry during the Holocaust, see Dan Michman, "The Place of the Holocaust of Dutch Jewry in a Wider Historical Fabric: Approaches of Non-Dutch Historians," in *Dutch Jews as Perceived by Themselves and Others*, eds. Chaya Brasz and Yosef Kaplan (Leiden: Brill, 2001).

29. Rabbi Zelmann's daughter, Yehudis Eichenthal, kindly showed me the Chumash with the dated inscription.

30. I originally found Rabbi Zelmann's calendar in the archives of the Ghetto Fighters' Museum (GFM). At the time I did not know, however, that it was his, since the GFM copy of the calendar was missing the title page bearing his name. See file Holland 6/11396.

31. Thomas Rahe, "Jewish Religious Life in the Concentration Camp Bergen-Belsen," in *Belsen in History and Memory*, eds. David Cesarani et al. (London: Cass, 1997), p. 91.

32. Yitshak Alfasi, *Gur: Toldot hasidut Gur*, 2nd ed. (Tel Aviv, 1978); Avraham Yitshak Bromberg, *The Rebbes of Ger: Sfas Emes and Imrei Emes* (Brooklyn: Mesorah, 1987). For a wartime description of Ger circa 1939, see Rabbi Shimon Huberband, *Kiddush Hashem*, pp. 235–37.

33. These included 139 from Warsaw, 108 from Lodz, 86 from Kracow, and 13 from Lublin. Email communication, related documents, and phone interview, Guido Abuys, Westerbork archivist, March 24, 2014.

34. For a classic statement of this belief, see Rabbi Shneur Zalman of Liadi, *Iggeret Hakodesh*, #27, in a letter sent to comfort the Israel-based followers of Rabbi Menachem Mendel of Vitebsk in the aftermath of his passing.

35. Both Asscher's biography and a number of the remarkable Bergen-Belsen sketches appear in Emanuel, *Dignity to Survive*.

36. See Chaya Brasz, *Transport 222* (Jerusalem, 1994); and A. N. Oppenheim, *The Chosen People: The Story of the '222 Transport' from Bergen-Belsen to Palestine* (London: Vallentine Mitchell, 1996).

37. In January 1945, Herbert Kruskal completed in German a memoir of his wartime experience, entitled *Two Years behind Barbed Wire*. An English translation prepared by him some six months later is archived at the Ghetto Fighters' Museum, Holland 73/11552.

38. The private archive was inherited by Rabbi Moshe Kruskal of Jerusalem, the youngest of the three Kruskal children to make it through the wartime ordeal. I am grateful for his sharing the materials with me and commenting on the collection.

39. My translation from the Hebrew original.

40. Rabbi Joseph Polak, Chief Justice, Rabbinical Court of Massachusetts, after viewing the calendar circa 2013.

41. Emanuel, *Dignity to Survive*, p. 150.

42. Ghetto Fighters' Museum Archive, Holland, 1697.

43. See Cecil Law, *Kamp Westerbork, Transit Camp to Eternity: The Liberation Story* (Clementsport, NS: Canadian Peacekeeping Press, 2000); Aad van As, *In the Lion's Den* (Dutch; 2004), pp. 91–98; and the seven eyewitness accounts at *The Holocaust—Lest We Forget: Camp Westerbork Liberation*, http://www.holocaust-lestweforget.com/camp -westerbork-liberation.html.

44. "The Summer of 1945," http://www.kampwesterbork.nl/en/geschiedenis /interneringskamp/de-zomer-van-1945/index.html#/index.

45. On Rabbi Zelmann's continuing inspiration during his tenure in Bergen-Belsen, see Rahe, "Jewish Religious Life in the Concentration Camp Bergen-Belsen," pp. 90, 105; fellow Belsen prisoner Abel Herzberg referred to him as "Rabbi S," apparently using the alternative spelling of "Selmann." *Between Two Streams: A Diary from Bergen-Belsen*, trans. Jack Santcross (London: Tauris, 1997), pp. 102–103. The Hebrew/Yiddish spelling used by the calendar's author is זעלמאן, which may be transliterated as *Zelmann* with a Z. This is also the spelling used on the Westerbork registration or information form.

46. David Cesarani et al., eds., *Belsen in History and Memory* (London: Cass, 1997); Suzanne Bardgett and David Cesarani, eds., *Belsen 1945: New Historical Perspectives* (Portland, OR: Vallentine Mitchell, 2006).

47. On the Star Camp, see, in addition to the general works on Bergen-Belsen cited previously, Eberhard Kolb, *Bergen-Belsen: Von Aufenthaltslager zum Konzentration Lager, 1943–45*; and the website of the former Westerbork Camp: http://www.kampwesterbork.nl/nl /jodenvervolging/het-oosten/bergen-belsen/index.html#/index.
Diaries of Star Camp prisoners include those of Loden Vogel (Louis Tas), *Dagboek uit een kamp*; Renate Laqueur, *Dagboek uit Bergen-Belsen maart 1944–April 1945* (the German translation was published in Hannover in 1983 under the title *Bergen-Belsen-Tagebuch 1944/1945*); Abel Herzberg, *Between Two Streams*; and Simon Heinrich Herrmann (one of the 222 Jews who, along with the Kruskals, were sent from Bergen-Belsen to Palestine in June 1944), *Austauschlager Bergen-Belsen* (Tel-Aviv, 1944).

48. Randolph Braham, *The Politics of Genocide* (New York: Columbia University Press, 1981); Randolph Braham and Brewster Chamberlin, *The Holocaust in Hungary Sixty Years Later* (Boulder: City University of New York Graduate Center and USHMM, 2006).

49. Israel Kasztner, *The Kasztner Report : The Report of the Budapest Jewish Rescue Committee, 1942–1945*, edited by László Karsai and Judit Molnár (Jerusalem: Yad Vashem 2013); Anna Porter, *Kasztner's Train: The True Story of Reszo Kasztner, Unknown Hero of the Holocaust* (Vancouver: Douglas and MacIntyre, 2007); Ladislaus Löb, *Dealing with Satan: Reszo Kasztner's Daring Rescue Mission* (London: Jonathan Cape, 2008); Szabolcs Szita, *Trading in Lives? Operations of the Jewish Relief and Rescue Committee in Budapest, 1944–1945* (Budapest and New York: Central European University Press, 2005); and Yehuda Bauer, *Jews for Sale? Nazi-Jewish Negotiations, 1933–45* (New Haven: Yale University Press, 1994). On the social make-up and relations of the group in Bergen-Belsen, see Thomas Rahe, "Die 'Kasztner-Gruppe' im Konzentrationslager Bergen-Belsen: soziale Struktur, Lebensbedingungen und Verhaltensformen," in *Bergen-Belsen-Neue Forschungen*, eds. Habbo Knoch und Thomas Rahe (Göttingen: Wallstein Verlag, 2014). For the viewpoints of

religious Jews who were members of the transport, see Esther Shulamis Bleier, *The Life and Times of Rabbi Yonason Steif: Living in the Illuminated Shadow* (Jerusalem and New York: Feldheim, 2009); and Rabbi Nachman Seltzer, *Heaven's Tears: Sima Halberstam Preiser's Journey to Life* (Brooklyn: Shaar, 2013). The latter biography, though moving and evocative, must be treated with caution with regard to the facts of the transport, since there are some conspicuous errors. For helpful comments on religious life in the Hungarian camp, see also Rahe, "Jewish Religious Life in the Concentration Camp Bergen-Belsen," who regularly notes how the Hungarian camp enjoyed exceptional privileges in terms of religious observance, and Löb, pp. 147–52, in a section entitled simply "Religion."

50. I am indebted to Yad Vashem archivist Emmanuelle Moscovitz, who supplied much of the information on Menachem Emil Neumann and copies of the documentation from which the information is culled, as well as forwarded scans of the calendar itself.

51. "The train," writes Esther Shulamis Bleir of the time of the group's arrival, "traveled through Germany until we arrived at a railhead near Hanover, the stop for the concentration camp Bergen-Belsen. It was Sunday morning, July 9, 1944—*shiva asar b'Tammuz* [the seventeenth day of the month of Tammuz; author's emphasis]." *The Life and Times of Rabbi Yonoson Steif*, p. 83. The date was actually the eighteenth of Tammuz. But because the conventional date of the fast fell on the previous day, a Sabbath, when fasting is not conducive to the enjoyment of the day's expansive menu of spiritual and material pleasures, the fast was moved to the following day. Though Esther Steir is factually mistaken, she is correct in attributing to the date of arrival the observance of the seasonal fast day. Rabbi Chaim Moshe Stauber's account of another member of the transport, the Satmar Rebbe, also refers to the arrival in Bergen-Belsen as taking place on "Shiv'ah Asar b'Tammuz," the seventeenth rather than the eighteenth day of the month. See *The Satmar Rebbe: The Life and Times of Rav Yoel Teitelbaum* (New York: Feldheim, 2011), pp. 110, 344.

52. The prayers can be viewed at the Yad Vashem website honoring Menachem Neumann's contributions: http://www.yadvashem.org/yv/en/exhibitions/rosh_hashana/jewish_calendar_bergen-belsen.asp.

53. Sudy Rosengarten, "Yom Tov in the Basunderlager [the Hungarian camp] in Bergen-Belsen," *The Jewish Observer* 36:8 (Tishrei 5764 / October 2003), pp. 36–38. The article relates the recollections of Kasztner transport passenger Rutie (née Bernfeld) Glick.

54. Löb, *Dealing with Satan*, p. 205.

55. Seltzer, *Heaven's Tears*, p. 154.

56. Rabbi Isaac Avigdor, "The Camp Calendar of Buchenwald," *Faith after the Flames* (New Haven: Rodgiva, 2005). Another article in the same volume, "Religious Observances in Buchenwald," deals in part with the calendar. A black-and-white reproduction of the calendar is included in the book. The original copy is archived at Yad Vashem: Yad Vashem Archives, O.48/96/1/4.

On the Buchenwald concentration camp, see *The Buchenwald Concentration Camp 1937–1945: A Guide to the Permanent Historical Exhibition*, compiled by Harry Stein (Goettigen: Wallstein, 2004); David Hackett, ed., *The Buchenwald Report* (Boulder: Westview, 1995); Kogon, *The Theory and Practice of Hell*.

57. Two autobiographical essays by Rabbi Yaakov Avigdor, narrating family and personal history through 1962, appear in *Faith after the Flames*, pp. 20–42. Two earlier accounts focusing on the Holocaust years appeared in 1949 and 1950, as prefaces to Rabbi Avigdor's books *Avir Yaakov* and *Chelek Yaakov*. An English translation of the 1950 preface can be found in Esther Farbstein, ed., *The Forgotten Memoirs* (Brooklyn: Shaar, 2011), pp. 39–61.

For a list of other discussions of Rabbi Avigdor's life and work, see Farbstein, p. 42. While the dating of events in the earlier 1949 and 1950 writings is according to the Jewish calendar and is accurate, the account in *Flames* switches from one calendar to the other and is marred by inaccuracies. No reference to the Buchenwald calendar or any of the others attributed to Rabbi Avigdor appears in these accounts. It may well have been the case that Rabbi Avigdor, in the midst recounting the tumult of wartime events, simply took in stride as an outgrowth of his rabbinic duties the fashioning of wartime calendar after wartime calendar

58. "Autobiography Written by Rabbi Dr. Yaakov Avigdor," *Faith after the Flames*, p. 39.

59. On religious observance in Buchenwald, see Rabbi Israel Meir Lau, *Out of the Depths* (New York: Sterling, 2011), pp. 56–59; Pesach Schindler, *Hasidic Responses to the Holocaust in the Light of Hasidic Thought* (Hoboken: Ktav, 1990), p. 102; and *Shema Yisrael*, pp. 206–8. Fellow Buchenwald inmate Joseph Friedenson recalled with great admiration these prayer services under Rabbi Avigdor's leadership. He did not, however, remember actually seeing the Buchenwald calendar (phone conversation, February 2012). Much information on religious life in Buchenwald can be gleaned from a biography of Chaskel Tydor's lengthy internment in Buchenwald from 1939–42 and again (following deportation and imprisonment in Auschwitz) in 1945. See Judith Tydor Baumel-Schwartz, *The Incredible Adventures of Buffalo Bill from Bochnia: The Story of a Galician Jew, Persecution, Liberation, Transformation* (Brighton: Sussex, 2009).

60. Rabbi Yaakov Avigdor, "The Camp Calendar of Buchenwald," p. 97.

61. Ibid.

62. Ibid., p. 98.

63. Ibid.

64. Rabbi Yehoshua Grünwald, "Wellspring of Tears," in *The Forgotten Memoirs*, p. 110.

65. In Jewish life in general, rabbinic authorities are divided regarding the significance of the Gregorian calendar year count and the degree to which a Jew should endeavor to avoid writing it down. See the survey of positions taken by rabbinic authorities in Rabbi Avraham Rosenthal, "Using the Secular Date," *Din*, http://dinonline.org/2011/12/20/using-the-secular-date/.

66. I am grateful to Marc Caplan for sharing his thoughtful observations on this particular omission.

67. Supporting evidence for this view can be found in the calendar's computation sheets, which do include the month of Elul.

68. Hence, Rabbi Isaac Avigdor's widow and son were taken by surprise when, in our February 2012 meeting, I pointed out to them the calendar's missing section.

69. Avigdor, "The Camp Calendar of Buchenwald," p. 98.

70. Tzvia Rosen, personal communication, Jerusalem, 5773/2013.

71. Judy Wilkenfeld, personal communication, Sydney, Australia, 5773/2013.

72. Joseph Czarnecki, *Last Traces: The Lost Art of Auschwitz* (New York: Athaneum, 1989).

73. p. 133.

74. p. xiv. For Potok, the etched calendars "marking time" in Auschwitz was one of the most interesting facets of the "last traces": "Particularly poignant, an apt and ghostly pair of metaphors for that charnel house, are two drawings. One depicts a clock without hands, the other shows us time floating away on a kite. . . . There was no time as we know it in Auschwitz. . ." Not only did Potok seem to miss the message of the calendars generally: he also did not mention Jewish time or the calendars that orchestrate it.

75. There is a formidable literature on most aspects of the Auschwitz concentration (or death) camp. For overviews, see Yisrael Gutman and Michael Berenbaum, eds., *Anatomy of the Auschwitz Death Camp*, (Bloomington: Indiana University Press, 1994); Sybille Steinbacher, *Auschwitz: A History* (London, 2005); and *Auschwitz 1940–1945: Central Issues in the History of the Camp*, 5 vols. (Auschwitz: Auschwitz-Birkenau Museum, 2000). On the broader history of Auschwitz, see Deborah Dwork and Robert Jan van Pelt, *Auschwitz, 1270 to the Present* (New York: Norton, 1996). For a detailed timeline of events at the camp, see Danuta Czech, *The Auschwitz Chronicle 1939–1945* (New York: Holt, 1997). It is important to note in this context that Czech almost always presents the chronicle of events according to the Gregorian calendar dates. For a rare exception and the possible significance thereof, see below, note 108.

76. Yisrael Gutman, "Auschwitz—An Overview," in *Anatomy of the Auschwitz Death Camp*, p. 19. I have drawn on Gutman's overview more generally concerning the prisoner's daily and weekly routine.

77. Rabbi Sinai Adler, "Celebrating Jewish Festivals in Auschwitz," *Organization of Partizans, Underground and Ghetto Fighters*,"Jewish Resistance in the Holocaust." http://archive.c3.ort.org.il/Apps/WW/page.aspx?ws=496fe4b2-4d9a-4c28-a845 -510b28b1e44b&page=5d675d48-68df-4fc3-833c-04a23648f70e&fol=fe71099d-270f-4c68-8def -25ee7cc7f81b&code=fe71099d-270f-4c68-8def-25ee7cc7f81b&box=3e0902e0-b315-412c-a5ec -927e5dab4302&_pstate=item&_item=8bbcebe7-5c27-4aca-ab7e-cbc92fb7cc85. A substantial primary and secondary literature as well as archives of oral testimony describe aspects of Jewish observance in Auschwitz, including studying Torah, reciting prayers and blessings, eating kosher food, wearing tefillin, and, in connection with the calendar, observing Shabbat and festivals. See for example Esther Farbstein, *Hidden in Thunder*; Rabbi Eliezer Berkowitz, *With God in Hell*; Rabbi Tzvi Hirsch Meisels, "Sanctifying His Name," in *The Forgotten Memoirs*, pp. 262–85; Rabbi Ephraim Oshrey, *Mi-Ma'amakim* (New York: 1958); and *Shema Yisrael: Testimonies of Devotion, Courage, and Self-Sacrifice, 1939–1945*, trans. Yaakov Lavon (Bnei Brak: Kaliv World Center / Targum, 2002).

78. Zahava Szász Stessel, *Snow Flowers: Hungarian Jewish Women in an Airplane Factory, Markkleeberg, Germany* (Cranbury, NJ: Associated University Presses, 2009), p. 181.

79. Anna Ornstein and Stewart Goldman, *My Mother's Eyes: Holocaust Memories of a Young Girl* (Cincinnati: Emmis, 2004), p. 89. Other written and oral memoirs that I have reviewed convey a similar diversity of—and challenge to—calendar knowledge in Auschwitz. For one example of the special conditions of Auschwitz, Katarina Spitzer reports that "in Auschwitz" (i.e., Birkenau) there was "no sense of time"; once relocated to a labor camp, in contrast, "we had a sense of time." Shoah Foundation Video Archive, interview code 3867, segment 57.

Another special case is that Rabbi Eliyahu Herman, who, when deported from Budapest to Auschwitz in 1944, hid strapped to his calf a pocket calendar, a set of tefillin, and a book of Psalms. The fact that the calendar was held on to with the same tenacity as these sacred articles reveals its significance in Rabbi Herman's eyes. The calendar remained with him through the end of the war. As recounted to Rabbi Nachman Seltzer and set down by the latter under the title "The Protection" in Rabbi Nachman Seltzer, *I Have an Amazing Story for You* (Brooklyn: Shaar, 2015), pp. 93–110. An earlier version of Rabbi Herman's testimony was written up by Debbie Shapiro and appears as "Tefillin in Hell," on Aish.com (July 7, 2012), http://www.aish.com/ho/p/Tefillin_in_Hell.html. Strangely, Shapiro's version contains no reference to the calendar (or to the book of Psalms)

80. *Shema Yisrael: Testimonies of Devotion, Courage, and Self-Sacrifice, 1939–1945*, trans. Yaakov Lavon (Bnei Brak: Kaliv World Center / Targum, 2002), p. 210–11. There have been reports of others whose mental command of the calendar was on this extraordinary level and who played a similar role. Israel (Sruleck) Starck noted that, as prisoners in the Melk labor camp in Austria, no one had any sense of the days of the week, much less the holy days— except for one man whom he called "Kopel the Calendar" who was able to calculate dates in his head and who knew when Yom Kippur was coming. Rabbi Nehemiah Polen, email, erev Rosh Hashana, 5776 (September 13, 2015).

81. Esther Farbstein, email, March 7, 2013.

82. I am indebted to Esther Farbstein for directing me to Sophie Sohlberg and her calendar. Farbstein refers to the Sohlberg calendar in *Hidden in Thunder* (Hebrew) (Jerusalem: Mosad HaRav Kook, 2002), p. 374. I received my copy of the Sohlberg Auschwitz calendar from the author herself, who today lives in a Jerusalem suburb. As far as I am aware, no archive possesses a copy of the calendar.
Sophie Sohlberg has recounted her wartime experience and its backdrop in Lore Shelley, ed., *Auschwitz: The Nazi Civilization* (Lanham, MD: University Press of America, 1992), pp. 164–77. The transcript of her Yad Vashem interview (Hebrew) can be found in the Yad Vashem Archives, 02/340, no. 492. I have benefitted by two personal interviews and close to a dozen phone interviews with her. In addition, Sohlberg kindly wrote up and shared with me a short overview of her calendar making in Auschwitz, with attention to the educational background that enabled her to accomplish this formidable task. A self-published memoir by another Auschwitz Stabsgebäude prisoner refers helpfully (if with some inaccurate background details) to Sohlberg's Auschwitz calendar and its special character. See Yael Stiefel, *Out of the Depths I Called to You* (Jerusalem: Yad Sarah, 5761), pp. 23–24.

83. Sohlberg's memoir in *Auschwitz* gives the last name as Kordheimer, seemingly a typo. It also lists the date of deportation as February 28, 1943, while other documents indicate March 1, 1943 (on Transport 31 from Berlin). Sohlberg writes poignantly of her sister Rosa that she was "very intelligent and gifted in every way." Sohlberg, *Auschwitz*, ed. Shelley, p. 165.

84. Chana C. Schultz, "In Spite of Everything: Zionists in Berlin," in *Jews in Nazi Berlin: From Kristallnacht to Liberation*, eds. Beate Meyer, Hermann Simon, and Chana Schütz (Chicago: University of Chicago Press, 2009), pp. 122–43; Horst Helas, "Eine Fürstenwalder Geschichte," Rosa-Luxemburg-Stiftung–Gesellschaftsanalyse und Politische Bildung–Seminarmaterialien.

85. The twenty-three accounts in Shelley's *Auschwitz: The Nazi Civilization* chronicle the various departments of the Stabsgebäude and the experiences of the inmates therein.

86. Estimates vary significantly on the number of Stabsgebäude women, ranging from one to three hundred. Though the lower figure seems closer to the mark, the population increased and decreased over time. I am indebted to Konrad Kwiet for information on the Stabsgebäude and for help in adjudicating the number of inmates therein.
Yeshaya Glick recounts that he, though a mere fourteen years old, had access to a calendar that he similarly shared with fellow inmates. Yeshaya Glick, *Mimachshichim Hoshianu*, ed. Benyamin Kluger (Jerusalem: David Ringel, 2009), p. 113.

87. The fifty-three divisions of the Five Books of Moses are mostly distributed a portion a week throughout the year. But in some cases, two portions are joined in the same week. Four points follow: (1) most portions are never joined; (2) certain portions are commonly paired with a regular partner, forming a familiar union to be recruited should the need arise; (3) the

second of the paired portions always comes directly after the first in the sequence of the Five Books; (4) and finally, commonly paired portions are not joined every year.

88. Phone interview, Motzei Shabbat, Sivan 21, 5775 (June 6, 2015).

89. Phone interview, 5774.

90. Chronology of Munich's Jewish History, http://www.rijo.homepage.t-online.de/pdf /EN_MU_JU_mueen.pdf.

91. The Würzburg Jewish Teachers Seminary was founded in 1864 by Rabbi Isaac Dov HaLevi Bamberger to train teachers for Jewish schools in Germany and had graduated well over four hundred students by the time of its forced closing in 1938. A brief overview can be found at http://www.yadvashem.org/yv/en/exhibitions/communities/wurzburg /beit_midrash.asp. For a more in-depth chronicle, see Max Ottensoser and Alex Roberg, eds., *Israelitische Lehrerbildungsanstalt Würzburg—1864–1938 by the Alumni of 1930–38* (Huntington Woods: Ilba, 1982). The seminary chronicle lists Julius as having begun his studies there in 1913, at the age of nineteen. A capsule biography of Kissinger's life and death, including the Jewish date of the murder in Kovno (Kislev 5) appears in Andreas Heusler, ed., *Biographisches Gedenkbuch der Muenchner Juden, 1933–1945*, vol. 1 (Munich: Stadtarchiv Muenchen, 2003), pp. 70–703. Thanks to Franny Schnall for providing information and resources related to the seminary and to Judy Wilkenfeld for similar generous help related to the family of Julius Kissinger.

92. To discover whether her second calendar would be that of a leap year and thereby have thirteen instead of twelve months, Sophie began with the year of creation, calculated intervals of nineteen years, and then reckoned correctly that the year in question, 5775, did not. She believes she wrote down the calculations but does not remember for sure. Phone interview, Sivan 20, 5775 (June 6, 2015).

93. Dr. Eric Bloch, phone interview and email, Kislev 5773 (November 12, 2012). Dr. Bloch studied at the Judische Volkshule from 1935 to March 1939, when he and his family immigrated to the United States. I located Dr. Bloch by way of the Yad Vashem "Page of Testimony" he had filled out in June 2008 on behalf of his teacher, Julius Kissinger. His "Page of Testimony" also serves as a remarkable kind of tribute. A classmate of Sophie Solhberg, Ruth Levi (née Gavrielowitz), has responded in kind. While she remembers their teacher with love and respect—and remembers him as being beloved by all—she doesn't recall the calendar lessons. Personal communication from Sophie Sohlberg, reporting on a conversation with Ruth Levi in Elul 5775 (August 2015).

94. Sohlberg, in *Auschwitz: The Nazi Civilization*, pp. 172–73.

95. Aloni-Borinski's account also appears in *Auschwitz: The Nazi Civilization*, pp. 179–92.

96. Email from Michael Tal, curator at the Yad Vashem Museum Archives, June 12, 2012.

97. *Auschwitz: The Nazi Civilization*, pp. 179–92; Anneliese-Ora Borinski, *Erinnerungen 1940–1943* (Nördlingen, Germany: Georg Wagner, 1970).

98. Phone interview with Yad Vashem archivist Riki Bodenheimer and Eldad Aloni, January 2013.

99. Anneliese-Ora Borinski, *Erinnerungen 1940–1943* (Nördlingen, Germany: Georg Wagner, 1970), p. 42.

100. Ibid., p.42.

101. *Auschwitz: The Nazi Civilization*, pp. 180, 184. In the same volume, Rachel Moses (née Inge Petzal), another Neuendorf deportee who worked in the Stabsgebäude mending room, also tells of the makeshift seder in the train car en route to Auschwitz, p. 195. Shoshana

Heyman (née Susanna Rosenthal), a Neuendorf deportee who worked in Stabsgebäude's "command post," does not refer to the Passover seder en route to Auschwitz but is emphatic about observance once there: "Every Friday night we celebrated Oneg Shabbat. We remembered the Jewish holidays and did fast on Yom Kippur. On Hannukka we lit candles; one of us always had to stand guard until the lights burned down" (p. 9). How the holidays were remembered she doesn't say; there is no reference to a calendar.

102. For a short summary of Zimche's biography, see "Zeitzeugengesprach in Israel mit Frau Zimche," http://hag-berlin.net/inhalt/zeitzeugengespr%C3%A4ch-mit-frau-zimche -israel.

103. On the Auschwitz women's orchestra, see Gabrielle Knapp, "Music as a Means of Survival: The Women's Orchestra in Auschwitz," http://www.feministische-studien.de /fileadmin/download/pdf/fem96_Translation_Knapp1.pdf; and Karen Kirtley and Richard Newman, *Alma Rose: Vienna to Auschwitz* (Portland, OR: Amadeus, 2000). On Zimche's leadership role with the orchestra women in Auschwitz and Bergen-Belsen, see Rachela Olewski's self-published memoir, "Crying is Forbidden Here!"

104. Phone interview with Hilde Zimche, Sivan 10, 5773 (May 19, 2013). The information appended by the Yad Vashem Museum Archive to the Borinski calendar conveys that the devout religious girls may have helped especially with culling the calendar's religious texts. My thanks go to David Silberklang for forwarding the museum description of the calendar. Despite what appears to be the close friendship between the two women, neither of Borinski's above-cited memoirs refer to Zimche.

105. Other diminutively crafted objects included those intended for ritual (prayer books, tefillin, shofars) as well as those intended for nonritual purposes (e.g., memorial medallions with the names of camps engraved on them that were bartered for food). For a ritual object of a size nearly comparable to that of the Borinski calendar, see for instance the prayer book in the Yad Vashem Archives written from memory by Haya Iren Weiss in the Sömmerda labor camp in Germany.

106. Rabbi Shimon Huberband, "Sacred Books," in *Kiddush Hashem* (Hoboken, NJ: Ktav, 1987), p. 216.

107. Elie Wiesel, *Night* (New York: Hill and Wang, 2006), p. 66.

108. The eve of this Rosh Hashana was also the occasion for the set of tragic events, including a large selection of boys slated to be sent in the following days to the gas chambers, chronicled by Auschwitz survivor Rabbi Tzvi Hirsh Meisels. For his account, see Rabbi Tzvi Hirsch Meisels, "Sanctifying His Name," in Esther Farbstein, ed., *The Forgotten Memoirs* (Brooklyn: Shaar, 2011), pp. 262–85; the chronicle originally appeared in Hebrew as the preface to his book of responsa, *Mekadshei Hashem* (Chicago: 1955). These tragic developments also may be related to a brief moment of recognition of the Jewish calendar that comes on this date in Danuta Czech's *The Auschwitz Chronicle*, a day-to-day chronicle of events in Auschwitz/Birkenau compiled by Czech in the aftermath of the war. Generally, Czech, a non-Jewish Pole whose father was imprisoned in Auschwitz, relies exclusively on the Gregorian calendar to chart events in the camp, including arrivals, murders, and rare escapes. On September 18, 1944, however, she breaks the pattern by alluding in one of the day's multiple entries to the Jewish calendar: "On the second day of the Jewish celebration Rosh Hashanah [sic] the SS Doctors conduct a selection in the prisoner's infirmaries." Two observations are in order. First, this entry is the thirteenth of a total of fourteen entries for this date. Yet it is only at this point, almost at the very end of the day's entries, that,

inexplicably, the fact of the "Jewish celebration Rosh Hashana" surfaces. Second, the Jewish calendar dating is mistaken. September 18 was not the second day of Rosh Hashana but the first. The gesture of trying to forge a link between the two calendars is nevertheless admirable if not quite fulfilled. The fact that Czech's "Auschwitz chronicle" "is not perfect" has been pointed out by Robert Jan van Pelt, but in a different vein than I am drawing attention to here. See *The Pelt Report*, p. 43. http://www.vho.org/aaargh/engl/report.pdf.

109. Emanuel Ringelblum, "Oyneg Shabbes," in *The Literature of Destruction*, ed. David G. Roskies (Philadelphia: Jewish Publication Society, 5748/1988), p. 389.

110. Sohlberg, "My Calendar," pp. 2–3; phone interview, Sivan 20, 5775 (June 6, 2015).

111. Moshe Flinker, *Young Moshe's Diary* (Jerusalem: Yad Vashem, 1979), p. 71. Saul Friedlander cites these words as an epigraph beginning the third and final section of his historical chronicle of the Holocaust entitled "Part III/Shoah/Summer 1942–Spring 1945." *The Years of Extermination: Nazi Germany and the Jews, 1939–1945* (New York: Harper, 2007), p. 397.

112. The special paragraph added to the daily prayers during the days of Chanukah amplifies these key features:

> For the miracles . . . which You have wrought for our ancestors in those days, in this time—In the days of Matityahu, the son of Yochanan the High Priest, the Hasmonean and his sons, when the wicked Greek kingdom rose up against Your people Israel to make them forget Your Torah and violate the decrees of Your will. But You, in Your abounding mercies, stood by them in the time of their distress. You waged their battles, defended their rights and avenged the wrong done to them. You delivered the mighty into the hands of the weak, the many into the hands of the few . . . Then Your children entered the shrine of Your House . . . kindled lights in Your holy courtyards, and instituted these eight days of Chanukah to give thanks and praise to Your great name.

113. As cited above, Borinski's later memoir mentions Chanukah observance; another Stabsgebäude inmate, Shoshana Heyman (née Susanna Rosenthal), also refers to the observance of Chanukah. But it seems that their observance was guided by a different calendar, since by the time Chanukah of 5705 had arrived, Borinski's calendar was already with her friend Zimche in Bergen-Belsen.

114. Notwithstanding the accumulated power of the eight days, the special nature of the first is brought out in Rabbi Sinai Adler's description of his Birkenau Chanukah lighting: "The first night of Hanukah we gathered together on the upper tier of one of the platforms, and we lit the candle which was so precious to us. The burning candle kindled in our hearts new hope for the future and strengthened our trust in the 'rock of our salvation.'" Quoted in Irving J. Rosenbaum, *The Holocaust and Halakhah* (Hoboken, NJ: Ktav, 1976), p. 118. Rabbi Sinai's concluding words allude to the title of the "Maoz Tzur" Chanukah hymn.

115. Translation into English of the Book of Psalms follows the Kohot edition: *Tehillim Ohel Yosef Yitzchok, with English Translation*, trans. Y. B. Marcus, Nissen Mangel, Eliyahu Touger (New York: Kehot, 2001). Other translations: *The Chumash* (Brooklyn: Mesorah, 1993); and *The Complete Artscroll Siddur*, trans. Rabbi Nosson Scherman (Brooklyn: Mesorah, 1984).

116. Three passages from Pirkei Avot (the Ethics of the Fathers), a tractate of the Mishna dedicated to epigrammatic ethical teachings, appear on pages 16, 21, and 26. While interesting in their own right, they do not explicitly deal with the theme of return. It seems

that, as the author went forward with the calendar—and as the dating of the Jewish calendar vanished—the theme of return came to progressively dominate. In my analysis that follows, I consider the interplay between the interrupted dating and the specific significance of the theme of return.

117. Yona Emanuel, *Dignity to Survive: One Family's Story of Faith in the Holocaust* (Jerusalem: Targum/Feldheim, 1998), p. 129–30. Elchanan Emanuel, who wrote the commentary on the psalm and was the brother of the memoir's author, was subsequently murdered.

118. Drawing on the past and fashioning a future have particular significance in light of what is argued to be the collapse of both dimensions during the Holocaust. See my discussion above of Engelking, Frankl, and Sofsky.

IV While in Hiding

Calendar Consciousness on the Edge of Destruction

Though prisoners in Auschwitz were cut off from the world at large, lacked most elements of civilized life, and were at risk for endeavoring to nurture any form of Jewish community, they shared this ordeal with other Jews. It was not for her sake alone that Sophie Solhberg made her calendars. They were a tool to enable the group of Jewish women among whom she lived and labored to track Jewish time and observe the holidays. In labor and transit camps where there was greater opportunity of using Jewish books and ritual objects, calendars could circulate in multiple copies, broadening the common consciousness of Jewish sacred days among the various prisoner groups. As is their wont, calendars created continuity with the past and bonds with those among whom one dwelled in the present.

Most Jews fortunate enough to find a place to hide did not suffer the radical privation or brutal oppression of Auschwitz. But the isolation, solitude, and non-Jewish environment in which they found refuge provided their own challenges. One of these was in tracking Jewish time, since sources of information were often even more difficult to come by in hiding than in ghettos or camps. For this reason, the experience of hiding—secreted outside of the Jewish community, compelled to follow the temporal rhythms of another—moved the victims to seek out ways to maintain Jewish time.

A Beautiful Ledger of Time and Memorial: Rabbi Scheiner's Polish Calendars

For Rabbi Shlomo Yosef Scheiner in Poland and Yehoshua Neuwirth in Holland, the making of calendars while in hiding created a Jewish domain whereby tradition could live and flourish. Rabbi Scheiner, a Chasid of Neustadt, ran a flour mill as well as a brick and roof tile factory in Debowka, Poland, before the war. He, his wife, and their four children lived in nearby Pinczow. The Pole who would become his rescuer during the war, Franciszek Matjas, was an employee of Scheiner's who built his home thanks to a loan from his boss. In early 1943, after two months spent hiding in the forest, the Scheiner family hid in the Matjas

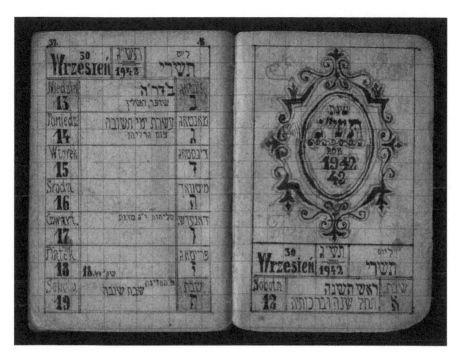

Fig. 4.1: In early 1943, after two months spent hiding in the forest, Rabbi Shlomo Yosef Scheiner, a Chasid of Neustadt, his wife, and four children, took refuge for the duration of the war in the house of a courageous employee, Franciszek Matjas, in Debowka, Poland. While in hiding, the family busied themselves with basic survival and the study of Torah, the latter of which included Rabbi Scheiner preparing beautifully calligraphed calendars for the years 5703 (1942–43) and 5704 (1943–44). Among other features, Rabbi Scheiner wrote with equal finesse the Hebrew, Yiddish, and Polish names and dates and color-coded the holidays.

home in Debowka behind a wall that Scheiner and Matjas built inside the house. While in hiding, the family busied themselves with basic survival and the study of Torah, the latter of which included Rabbi Scheiner preparing a calendar according to his own calculations.

Scrupulously noting Shabbat, holidays, Rosh Chodesh, and the precise time of sunset that ushered in these special days, Rabbi Scheiner at first only schematically set down these calculations. But the final product, rendered on a checkerboard notebook, was a full-blown, beautifully calligraphed calendar, with equal finesse given to the Hebrew, Yiddish, and Polish names and dates. And even the nuanced errors that crept into the definitive version—mistaking the onset of night for the time of sunset, for example—testify to the remarkable pains taken to craft a meticulous guide to Jewish life in the midst of carnage.[1] The calendar, moreover, had both a shared and hybrid identity. It was one of several sacred writings that

Shlomo Yosef and his son Yisrael penned in hiding, the others being a book of psalms and prayer books. The calendar thus served together with these sacred writings to outfit the family, bereft of home and possessions, with the equipment of daily religious existence.

While Rabbi Scheiner's calendars usually follow standard conventions, he nonetheless also developed his own idiom. This is especially conspicuous when it comes to his practice of coloring, in pastel red, the square with the date in order to honor the weekly Sabbath and the periodic holidays. In this way, the days of special sanctity were color coded. Following in the same vein, the days of somewhat lesser sanctity—Rosh Chodesh and Hol Hamoed (the intermediate days of Passover and Sukkoth)—had the square half colored in, as if to publicize the two-sided character of the day. Operating at another level, he devised a singular mark for the day known as Lag b'Omer, the thirty-third day of the Omer count falling on the eighteenth day of the month of Iyar—which, though not imbued with ritual sanctity to the degree of even a so-called half holiday, still was given through custom and history something of a sacred aura. The date thereby earned a single stroke of the red pen, enough to distinguish it from the run-of-the-mill days without confusing it with the days imbued with true sanctity.

Up to this point, Rabbi Scheiner's technique is idiosyncratic but unsurprising, novel but conventional in its essence, creating by way of color a pictorial means to distinguish the sacred from the mundane as well as the more sacred from the less. But the next step, the elaboration and extension of the color-coding system, is startling, unexpected, and indeed unparalleled in any other wartime Jewish calendar. Not only are the squares for the dates and days of special sanctity in the Jewish calendar filled in with the color red, but so in similar fashion are such days and dates in the Gregorian calendar. This means that Christian holidays, specified by name on the calendar's left side, are also filled in with the color red; and, consistent to a T, on every Sunday, the box with the day's Polish name (*niedziel*) and the date is completely colored in as well. One curious element differentiates the system of coloring in the Gregorian calendar: there are no half-shaded boxes, no sacred days, in other words, in which the degree of sanctity is less than full blown.[2] Only in the Jewish calendar was there a need for gradation.

Be that as it may, it seems extraordinary that Rabbi Scheiner, crafting Jewish calendars as he hid from an enemy bent on the destruction of his family and his people, would confer upon Christian holy days such stature. As mentioned above, in no other wartime Jewish calendar do we find a similar gesture. Moreover, nowhere else do we find reference to even the most conspicuous Christian holidays dated by the Gregorian calendar. It was as if Jewish calendars in wartime Europe, forged in order to track Jewish time amid upheaval and isolation, simply had no spiritual room to record that which did not carry meaning within a Jewish sphere of existence. For most wartime Jewish calendars, the

Gregorian calendar itself *did* carry such meaning, did play an orienting role for Jewish life in relation to the world at large. But Christian holidays dated according to that calendar did not play a similar role and hence were studiously omitted.

Why then did Rabbi Scheiner include these holidays when others excluded them? Why did he go a step further and honor the holidays with special marks of distinction? The reason could well be a gesture of goodwill toward the Matjas family. At great risk to their own safety, the family was providing sanctuary for the Scheiners, and it was the Matjas who, in connection with the timekeeping matter at hand, were even furnishing the materials necessary to compose the calendars. In this vein, Rabbi Scheiner may have shared with his hosts the fruits of his labor, the calendars themselves, on which the Matjas family would have recognized the Gregorian calendar more or less as they knew it. Indeed, they would likely have assumed that the special Christian days would be colored red; this is the case, as we have seen, with the Kodak Pocket Calendar Companion, where all holidays are printed in red. If that was the convention with which they were familiar, Rabbi Scheiner may have decided he would not be one to disappoint his generous hosts. Understandably, the Gregorian calendar that Rabbi Scheiner scripted was not the typical Polish version, which incorporated on every day of the year the saint's name associated with it. In a number of respects, that would have been beyond the Rabbi's reach. His version included just the basics. But that was clearly a formidable gesture in its own right, carving out a space for eight Gregorian-dated holidays. It may have been that listing these days also had the practical benefit of keeping the Scheiners alert to days meaningful to their hosts, and on which the Jewish guests could thereby act with the requisite sensitivity.[3] In any case, the singular inclusivity of Rabbi Scheiner's Debowka calendars testifies to the extraordinary circumstances in which the calendars came into being.

They do this in yet another way. Each calendar doubled as a kind of diary, Rabbi Shlomo Yosef noting on a substantial number of dates (eighty-two in 5703 and eighty-six in 5704), in red-inked Yiddish script, tragic events that had affected neighbors and friends.[4] The entries spanned the calendar time frame: the first appeared on the holiday of Shemini Atzeret, Sunday, Tishrei 22, 5703, twenty-two days into the year; the final one appeared on the next to last day of the following year, the twenty-eighth day of the month of Elul. There was unfortunately too much bad news to report; almost every fourth day Rabbi Scheiner felt called upon to report on dire events. On Iyar 22, 5703 (May 27, 1943), for instance, Scheiner wrote that an underground unit had "killed four Jews near Wisnicz."

These red-inked notations, which punctuate the calendars at intolerably regular intervals, transform the blank spaces of the dates into an unfolding martyrology of the local Polish Jews. Calendars had performed such double duty at earlier stages of Jewish life and experience, commemorating previous catastrophic events and those who were compelled to endure them. These hybrid chronographs, as they are known, fused commemoration of the historical past with the calendar's task of marking present and future time. In some cases, the commemorated past may have been within memory's reach. "The last lines of chronographs," notes Elisheva Carlebach, "incorporated local and recent events such as expulsions, salvations, fires, wars, and plagues."[5] Rabbi Scheiner's impulse to record local tragedies in the seams of the calendar thus has general precedent. And we saw how the author of the Jewish calendar layered onto the *Kodak Pocket Companion* put his time-keeping materials to similar commemorative use, listing victims' names and telling in shorthand how the losses occurred. Admirable though the accomplishment was, the listing in the *Kodak Companion* was occasional and erratic. For Rabbi Scheiner, in contrast, noting down tragic events was regular activity, an almost systematic endeavor. His nearly simultaneous documenting of such crimes, bringing the calendar closer to the diary or log, may be his own innovation.

The Scheiner family was gratefully liberated in January 1945 by the Red Army, and they returned to their hometown of Pinczow to find that other than themselves the streets were empty of Jews. Before Rosh Hashana of 5705 (which corresponded to September 18, 1944, in the Gregorian calendar), Rabbi Scheiner was troubled that he had been mistaken in his calculations (he apparently had no access to a Jewish calendar while in hiding), so he formed with his sons a *beit din*, or Jewish rabbinical court, to establish the proper date.[6] Later on, he became more convinced that he had made a mistake, so he fashioned another calendar, but after the war it turned out that the first calendar had been correct.[7]

Occupying Time in Amsterdam: Rabbi Yehoshua Neuwirth's Calendar Projects

At roughly the same period in western Europe, Rav Yehoshua Neuwirth, renowned in the postwar world for his book on the laws of Shabbat, spent the war years in Amsterdam in hiding with his parents and three siblings; he was twelve years old when the war began.[8] The Neuwirths were based in Berlin in the 1930s, but after Kristalnacht they sent three sons, including Yehoshua, to Belgium, where he celebrated his bar mitzvah with a foster family. The parents also soon fled Germany, and the family was reunited in Amsterdam, where they eventually went into hiding. Under constant threat of arrest, as Rabbi Neuwirth later expressed it, miracles protected the family time and again. Somehow they escaped even a major deportation in spring 1943:

> The central gathering point was right opposite our window. The cursed Germans began at one end of the city and worked toward the center. We saw lines upon lines of Jews being led to the train station. We sat at home with pounding hearts, waiting for the inevitable knock at the door. For several hours the buildings were combed for Jews. Armed with official lists, the Germans

reached our building. But instead of coming up to knock at our door, they sufficed with standing in the entrance of the courtyard and calling "Are there Jews here?" They did not comb the building . . .[9]

Yehoshua Neuwirth was around sixteen years old when he made his first calendar, which he did both to keep busy and also to keep track of sacred time. While in hiding, writes Rabbi Neuwirth, "we did not have a Hebrew calendar that would have enabled us to know the dates of the holidays."[10] Relying for a guide on one of the few sacred books in the Amsterdam bunker, he was able to figure out how to craft a Jewish calendar from scratch; following this template, he fashioned a calendar "for the years we were in hiding" (5703 and 5704) with "information about Shabbos, holidays and fasts."[11]

Here, too, time was lived according to two calendars: despite the danger from the outside world constantly bearing down upon them, Rabbi Neuwirth is careful to note that he "placed the Hebrew dates opposite the Gregorian for duration of the war."[12] The calendars ended up circulating outside the family's hiding place, since word of their existence spread to the Dutch Jewish underground, which took steps to photograph them and disseminate the reproductions to "Jews in the camps."[13] In this case, the private act of salvaging Jewish time in hiding turned out to be of benefit to those suffering greater deprivation. Rabbi Neuwirth's sense of responsibility for such artifacts extended, moreover, beyond his own creations. When told of a nearby collection of prewar calendars that the owner had been obliged to abandon, he went to the site, gathered them up, and stored them in the family hiding place. His family still has the collection today.[14] As the Neuwirths were hidden and kept out of harm's way, so the young Yehoshua, attentive to the imperiled techniques of timekeeping as well as for sacred time itself, hid the calendars and preserved them.[15]

Rabbi Neuwirth's is among the most detailed of wartime calendars, including, for example, reading the biblical book of Kohelet on the Sabbath of the Sukkoth holiday and reciting the Barchi Nafshi psalms on the Sabbath following. Everything in Jewish calendar life was seemingly accounted for. But for all of the detail and finesse, the real key is Shabbat. It stands at the center of the calendar, set apart in three ways: (1) while Rabbi Neuwirth abbreviates the first six days of the week, he writes "Shabbat" out in full; (2) while he scripts the other days in Dutch, he writes Shabbat in Hebrew; (3) and for the Hebrew script he uses not, as one would expect, cursive but rather block letters, giving the weekly Shabbat listing the appearance of a proclamation.

The calendar's singling out of Shabbat presented both the ideal and the actual. Like other wartime Jewish calendars, Rabbi Neuwirth's portrayed Jewish life as it ideally should be lived. Whether Jews could carry out all the observances had no bearing on their being included in the calendar. Yet the Neuwirth family, secreted behind closed doors for more than a year, was able to keep Shabbat with fidelity; throughout their time in hiding, the actual experience of Shabbat nearly always conformed to the ideal. Problems with Shabbat began only when the war ended and the Neuwirths gained their freedom. It was then and only then, while trying to make his way to a safe haven out of war-ravaged Europe, that Rabbi Neuwirth was confronted with a situation that forced him to desecrate Shabbat. He later stated that his postwar commitment to bring meticulous Shabbat observance within the reach of every Jew by authoring his compilation of Shabbat laws arose from a desire to atone for this desecration. One might surmise, however, that his wartime calendar already revealed such a commitment, publicizing in the very script and strategies he chose the centrality of Shabbat in the life of a Jew—whether in hiding, or in freedom.

Rabbi Neuwirth's efforts had their near parallel in a handwritten calendar for 5703 (1942–43) produced by a senior figure in the Amsterdam Jewish community, Rabbi Shimon Hammelburg. Born in 1884, Rabbi Hammelburg was noteworthy for his translation of the Mishna into Dutch; he served as a member of the Jewish Burial Society and as a teacher in an Amsterdam yeshiva. He was apparently well-known for his calendrical prowess; it was his calendar collection that came into the possession of Rabbi Neuwirth. In Rabbi Hammelburg's case, however, the 5703 calendar was tragically his last: he was deported to the Sobibor death camp and murdered there on June 4, 1943 (Rosh Chodesh, Sivan 5703). His meticulous calendar thus eerily included the day of his own demise.

Dwelling Alone in Jewish Time: Adela Levisson

Others fortunately lived to bring their homespun wartime calendars to a postwar world. Though composing a Jewish calendar usually demands rabbinic expertise, knowledgeable women and girls also, as we have seen, had a role in tracking calendrical time during the Holocaust, either producing full-fledged calendars or, like many men under restrictive conditions, using more basic modes of keeping track of the days.[16] For example, Adela (née De Beer) Levisson, wife of Rabbi Avraham Salomon Levisson, fashioned a calendar for the year 5705 (1944–45) while in hiding in the north of Holland with her oldest child. Seemingly dedicated to outfitting her life in hiding with as much of Jewish tradition as possible, she also resourcefully translated a Dutch Bible's book of Esther into Hebrew. She and her three children (the one in hiding with her and two others who were hidden separately) survived with the help of the Dutch underground. Her husband, chief rabbi of Holland's Friesland region, unfortunately did not fare as well. Devoting himself to Jews imprisoned in Westerbork, he too was eventually made a prisoner in the Dutch transit camp, was deported from there to Bergen-Belsen, and perished on the "Lost Transport" train in Tröbitz, Germany, shortly after liberation.[17]

Adela Levisson's calendar covers the Jewish months of Tishrei–Iyar 5705 (September 1944–May 1945), with the Jewish year written in Arabic numerals. There is a separate column for every Jewish month, with the sequence moving from left to right. The names of the Jewish months are written in Hebrew script, the days and Gregorian months in Dutch. The calendar is finely detailed, including the weekly Torah portion, the onset of the new month, fast days, holidays with candle-lighting times, and even the numbering of the Omer count.[18]

As was the case with Adela Levisson, Rabbis Scheiner, Neuwirth, and Hammelburg were unwilling to settle for a scrap of time or the rhythms of a different culture that would accompany the predicament of hiding, choosing instead to resurrect the most conventional template of Jewish time as set forth in a day-by-day or week-by-week calendar. Indeed, these pocket-size calendars were similar in most respects to those produced a hundred or two hundred years before. Even the fact of their being handwritten rather than printed was not an unheard-of departure from the norm, since handwritten calendars continued to be fashioned by European Jews long after printed editions came to the fore.[19] Yet in this case the oppressive solitary conditions that the calendar's authors endured meant that they had no alternative but to pen their own.

A Calendar of a Life: Tsewie Joseef Herschel

This refusal to forego Jewish timekeeping was achieved by different means in another calendar produced in hiding in wartime Holland. In this case, a father designed an unconventional calendar to accompany his infant son into hiding. The hand-drawn calendar of Nico Louis Herschel was actually an innovative sequence of twenty-four panels imagining the child's evolution at various intervals of early life, from Tsewie Joseef Herschel's birth in December 1942 to the projected birth of Tsewie's son in November 1967.[20] The final panel proclaims "mazel tov" as Tsewie, dressed with ceremonial top hat, attends the son's bris. The father sent the life-stage calendar to accompany Tsewie into hiding in April 1943, as the family was threatened with imminent deportation.

As with the Scheiner and Neuwirth calendars, the artifactual status was important, predominantly so in this case: the life-stage calendar remained with the child when the parents were no longer present and, in a matter of months, had been sent to their death. Again, like the other calendars, its graphic representation of time was a response to crisis, envisioning a future when its collapse seemed imminent. But the multipanel Herschel calendar differed profoundly in that it did not articulate, as the conventional calendars did, a future shared by Jews throughout the world and throughout history. The Herschel life-stage calendar rather customized the future for an individual Jew—a future that included not only survival but also aliyah to Israel, marriage, and family.

Fig. 4.2: The hand-drawn calendar of the Amsterdam-based Nico Louis Herschel was actually an innovative sequence of twenty-four panels imagining the child's evolution at various intervals of early life, from Tsewie Joseef Herschel's birth in December 1942 to the projected birth of Tsewie's son in November 1967. The father sent the life-stage calendar to accompany Tsewie into hiding in April 1943, as the family was threatened with imminent deportation. Whereas Tsewie survived the war, his parents were murdered in the Sobibor death camp. Courtesy of the United States Holocaust Memorial Museum.

The Jewish Calendar of a Catholic Priest

One of the most remarkable, generous, singular—and puzzling—wartime Jewish calendar projects was that undertaken by the Italian priest, Don Gaetano Tantalo.[21] The circumstances under which this project took place are special in their own right. For some ten months (September 1943–July 1944), Tantalo sheltered seven Italian Jews. He and the head of one of the families, Enrico Orvieto, had become friends while vacationing in the same locale in the summers of 1940, 1941, and 1942. When the Germans occupied Italy in September 1943, the Orvietos and another family fled Rome seeking a safer haven. They traveled to Tantalo's residence and were readily taken in.

Beyond material provisions, Tantalo also endeavored to create a hospitable Jewish environment where the Sabbath and holidays could be kept, at least in a rudimentary fashion. Information about just how he was able to accomplish this is sketchy. But one example having to do with Passover is cited: he obtained new dishes for the holiday (in order for his guests to observe the stringencies of avoiding leaven) as well as acquired all the ingredients necessary—matzah included—to enable them to properly conduct a Passover seder.

For our purposes, especially resourceful were Tantalo's efforts to ascertain exactly when Passover fell in the calendar. His Jewish guests evidently lacked the means to know, having been compelled to leave home in early September without being able to take with them a Jewish calendar for the coming year of 5704, which began only at the very *end* of September. Their place of refuge was in an area where there was no organized Jewish community to speak of, and hence there was little opportunity of obtaining from anyone close by the information regarding the corresponding date in the Gregorian calendar when Passover was scheduled to take place. Tantalo thus had to resort to his own calculations, which were based on the cycles of the moon and the relevant knowledge that Passover occurs at midmonth, when the moon is full. The sheet that Tantalo used to make the calculations survives; the families conducted their seder (or perhaps seders) at the time determined by the priest's reckoning.

Uniquely resourceful, Don Tantalo's remarkable gesture nevertheless begets several questions—most of which no doubt arise because of the sketchy information concerning the events. Why did the attempt to acquire information about the Jewish holidays not come about earlier in the Jewish year of 5704 (1943–44), particularly for Rosh Hashana? Were there events that transpired during the Jewish families' stay that occasioned Don Tantalo's endeavor to determine the date only with the approach of Passover? Did Don Tantalo carry out his reckoning of the Passover date on his own, or did he involve his Jewish guests? This question also bears on the sheet of calculations, which, though clear and well-ordered, turns out to be one day off: Passover began in 1944 not on the night of April 8 (as his calculations show) but rather on April 7, a mistake made because a date in the Gregorian calendar (March 30) was skipped over. Did no one notice? Did no one check?[22]

Of course, one should not lose sight of what was gained. If the calculations were followed, they imply that the seder took place a day late—which was, in any case, also a seder night (the second of two that are conducted in the diaspora). And whatever errors crept in do not obscure Don Tantalo's heroic efforts to reckon the Jewish calendar for the sake of his wartime guests. In no other case that I am aware of did the tracking of Jewish time move so fully into the domain of a non-Jew. In his case, he opened his doors widely not only to his Jewish friends but also to Jewish time.

Notes

1. The times listed as קש/*shkia*, sunset, were actually the hour of צאת הכבים/nightfall.

2. *Full blown* here refers to the wholesale restrictions on work characteristic of the Jewish Sabbath and major holidays—that is, technically speaking, how Jewish tradition, and in the present instance Rabbi Scheiner, determined the measure of sanctity.

3. For similar reasons, reference to Christian holidays were found in Jewish calendars in earlier periods. See for example Carlebach, *Palaces of Time,* ch. 5 and 6; and Elisheva Baumgarten, "Shared and Contested Time: Jews and Christian Ritual Calendar in the Late Thirteenth Century," *Viator* 46 (2015), pp. 253–76.

4. According to Yisrael Scheiner, his father did not keep a separate diary or log of events while in hiding. Personal communication, February 2011.

5. Carlebach, *Palaces of Time,* p. 195.

6. Yisrael Scheiner, February 2011. Secular dates were periodically available, says Rabbi Y. Scheiner, by way of Polish newspapers.

7. The original calendar remains in possession of Rabbi Yisrael Scheiner, son of Rabbi Shlomo Yosef Scheiner. I have used a reproduction in the holdings of the Yad Vashem Museum and have drawn on information on the circumstances of its composition generously provided by Sara Shor and Michael Tal. See also Mordechai Paldiel, "Keeping the Faith," *Yad Vashem Magazine* 35 (2004). Paldiel's helpful overview is flawed, however, due to the fact that two of the three dates that he cites as used by Scheiner to record tragic local events do not actually contain the notations. On Matjas' rescue of the Scheiners in wartime Poland, see *Encyclopedia of the Righteous Among the Nations: Rescuers of the Jews during the Holocaust* in *Poland*, eds. Sara Bender and Shmuel Krakowski (Jerusalem: Yad Vashem, 2004), pp.495–96.

8. See "Introduction," *Shimiras Shabbes C'Hilchasa* (Hebrew) (Jerusalem, 2010); for an English translation of Rabbi Neuwirth's chronicle, see "It Is Good to Thank Hashem," in *The Forgotten Memoirs*, ed. Esther Farbstein (Brooklyn: Mesorah, 2011), pp. 293–316. See also Tuvia Freund, "The Forced Desecration that Led to Shmiras Shabbos: An Interview with Harav Yehoshua Neuwirth," *Hamodia* (March 25, 2010), pp. 7–9; I am indebted to R. Dov Teitz for directing me to the *Hamodia* article. One of the earliest sources to discuss Rabbi Neuwirth's wartime calendars appeared in Tuvya Ferschel, *HaDo'ar* (Tishrei 9, 5727),

p. 643; a portion of the article has been excerpted under the title of "Calendars" in *Shema Yisrael*, trans. Yaakov Lavon (Bnei Brak: Kaliv World Center / Targum, 2002), p. 91. I have supplemented written sources with interviews of the author, his family and friends: Rabbi and Rebbetzin Neuwirth, February 2011; Rebbetzin Neuwirth, January, 2011; Yosef Roosen, fall 2010; and Rebbetzin Nechama Shirkin (daughter of Rabbi Neuwirth), January 2011.

9. "Interview with Harav Yehoshua Neuwirth," *Hamodia*, p. 7.

10. "It Is Good to Thank Hashem," pp. 307.

11. "It Is Good to Thank Hashem," pp. 307

12. While many wartime calendars fashioned by Jews in hiding incorporate both Jewish and Gregorian calendars, there are exceptions. For example, Max Amichai Heppner's 1944 wall calendar, produced at the age of ten while hiding on a farm in Deurne-Zeilberg, Holland, presents only Gregorian dates.

13. R. Yehoshua Neuwirth, *Shimiras Shabbes C'Hilchasa*, p. 36. My translation.

14. Personal communication, R. Yosef Roosen, fall 2010.

15. See *Shema Yisrael*, p. 91. I am indebted to Bernard Hammelburg, grandson of Rabbi Shimon Hammelburg, and Yehuda van Dijk for their personal communications with me.

16. For a brief overview of women's wartime tracking of time, see Rosen, "Calendars and the Holocaust."

17. On Rabbi Avraham Levisson's biography and extraordinary contributions, see Farbstein, *Hidden in Thunder*, pp. 297–99, 306, 315. Although Farbstein notes that Rabbi Levisson himself made a calendar in Bergen-Belsen, Levisson family sources say they are not aware of it.

18. I am grateful to the Levisson family for supplying me with a copy of the calendar and for sharing their (admittedly partial) knowledge of its genesis.

19. Elisheva Carlebach, *Palaces of Time*, p. 69.

20. The original is in the archives of the United States Holocaust Memorial Museum. I am indebted to Judy Cohen, curator of the photo archive, and Teresa Pollin, curator of arts and artifacts. I am grateful to Tsewie and Annette Herschel for information and commentary on the calendar, including Tsewie Herschel's unpublished memoir, "The Son of My Son."

21. Accounts can be found in the following sources: Ugo Pacifici Noja and Silvia Pacifici Noja, *Il cacciatore di giusti: storie di non ebrei che salvarono i figli di Israele dalla Shoah* (Cantalupa [Torino]: Effatà, 2010), pp. 47–48; G. De Rosa, "Don Gaetano Tantalo," *La Civiltá Cattolica* (1972), pp. 414–15; Sara Bender and Pearl Weiss, eds., *The Encyclopedia of the Righteous of the Nations* (Jerusalem: Yad Vashem, 2007), p. 411; and Nicolino Sarale, *Don Gaetano Tantalo: un sacerdote amico, umile, eroico, esemplare* (Cinisello Balsamo [Milano]: San Paolo, 1995).

22. No source refers to the error in dating. Responding to my question whether the families ever became aware that the date was mistaken, Iael Nidam-Orvieto, granddaughter of Enrico, writes, "My father [who was present at the Passover seder] has no clue if the date they celebrated was correct or not, since they didn't check it after the liberation" (email, October 2, 2016).

V At the Top of the Page
Calendar Dates in Holocaust Diaries

Trying to keep out of harm's way in a Brussels refuge, Moshe Flinker, at sixteen years—the oldest son in a family of seven children—began his diary by inscribing the date at the top of notebook's opening page the fifteenth day of Kislev 5703, in the Jewish calendar, the twenty-fourth of November 1942, in the Gregorian. Tellingly, both dates are duly recorded. He continues in the most clear-cut way imaginable: "For some time now I have wanted to note down every evening what I have been doing during the day. But, for various reasons, I have only got round to it tonight." As the diary unfolds, he indeed notes down the day's events. But he also reflects on his own way of dealing with confinement and danger, on the reading and religious study he regularly pursues to pass the hours, on the disarming disappearance of fellow Jews, and on trying to decipher God's message in such difficult times. As we will come to see, crucial as well to his diary was its role as a calendar.

To focus on diaries swerves a bit from the course I have thus far pursued. Up to this point, my discussion of wartime calendars has been relatively straightforward; no matter how various the circumstances in which the calendars came into being, and no matter how much the approaches diverged in carrying out the task, calendars have been the subject at hand. Undoubtedly, I have included some eccentric examples (for instance, the life-cycle calendar made in Amsterdam on behalf of the infant Tsewie Herschel and the canvas painted by Hilda Kalikow in Theresienstadt). So not every example served as a true calendar, nor could every one likely be strictly defined as such. Nevertheless, they all used the medium of drawing or printing to present in columns or boxes time's structured flow. And most could be easily recognized as a day-to-day calendar, similar to those we use to organize our lives and to celebrate and commemorate personal, family, and communal events.

At first glance, diaries may seem like another creature entirely. More than anything, they are narrative, a shorter or longer chronicle about one's life as it unfolds in the present. If calendars are largely columns or boxes of numbers, diaries are mainly pages of words, sentences, and paragraphs. During the Holocaust, chronicling such pages of words became an urgent and widespread occupation: "Everyone" wrote diaries, Warsaw-based historian Emanuel Ringelblum reported in 1943: "journalists, writers, teachers, community activists, young people, even children."[1] No doubt driven by the desire to record in words what seemed beyond them, the collective impulse to keep a diary may have also been drawn to the act of forging an informal calendar.

Indeed, diaries are usually structured around a series of dated entries.[2] Like most calendars, they revolve around the day, week, month, and year—which are often the first things noted at the top of the diarist's page. Though diaries need not be, and often are not, as rigorously dedicated as calendars to a disciplined sequence of days, they nevertheless chart a progressive movement of time according to one or multiple calendars. They draw on calendars as well as serving as surrogates for them.

Clearly, proportions and purposes differ. In a calendar, the date (or dates) stand out, overshadowing any annotation; one owns, views, or fashions a calendar toward the end of systematically tracking time's flow. In a diary, the date serves as a lead-in to the narrative account, interpretation, reflection, or introspection that constitutes the essence of the genre. That said, the authors of diaries, aware of the calendrical link, are usually careful about noting down the date, or in some cases (like that of Chaim Kaplan or the opening entry of Moshe Flinker's) the multiple dates on which the entry was recorded. Such a link is also incorporated in the word *diary*, which in Yiddish, Hebrew, German, French, English and various other languages is associated with *day* or *daily*. At times, the bridge between the two has been made explicit, with *diary* referring to a daily dated planner or, with the cover title "Pocket Diary," to a calendar itself.

Most commentators on Holocaust diaries have noted but not investigated their special timekeeping dimension. Alexandra Zapruder, for instance, refers to diaries as "records of events recorded contemporaneously, usually composed of periodic dated entries." While she usefully shows how some diary writing came at a later stage than the periodic dating would lead one to believe, she doesn't take up the issue of dating (or the diary's relation to calendars) as such. [3] Alexandra Garbarini, for her part, notes the dating of entries that typically (though, to her mind, unsatisfactorily) defines a diary and reflects on the "attention to time" that emerges from reading Holocaust diaries. But the importance of such dating, and the fact of multiple calendars, does not surface in her discussion.[4]

David Patterson has gone furthest in arguing that Holocaust diaries appear when "the measure of time itself is under assault" and that they serve as an effort to retrieve that measure of assaulted time.[5] Referring for instance to Mirjam Korber, a Romanian teenager who kept a diary while she and her family took flight from their home in Iasi, Patterson notes that Korber "does not inscribe her diary in time; rather, she takes up an effort each day to inscribe time into her diary."[6] While Patterson includes the way the Jewish holidays played a role in the diarists' struggle to "inscribe time," the calendars and the dating of entries serve only as background.[7]

But when viewed alongside our study of wartime calendars, the timekeeping elements of Holocaust-era diaries move to the foreground. In some respects, the diaries resemble the calendars. Occasionally, for example, they place two calendar dates side by side at the top of the page (as we recall, Moshe Flinker begins his diary in this fashion). More often than not, however, two calendars are not lined up at one go; rather, the diaries opt for a date from a single calendar. Another point of contrast is that, while those who fashion wartime calendars generally set down the dates a year (or more) in advance, diarists inscribe the date only as the entry is about to be written. This progressive approach to dating offers the diarist a crucial flexibility: the calendar system used to date the entries can be changed from one day (or week or month) to the next. And, as we will see, some wartime diarists exploit this flexibility to the hilt, changing from the Gregorian to the Jewish calendar (and then sometimes back again) to underscore the significance of any given day and of the events that occurred on it. Finally, the narrative that follows the entry's date can serve as a complement to it, illuminating explicitly or between the lines the diary's dynamic interplay of calendars and dates.

The Warsaw Ghetto and Jewish Time

We begin with a revered wartime diary, but one of which, like most, little has been said about its special way of tracking Jewish time. Chaim Kaplan's Hebrew-language Warsaw diary gives an exceptional insider's view of the fate of Warsaw's Jewry during the war and in the Warsaw ghetto.[8] He kept a diary intermittently through the 1930s. But the published editions in the original Hebrew and in translation (all of which are missing substantial material from the original twelve notebooks) begin with his wartime entries and continue into the Great Deportation in summer 1942. He perished soon after he arranged for his diary to be smuggled out of the ghetto. Born in Horodyszcze, Belorussia, in 1880, Kaplan was brought up in a traditional home with a yeshiva education. He then modified these traditional interests to square with a modern passion for Hebrew and Palestine. In 1902 he founded an elementary school and thereafter served as its director for forty years. His devotion to Hebrew while nonetheless being immersed in the European culture of his day mark him as straddling these two worlds.[9]

Regularly dating entries by both the Jewish and Gregorian calendars, Kaplan brought this dual perspective to bear on the cruel events unfolding in wartime Warsaw. In a month of entries in the fall of 1940, for instance, Kaplan heads twelve of them with both calendar dates:[10]

2 October, 1940/evening of first day of Rosh Hashana 5701
3 October, 1940/evening of second day of Rosh Hashana 5701
4 October, 1940/Motezi (the night following) Rosh Hashana 5701
6 October, 1940/Tzom Gedalia Nidha
8 October, 1940 (second entry)/evening of 4th day, 7 Tishrei, 5701

10 October, 1940/evening of the day before Yom Kippur, 5701

12 October, 1940/Motzei (the night following) Yom Kippur, 5701

22 October, 1940/Night of Hoshana Rabba, 5701

24 October, 1949/Night of Simchat Torah, 5701

25 October, 1940/Motzei (the night following) Hag haSukkos, 5701 (not accurate)

2 November, 1940/Motzei (the night following) Shabbat Kodesh, Parshat Noach, 5701

5 November, 1940/4 Marchesvan, 5701

Taking stock of the regular dual-calendar dating conveys Kaplan's consistently Jewish orientation throughout this period. The Jewish calendar and the time perspective it bequeathed did not erupt occasionally into Kaplan's consciousness. They were rather a ready lens through which he confronted wartime Poland. And while the fall holiday season certainly increased the density of these bicalendar citations, we see that it didn't stop there but rather continued into the next month of Marcheshvan. The citation of "Parshas Noach" on November 2 is particularly intriguing, since it refers to the Sabbath reading of the Torah from the book of Genesis that describes the destruction of the sinful world by a flood and the survival of Noach and a retinue of the world's creatures aboard an ark. Though Kaplan does not comment directly on the intersection between this reading and the circumstances of Warsaw's Jews at that specific moment, he does in this entry ruminate on the soon-to-be enacted isolation of these Jews in a ghetto, an edict of incremental rather than wholesale destruction. Perhaps in Kaplan's allusive reckoning, the ghetto-to-be served as Europe's contorted version of an ark, ingathering a saving remnant fragilely sheltered against the mad forces raging without.

Other diaries bring out the importance of the Jewish calendar dating in more dramatic fashion. Abraham Lewin's Warsaw ghetto diary has a stature similar to that of Kaplan's.[11] Born in Warsaw in 1893, Lewin was nearly fifty when he began to keep a diary in spring 1942. He was a teacher at a Jewish girls' high school in Warsaw, had penned a history of the cantonists (Jewish boys conscripted into the Russian Army), was a dedicated Zionist and was steeped in Jewish culture and Hebrew letters. He was a member of the Oyneg Shabes group's inner circle in wartime Warsaw; the group's leader, Emanuel Ringelblum, in turn, viewed Lewin's diary as an outstanding, measured documentation of Warsaw's Jewry plight:

> A valuable document is the diary of A. L-n, the author of the book "The Cantonists." The author has been keeping a diary for a year and a half and has poured all of his literary talent into it. Every sentence in the diary is measured. L. has packed the diary not only with everything he has managed to learn about Warsaw, but also with the terrible suffering of the provincial Jews. . . . The clean and compressed style of the diary, its accuracy and precision in relating facts, and its grave content qualify it as an important literary document.[12]

Lewin continued to keep his diary during the Great Deportation, the period in summer 1942 when the vast majority of Warsaw's Jews—some 275,000, including 50,000 children—were deported to the Treblinka death camp or murdered in the ghetto itself.[13] Persevering during this period of unprecedented loss and upheaval, Lewin marked the beginning of the watershed events by several means. First, he switched from writing in Yiddish to writing in Hebrew; second, his prose became more fragmented; and third, he registered the pivotal nature of this period by switching from the Gregorian to the Jewish calendar.

The shift to the Jewish calendar was set in motion both by the horrible devastation begun on that day and also by the ominous date of the Jewish calendar—the ninth day of the month of Av. According to Jewish tradition, numerous destructive events in Jewish history took place on the ninth of Av, including the destruction of the ancient temples in Jerusalem and the exile of the Jewish people from their homeland. In consequence, the sages of antiquity fixed the date as a singular day of mourning in the Jewish calendar, marked by a round-the-clock fast together with a public reading of the biblical book of Lamentations and of a special set of commemorative poems. For Lewin, then, what was unfolding in Warsaw on that day and date had its precedent in pivotal disasters in Jewish history and was linked to the mournful character of the day.[14] He thus dates the first Hebrew entry "Erev Tisha b'Av" (the day before the onset of the ninth day of the month of Av) and the second entry "Tisha b'Av." He thereafter returns to dating the entries according to the Gregorian calendar. For Lewin, time on that day had taken on a profoundly Jewish character such that the ancient and medieval Jewish experience of catastrophe was the only possible referent. The special heading of these two entries was meant to merge the profound suffering of Warsaw Jewry with that of Jews throughout history.

The English translation of Lewin's heading for that day—"Wednesday, 22 July—The Day before Tishebov"—does not ignore his gesture, but it also doesn't do justice to it.[15] The translated diary heading indeed refers to the Jewish calendar, yet it does so in such a way as to obscure the reference: *Tishebov* conflates into a single unknown word the two words (*Tisha*, or "ninth," and *Av*) indicating the day and month. The translation also adds the Gregorian date, something that Lewin apparently felt was superfluous to the nature of this day of unprecedented upheaval. In what seems to be the only case in the diary, he simply omitted the Gregorian date. The translation thus misses on two scores Lewin's powerful judgment of the first two horrendous days of the Great Deportation: first, as marking a turning point so exceptional as to demand a different system of dating, and second, as referring to an event so historically formidable as to demand to be viewed in light of what according to tradition was the most devastating instance of Jewish loss and suffering.

Much like Lewin, the Warsaw-based poet Yitzhak Katzenelson also dated his "Vittel Diary" generally according to the Gregorian calendar but switching in key entries to the Jewish one.[16] A leader of Warsaw's literary and cultural community, Katzenelson and his son, having obtained Honduran passports, gained a temporary reprieve and, in May 1943, were sent to the Vittel transit camp in France. He began his diary the day he arrived and continued into the fall, with the final entry being written on "16.9.43." The reprieve ended the following spring. In April 1944, Katzenelson and his son were included in a group deported first to Drancy and then to Auschwitz, where they were tragically murdered.

Dated "22.5.1943," the first entry sets the scene: "My son Zvi and I are now in Vittel. We came with a small group of Jews, all of whom were nationals of different countries of South America. Zvi and I are nationals of Honduras." So continue the entries that follow, chronicling day-to-day events and tracking them by means of the Gregorian calendar. But at the peak of summer, a year after the destruction of Warsaw Jewry was set in motion, the everyday was consumed by the past: "On July 21," as David Roskies powerfully observes, "the dam burst, with the following day marking the first anniversary, the *yortsayt*, of the start of the Great Deportation. From then on, Katzenelson backtracked to the slaughter, as if reliving it in real time, back to the liquidation of the Little Ghetto with all its orphans, who had performed the plays he had written for their benefit; back to the discovery that his loved ones had been taken to Treblinka; back to the cellar at Karmelicka 9, on the eve of the first armed resistance; back to finding his works strewn about the abandoned ghetto streets."[17] Katzenelson turns the diary into a memoir to work his way back in time.

But even Roskies, master reader of Holocaust diaries, doesn't refer to the poignant shift of calendars heralding the anniversary: not July 21 but the *eighth of Av* heads the entry. Like Lewin, Katzenelson predominantly dated his entries according to the Gregorian calendar. So again like Lewin, the shift to the Jewish calendar proclaims the momentous nature of the day and date; a *yortsayt*, the first anniversary of the Warsaw ghetto's demise, can only be truly observed by using the Jewish calendar date. Orthography reinforces the date's importance. In his manuscript, Katzenelson spells out the number, writing not the cardinal *8* or its ordinal *8th* but rather *eighth*, just as in those calendars that wish to elevate the nomenclature in order to honor the day at hand.[18] By bringing the Jewish calendar to the fore, Katzenelson shows unequivocally that assessment of the event's significance must be viewed through the lens of Jewish history and thereby must be linked to the Jewish calendar date marking the destruction of the ancient temples. Katzenelson's gesture is the same as Lewin's. He too chose to switch from one calendar to another to activate a set of associations that would otherwise be missed. To be sure, Lewin wrote in real time, chronicling the sad destruction as it occurred; Katzenelson wrote a year after, memorializing the loss by retrieving it from oblivion. Yet each knew the shift of calendars was necessary to come close to giving Warsaw's eclipse the weight it deserved.

Only by knowing the diary entry's Jewish calendar date, as it turns out, can one appreciate Katzenelson's contentious gloss: "Today is the eighth [of] Av, no less a day of mourning for all the Jews, wherever they be, than the ninth of Av."[19] The ninth of Av, commemorating the destruction of the ancient Jerusalem temples, clearly sets the standard as a day of mourning. But the scale of Polish Jewry's present ordeal could not be contained by a single day. "Indeed, yesterday and all the foregoing days of the year, likewise all the days that are to follow until the end of time, are evil days. Never will the sun shine upon us again and never will there be any consolation for us on this earth." Having seen the terrible affliction affecting Polish Jewry over the past year—likely the worst in Jewish history—and the consequences it had continued to suffer in his temporary haven, Katzenelson posits the calendar's transformation into a ceaseless record of "evil days."

But he soon returns to a traditional focus: "Tomorrow is the 9th of Av, and it will be a whole year since the killing began in Warsaw itself." Indeed, the force of the traditional day of Jewish mourning is such that Katzenelson joins Warsaw's bitter fate to it—even when "the killing" that initiated the Great Deportation of Warsaw Jewry actually began a day earlier. Yet, as Katzenelson elaborates, the fact that the anniversary falls (more or less) on the traditional day of mourning allows for both analogy and contrast. True, the Jews of ancient Jerusalem suffered death, destruction, and exile. But, to Katzenelson's mind, the earlier cruelties were unleashed as acts of war. In contrast, the present-day ones were perpetrated against those residing in peace. Moreover, he believed the current devastation, even to the degree he could be aware of it in summer 1944, to be far more comprehensive than the ancient one. The shift to the Jewish calendar date thus links the ancient and modern-day tragedies, thereby occasioning a chronicle of mourning. But it also illuminates by way of pointed contrast the terrible predicament of Warsaw Jewry. Such disparity between ancient and modern catastrophe can only be reckoned, the Vittel diarist implies, by charting the coordinates of time according to the Jewish calendar.

The Eve of Rosh Hashana and Herman Kruk's Final Words

The Jewish calendar also made its way into ghetto diaries where one would least expect it, including diaries written by arch-Bundists, who generally rejected what they saw to be the Jewish calendar's parochial nature. Yet in the diary of Herman Kruk, noted Vilna ghetto librarian and Bundist activist, the Jewish calendar orients several entries and plays a key role in the last.[20] Born in Plock in 1897, Kruk joined the Bund in his twenties, first organizing seminars and then dedicating himself to library work. Initially, he did this for almost a decade with Warsaw's Grosser Library, making it the city's largest and most popular worker's library. With the German invasion of Poland, he fled Warsaw and, after a difficult journey of three months, was able to find his way to Vilna. Once the Vilna ghetto was formed in fall 1941, Kruk cobbled together a library and turned it into a cultural center. The library also served as a personal refuge where he could daily dictate his diary.

Begun at the time of the German invasion of Lithuania in June 1941, the diary was designed to be the "chronicle of a city" and become "the mirror and the conscience of the great catastrophe and of the hard times." Indeed, the diary chronicled the sad fate of Vilna in the aftermath of the invasion, during the ordeal of the ghetto, and even beyond. Once the ghetto was destroyed in fall 1943, Kruk hid the diary in the ruins of Vilna before he was deported to the Klooga concentration camp in Estonia, where he spent the final year of his life. There, too, he continued to keep a diary, dedicated as he was to setting down a record of the onslaught.

Indeed, he kept it almost to the very end. Kruk's sporadic references to Jewish holidays culminate in the diary's final entry: "Today, the eve of Rosh Hashanah [5705/1944], a year after we arrived in Estonia, I bury the manuscripts in Lagedi, in a barrack of Mrs. Shulma, right across from the guard's house. Six persons are present at the burial."[21]

Although overlooked by even the best of commentators, Kruk's decision to enter the date according to the Jewish calendar is clearly charged with meaning. As we have seen, the eve of Rosh Hashana is both the last day of the previous year and the gateway to the new one. Moreover, its position as a lead-in to the holiday of Rosh Hashana, the Day of Judgment, was also significant, in all likelihood reflecting the role of the diary itself as a form of taking stock. Kruk adds to these layers of meaning by noting that the day marks the anniversary of his imprisonment in the Estonian camp. He thus sees his fate as running parallel to that of the Jewish year; just as the Jewish calendar had traversed a year, so had he. Practical concerns no doubt also played a crucial role. Time was running short. Kruk knew that he had to act fast if the diary was going to stand a chance of being securely hidden. Nevertheless, beyond the practical concerns that led to the burial ceremony taking place at this specific time, the Rosh Hashana association also gave an honorable conclusion to the life of the manuscript.

As it turned out, the decision to seize this auspicious opportunity occurred at virtually the last possible moment. The next day, the first day of the Jewish New Year, the holiday of Rosh Hashana, Kruk and those with him were murdered. The liberating Soviet forces arrived at the camp several hours later.

Kaplan's and Lewin's diaries, straddling tradition and modernity amid the annihilating conditions of the Warsaw ghetto, alternate between two timekeeping systems, a strategy that is crucial to recognize in order to fully follow their resolutely insider perspective. For his part, Herman Kruk, ideologically committed to a path freed from the constraints of Jewish particularity, nonetheless ends his diary—and his life—reckoning time according to the Jewish calendar date of

Rosh Hashana: the Day of Judgment for Jews everywhere and always, including a Bundist librarian on the outskirts of an Estonian hell.

Revisiting Moshe Flinker's Diary: The Definitive Choice of Jewish Time

Moshe Flinker's diary dramatizes in a starker way the significance of the issues bound up with calendar dates. Born in 1926, Flinker, as we recall, hailed from a Dutch Jewish family and had spent his early years in The Hague, Holland, the oldest boy in a religious Jewish family of five sisters and a younger brother. The parents had emigrated from Poland, and the household languages were Yiddish and Dutch. It was after the German occupation of Holland that the family had fled to Brussels.

Moshe Flinker began his diary in the fall of 1942, choosing, as an ardent Zionist and competent student of sacred Jewish literature, to write mainly in Hebrew. Persevering through months of hiding, the family was betrayed and those in the house arrested on the eve of Passover 5704/1944. His mother was murdered in Auschwitz; Moshe and his father perished in Bergen-Belsen. His siblings managed to survive and, returning to Brussels, found the three diary notebooks. The surviving Flinker children eventually all immigrated to Israel, bringing the notebooks with them, and today they continue to keep the original diary in their possession.

The diary has been a topic of interest since its initial publication in 1958. Flinker's age and Dutch origins have spurred comparisons to the diary of Anne Frank, with Flinker's religious identity complementing Anne Frank's secular one. Though out of print in the Hebrew original and English translation, a significant portion of the English translation was included in Alexandra Zapruder's 2002 collection of children's Holocaust diaries. More recently yet, Saul Friedlander draws on Flinker's diary in his 2007 Holocaust chronicle, *The Years of Extermination*, and features a particularly arresting paragraph from the diary as the book's final epigraph.[22] Translations have appeared in English, Yiddish, Dutch, Russian, Italian, and, most recently, German and French (with a foreword by Friedlander), in some cases based on the original Hebrew, in other cases on previous translations.

Flinker's education and industry made him attuned to both Jewish and secular culture and calendars. It is thus no surprise that, as noted earlier, he begins by citing the date in both calendars—"15 Kislev, 5703," in the Jewish and "November 24, 1942," in the Gregorian. This is a striking statement of bicultural affiliation. At this departure point, in spite (or perhaps because of) the choice to write in Hebrew, Flinker demonstrates his allegiance to both his Jewish and European identities.

Flinker complements the dual date heading with the location "Brussel," written not in one but two scripts, Hebrew and Latin. To inscribe the location here had powerful associations beyond the everyday. Brussels was the site of the

family's hiding place, providing shelter and safety. But it also demanded a divided existence, where they lived as Jews in the privacy of the home while posing
as gentiles in public. The double-scripted location, with the Latinized spelling enclosed in parentheses, thus conveys the ambiguity of a life in hiding in Brussels.
Moreover, the diary itself, as the first lines set forth, had its origins in the flight
to Belgium's capital: "I must start," notes Flinker, "by describing why I came here
to Brussels." All in all, the importance of time and place may be why the Hebrew
original reproduces so precisely the orthographic features, including the parentheses around "(Brussel)" and the abbreviated spelling of "Novemb."

Flinker's use of two calendar headings was a onetime occurrence; he, too,
likely felt that the first page required something special to mark the launching of
the diary project. As we recall, the first entry explains why he decided to keep a
diary:

> For some time now I have wanted to note down every evening what I have
> been doing during the day. But, for various reasons, I have only got round to
> it tonight.
>   First, let me explain why I am doing this—and I must start by describing
> why I came here to Brussels.

Flinker shows an acute sense of being at the beginning and of conforming to the
obligations that come with such an endeavor. The dual calendar heading, a surrogate title of sorts, is in keeping with such a sense of responsibility.

Once underway, he deemed a single date heading enough. He thus begins
the next five weeks of entries, from November 26 to December 28, solely with the
Gregorian calendar date.[23] But a few days later he dates the entry ד"כ טבת
(the twenty-fourth day of the Jewish month of Tevet), for the first time using
exclusively the Jewish calendar. Thereafter he follows this pattern, dating the remaining eight months of entries according to the Jewish calendar alone. In his
estimation, what happens thereafter can apparently only be properly viewed by
way of a Jewish measure of time. Writing his diary in Hebrew, his decision to date
by the Jewish calendar thereby makes a seamless artifact of Jewish time and Jewish language, creating a symbolic Jewish domain, even as he passes for a non-Jew
in his wartime public life.[24]

The diary entry for this day gives a clue as to why Flinker changed to the
Jewish time system, since he lists as one recent reading a particularly exhaustive
study of the Jewish calendar authored by Chaim Bornstein, a noted expert in the
field.[25] The article certainly gave him a push to believe that the Jewish calendar, at
least in this juncture in history, was the one that mattered most. But his switch to
a different time register also reveals a special drama. The twenty-fourth of Tevet,
the date that marked the change of calendars, corresponded that year to January
1, 1943. It was thus on the day that the Gregorian calendar ushered in a New Year

that Flinker chose to switch allegiances, as it were. His embrace of the Jewish calendar as a mode of dating his diary was exquisitely timed to coincide with a rejection of the secular/Christian one.

The drama was undoubtedly heightened by the fact that in Brussels the Flinkers resided over a café, the patrons of which, as the end of the secular year drew near, were in the throes of celebrating the occasion. The noise of the festivities could clearly be heard in the Flinkers' apartment. Moshe Flinker's parents, in order to not raise any suspicions about their Jewish identity, felt called at some point in the evening to put in an appearance at the café. Their lives at stake, they were pro forma compelled to join the crowd in honoring the incoming January 1 secular New Year. Meanwhile, their son went in the other direction. Moshe Flinker's shift in dating his diary from one calendar to the other presumably countered the family's obligatory public subservience to the Gregorian calendar with a private gesture of loyalty to the Jewish one.[26] The diary was the place where one did not have to put on appearances. From this point forward there was no retreat; the shift to a Jewish mode of tracking time was irreversible. Writing every few days or, as time went on, every few weeks, he dated each and every entry according to the Jewish calendar. The final dated entry was the sixth of Elul, 5703, some eight months after his personal revolution in time.

Translation of calendar dates in this remarkable diary is thus no simple task, demanding as it does that one weave between calendars and, beyond that, bring to the reader's attention their pivotal interplay. And even more fundamental would be the conviction that the date that heads the entry has significance in its own right. As it stands, most translations miss the change of calendar and the drama that attends it. The English translation, for example, neither changes to the Jewish calendar nor refers to the change that takes place in the original but rather blithely continues to use the Gregorian calendar date throughout, as if no change ever occurred. Moreover, it also mistakenly heads the the twenty-fourth of Tevet entry with the date "January 4" rather than the correct, and pivotal, date of January 1.[27] Flinker's strategic playing off of one calendar against the other is thus blunted in two ways.

Other translations are more accurate but, in most cases, not completely so. Translated from the Hebrew, the 1973 Dutch edition records the Jewish calendar date and even adds an editorial note signaling the change from one calendar to another.[28] But it tries to encompass Flinker's bifocal calendrical approach by adding the secular date in parentheses alongside the Jewish one. This version had the potential not only of doing justice to the multicalendrical dimension of the diary but of enabling the reader to track the drama of the shifting calendars. Indeed, it goes so far as to append a brief overview of the Jewish calendar, which includes a list of the names of the months. Yet the drama of Flinker's strategic shift in dating is missed because the Dutch version reproduces the secular calendar dates from the flawed English edition, which erroneously cited January 4 instead of January 1. Curiously, the English version, which included almost nothing of the diary's multicalendrical facility, becomes at this stage an authoritative calendar on which (wrongly, as it turns out) to base the corresponding Gregorian dates.[29]

The recent 2008 German version goes a step further while continuing to miss the crucial drama.[30] Translated in this case from the Dutch version, the German follows the earlier edition by including the switch to the Jewish calendar date, parenthetically inserting the Gregorian date alongside—and, once again, citing the wrong corresponding date (January 4 instead of January 1) on the twenty-fourth of Tevet. Yet the German version demonstrates an even greater degree of calendar consciousness than its counterparts, placing as it does the date of an entry (in tandem with the book title, *Auch Wenn Ich Hoffe* [Even as I hope]) at the top of every page as a running header. But with this feature the multicalendrical facet can go only so far. Despite the fact that, beginning with the pivotal date of the twenty-fourth of Tevet, the Jewish calendar plays the lead role in every entry, the running header at the page's top only accommodates the parenthetical, editorially added Gregorian date. So at the point when the calendar date in Flinker's original diary reaches the highest point of visibility, the Jewish date becomes poignantly eclipsed, likely because it was deemed too exotic to serve as a top-of-the-page guide to readers.

The problem actually precedes translation, since the drama of switching from one calendar to the other on January 1 is lost to nearly all readers, even those who encounter the diary in the original, since the Hebrew edition contains no annotations conveying the parallel calendar dates. Only a multicalendar awareness could enable an appreciation of Flinker's extraordinary gesture. The exception to this obfuscating rule appears, of all places, in the 1988 Russian edition.[31] Meticulous to a T, this edition reproduces the shift to the Jewish calendar and heads each entry following the twenty-fourth of Tevet with that date alone. In a footnote at the bottom of the entry, moreover, it cites the corresponding date in the Gregorian calendar—even, in this single case, the "January 1" date, the addition of which allows the reader to appreciate Flinker's gesture.[32]

Flinker reinforces the Jewish calendar's importance when he inscribes the illustrated cover of the third and final diary notebook with *only* the Jewish calendar date: 5704/ד"שת. Hence, even though he did not date the individual entries in this third notebook, his determination to date the notebook's cover with the Jewish calendar date alone again points to his continued dedication to the shift to the Jewish calendar set in motion months earlier. The layout of the inscription —"Eretz Yisrael" (the Land of Israel) above, "Zion" below, and the

Jewish date in the middle —shows graphically how precious the Hebrew calendar had become: it stood in the center, the pivot around which Jewish life turned.[33]

Jewish Time's Evolution in Rabbi Chaim Stein's Diary

Rabbi Chaim Stein's wartime Hebrew-language diary did not serve as a calendar per se; he had one at his disposal throughout his flight from the blood lands of Lithuania to the wartime oasis of Samarkand. But, like with Moshe Flinker's diary, the dating of Rabbi Stein's underwent a stunning revolution, shifting over the course of time (like Flinker's) from the secular to the Jewish. Certainly, the change from one system to the other doesn't go quite as far as Flinker's did; Rabbi Stein never eliminated completely Gregorian calendar dating. Nor did the transformation from one system of dating to the other occur as quickly, in overnight fashion, as did that of his young Dutch counterpart. But the movement was nonetheless steady, dramatic, and revealing.

Rabbi Stein was born in 1911 in western Lithuania, then part of the Russian Empire.[34] When he was nine years old, he was sent to study in Kelm, and two years later was brought to the Telshe yeshiva, one of the oldest, largest, and most respected yeshivas in Lithuania. Over time, he became one of the yeshiva's outstanding students, teaching as well as studying, and developing close relationships with the rabbis who administered the institution. In this period, the yeshiva numbered some five hundred students.

In addition to its rigorous Talmud study, the yeshiva also became an outpost of the musar movement, a state-of-the-art program of ethical refinement and intense devotion. Evidence of Rabbi Stein's passionate embrace of the philosophy and practice of this movement appears regularly in his diary, and clearly provided uncommon spiritual strength to confront the ordeal that he and his companions were subjected to during the war years.

The upheaval was set in motion in June 1940, when the Soviet Union occupied and soon annexed Lithuania. Some students remained with the yeshiva's head, Rabbi Avraham Yitzhak Bloch, in Telshe, while others relocated to four neighboring locales. Rabbi Stein led the group that went to the town of Tryskiai. Difficult though life may have been under the Communist regime, the Soviet occupation turned out to be but a prelude to the comprehensive disaster wrought by the Nazi invasion of Lithuania a year later. In the weeks that followed the summer 1941 invasion, almost all of the yeshiva's students and faculty, together with their families, were murdered en masse.

A small number, however, gratefully escaped the onslaught, including members of Rabbi Stein's Tryskiai group, who fled eastward. Thus began a trek of some three years, during which time the group was compelled to endure harsh physical labor in the kolkhoz farms of the eastern Soviet Union. Eventually, along with many other refugees, Rabbi Stein's group traveled to the southern Soviet republics, and they stayed in Uzbekistan until summer 1944. In Elul 5704 (September 1944), they reached Samarkand, remaining there until the war's end. In the aftermath, Rabbi Stein married the daughter of another refugee, Rabbi Chaim Aryeh Leib Sachs, and together with his wife and father-in-law immigrated by way of Europe to the United States. In Cleveland, Ohio, at the site of the transplanted Telshe yeshiva, he took up where he had left off just a few years before.

Rabbi Stein apparently began to keep a diary with the outbreak of the war in September 1939; the date has to remain speculative because the first of the six diary notebooks has disappeared. The second notebook commenced at Chanukah 1939; the sixth continued until the end of August 1944. At the outset, while still based in Lithuania, he mostly reported on what he knew of the events of the war (up through notebook 3). As time went on, and he and his Tryskiai study group were forced to take flight, his focus became more personal, documenting the group's journey as well as noting the spiritual strategies he enlisted to meet the formidable challenges the group encountered.

Rich in bringing together the description of an extraordinary journey of survival with the learning of a young Torah sage, the diary uses a system of dating that, on the face of it, runs counter to what one would expect. While still at his home base in Lithuania, immersed in a Jewish environment, Rabbi Stein dates the entries almost exclusively according to the Gregorian calendar. Clearly, the Jewish calendar is not absent; some holidays (the eighth day of Chanukah, for example) are referred to and the Jewish date on which they occurred shares the spotlight at the head of the entry. But by and large the Gregorian calendar dominates. One way to account for this is that opting for the Gregorian calendar paralleled the content that filled most entries—that is, the events of the war. And the course of the war that Rabbi Stein endeavored to chronicle related, at this point in time, to the world at large. In Lithuania, in contrast, life (including Jewish life) at the end of 1939 remained much as it had been. Indeed, many Polish Jews had fled east, believing that Lithuania, untouched by German aggression, provided a secure haven and a large welcoming Jewish community to boot.

That was no longer the case come the Nazi invasion of Lithuania on June 22, 1941. Having launched a surprise attack on Russia in the early hours of the day, the Germans quickly entered Lithuania. The threat that had been at a distance became local and intimate; the zone of safety insulating Lithuanian Jewry terrifyingly disappeared. "The war suddenly broke out," wrote Rabbi Stein on the day of the invasion, and "the panic among the residents was terrible. They fled for their lives, with only the clothes on their backs."

Chronicling the panic and flight of his fellow Lithuanian Jews, Rabbi Stein altered the dating of the calendar in two ways. First, from this point forward the Jewish calendar date is joined to each entry. Knowing something of what had occurred in Poland and elsewhere in the previous twenty months, only at this juncture did Rabbi Stein himself witness the imminent threat to Jewish life and limb. Along with the fear and panic ushered in by the enemy's proximity, it also changed how time was to be construed. Once Jewish existence was at stake, Jewish time became the idiom by which to chronicle the Jewish community's fate.

The second alteration in dating is likely related to the first. Rabbi Stein initiates here a count of the days of "the war"; each subsequent day ticks off one more in the count. The diary is recruited to track how many days the war (here understood as the watershed moment of the invasion of Lithuania on June 22, 1941) has thus far lasted. So "June 26, the second day of Rosh Chodesh Tammuz," marks "day five of the war"; "July 18, 25 Tammuz," marks day "27 of the war"; and so on, until toward the conclusion of notebook 4, in mid-December 1941, he sets down the number "148"—and then ends the count.

With the arrival of the notorious enemy, nothing was the same. War took over, danger penetrated every aspect of life—and the diary's calendar had to be calibrated anew to reckon with the changed circumstances. In order to reflect these circumstances accurately, Rabbi Stein, acting seemingly by reflex rather than by deliberation, twined together Jewish time and war time, pairing the twenty-seventh day of the month of Sivan and day number one (actually the letter *aleph* in the Hebrew script in which he wrote) of the outbreak of war in Lithuania.

From the third day on, Rabbi Stein and his group of sixteen fellow students were on the run, trying to decipher where and when to go. "We went some two kilometers outside of the city," he notes on June 24, "stopped in the forest, prayed the morning prayers, ate breakfast, and once again tried to determine where to go and how to proceed." This became a typical refrain, along with the sighting of refugees in flight and scouting out a place to sleep. Unsure at almost every juncture of what to do next, the group nevertheless made progress, and by the time of Tisha b'Av some six weeks later, they continued at a steady pace their eastward flight.

It was then, on the tenth day of the month of Menachem Av, 5701 (August 3, 1941), that Rabbi Stein made another telling change in the manner of dating his entries: the Jewish calendar date, which had been largely omitted from the diary entries for almost two years and had begun to appear regularly only with the outbreak of the war in Lithuania six weeks before, was now placed in the first and primary position.[35] The shift is of course subtle and nuanced, easily overlooked by the reader, and seemingly concerns a minor detail amid the welter of life-threatening phenomena that Rabbi Stein and his cohort were daily contending with.

Yet for all that, the change in sequence couldn't have been casual, since from here on out it stuck. Timed to coincide with a weighty date in the Jewish calendar, highlighting the Jewish date in such a manner could have been exceptional, something done on a special occasion (such as the ninth or tenth day of Av) or to mark a new point of departure; once the day passed, the diarist could well have returned to his conventional practice. As we saw, this indeed was the approach of Abraham Levin and Yitzhak Katzenelson, who featured the Jewish calendar date in order to align their wartime experience of catastrophe with the traditional meaning of the date in Jewish history and commemoration. Afterward, they reverted to their default practice of dating according to the Gregorian calendar. For his part, Rabbi Stein did not backtrack. Having altered the sequence and set the Jewish calendar date in a place of honor, he held to it. He doesn't comment on what moved him to emend his previous well-established practice of beginning each entry with the Gregorian calendar date. But we can surmise that the more distant became the life and land that had provided for a rich study and practice of Jewish tradition, the more the Jewish calendar was viewed as playing a key role in carrying forward what from the world of Lithuanian Jewish could be salvaged.

Rabbi Stein's diary helped him cope with the ordeal of flight and of being uprooted from the Torah-centered life that he had cultivated and the yeshiva halls where he could pursue that ideal unstintingly. In a fashion, the diary stood in for the yeshiva, summoning forth a regimen of religious study and practice and providing a forum for the author to air his insights. The fact that the Jewish calendar should progressively come into the limelight is thus in keeping with the special nature of this diary, saturated as it is with the spirit of Torah learning and prayer. From this angle, it is no wonder that the Jewish calendar came out on top. But the real story is told not by the ultimate triumph but by the slow but sure switch from one calendar to the other—a change brought about only once the Lithuanian Jewish world that had been ceased to exist. Hence the three-layered dating of Rabbi Stein's diary tells a story of its own, assuredly schematic and compressed compared with the narrative that surrounds it, but nonetheless symbolic of the struggle the author waged to continue to prize Torah and God in the wartime wilderness of the eastern Soviet Union.

In the aftermath of the war, Rabbi Stein settled back in the halls of the Telshe yeshiva, albeit transplanted to a different country and continent. With a few senior figures at the helm, the yeshiva, now based in Cleveland, Ohio, grew into a formidable institution in its own right, even while forever mourning the rabbis, students, and families whose bitter fate and heroic response were all too succinctly recalled by the few witnesses to survive.[36] Rabbi Stein himself was blessed with a long life, a great family, and many students. The diary, relic of a lost world, was put away, like so many others, in a drawer.

But once a year the drawer, and the diary, were opened. On the ninth day of the month of Av, the fast day dedicated to commemorating Jewish tragedies, Rabbi Stein would read passages from the diary aloud in the yeshiva, weaving his wartime deposition into the tapestry of ancient poems ritually recited on that day. The occasion, sober in tone and singular in allowing communal grief open expression, was clearly suited to the subject matter at hand. In terms of the diary itself, there was also a kind of poetic justice in choosing this day to read from the wartime diary, for the ninth of Av was, we recall, the day on which the Jewish calendar date was first given top billing. The diary was hence linked to the date internally and externally, at the moment of its composition and at the time of its later recitation. "On the day of the fast," Rabbi Stein wrote then, "we poured forth words before the Master of all concerning all of our travail, and our prayers and our hopes were strengthened that soon we would merit the complete redemption." One imagines that, spoken aloud by Rabbi Stein year after commemorative year, the words only gained in strength.

The Moon's Phases: Illustrating Jewish Time in Otto Wolf's Diary

A different kind of multicalendar dating surfaced in the diary of the Czech teenager Otto Wolf. The fifteen-year-old Wolf began to keep a diary in Czech when his family went into hiding in Moravia in June 1942. He continued for some two and a half years, making his final entry the day he was taken captive in April 1945. His sister took over the task in his stead, maintaining the diary at least to the end of the war. While she and her parents survived the war, Otto and his brother Kurt did not.[37]

Otto's diary tracked time on multiple levels. He was finely sensitive to recording a range of calendar dates, supplementing the dated headings with calculation of the number of weeks the family was in hiding. When they were forced to find a new hiding place in April 1944, he noted the number of days they spent in the new location. The diary entries served as a counterpoint to the headings, conscientiously alluding to major Jewish holidays, including the start of the Jewish month, anniversaries of notable deaths and birthdays, and, because special occasions increased his family's food allotment, Christian holidays and the start of the secular year. The datings are accurate, or nearly so.

But the printed editions of the diary omit a remarkable visual complement to his fine-tuned calendar consciousness: Wolf drew the phases of the moon next to the diary entry at the appropriate time in the lunar cycle: a half-moon for his first entry, on June 22, 1942; a full moon on June 28; a new moon on July 13; and continuing through to the full moon drawn on February 20, 1943, in the thirty-fifth week of hiding.[38] These are the diary's only illustrations. As Wolf chronicled the day-to-day fortunes of his family in hiding, he measured time also according to the lunar cycle, his illustrations echoing in their boyish way the pedagogic drawings used by the Mishnaic sage Rabban Gamliel to keep the ancient Jewish calendar on track.[39] While it is not likely that Otto deliberately mimicked the sage's drawings, both sage and boy turned to a visual lunar vocabulary in their respective commitments to keeping track of Jewish time.

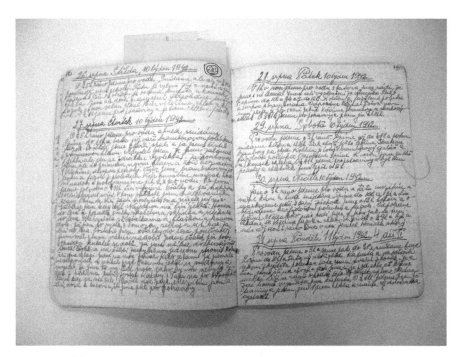

Fig. 5.1: The fifteen-year-old Otto Wolf began to keep a diary in Czech when his family went into hiding in Moravia in June 1942, and he continued to write in it for some two and a half years, making his final entry the day he was taken captive in April 1945. His diary tracked time on multiple levels, including drawing the phases of the moon next to the diary entry at the appropriate time in the lunar cycle. United States Holocaust Memorial Museum, Courtesy of the heirs of Felicitas (Lici) Garda, sister of Otto.

It may be that a local calendar could have inspired Otto Wolf to add his drawings of the moon's phrases. As Bina Greenwald notes in reference to her wartime experience of trying to keep track of Jewish time, even some wartime Gregorian calendars included such diagrams, which offered guidance for those bereft of Jewish calendar dates: "Of course we didn't have a Jewish calendar there and we couldn't know when any particular festival fell. But there was a secular calendar in the factory and it had little pictures of the new moon, when the moon would be full, and so on. So I did a reckoning and realized that it was almost Purim. I tried to find a way to celebrate the festival in this vale of tears."[40] Guided by the factory calendar's "little pictures," Bina Greenwald carried out her celebration in an improvised manner: "In the yard I found a small but whole potato. I sliced it and baked it in the little stove that we still had as a refuge from the winter. Those slices became Purim food gifts for my good friends."

Otto Wolf may have remembered a calendar with "little pictures of the new moon" like the one Bina Greenwald describes. But he also could have relied on his own disciplined observation to render the moon's phases. Endeavoring to make his way in his own vale of tears, he thereby bestowed upon his diary the capacity, in a rudimentary fashion, to chart the course of the Jewish month.

When Wolf was apprehended and his sister took over the diary, the reference to Jewish time became both more nuanced and strangely less accurate. Her April 20, 1945, entry exemplifies this change. "It is Yom Kippur Qatan," notes Felicitas Wolf, invoking the name given to the final day of a Jewish month. "We fast until 1pm." The special observance of the day before the onset of a new Jewish month is indeed marked by fasting among some groups of particularly devout Jews. Yet the secular date does not in this case square with the onset of the Jewish month, which occurred more than a week earlier. It is as if Otto's sister wished to use, and even expand, the diary's calendrical nature. But the oppressive nature of the family's ordeal at this stage, and particularly the loss of Otto himself, made it no longer possible to do so with the former fidelity.

Recording the Dates of Martyrdom: Leyb Rochman

From an altogether different, eastern European vantage point, Leyb Rochman, a twenty-six-year-old yeshiva student turned writer, commenced with his diary while hiding in a narrow bunker in dire conditions with four other Jews, including his wife and sister-in-law, in a cottage in the countryside outside of Warsaw.[41] Writing in Yiddish and regularly referring to Shabbat and holidays, Rochman nevertheless dates the entries according to the secular calendar, beginning with February 17, 1943, and ending with July 30, 1944. The special nature of time while in hiding and the role of the calendar are fused from the diary's outset. The first entry begins by fracturing time into its smallest components, as if the calendar date's significance itself demands investigation: "Today is Wednesday, February 17, 1943. Exactly twelve weeks have passed since we went into hiding here at Felek's. Twelve weeks are eighty-four days and, if my arithmetic is correct, 2, 016 hours. That's my count. All of us are constantly reckoning the time. We count even the individual minutes and seconds."[42] In Rochman's formulation, hiding has its own calendar and its own "constant" way of counting time passed.

The isolation of these five Jews in hiding was profound. This was not so much because they "los[t] touch with the outside world," as Michael Marrus has characterized the experience of wartime hiding. It was rather because the desperate fate of Polish Jewry was filtered through the reports of Polish gentile visitors to the cottage, who, in 1943, argued over whether there were any Jews left in Poland. Rochman and his companions had few opportunities to leave the attic bunker, so the bleak message they heard from the visitors' reports was overwhelming. Whereas Moshe Flinker strained to imagine what the deported Jews were going through in the East, Rochman and company were regularly faced with the anguished prospect that there were a diminishing number of Polish Jews left about whose fate they could speculate on.

The Jewish calendar, for its part, plays a role in three notable ways. First, the group composed a Jewish calendar so that, even in the undersize attic hideout, they could properly observe Shabbat and the holidays. Second, the diary concludes with a martyrology that lists both dates, secular and Jewish, side by side. And third, the two entries with a Jewish calendar date—the eighth and tenth of Elul 5702—head Rochman's two-day retrospective chronicling of his town's destruction. Even in the midst of hiding, the watershed of the community's destruction stands at the center of the diary's narrative—and with it, the Jewish dates that mark its demise.

Zelig Kalmanovitch: The Beginning of the Jewish Month as Point of Reference

On the surface, Zelig Kalmanovitch's Vilna ghetto diary also seems content to date with the secular calendar. But beneath it, the Jewish calendar plays a formidable role. It is a combination not unlike Kalmanovitch himself. Born in Latvia in 1881, he enjoyed a traditional Jewish education but then went on to pursue the academic study of Yiddish. He arrived in Vilna in 1929 and became a central figure in the founding and leadership of the Vilna YIVO Institute of Jewish Studies. During the war, he underwent a change of heart, embracing a life of Torah and devotion. This blend of an expertise in the scientific study of Judaism and articulate faith gave his voice a particular moral authority in the ghetto. In historian Lucy Dawidowicz's formulation, he was one of the wartime Jewish intellectuals who "saw Jewish fate in the light of millennial Jewish history and under the aspect of eternity."[43] Indeed, he chose to write his wartime journal in Hebrew, as if the vehicle of the sacred Jewish language was meant to underscore "the aspect of eternity." Like Herman Kruk, Zelig Kamanovitch was deported to Estonia and perished there in 1944.

Though his religious commitment plays a moving part in the diary, it is not conspicuous in the dating.[44] With entries spanning June 1942 to the end of August 1943, he dates most of them according to the secular calendar. Yet sensitivity to the calendar is present from the outset: the diary begins by noting that it is the anniversary of the commencement of war in Lithuania: "On the day that marks a full year since the outbreak of the war I begin to set down my account of the days that have past." From that point forward, dating becomes laconic—"First day of the week, 26 July [1942] . . ."—and more telegraphic, sometimes not including even the month: "6th day of the week, 31th [July 1942]." Yet there are telling exceptions where the Jewish calendar rises to the surface.

One of these is an entry that at first glance appears like most others: "11th of the 10th," a shorthand way of referring to the eleventh day of October. But this is followed by invoking the Jewish calendar—and a special date at that: Rosh Chodesh Marcheshvan, the first day of the second month of the Jewish year. Exceptional in its own right, the date leads off a passage that focuses on a number of celebrations from the string of holidays filling the previous month, particularly a Simchas Torah celebration that Kalmanovitch attended and spoke at. His entry includes at least some of his inspired comments: "Our song and dance are a form of worship. Our rejoicing is thanks to the One who decrees life and death." Though written a week after the events it recounts, the entry filters the special character of the festival, even in the shadow of the oppressor, through the Jewish calendar date, the celebratory beginning of the next Jewish month. Yet it is likely that the sequence was the other way around, that the Simchas Torah account also elicited the dating that would fit the sublime nature of the entry, as the formulation of a title often comes after, rather than before, the story it heads.

Like Saying Kaddish: A Jewish Calendar's Legacy in Rabbi David Kahane's Diary/Memoir

Multiple dates that head diary entries make conspicuous the calendar's importance. But, in certain cases, the astonishing presence of a Jewish calendar plays a pivotal role within the diary's narrative. Rabbi David Kahane's diary/memoir of his wartime ordeal in Lvov, a well-known primary source, serves as a powerful example.[45] Rabbi Kahane endured not only the decimation of the Lvov ghetto but also the terrible rigors of the Janowska concentration camp, both of which he chronicles in significant detail. He escaped the camp and, with his wife and child, was hidden by leaders of the Ukrainian Greek Catholic Church. Following the war he served as a rabbi in Poland before immigrating to Israel, where he became the chief rabbi for the Israel Air Force. He passed away in 1998.

Rabbi Kahane details a particularly moving episode in the Janowska camp that pivots on the calendar. Returning to the camp with his work detail, he sees that two friends have not come back, having apparently been murdered for not being able to keep up the pace. He takes out of a bag a "fifty-year calendar" that he received from one of the men. Leafing through it, writes Kahane, "was like saying kaddish" for the murdered friend who had first presented him with the gift. "Whom will I inform of the day of his passing?" wonders Kahane, clearly distraught by the vacuum in marking his friend's death. Replaying in his mind the anguished scene, he turns to his readers as those whom he will inform: "The day, the fifth day of the week, 24 Kislev 5703, 2 December 1942, Mar and Shapiro were certainly shot."[46] By way of the calendar and calendar date, he fills the vacuum that leaves a death unknown and unmarked.

Meant initially to give meaning to a friend's senseless death, the Jewish calendar date initiates a sequence of commemoration. "Suddenly," notes Kahane, "I remembered: Master of the Universe, is today not the first light of Chanukah, the evening of the sixth day of the week, 25 Kislev?" Even with the friend's calendar in his bag, Kahane was so submerged in the camp's brutal routine that he couldn't keep track of time. "The first light of Chanukah," he records with chagrin, "and I forgot." Checking the calendar has unearthed more than one meaning for this date, a discovery that then crescendos toward an attempt to rectify what was forgotten: Kahane shares his calendar revelation with his fellow prisoners, is able to organize material to light a makeshift menorah, rallies his blockmates, intones the blessings, says words of encouragement, and feels spiritually cleansed by the experience. The finale comes with the singing of "Maoz Tzur," the medieval Chanukah hymn chronicling the Jew's triumph over ancient enemies, a culminating act of recovery eventually suppressed by the kapos. Confronted with the sorrowful prospect of uncommemorated death, Kahane ends up retrieving from oblivion a crucial time of spiritual resistance on the Jewish calendar. All in all, it is the "fifty-year calendar," presumably kept in secret and presented as a gift by one inmate to another, that sets in motion the preservation of the Jewish calendar dates per se.[47]

Yet Rabbi Kahane has trouble moving between calendars. His original diary/ memoir reference to "December 2" as the day on which his friends were murdered does not align with the Thursday Jewish calendar date, which turns out in 5703/1942 to have been December 3. Though in this case the actual fallout from the error of a day is seemingly minimal, the gap between the calendars leaves a dissonance, especially because the incident in question pivots so forcefully around the calendar once owned by one of the victims.

Indeed, this precious calendar plays an orienting role from the first page of the book. Having been spirited out of the Janowska camp in spring 1943, first to one hiding place and then another under the watchful eye of Andrei Sheptyts'kyithe, the Greek Catholic archbishop of Lvov, Kahane tries to locate himself in Jewish time: "It is a lovely sunny morning, awash with light, as beautiful as a day can be in our parts, in Podolia, in early fall. According to my calculations, today Jews rise at dawn to say Selikhoth."[48] Kept out of harm's way in a Christian citadel, Kahane links himself by way of his "calculations" based on his inherited calendar to Jewish life and time: the special early morning Selikhoth prayers recited by Ashkenazi Jews that commence a few days before Rosh Hashana. But the vast isolation insinuates doubt where normally none would arise; the calendar becomes suspect, orchestrating as it does community ritual for those who no longer exist to carry out the precepts: "I am not certain about my calculations but according to the thousand-year calendar given to me by an old man in the camp last winter, the first day of Rosh Hashana falls on September 30. Besides, the whole matter seems a bit ridiculous to me since the question is, Are there any Jews left in the world? Are there any people left, free to come and go as they wish? Do Jews still rise to say Selikhoth somewhere?"[49] Rabbi Kahane's searching reflections probe the essential link between calendar and community, asking whether there can be a Jewish calendar without a Jewish community observing the holidays, precepts, and customs it sets forth. The question strikes at the heart of Jewish timekeeping during the Holocaust. Strikingly, we have regularly seen that wartime Jewish calendars often included observances that few, if any, Jews in ghettos or camps would be able to honor. In these cases, the calendar itself would do the observing, would articulate the precept, would carry forward the custom, irrespective of the wherewithal of the Jewish community it addressed to actively perform them. Rabbi Kahane, alone and having just witnessed the decimation of one of Europe's great Jewish communities, is led to wonder, ponder, and question. And yet he, cloistered in a hideout administered by the region's Christian elite, turns to the Jewish calendar to get his bearings. Whatever the questions that arise, the calendar is his compass. It is the guide that transports him beyond his immediate circumstances to a Jewish world preparing, by way of the Selichot prayers, for the entry into a New Year. The calendar at hand, moreover, tracks time for a "thousand year[s]," an extraordinary reckoning by any standard. Especially in the midst of Rabbi Kahane's desperate isolation, the reference to a calendar of such duration conveys a sense of immense longevity—and of a future extending well beyond the confines of the moment.[50]

The Jewish Calendar as *the* Calendar in Rabbi Wolgelernter's Diary

The Jewish calendar was not only an *alternative* system of dating. For some, it was *the* system. In these cases, the war unfolded first and foremost as a Jewish experience. In this respect, the years of the war were no different from the time that preceded it. Blessed or cursed though life may have been for Jews in Poland and elsewhere, time remained constantly recognizable. To continue to perceive daily reality through the lens of the Jewish calendar was normal and pervasive. No tragedy was needed in order to hurtle the Jewishness of the experience into the foreground. It was there all the time.

The dating of a diary according to the Jewish calendar served as both symptom and signpost of such experience—symptom because it objectified time as Jewish and signpost because, like a calendar, it kept track of the days. It often did this sporadically, diary dates often being far less consistent than those of a calendar. And to a certain extent this inconsistency in daily dating was an obligatory omission for an Orthodox Jew, who followed the prohibition against writing on the Sabbath and certain holidays. But even or especially with these patterned omissions, the diary too tracked time.

For Rabbi Chaim Yitzchok Wolgelernter, then, to date his wartime diary according to the Jewish calendar flowed from his pen.[51] Born in 1911 in a shtetl outside of Kracow, Rabbi Wolgelernter grew up in a Chasidic family of six children, in the town of Dzialoszyce. His father was a ritual slaughterer who trained his sons in kind. Chaim Yitzchok studied in yeshivas in Kracow and then became an ardent Chasid of the Ostrozve Rebbe. His gift for writing found expression early and in a number of different forums, including as editor of the yeshiva journal and as contributor to others. With the cruel destruction of the town's Jews in September 1942, he hid over the next twenty months with Polish contacts. Shortly before the area was liberated by Russian troops, he was betrayed and murdered by Polish nationalists. His wife, a young child, and his brother managed to survive.

While in hiding, Rabbi Chaim Yitzchok kept a diary in Yiddish in a lined ledger writing tablet. He recorded events but also memorialized in Hebrew poems of lamentation, his town, his Rebbe, and his family members who were deported and murdered.

"The yahrzeit of the *kedoshim* of Dzialoszyce," writes Rabbi Wolgelernter, "falls on the twenty-first of Elul." Marking the day when the Jews of his town were slaughtered, the author keeps track of the movement of the Jewish calendar even when in constant trepidation over his own fate. Reference to the Jewish calendar is ubiquitous. Whether dating the entries, chronicling events within them, or concluding the poems that pay tribute to the murdered, the Jewish calendar date locates the events in Jewish time.

Yet for Rabbi Wolgelernter to maintain a sense of time and occasion is itself an achievement, for the cruelty of the events constantly threatens to overwhelm any attempt to cleave to tradition. Religious practices can be carried out only piecemeal, without the ritual objects and texts that allow for even rudimentary observance:

> We spent Rosh Hashanah 5703 [September 12–13, 1942], in the mayor's barn [in Szyszczyce]. Although we were more than a *minyan* of men, we had neither a *tallis* nor even a siddur, and, needless to say, no *shofar*. Each person pieced together the holy words of the *tefillos* from memory as best as he could.
>
> No one had any individual, personal pleas. Just one collective request from the Master of the Universe that the new year should bring relief and an end to the plague, at least for the few remaining *Yidden*.[52]

Piecing together fragments of holy words as best they could, the barn-based prayer quorum still made Jewish time the index for life and hope.

Even when suffering the most intimate loss, Rabbi Wolgelernter yokes the Jewish calendar to his poignant lyrics as the natural means to bring meaning to what seems hopeless:

> My heart is searching in the east; my spirit roaming the world.
> Alte'le, my beloved daughter, I sought you but could not find you.
> O, how I yearn for you —will I merit seeing you again?
> *In memory of my three-year-old daughter Altele who was taken on a transport on Thursday, 21 Elul, 5702. Chaim Yitzchok Wolgelernter Tishrei 5703*[53]

Writing a month or so after his daughter's disappearance, Rabbi Wolgelernter makes sure the exact date and day in the Jewish calendar are recorded. Generalities are not enough; specificity offers a refuge in time for those dislodged from place. The world at large may operate according to another calendar. But it exists outside of the author's frame of meaningful reference.

Moreover, the frame did not shift as things became worse. This differs from those for whom the Jewish calendar served as an alternative. For them, the decision to invoke the Jewish calendar, the alternative system, came at moments of crisis. To switch to Jewish dates aligned the diary chronicle with Jewish time. It also demonstrated that the mainstream secular calendar was not altogether neutral but rather filtered out the associations latent in Jewish life and history. For a period, Jewish time was given center stage and then retreated again to the wings. In the exceptional cases of Rabbi Chaim Stein and Moshe Flinker, the alternative system became the system of choice. For Rabbi Wolgelernter, nothing shifted, every coordinate remained in place; from beginning to end, time was defined singly by the Jewish calendar.

Notes

1. Emanuel Ringelblum, "Oyneg Shabbes, " *The Literature of Destruction: Jewish Responses to Catastrophe*, ed. David G. Roskies, trans. Elinor Robinson (Philadelphia: Jewish Publication Society, 1989), p. 386.

2. See Philippe Lejeune's thoughtful remarks on the subject in *On Diary*, eds. Jeremy Popkin and Julie Rak (Honolulu: University of Hawaii Press, 2009), particularly the section "The Clock and the Calendar" and the chapter "Today's Date." Despite the fact that Lejeune helpfully includes both calendars and diary dating, his focused discussion of diary dating in "Today's Date" strangely makes no reference to calendars. And while he nicely endeavors to give the emergence of diary dating a wide historical lens, his assertions about the history of calendars seem off base.

3. *Salvaged Pages: Young Writers' Diaries of the Holocaust* (New Haven: Yale University Press, 2004), p. 444.

4. *Numbered Days: Diaries and the Holocaust* (New Haven: Yale University Press, 2006),

5. David Patterson, *Along the Edge of Annihilation: The Collapse and Recovery of Life in the Holocaust Diary* (Seattle: University of Washington Press, 1999), p. 68. See also his more recent comments on wartime diaries (and letters): David Patterson, "Wartime Victim Writing in Western Europe," in *Literature of the Holocaust*, ed. Alan Rosen (Cambridge: Cambridge University Press, 2013), pp. 33–47.

6. Patterson, *Along the Edge of Annihilation*. p. 71.

7. See also Amos Goldberg's comments in *Trauma in the First Person: Diary Writing during the Holocaust* (Bloomington: Indiana University Press, 2017), pp. 43–44, and p. 114. For Goldberg, the calendar (seemingly any kind of calendar) places the diary writer in time, but because it offers a "geometrical and objective framework," does not provide a "framework for human experience." His remarks seem to mirror Engelking and others I discuss in

my introduction, who view the calendar in a negative light in terms of the Jewish victim's experience of time during the Holocaust.

For studies that explore the diary's special timekeeping aspects, see Anna Jackson, *Diary Poetics: Form and Style in Writer's Diaries, 1915–1962* (New York: Routledge, 2010); Stuart Sherman, *Telling Time: Clocks, Diaries, and English Diurnal Form, 1660–1785* (Chicago: University of Chicago Press, 1996); Paul Glennie and Nigel Thrift, *Shaping the Day: A History of Timekeeping in England and Wales 1300–1800* (London: Oxford University Press, 2009); J. A. Baggerman, R. Dekker, and M. Mascuch, *Controlling Time and Shaping the Self: Developments in Autobiographical Writing Since the Sixteenth Century* (Leiden: Brill, 2011); Molly A. McCarthy, *The Accidental Diarist: A History of the Daily Planner in America* (Chicago: University of Chicago Press, 2013); Rachael Langford and Russell West, eds., *Marginal Voices, Marginal Forms: Diaries in European and History* (Amsterdam and Atlanta, GA: Rodopi, 1999). Although the latter volume casts a wide net, a number of contributions (including the editors' introduction) deal with Holocaust-era diaries. See also Salim Tamari and Ihsan Turjman, *Year of the Locust: A Soldier's Diary and the Erasure of Palestine's Ottoman Past* (Berkeley: University of California Press, 2011), pp. 37–38. Turjman drew on three calendars for dating all diary entries.

8. Chaim Aharon Kaplan, *Megilat Yesurim*, ed. Nachman Blumenthal (Tel Aviv and Jerusalem: Am Oved and Yad Vashem, 1966); Chaim Kaplan, *Scroll of Agony: the Warsaw Diary of Chaim A. Kaplan*, ed. Abraham Katsh (New York: Macmillan, 1965); *Buch der Agonie: Der Warschauer Tagebuch des Chaim A. Kaplan* (Frankfurt: Insel Verlag, 1965); and *Chronique d'une agonie: Journal du Ghetto de Varsovie* (Paris: Calmann-Levy, 1966).

9. See the introductions to the respective editions. Most commentators on Holocaust diaries, and on wartime Warsaw Jewry, refer to Kaplan's diary. See for example Yisrael Gutman, *The Jews of Warsaw, 1939–43: Ghetto, Underground, Revolt*, trans. Ina Friedman (Bloomington: Indiana University Press, 1982); George Steiner, "Postscript," *Language and Silence: Essays on Language, Literature and the Inhuman* (New York: Atheneum, 1977 [1967]); Irving Halperin, "'To Save Alive a Whole World': Chaim Kaplan's Warsaw Diary," in *Messengers from the Dead: Literature of the Holocaust* (Philadelphia: Westminster, 1970); Alvin Rosenfeld, "Holocaust and History," in *A Double Dying: Reflections on Holocaust Literature* (Bloomington: Indiana University Press, 1980); and Patterson and Garbarini's more recent reflections in the context of Holocaust diaries.

10. It is worth noting that the Jewish calendar dates appear only sporadically in the English-language translation; in this fall, 1940 period, for example, the translation into English incorporates only five of the twelve examples (highlighted in bold).

11. *Bletter far Geschichte* V:4 (1952), pp.22–68; VII:1 (1954), pp. 42–99; VII:2–3 (1954), pp. 210–40; *From the Notebook of the Yehudiya Teacher: Warsaw Ghetto, April 1942–January 1943* (Tel Aviv: Ghetto Fighters' House and Ha-Kibbutz ha-Meuhad, 1969); *A Cup of Tears: A Diary of the Warsaw Ghetto*, ed. Anthony Polonsky, trans. Christopher Hutchins (Oxford: Blackwell, 1988).

12. Ringelblum's well-known approbation was written in 1944. Joseph Kermish, ed., *To Live with Honor and Die with Honor: Selected Documents from the Warsaw Ghetto Underground Archives 'O.S.'* [Oyneg Shabbes] (Jerusalem: Yad Vashem, 1986), p. 18.

13. On the Great Deportation, see Israel Gutman, *The Jews of Warsaw*, particularly the chapter "The Fateful Deportation"; and Samuel Kassow, *Who Will Write Our History?: Emanuel Ringelblum, the Warsaw Ghetto, and Oyneg Shabes Archive* (Bloomington: Indiana University Press, 2007), particularly pp. 299–311.

14. See David Roskies on the archetypes of traditional responses to catastrophe that figured centrally in the writings of Holocaust ghetto chroniclers. *Against the Apocalypse: Responses to Catastrophe in Modern Jewish Culture* (Cambridge: Harvard University Press, 1984).

15. pp. 135–36 in the English translation, pp. 87–88 in the Hebrew.

16. Yitzhak Katznelson, *Pinkes Vittel* (Hebrew); *Vittel Diary* (Tel Aviv: Ghetto Fighters' House, 1964).

17. David Roskies, "Wartime Victim Writing in Eastern Europe," in *Literature of the Holocaust*, ed. Alan Rosen (Cambridge: Cambridge University Press, 2013), pp. 28–29. See within the essay (pp. 15–32) for Roskies's valuable remarks on other wartime diaries, particularly the Auschwitz Sonderkommando journal of Zalman Gradowski.

18. This is how Katznelson's holograph of the diary renders it; the Hebrew edition follows suit; the English translation ignores it and substitutes a numeral.

19. *Pinkes Vittel*, p 163–64; *Vittel Diary*, p. 100–102. I have modified the orthography to reflect the original.

20. Herman Kruk, *Diary of the Vilna Ghetto* (Yiddish) (New York: YIVO, 1961); Herman Kruk, *The Last Days of the Jerusalem of Lithuania: Chronicles from the Vilna Ghetto and the Camps, 1939–1944*, ed. Benjamin Harshav, trans. Barbara Harshav (New Haven: Yale University Press; YIVO). In addition to the editors' introductions to the above cited editions of the diaries, see Samuel David Kassow, "Vilna and Warsaw, Two Ghetto Diaries: Herman Kruk and Emanuel Ringelblum," in *Holocaust Chronicles*, ed. Robert Moses Shapiro (Hoboken, NJ: Ktav, 1999), pp. 171–215.

21. Herman Kruk, *The Last Days of the Jerusalem of Lithuania*; see Saul Friedlander, *The Years of Extermination: Nazi Germany and the Jews, 1939–1945* (New York: Harper, 2007), p. 633.

22. Friedlander, *The Years of Extermination*, p. 397. The epigraph begins the final section entitled "Part III/Shoah/Summer 1942–Spring 1945." It reads as follows: "It is like being in a great hall where many people are joyful and dancing and also where there are a few people who are not happy and who are not dancing. And from time to time a few people of this latter kind are taken away, led to another room, and strangled. The happy dancing people in the hall do not feel this at all. Rather, it seems as if this adds to their joy and doubles their happiness." Flinker's diabolical "great hall" image, formulated on the heels of his shocking discovery of the disappearance of another Jewish family in Brussels, thus symbolizes for Friedlander the heart of the Holocaust. I quote and comment on Flinker's remarkable parable in my discussion of Borinski's Auschwitz calendar.

23. Moshe Flinker, *Hana'ar Moshe: Yomano shel Moshe Flinker*, ed. Shaul Esh, intro. Dov Sadan (Jerusalem: Yad Vashem, 1958).

24. Jacob Boas has noted the Jewish calendar's role in Moshe's diary: "Every page of his diary is a Jewish page, from the dating by the Hebrew calendar and the mournful prayers that close many of the entries, to the classical Hebrew he used to express himself." Jacob Boas, *We Are Witnesses: Five Diaries of Teenagers Who Died in the Holocaust"* (New York: Square Fish, 1995), p. 85. Boas doesn't, however, refer to the calendar change in dating the entries, missing the evolution that takes place over time and the strategic moment in which the change occurs.

25. H. Y. Bornstein, "Ta'arichei Yisrael" (The Dates of Israel), *HaTekufah* 9 (1935), pp. 202–64.

26. I am indebted to Rivka Schweber, Moshe Flinker's sister, who shared with me her recollection of the events surrounding January 1, 1943. She (and her sisters and sister-in-law

listed in note 33 below) also elaborated on the biographical information available in the introductions to the diary's various published editions. Personal communication, July 11, 2010 (Tammuz 29, 5770).

27. *Young Moshe's Diary: The Spiritual Torment of a Jewish Boy in Nazi Europe*, intro. Shaul Esh and Geoffrey Wigoder (Jerusalem: Yad Vashem 1979), p. 56. The Italian edition, because it is translated from the English, reproduces the same errors. *Diario Profetico (1942–1943)*, intro. Shaul Esh and Geoffrey Wigoder, preface Alighiero Chiusano, trans. Gabriele Bonetti (Rome: Citta nuova, 1993).

28. *Dagboek van Mozes Flinker*, trans. J. Soetendorp, intro. H. Van Praag, Baarn, 1974.

29. Translations take on a life of their own, independent of the original. Thus the skewed dating of the English translation has been reproduced in several places. Alexandra Zapruder's outstanding collection of children's diaries from the Holocaust reprints the English translation with no critical attention to the dating. And Saul Friedlander's epigraph, which I cited above, is culled from the English translation and hence follows that edition in using the Gregorian rather than (as Flinker himself did) the Jewish calendar. On top of that, the date given in Friedlander's epigraph (January 21, 1943) is off by a day from the Gregorian calendar date given in the English translation (January 22, 1943; it is this latter date that corresponds to the Jewish calendar date in the original Hebrew edition). See Friedlander, *The Years of Extermination*, p. 397.

30. *"Auch Wenn Ich Hoffe": Das Tagebuch Des Moshe Flinker*, foreword by Saul Friedlander (Berlin: Berlin University Press, 2008).

31. *The Diary of Moshe Flinker*, trans. Avraham Beilov (Jerusalem: Amaha, 1988). The most recent edition, a French translation from the Hebrew manuscript, also records the change to the Jewish calendar. Like the German translation, it accompanies the Jewish date with the Gregorian in parentheses—in this case, however, noting the correct January 1 date on which the shift took place. But, alas, the translation begins on the wrong foot: it encloses the initial Gregorian date—24 Novemb. 1942 —with parentheses, thereby giving the mistaken impression that the Jewish date had from the outset the primary role. Moshe Flinker, *Carnets de clandestinié: Bruxelles, 1942-1943*, trans. Guy-Alain Sitbon (Paris: Calmann Levy, 2017).

32. The fact that readers of Russian, straddling Western and Eastern timekeeping modes, are used to negotiating multiple calendar dates may have set the stage for this breakthrough.

33. Here, too, the English translation is less than faithful to the original. The English edition reproduces at the very beginning of the volume a photograph of the third notebook's illustrated cover, with a caption stating, "Cover of Moshe Flinker's Notebook." Unlike the accurate rendering of the Hebrew edition, the English one does not indicate that the cover is that of the third notebook. Nor does it translate Flinker's Hebrew inscription ("Eretz Yisrael" [the Land of Israel] above, "Zion" below, and the Jewish date in the middle). And by placing the cover reproduction at the beginning of the volume, it wrongly conveys the impression that this is the cover for the diary entries that follow, culled mainly from the first notebook. I am indebted to Gittel Vidoslovsky and Esther Flinker, sister and sister-in-law respectively of Moshe Flinker, for the opportunity to review the original notebooks. In spring 2010, a third sister, Rochel Shmuelevitz, was also kind enough to share recollections of the Flinker household in general and the time in Brussels in particular. Four of Moshe's sisters tell the family's story in the documentary film *B'tzel K'nafecha*, (Jerusalem, 2006).

34. See Rabbi Chaim Stein, *From Telshe to Telshe: The Diary of Rabbi Chaim Stein, 5700–5704/1940–1944* (Hebrew), ed. and intro. Esther Farbstein (Jerusalem: Michlala Center for the Study of the Shoah, 2015), pp. iv–xxlii For further context see the interview with Rabbi Isaac Ausband by David Boder, 1946 (Hénonville, France). Rabbi Ausband was a member of the Telshe group of students who took flight; he too survived and joined the staff of the transplanted Telshe yeshiva in Cleveland. His interview first appeared in printed form in David Boder, *Topical Autobiographies of Displaced People* (Chicago: self-published, 1950), vol. 2, pp. 202–43; the audio and text of the interview can be accessed at http://voices.iit.edu/audio.php?doc=ostlandI. Website biographies of Rabbi Stein give inaccurate information, claiming that he was among those rescued by the Japanese consul in Kovne, Chiune Sugihara. For general background, see *Sefer Telshe* (Hebrew), ed. Yitzhak Alporovitz (Tel Aviv: Telz Society, 1984); and *Pinkas HaKihilot Lita*, ed. Dov Levin (Jerusalem: Yad Vashem, 1996).

35. The day usually designated for the twenty-four-hour communal fast, the ninth of Av, took place in 5701 on Shabbat, when it is prohibited to fast. Hence the fast day, and the special prayers that accompanied it, was deferred to Sunday, the tenth day of Av.

36. Naomi Bloch, "Testimony on Telsiai" (Yiddish) (Israel Kaplan Collection, Ghetto Fighters' Museum Archive, no. 20857); Chana Bloch-Ausband, "Last Confession," *Beth Jacob Monthly* 26 (Tammuz 5721 [1961]), pp. 24–25; excerpts from this testimony appear in *Shema Yisrael*, pp. 62, 123–25. Both were daughters of the heads of the yeshiva, Avraham Yitzhak Bloch (Chana) and his brother Rabbi Zalman Bloch (Naomi). They witnessed the horrific decimation of the Telshe community but were able to escape the final slaughter. Chana married Rabbi Isaac Ausband; Naomi married Rabbi Pesach Stein, a Lithuania survivor and noted Torah sage, who joined the staff of the Cleveland Telshe yeshiva in the late 1940s.

37. See *Denik Otty Wolfa 1942–1945* (Prague: Sefer, 1997); a partial translation by Michael Kubat is included in Alexandra Zapruder, *Salvaged Pages: Young Writers' Diaries of the Holocaust* (New Haven: Yale University Press, 2004), pp. 122–59. I have benefited from Kubat's full English translation generously provided by the United States Holocaust Memorial Museum (USHMM) and from on-site review of the original notebooks, which was also generously aided by the USHMM.

38. After six months or so, Otto, for unknown reasons, began to limit the drawings to new and full moons and then left off with the lunar illustrations entirely, perhaps because of decreasing winter visibility or increasing preoccupation with the demands of hiding.

39. Mishna Rosh Hashana, 2:8.

40. Bina Grünwald, *Light from the Darkness* (Hebrew) (Me'orei Or, 1998), pp. 61–63.

41. Leyb Rochman, *Un in deyn blut solstu lebn* (Paris: Friends of Mintz-Mazowiecski, 1949); English trans., *The Pit and the Trap* (New York: Holocaust Library, 1983). A copy of the holograph of the diary can be found in Yad Vashem Archives, 033. I have benefitted by Jan Schwarz's comments on Rochman's diary in a chapter of his book *Survivors and Exiles: Yiddish Culture after the Holocaust* (Detroit: Wayne State University Press, 2015).

42. Rochman, *The Pit and the Trap*, p. 11.

43. Lucy Dawidowicz, *A Holocaust Reader*, p. 175.

44. Zelig Kalmanovitch, *Diary from the Vilna Ghetto* (Hebrew) (Tel Aviv: Moreshet, 1977); "A Diary of the Nazi Ghetto in Vilna," *YIVO Annual of Jewish Social Studies* 8 (1953): 9–81; the earliest publication of the diary appeared in a Yiddish translation in *Yivo-bleter* 35 (1951), pp. 18–92.

45. David Kahane, *Yoman Ghetto Lvov* (Jerusalem: Yad Vashem, 1978); *Lvov Ghetto Diary*, trans. Jerzy Michalowicz; foreword by Erich Goldhagen (Amherst: University of Massachusetts, 1990).

46. *Yoman Ghetto Lvov*, p. 119

47. The English translation, almost entirely omitting Jewish calendar dates, misses this pivotal connection. See Rosen, "The Languages of Time."

48. *Lvov Ghetto Diary*, p. 3.

49. Ibid.

50. The "fifty-year calendar" that Kahane refers to when chronicling the Chanukah commemoration in Janowska and "the thousand-year calendar" that he alludes to here in the book's opening pages are apparently one and the same.

51. Rabbi Chaim Yitzchok Wolgelernter, *The Unfinished Diary: A Chronicle of Tears* (Lakewood, NJ: Israel Book Shop, 2015). My thanks to Feival Wolgelernter, the author's son, for sharing with me copious information about his father's ordeal and providing me with a copy of the Yiddish original of the diary.

52. Ibid., p. 147

53. Ibid., pp.136–37

VI The Holocaust as a Revolution in Jewish Time

The Lubavitcher Rebbes' Wartime Calendar Book

A New Beginning

Most wartime calendars, as we have seen, were conventional; they looked much like Jewish calendars produced under less dire conditions. Indeed, their very greatness can be seen in how firmly they stuck to convention. In order to do that, their authors felt obliged to produce a familiar guide to traditional practice and custom. Hence, the calendars usually encompassed a Jewish year, which began in the month of Tishrei with the holiday of Rosh Hashana. Through the year, they highlighted the Sabbath day, enumerated holidays and fast days (often with accompanying times specifying the entry and exit of the special day), indicated the onset of the new Jewish month, and occasionally augmented the facts with illustrations. And in nearly every case (Kalikow's painting is the exception), the Jewish calendar was paired with the Gregorian one. Joining together the two calendars demonstrated that, even when the world at large had gone awry, had come undone, had with relentless fury turned against the Jewish people or had abandoned them, Jews nevertheless continued to be linked to it through the calendar.

As we know, these wartime calendars were not uniform but rather appeared in various sizes and designs, drew on a wide range of materials, and exhibited different degrees of sophistication. In certain cases, the calendars seemed to introduce nuanced innovations, omitting, for example, key dates at pivotal junctures of the year. Sometimes the calendars doubled as ledgers on which to record the heartbreaking losses of the moment. And there were ingenious attempts to picture Jewish time, as for example in the painting of Hilda Kalikow and the life-cycle drawings of Tsewie Herschel's father. These productions were not calendars per se but rather hybrid creations that nevertheless harnessed an artistic medium to envision Jewish time—or, in the latter case, the time of a single Jew.

The truly unconventional calendar came, however, in a surprisingly original garb: a 1943 book fashioned as a calendar.[1] Entitled in Hebrew *Hayom yom* (Today is the day) and compiled by Rabbi Menachem Schneersohn (who would

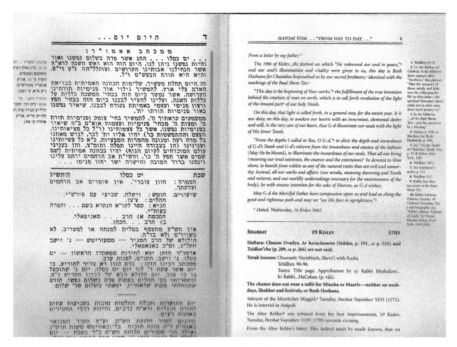

Fig. 6.1: *Hayom yom* ("Today Is the Day") was a Chasidic calendar book for the years 5703–4 (1943–44). A collaboration between the Lubavitcher rebbe and his son-in-law Rabbi Menachem Mendel Schneersohn, the Yiddish/Hebrew calendar was produced in New York, out of harm's way. But the teachings contained therein were intended to guide a spiritual revolution in response to the desperate situation of European Jewry. Courtesy of Kehot Publications.

later become the seventh Lubavitcher Rebbe), the revolutionary character of the calendar was brought home by its absolutely unique starting date. It did not begin on January 1, New Year's Day in the Gregorian calendar year; indeed, January 1 is nowhere to be found in the pages of the calendar. Nor did it begin on Tishrei 1, the date of the conventional Jewish New Year, Rosh Hashana, the fall day that does double duty by inaugurating the Jewish year as well as leading off the high holiday season. Nor did it begin, as a few wartime calendars did, on Nisan 1, which starts the month in which the momentous holiday of Passover occurs.

This calendar set out on an entirely new course.[2] The starting date was the nineteenth of Kislev, a date that had never before headed a calendar. The date fell in the latter part of what was usually deemed to be the third month in the Jewish year, some six days before the onset of the holiday of Chanukah, which begins on the twenty-fifth of Kislev. Ensconced in the third week of the third month, the date on the face of it had little to recommend it as a beginning; it would roughly compare to starting off the Gregorian calendar with the nineteenth day of the month of March! In other words, it seemingly came out of nowhere.[3]

Unlikely though the choice of starting date was, the innovation had behind it a history and logic. First and foremost, it marked the liberation from a St. Petersburg prison in 1798 of the founder of Chabad Chasidism, Rabbi Shneur Zalman; later, the date was given the name "Chasidic New Year," an honorific title that clearly set the stage for its being recruited for its prestigious opening position in Rabbi Menachem's wartime calendar. But most important for our purposes was the way this revolutionary starting date served as a sign that time was being newly conceived and configured. This was a wartime calendar that would not only help track time but also compel one to meditate on its nature and purpose. One knew it simply by looking at the calendar's first page.

A Holocaust-Era Calendar from Outside of Europe

This wartime calendar—all of 128 pages in a pocket format—was first published around Passover of 5703 (April 1943).[4] This put its genesis right in the middle of what historian Saul Friedlander has starkly referred to as "the years of extermination." Hundreds of thousands of Russian, Ukrainian, and Lithuanian Jews had been shot in mass graves; labor, concentration, and death camps were operating with unprecedented malevolence; the Great Deportation of Warsaw Jewry, whereby most of the ghetto's Jews were sent to the Treblinka death camp, took place some six months before, from July to September 1942 (in the Jewish calendar, from the summer fast day of Tisha b'Av to the fall holiday of Yom Kippur). This was the grim era in which *Hayom yom* first saw the light of day. Yet what was it that made this calendar, among all others that emerge from this period, reckon Jewish time differently than ever before?

The question looms even larger when noting a crucial fact. This wartime calendar was conceived, assembled, and published *outside* of Europe, a characteristic that distinguishes it from those surveyed thus far—and which, presumably, allowed it to take the shape that it did. Those responsible for its production were not (or, rather, were no longer) immediately under siege, were not, as they sought to track Jewish time circa 1942–43, compelled to suffer debilitating privation of all sorts, and were not threatened with imminent imprisonment, torture, or death.

The two individuals responsible for *Hayom yom's* content and production, the Rebbe Rabbi Yosef Yitzchak Schneersohn and his son-in-law, Rabbi Menachem Mendel Schneersohn, had been subject to such ordeals. They had recently fled Europe and, equally important, remained literally and spiritually tied to the devastated continent. But from a practical vantage point, their newly established American base of operations gave them opportunities that no longer existed in most of Europe. They had the liberty and resources to publish Jewish books; had at their disposal libraries to check references; had available other calendars and the rabbinic literature necessary to research whatever questions might arise regarding the computation of dates; and had at hand the trove of letters and writings that could constitute such a volume as they had ambitiously conceived it. Without such an array of resources, a project of this kind would likely never have been imagined, never have gotten off the ground, and certainly never would have been carried out.

There was thus a world of difference—literally, geographically, circumstantially—between this wartime calendar and those considered up to this point. Indeed, the distinctive mark of the wartime calendars fashioned in Europe was the perilous predicament their authors were compelled to endure as they labored to bring the calendar into being; the very act of fashioning a Jewish calendar, moreover, often increased the risk to life and limb. What defined their special accomplishment was the resolute commitment to track Jewish time in circumstances of profound adversity. The same cannot be said for a wartime calendar such as *Hayom yom*, produced out of harm's way in the then upper-middle-class Brooklyn neighborhood of Crown Heights.

The Legacy of Chabad and the Ties to Wartime Europe

Yet from an internal vantage point, the authors' ties to wartime Europe defined the character and mandate of this calendar through and through. First, the languages of the calendar were Hebrew and Yiddish; not a word of English appeared on its pages. This was true not only of the calendar's headings but also the voluminous number of teachings distributed through the calendar—teachings which at times comprised several paragraphs or more. The reader took it for granted that he or she was to swim and stay afloat in the sea of eastern European Jewish languages. The teachings targeted followers born and bred in Europe or their American-born offspring who continued to dwell in the ambience of Old World mores and who possessed the linguistic skill to find their way in them.

The source of all of the calendar's epigrammatic teachings—380 or so in number—were the writings of Rabbi Yosef Yitzchak, the incumbent Lubavitcher Rebbe. The Rebbe Raya"tz, as he was known, was the sixth dynastic leader of the Chabad Chasidim. For roughly a century, the headquarters had been located in the White Russian town of Lubavitch; the Raya"tz was born there in 1880 and grew up largely in its environs. But as with so much of Jewish eastern Europe, the immense disruptions of World War I compelled his father, the Rebbe Rabbi Shalom Dovber Schneersohn, to relocate the community's headquarters, in this case to the city of Rostov. It was there that the Raya"tz took over the reins of leadership with his father's passing in 1920. He spent the next seven years in a tenacious struggle to preserve traditional Jewish life in the midst of the increasingly draconian policies of the Soviet Communist regime. He saw it as his task to persevere, no matter what the risks and dangers. When in 1927 he was arrested, sentenced to death, and eventually subjected instead to internal exile, he became aware that his time in Russia was drawing to a close. He was forced to leave the Soviet Union in the summer of 1927, finding over the next decade temporary havens in Riga and Warsaw.

The Warsaw base, however, also became perilous. With the German invasion of Poland threatening especially highly placed Jewish leaders, Rabbi Yosef Yitzhak took flight in fall 1939. Escaping by way of Latvia and Sweden, he arrived in New York a few months later, where he once again reestablished the court of Chabad. He quickly divided his activities along multiple fronts, founding various Torah-centered institutions in the United States and Canada, spearheading efforts to rescue followers languishing in eastern Europe, and setting in motion programs of spiritual devotion to address the urgent needs of world Jewry.

A prolific author in a gamut of religious genres, the Raya"tz made sure that as many of his writings—letters, speeches, lectures, and Torah commentary—as possible had made the journey to the New World as well. It was these that furnished a part of *Hayom yom's* teachings; another sizable portion were authored by the Raya"tz in America, written in support of his specially conceived programs on American soil.

While almost every word of each and every teaching had its source in the pen of the incumbent leader, the Raya"tz gave the actual task of assembling the calendar—including choosing which teachings to incorporate and selecting the date and day on which to place them—to his son-in-law and Chasid, Rabbi Menachem Mendel Schneersohn. As close to his father-in-law as the intimate collaboration on the calendar suggests, Rabbi Menachem had ascended through the ranks of the Chabad movement by an unusual path.[5] Ukrainain-born, he had largely been self-schooled, guided in his studies by his gifted father, Rabbi Levi Yitzhok Schneersohn. A prominent Jewish leader, Rabbi Levi Yitzhok was staunchly dedicated even under Stalinist rule to preserving observant Jewish life; he was at the time the calendar was composed eking out an existence in exile in Central Asia. Having first met the Raya"tz in 1923, Rabbi Menachem soon became a member of his inner circle and eventually became engaged to his daughter, Rebbetzin Chaya Mushka, whom he married in fall 1928.

Residing in Berlin since that year, Rabbi Menachem saw firsthand the rise of Nazism. He and his wife managed to evade the enemy's widening net by moving first to Paris in 1933 and, after the occupation of France in spring 1940, to Nice in unoccupied Vichy. The couple's safety, however, remained tenuous at best. They had hoped to join the Raya"tz in New York, but, time and again, obstacles intervened. Even while trying to press for life-saving emigration, Rabbi Menachem continued during this fraught period to pursue a high level of Jewish study, writing, and teaching. Of special interest for our purposes are Rabbi Menachem's annotations in his copy of the Paris rabbinate's final wartime Jewish calendar compiled for the year 5701. Commenting on aspects of fast days and the practice of determining the onset of the new Jewish month, the annotations show that the significance of the calendar as a key for orchestrating Jewish life was never far from Rabbi Menachem's mind.[6]

Study was interwoven with attempts to obtain the much sought after visas, and, after repeated efforts, the prized documents were finally secured in April 1941. Like many of those fortunate enough to leave Europe during these difficult hours, Rabbi Menachem and Rebbetzin Chaya Mushka embarked from the port of Lisbon, in neutral Portugal. After an eleven-day journey, they arrived in New York on Sivan 28, 5701 (June 23, 1941). Out of harm's way, the Chabad leaders continued to feel acutely the war's intensifying threat to the well-being of Europe's Jews, of their Chasidim, and of family members. The horrible persecutions in Europe were for them anything but abstract. Indeed, the Raya"tz's youngest daughter and her husband, Rebbetzin Sheina and Rabbi Menachem Mendel Horenstein, were at this stage imprisoned in the Warsaw ghetto, having remained behind to care for Rabbi Horenstein's ailing father. Tragically, the couple would end up just over a year later sharing the brutal fate suffered by most of Warsaw Jewry: deportation to the Treblinka death camp.[7] The shadows cast by these losses would still be visible years later when Rabbi Menachem would annually recite the mourner's Kaddish for his murdered sister-in-law and brother-in-law. And when Rebbetzin Chaya Mushka passed away close to a half century down the road, in 1988, one of the two items Rabbi Menachem placed in the coffin was a ring that had belonged to Rebbetzin Sheina, his wife's murdered sister.[8] Time did little to overcome her palpable absence.

In the midst of the war, other losses came as well. As the enemy advanced in the East, relatives back at home were equally at risk. Rabbi Menachem himself had a brother and grandmother who continued to reside in his native region of Ukraine; their lives too would be snuffed out within the year.[9] The sense of urgency to act of behalf of those trapped in Nazi-occupied Europe was profound.

Collaborating on a Program of Immediate Redemption

Rabbi Menachem's arrival in New York in 1941 made collaboration possible between the Raya"tz and his son-in-law on a number of important initiatives. One of those was *Hayom yom*, which became a reality less than two years later. What had to happen in order to bring out a calendar/book that measured time not only during, but according to, the Holocaust?

The idea of a calendar as a response to cataclysm had to come to the fore. From a spiritual point of view, the war's great disruptive force offered the departure point. The Raya"tz believed the massive upheaval of Jewish life in Europe—the upheaval that had made it necessary for him to flee and that had already annihilated countless Jewish lives and put so many others in mortal danger—signaled a radical transformation of time and history. The events were surely terrible, the loss of life tragic, the persecution of Jews and Judaism despicable. But, seen from this angle, they also had a purpose and goal: promoting a universal climate of repentance and ushering in a new era, one that would welcome the redeeming Messiah.

With most of Europe in the throes of war, time was in the process of being revolutionized. Like with most revolutions, intense suffering—known in the nomenclature of traditional Jewish teaching as the birth pangs of the Messiah—would have to accompany the transition to a new era. But the intensity of the birth pangs could be eased. The Raya"tz believed that righteous action could lessen the suffering associated with them. He thereby established under the organizational banner of "Machene Yisrael" (the camp of Israel) special programs of spiritual devotion. Its mandate was "to publicize the truth [that] immediate repentance [will bring the] immediate complete redemption by means of the righteous Messiah." From this directive was distilled the motto with which the Raya"tz would end his wartime letters: "immediate repentance, immediate redemption." It implied that action would be sure to bring far-reaching results—and that the moment to act was now.

The aim was to lessen the suffering—the birth pangs of the Messiah—by recruiting as many Jews as possible to participate in the programs of spiritual devotion. One program was a Psalm Fellowship, whereby groups would recite the entire book of Psalms at regular intervals. Another program was dedicated to the study of Mishna, the basis of the Oral Torah, the review of which could also enhance the purity of the participants and those in their vicinity. Heightened care in Sabbath observance was another dimension. All of these were tried-and-true, centuries-old methods for endeavoring to avert crisis. What was special was the combined systematic character of the approach. Moreover, the Raya"tz founded two journals, among whose highest priorities were warning the Jewish world about the birth pangs and publicizing the ideas behind the programs of spiritual devotion.[10] Intensifying areas of traditional practice were thus championed as paths leading toward a climate of universal repentance.

One tactic was more unusual: commencing writing a "Torah scroll to Welcome the Messiah." The Raya"tz fittingly announced the plan for the project on the fall holiday of Simchas Torah 5702 (1941). Steps were thereafter taken to secure special materials and to employ premier scribes. The actual writing began on Iyar 2, at which time the Raya"tz explained his decision to proceed with this remarkable enterprise:

The Cause of all causes and the Reason of all reasons,
may He be blessed, has conferred upon me the
merit, which I owe to my sainted ancestors, to be
awake, and awaken others, to the necessity of *teshuvah*

now, without delay. We must hold ourselves in
readiness for the deliverance which is at hand, and, in
particular, to write a *Sefer Torah* with which to welcome
our righteous *Mashiach*.[11]

The plan was no doubt exceptional as it was cast. Yet it too followed in line with traditional mores. The writing of a Sefer Torah to mark an auspicious occasion—for example, the anniversary of the passing of a noted personage or the dedication of a synagogue or school—occupies an honored place in the customs of Jewish life; there was nothing novel in the medium of commemoration at hand. And it seems that the Raya"tz drew on an incident in the early days of Chasidic life to serve as a precedent for catalyzing repentance by way of writing a new Torah scroll. Yet the idea shows how the Raya"tz would leave no stone unturned in his quest to prepare the world for the imminent coming of the Messiah, heralded by the harrowing persecution being endured by European Jewry.[12]

Organized as a means to spiritually empower world Jewry in the midst of crisis, the Machene Yisrael programs embodied concerns eminently relevant to *Hayom yom* as well. Indeed, a "brief review" of these programs was featured on the inside front cover of the calendar/book. At a deeper level, the teachings set forth in *Hayom yom* took up the cause of these programs, devoting numerous entries to the extraordinary potential of psalm recitation (eighteen entries), the purifying effect of Mishna study (twelve entries); and the desirability of repentance for all Jews (sixteen entries). But, as we will see, the relevance of the Machene Yisrael mandate to *Hayom yom* was broader and more pervasive. Both were driven by an agenda that sought not only to reduce the suffering and to wring from it God's urgent message but also to seize what was perceived to be the opportunity at hand. The philosophy that nurtured the agenda was Chasidism.

"A Truly Chasidic Cultural Work"

We saw how Chasidic values shaped an exceptional aspect of the calendar Rabbi Yisrael Simcha Zelmann fashioned in the Holland-based Westerbork transit camp. Listing the dates of the yahrzeits, the anniversaries of the passing of the three leaders of the Ger Chasidim, Rabbi Zelmann's calendar gave pointed expression to the devotion of a Chasid to a rebbe, a disciple to his master, one of the cornerstones of Chasidic life and philosophy. This surely would have been a sign of devotion at any time and in any place. But this was a time and place of travail. As Rabbi Yisrael Simcha makes clear in the calendar's introduction, carrying out the basic precepts of religious life under such circumstances took unusual zeal. He forged his calendar for the year 5704 to help Jews imprisoned in Westerbork observe tradition to the greatest possible degree. The listing of the yahrzeits went a step further. Stranded in Holland, cut off from the living wells of Chasidic society, he nevertheless imported into the calendar the element of Polish Chasidic devotion that, even under punishing conditions, enabled him to maintain the zeal necessary to fulfill whatever precepts he could—and to author the calendar that made such observance available to a wider circle. It did not matter that the wider circle may not have bestowed upon the yahrzeits the same degree of significance as did Rabbi Zelmann. His Jewish calendar would bear witness to his continued bond to his masters.

Like Rabbi Zelmann's calendar, *Hayom yom* pays homage to many leaders by referring to the anniversary of their passing. Indeed, the unusual opening date of Kislev 19 has the distinction of being such an anniversary, commemorating the passing of the Rebbe Rabbi Dov Ber of Mezeritch, the master who took over the leadership of the movement after the passing of its founder, Rabbi Israel Ba'al Shem Tov. And clearly the starting date is partly inspired by the legacy left by this pivotal figure.

But in the case of *Hayom yom*, the Chasidic dimension is not limited to yahrzeits; it rather pervades every facet of the calendar. Indeed, one could emphatically say that without it the calendar wouldn't have been—and wouldn't have measured time according to the Holocaust.

With this proviso in mind, it is important to note that *Hayom yom* was preceded by another calendar that appeared under Rabbi Menachem's name and auspices. A short time earlier, he was in charge of bringing out a like-minded calendar, also for the year 5703 (1942–43).[13] This earlier calendar, however, was guided by principles different from those that came to distinguish *Hayom yom*. It also targeted a different audience. First of all, it was in English and geared toward an exclusively American readership. The straightforward title was *Young Scholar's Pocket Calendar, 5703 (1942–43)*; "Young Scholar" referred to younger students—that is, school children, perhaps those nearing the middle-school age of bar and bat mitzvah. Indeed, Rabbi Menachem opens his introductory greeting with "Dear Children," and when later he explains the broader implications of using such a Jewish calendar, he tells them that "you, the children of today, are the grown-ups of tomorrow." As with *Hayom yom*, this earlier production combined a calendar with daily teachings: of the sages, laws, customs, witticisms, and more. It included Chasidic references but did not explicate or elaborate them. These references formed not the centerpiece but rather one piece of the pie.

Though straightforward and friendly, such a calendar, Rabbi Menachem made clear, was nevertheless a tool that needed to be used properly: "Make this Calendar [with a capital *C*] your constant companion and take full advantage of the knowledge and wisdom it contains. This Calendar should not merely tell you the date of the month, but, what is more important, the significance of each day." Behind the concern with each day, notes Rabbi Menachem, lies the nature and challenge of time: "Time is a very great treasure. A minute lost or wasted can never be restored. Time can be very valuable, but it can also be absolutely valueless—all depending upon how you use it. Therefore, you must not let your time pass by without making full use of it, giving it the fullest measure of meaning and worth—Jewish meaning and worth."[14]

A rudimentary philosophy of time was, as we see, already joined to Chabad's wartime calendar project. Yet in many respects, this *Young Scholar's Calendar* was a primer. The American and English-language-oriented audience whom this calendar addressed had to be schooled in Jewish time from the ground up. It thus begins with an explanation of the Jewish day, week, month, and year. One could assume nothing about what was known, so it was necessary to start with the basics. In this respect, the calendar could not introduce revolutionary concepts or formats. Instead, it had to convey that there was an alternative to the Gregorian calendar— the calendar of choice for most Americans, and likely for many American-based Jews. Hence, the starting point for the *Young Scholar's Pocket Calendar* was, as with most Jewish calendars of this period, the first day of the month of Tishrei. For these American "young scholars," to begin a calendar with the *Jewish* New Year must have felt radical enough. For them, the Gregorian calendar likely had unimpeachable authority. They had to be persuaded that January 1 had to take a back seat. It would take the vastly different kind of initiative of *Hayom yom* to intrepidly formulate an entirely new point of beginning, one that diverged from standard Jewish practice. In Rabbi Menachem's earlier calendar, in contrast, the challenge was to train young American Jews in what the standard practice ought to be.

For our purposes, the essential point is that the *Young Scholar's Calendar* makes *no reference* to the tragic events in Europe circa September 1942. Neither in the foreword, in the footnotes, nor in the calendar itself does the perilous fate of European Jewry receive attention. American through and through, the calendar could have just as well been produced in 1922 or 1932. Tracking Jewish time, it is, like most calendars, oblivious to the specific historical moment in which it came into being. Clearly, the calendar views its goal as cultivating an appreciation for Jewish history, with the dates calculated according to a Jewish calendar reckoning. To that end it appends a list of "some outstanding events in early Jewish history," beginning with the creation of Adam and Eve in 930 and ending with the "Conclusion of the Babylonian Talmud" in 4260.[15] But the list was obviously compiled with an eye toward teaching about the "outstanding events" in *ancient* history, viewed from a Jewish perspective. It was not, however, concerned with presenting an approach to the European debacle and with laying out how such a calendar might serve as a response to these tumultuous events.

This is exactly what *Hayom yom*, a calendar that was "truly a Chasidic cultural work," was designed to do. The very idea of a book qua calendar was an innovation. No such calendar existed in Chasidic literature, or likely in Jewish religious literature altogether.[16] There had been attempts to adapt the non-Jewish idea of a "book of days" to the Jewish calendar. In 1931, for instance, a little over a decade before *Hayom yom* was published, the prolific English Jewish historian Cecil Roth brought out *A Jewish Book of Days*.[17] Yet Roth's book contrasts with Rabbi Menachem's in almost every respect. For instance, it is organized according to the Gregorian calendar, beginning on January 1 and ending December 31, a decision he (a religious Jew) explains as facing the reality of what Jews generally referred to. "The fact must be faced," argues Roth, "that, for the vast majority of us," the "Gregorian calendar is an actuality, while the lunar year is not." For what Roth calls the "layman," the "Gregorian system of reckoning is infinitely more familiar and infinitely more significant."[18]

In contrast, *Hayom yom* not only begins on the Chasidic New Year and is organized from "Yom Rishon" (the first day—i.e., Sunday) to "Shabbes" but also eschews the non-Jewish calendar completely. Every entry begins simply with the day of the week, the date of the Jewish month, and the Jewish year. There is no spiritual room, as it were, for the secular calendar. Time as *Hayom yom* projects it is Jewish time, Chasidic time, Messianic time. The novel idea of a teaching calendar—a truly Jewish book of days—was the way to harness time to the project of repentance, which was the key to releasing the redemptive power in the historical moment.

The special urgency of time is associated with the book's title. Taken from the phrase in the prayer book that announces the psalm of the day, *Hayom yom* is commonly translated "From Day to Day." But the Raya"tz understood it differently: the calendar communicates "the true *Hayom yom* ('today is the day') for its every day is indeed a day" (es iz der emeser *Hayom yom*, jeder tag iz a tag).[19] On Cheshvan 17, Rabbi Menachem chose a teaching that challenges what should serve as a standard for measuring time and in the process redefined what constitutes a "day": "One must be vigilant with time . . . every day that passes is not just a day but a life's concern . . . My father [the fifth Lubavitcher Rebbe, Rabbi Shalom Dovber Schneersohn] quoted the Alter Rebbe [the first Lubavitcher Rebbe]: *A (long) summer day, a (long) winter night—is a year!*"[20] Via the calendar and its teachings, time was stretched, reorganized, and measured according to a rigorously spiritual standard.

Hayom yom was meant to be a Chasidic calendar in form as well as in content. Assuredly, the teachings are anchored in the concepts and expressed in the vocabulary of the Chasidic movement and the rabbis who are cited as the source for the teachings are leading figures from the early generations of Chasidism (for example, the Baal Shem Tov, the Maggid of Mezeritch, the Rebbe Reb Zusia of Anapoli, the Shpola Zeide, Rabbi Nachum of Chernobil). But also the very manner in which the teachings are presented bears witness to an integral dimension of Chasidic mores.

Rabbi Menachem culled all the entries verbatim from the teachings of his father-in-law, his Rebbe and master. This was by no means something to take for granted. Indeed, on the face of it, the decision to proceed in this way seems to bypass the sources of the teachings. In other words, one could have quoted from the books authored by each of the masters: the Besch"t, the founder of the Chasidic movement; his disciple, the Maggid; his student, Rabbi Shneur Zalman, the founder of the Chabad movement; and each of the subsequent Chabad rabbis whose teachings are cited. The books and material were voluminous; there was no lack of primary sources. Yet Rabbi Menachem chose to draw not on the books but rather solely on the teachings transmitted by the Raya"tz. As a number of the *Hayom yom* entries show, the transmission of Chasidic teachings and customs proceeded step by step. The Raya"tz came at the end of a more or less lengthy chain of transmission. But the entries contain his words alone.

Going against the grain of standard protocol, Rabbi Menachem's decision to draw solely from the words of the Raya"tz demonstrated several aspects of Chasidic values and culture: (1) the bond of connection that Rabbi Menachem felt toward him as his spiritual master and mentor; (2) the presumption that the Raya"tz's teachings could serve as a funnel for the authentic and comprehensive transmission of Chasidism; (3) the confirmation that despite the upheaval that wrenched the court of Lubavitch Chasidim from its home base in Russia and Europe, the Raya"tz maintained the tradition in full; and (4) the conviction that his words provided a recipe for responding in appropriate fashion to the special claims put on the Jews by the terrible ordeal they were currently enduring. The corollary to this last point put forward the belief that the Raya"tz's assuming the helm of the Chabad court at the time when he did indicated, by way of Divine Providence, that he possessed the specific attributes to steer the movement and world Jewry at large through the wartime ordeal. The Raya"tz was the one, in Rabbi Menachem's estimation, ready to do all in his power to bring about the "immediate redemption." This included the completely novel idea of fashioning a Chasidic calendar.

When All the World Shudders: The Calendar's Call to Action

When turning to the calendar itself, we may miss this essential dimension, because we may be looking for the wrong kinds of references.[21] No war events are mentioned, no battles singled out, no secular leaders praised or condemned, no sites of evil alluded to. There are certainly no references to the enemy. In this respect, Rabbi Menachem's strategy is similar to that of other great spiritual responses from the period—the Warsaw ghetto sermons of the Piaseczner Rebbe, for example, or, closer to home, the wartime sermons of the Raya"tz himself— which chose to confront the tragedy exclusively from within the framework of the Torah and the Torah community.[22]

But the signposts of the war and destruction are there for those that wish to see them. The first appears just before the beginning of *Hayom yom*'s calendar, in

a Yiddish letter (dated Tammuz 11, 5702) of the Raya"tz that spiritually characterizes the terrible era:

> At the present time, when the world trembles, when all the world shudders with
> the birth-pangs of the Messiah, for G-d has set fire to the walls of the Exile…it
> is the duty of every Jew, man and woman, old and young, to ask themselves:
>
> **WHAT HAVE I DONE AND WHAT AM I DOING TO ALLEVIATE
> THE BIRTH-PANGS OF THE MESSIAH, AND TO MERIT THE TOTAL
> REDEMPTION WHICH WILL COME THROUGH OUR RIGHTEOUS
> MESSIAH?**[23]

The world out of which these terms come is in upheaval: trembling, shudder-
ing, spiritually (and literally) on fire. Yet the graphic portrait is not meant to
stand on its own; it certainly does not paint a picture of horror simply to horrify.
It rather translates the Holocaust into a spiritual idiom of cosmic dimensions.
The Raya"tz's vivid words, moreover, charge the reader to address this upheaval
directly, through action. It was no time to be a casual bystander. Indeed, the second paragraph appeared in larger and bold print to emphasize the call to action:
"**WHAT HAVE I DONE AND WHAT AM I DOING?**" Multiple strategies, as
we recall, were enlisted to this end, among them memorizing Psalms and the
teachings of the Mishna and writing a Torah scroll to welcome the Messiah. The
Chasidic calendar entitled "Today Is the Day" was another crucial facet of this
urgent enterprise.

Rabbi Menachem returned to this message several times in the *Hayom yom*
calendar itself. Less than a month later, on the fifteenth day of the month of Tevet, he chose a teaching that applied the day's biblical passage from the book of
Genesis heralding the Messiah's arrival: "The scepter," reads the blessing of the
patriarch Jacob, "shall not depart from Judah nor a scholar from among his de-
scendents until Shiloh arrives." The latter phrase—"until Shiloh arrives"—is understood by the classic commentators to refer to the arrival of the King Messiah.
One of the central Torah passages proclaiming his coming, the biblical blessing
gives rise to the teaching in *Hayom yom* wherein the Messiah's arrival is viewed
as catalyzed by current events: "Hearken and hear Israel, this is the time marked
for the redemption by the Messiah." Culled from a letter penned the previous
spring, the author was clearly responding to the convulsive events in Europe,
the message of which was clear: "The sufferings befalling us are the birth-pangs
of the Messiah. Israel will be redeemed only through repentance." These lines
contain virtually the same message as had appeared in the preface. Yet the continuation adds two elements: a warning and an explicit reference to the conflict
at hand. The teaching cautioned, "Have no faith in the false prophets who as-
sure you of glories and salvation after the War." Instead, "return Israel unto the
Eternal your God; prepare yourself and your family to go forth and receive the

Messiah, whose coming is imminent."[24] The "war" was not something merely to win; it also, and perhaps mainly, was meant to convey a stirring message, and heeding it presented an opportunity not to be missed.

A multilayered message thus infused the calendar date; that the biblical passage fell on Tevet 15 was anything but arbitrary. It rather elevated the date to a position of highlighting a theme prominent in the calendar as a whole yet especially relevant to the date: "This is the time marked for redemption."

The special opportunities the current time afforded found further expression in the entry for Shevat 8, drawn from in a letter written in late summer 1942: "Particularly in these times, when thanks to God's kindness we stand at the threshold of redemption. . . . it is a mitzvah and duty of every rabbi in the Jewish community to inform his congregation that the current troubles and sufferings are the 'birth-pangs of the Messiah.'"[25] The biblical passage for the day—which tells of the Jews in Egypt preparing for the exodus from Egyptian slavery—again emphasizes being on "the threshold of redemption." Just as the Jews of ancient Egypt were soon to experience redemption from their oppressors, so the Jews afflicted by the "current troubles and sufferings" would soon experience redemption. The exodus from Egypt was the first such redemption; the "birth-pangs of the Messiah," understood to be taking place as the Raya"tz drafted his letter and as Rabbi Menachem culled it for the calendar some months later, was to be the final redemption. The calendar did all that it could to show that past "troubles and sufferings" associated with specific dates were meant to serve as a springboard for hope, action, and relief.

Changing the idiom slightly, the entry for the eighteenth day of the month of Sivan carries through the theme of the current time being especially opportune for redemption: "This is the actual time of the footsteps [rather than the 'birth-pangs'] of the Messiah." In this context, not only the leaders but "every Jew" plays a central role in taking advantage of the fraught circumstances: it is imperative for "every Jew to seek his fellow's welfare . . . to inspire the other to repentance, so that he will not fall out—God forbid—of the community of Israel who will shortly be privileged, with God's help, to experience complete redemption." The biblical reading for the day again offers a guide, telling as it does of the tragic error of the spies who, sent by their leader Moses to scout out the land of Israel, are cowed by the prospect of battling the local population. On their return, they therefore discouraged the community from going forward, a failure of nerve that brought in its train a punishment of remaining in the desert for forty years. The eighteenth of Sivan's teaching replays with a twist the scenario in the current climate of wartime upheaval, exhorting "every Jew" to "seek his fellow's welfare"—a gesture of generosity that can overturn the discouraging message communicated by the biblical spies generations ago and bring about in the present (circa 1943) repentance and a "complete redemption."[26]

A central goal of the calendar, then, was to induce a *heshbon nefesh,* a spirit of introspection and "complete repentance," among all Jews. This would, in turn, catalyze action which would alleviate the immense suffering and bring forth the much yearned-for redemption.

Reading Between the Lines of Catastrophe

This message was at the heart of the calendar as a whole. Yet the calendar dates most likely to give further guidance in how to respond to the European catastrophe were those that commemorated past catastrophe. As we recall, the preeminent commemorative date falls on Tisha B'Av, the ninth day of the month of Av. Yet the date's influence is so great that it colors a ten-week period before and after the day itself. The three weeks preceding the ninth of Av are known as *Bein Hametzarim* and choreograph a gradual adoption of mourning customs. Prophetic readings highlighting repentance distinguish the Shabbatot during this period. On Tisha b'Av, the day commemorating the destruction of the ancient Jerusalem temples, the customs of mourning are given their most intense expression, letting up in the afternoon. The seven weeks that follow, referred to as *Sheva D'nhamasa,* the seven consolations, feature Shabbat readings with words of comfort. These ten weeks, pivoting on the demanding mourning customs of Tisha b'Av, constitute a significant period leading up to Rosh Hashana.

As we have seen, wartime calendars vary in their graphic presentation (or omission) of this weighty occasion. Some draw attention to the day by writing out the date, while others indicate it is to be observed (or perhaps observed in the breach) as a fast day, and still others do both. More striking—if more puzzling— are those calendars (such as the *Luach Katan* fashioned in Theresianstadt and that of Rabbi Avigdor composed in Buchenwald) that omit any special designation. Finally, a number of wartime diaries highlight the date or weave its specially fraught meaning into their unfolding chronicle. In nearly every case, the tragic character of the day's commemoration intersects with the tragic events being endured as the calendar or diary was being composed.

On the face of it, *Hayom yom*'s teaching for Tisha B'Av, detailing relevant customs, seems to focus merely on the observance of the day. But on closer inspection, *Hayom yom*'s configuration of the three weeks leading up to the ninth of Av, the day itself, and the seven weeks following reveal an extraordinary calendrical response to Jewish suffering.

Rabbi Menachem chose a teaching for the eighteenth of Tammuz, the virtual onset of this delicate catastrophe-burdened period, that by way of allusion gives new meaning to these ten weeks—and, by implication, to the tragic events in Europe more generally.[27] A word should be said in advance. As with many of the teachings, this one draws on personages from the Chabad movement's early days, outlining in condensed fashion the drama that attended their quest for spiritual growth; it also invokes practices and concepts central to Chasidic life. The first part describes the accomplishment of a premier follower of the Alter Rebbe, the movement's founder and first leader: "The Alter Rebbe said of Rabbi Moshe Vilenker: 'Moshe has *mochin d'gadlut*, magnitude of intellect, and in his **ten years of toil**, he has attained through his labors a powerful, capacious, wide-ranging intellectuality [*mochin rechavim*].'" A lengthy ten-year period of toil and labor has secured these enviable traits. But how exactly did he do it? The second part of the teaching provides this crucial information: "For three years Rabbi Moshe Vilenker prepared himself for *yechidus* [an intimate meeting] with the Alter Rebbe. Afterwards he remained in Lyozna [his master's home base] for seven years to translate [auf brengen] the *yechidus* into actual spiritual practice." The time frame is crucial. Rabbi Vilenker's remarkable accomplishments took place over a ten-year time span, divided into three- and seven-year periods. In the middle came the defining event: the *yechidus*, the intimate meeting with his master, the Alter Rebbe. This time frame of three and seven matches to a T the period in the calendar that this eighteenth of Tammuz teaching initiates. And the correspondence between the time frame of the calendar's "Rabbi Moshe Vilenker" teaching and that of the summer period commemorating catastrophe is meant to carry over to the spiritual meaning. The ten years of Rabbi Moshe Vilenker's toil parallel the ten weeks that precede and follow the ninth of Av; the three years of preparation parallel *Bein Hametzarim*, the three weeks of intensifying mourning; the seven years of translating the meeting's momentous import parallel the seven weeks of consolation.

What then parallels the *yechidus*, the decisive encounter of Rabbi Moshe Vilenker with the Alter Rebbe, his master and teacher, that confers meaning and purpose to the time before and after? It is the ninth of the month of Av, the day that commemorates the destruction of the ancient temples but also, traditionally, the day on which the Messiah is born. Tisha b'Av is thus also, according to *Hayom yom*, a day of *yechidus*, a day of meeting, not as in Rabbi Moshe Vilenker's case, with the rebbe and master (though perhaps that too), but rather of the Jewish people with the Almighty, with God. That destruction-filled day does not signify the remoteness of the Almighty but rather God's intimate involvement with the Jewish people. This message was clearly geared for a time when the anguish of world Jewry was at a height. Seeing the worst imaginable disaster as a time of *yehidus*, of spiritual bonding and of translating that bond into daily life, gave a way to confront the suffering of European Jewry. In *Hayom yom*'s Chasidic idiom, commemorating past catastrophe became a guide to reckoning with—and to transforming the meaning of—the current one.

This approach goes hand in hand with the Chasidic calendar's introductory teaching, wherein the task at hand was to alleviate the pain that comes with the birth pangs of the Messiah. The eighteenth of Tammuz teaching outlined this redemptive project in terms that the individual Jew could grasp.[28]

A Revolution in Jewish Time

On the surface and beneath it, *Hayom yom* then is geared to respond to terrible, overwhelming suffering. It presumes that during such a confrontation doubts arise as to the reasons for the vast suffering (how could they not?) and what to do in the face of it. Much of the time, the response set forth is indirect: know and maintain the tradition scrupulously; see oneself and one's religious observance as a link in the chain of that tradition; build up Chasidic life at the very moment that it is undergoing unprecedented persecution; and, in the calendrical terms of "today is the day," understand this as a daily task.[29]

This program clearly orchestrates a sacred response. *Hayom yom* was brought into the world at a moment when the potential for both material and spiritual loss was at its peak. Instead, by way of a calendar, Rabbi Menachem sought to see every day as an opportunity to transform the nature of time as such. By so doing, the nature of the world—a world at war, a world "shudder[ing] with the birth-pangs of the Messiah"—would be transformed as well.

Conveying a bracing message to its wartime audience, Rabbi Menachem's Chasidic calendar has attained even greater prominence in its postwar incarnations. At first, Rabbi Menachem had hoped to bring out a sequel the next year, but other pressing commitments intervened. Instead, the original "Today Is the Day" was reprinted three years down the road, for the Chasidic year 5706–7 (1945–46); ten years later it was again reprinted; in the 1970s and 1980s, it was brought out in a flurry of editions and translations. Finally, in 1989, the Lubavitcher Rebbe (the title by which Rabbi Menachem became known after becoming Chabad's leader in 1951), some forty-five years after its first wartime publication, called for regular study of the volume's teachings, a directive often fulfilled by reading the day's entry following morning services in Chabad synagogues throughout the world. What was conceived as a thoroughly innovative response to a crisis precipitated by the Holocaust has shown itself relevant to those for whom the Holocaust is at most a distant shadow.

How do we explain the continued—nay, increasing—significance of a wartime calendar produced to meet the needs of the moment? How do we account for the fact that its success has been so great that the discrepancy between the dating of the current Jewish calendar with that of the original is simply overlooked? Without doubt, the Lubavitcher Rebbe's continued supervision of the calendar's postwar fate has played a formidable role. As the leader of the Chabad movement (and as *Hayom yom*'s original compiler/author), he saw the enduring relevance of the calendar/book and took the practical steps necessary to ensure its circulation. Added to this is the calendar's literary/pedagogical dimension. The daily epigrammatic teaching supplies invaluable information and challenging study that transcends the crisis that brought forth its creation. That said, I want to suggest that, perhaps on a subconscious level, "Today Is the Day" continues to be enmeshed with the Holocaust. Both form and content link the reader or listener with the urgent program ("immediate repentance, immediate redemption") meant to see the wartime conflagration as an opportunity to transform the world—a program of which the calendar was to play a crucial role. And its role was that of turning time inside out: from conjuring a new calendar starting date to showing the promise borne within the days most deeply associated with catastrophe to living on the edge of the Messiah's fraught arrival. Even today, *Hayom yom* cannot be encountered without the reader being thrust into a world where time, as defined by a calendar forged in the fire of wartime faith, has undergone its nearly final revolution.

Notes

1. *Hayom yom* ("Today Is the Day") (New York: Kohut, 5703 [1943]). As of 2017, twenty-nine editions have been printed. An English translation of *Hayom yom* (which included the original Yiddish/Hebrew text) was first published in 1988. In 2010, *Hayom yom* appeared in a new English translation and newly organized format bearing the title *Tackling Life's Tasks*, eds. and trans. Uri Kaploun and Rabbi Eliyahu Touger (Brooklyn: Sichos in English, 2010).
   Background sources include Rabbi Sholem DovBer Levin, *Toldos Chabad b"Artzot HaBrith* (Brooklyn: Kohut, 5748); Igros Kodesh Mohara"tz; "Paths of Providence," http://www.chabad.org/therebbe/article_cdo/aid/2317686/jewish/Overview.htm; Rachel Altein, with the editorial assistance of Eliezer Zaklikovsky, *Out of the Inferno: The Efforts that Led to the Rescue of Rabbi Yosef Yitzchak Schneersohn of Lubavitch from War-Torn Europe in 1939–1940* (Brooklyn: Kohut, 2002); Gershon Greenberg, "Redemption after Holocaust according to Mahaneh Yisrael-Lubavitch, 1940–1945," *Modern Judaism*, vol. 12 (1992), pp. 61–84; "Mahane Israel-Lubavitch, 1940–1945: Actively Responding to Khurbn," in *Bearing Witness to the Holocaust, 1939–1989*, ed. Alan L. Berger (Lewiston, Maine: Edwin Mellen, 1991), pp. 141–62; and "[Rabbi] Menachem Mendel Schneersohn's Response to the Holocaust," *Modern Judaism* (2013), pp. 1–37.
   2. Rabbi Michael Seligsohn's three-volume commentary (5742 and 5744/1982 and 1984), has demonstrated the rich web of allusions that run through *Hayom yom*'s daily teachings, the day's specific learning in Chumash, Tehillim, and Tanya, and the broader range of the Chabad Rebbes' discourses and teachings. Rabbi Seligsohn also speculates on a number of thematic patterns in *Hayom yom* in his class. Rabbi Michoel Seligson, "The Hidden Treasures of 'Hayom Yom,'" International Conference of Shluchos, 2011, Shevat 23, 5771 [2011], CD GPO6. I'm concerned almost solely with *Hayom yom*'s intersection with the Holocaust. R. Seligsohn briefly alludes to this intersection in "The Hidden Treasures of 'Hayom Yom.'" He suggests that the Rebbe chose *Hayom yom*'s entry for Tevet 21, a teaching of the Ba'al Shem Tov that encountering water is a *siman bracha* (sign of blessing), to coincide with the birthday of Rebbetzin Sheina Hornstein—the purpose being to convey a wish of blessing to her at a time when her precarious fate in wartime Warsaw was still unknown. Powerfully suggestive as this example is, R. Seligsohn does not address in other entries or more generally the Holocaust's influence on *Hayom yom*.

The more recent commentary by Rabbi Shmuel Raskin, *Hayom yom Hamevuor* (Brooklyn: Kehot, 2016), while explicitly linking *Hayom yom* to the Holocaust, does not pursue general implications for understanding the role of *Hayom yom* as a calendar. Another recent article (by an unnamed author), "Hayom Yom: The Chossid's Calendar," gives substantial information on the postprinting history of the calendar book. But it does not refer to the historical importance of the publication date. "Hayom Yom: The Chossid's Calendar," *A Chassidisher Derher* 37 (Kislev 5776 [2016]), pp. 38–47.

3. The date was also innovative in that it broke with astronomical phenomena—such as the beginning of a lunar month or solar year—in determining a starting point.

4. Rabbi Sholem DovBer Levin, *Toldos Chabad b"Artzot HaBrith*; Rabbi Seligson also refers to the Pesach 5703 date. Rabbi Michoel Seligson, "The Hidden Treasures of 'Hayom Yom.'"

5. I use the name "Rabbi Menachem (Schneersohn)" because that is how he is referred to on the title page of the first edition of *Hayom yom*. If I used the name "Rabbi Schneersohn," he could be confused with his father-in-law, the Rebbe Rayaatz, who shared the same last name.

6. See Rabbi Sholem Dov Butman, *The Rebbe in Paris* (Hebrew) (Jerusalem: Hechal Menachem, 2015).

7. See Yosef Y. Kaminetsky, *Days in Chabad: Historic Events in the Dynasty of Chabad-Lubavitch*, trans. Yosef Cohen (Brooklyn: Kohut, 2005), Elul 2, 5703/1942, pp.2 –3; and Marcheshvan 25, 5703/1942—the dates when Rebbetzin Sheina and Rabbi Menachem Mendel Horenstein were respectively determined to have perished. The initial English translation of *Hayom yom*, entitled *From Day to Day* (1988), notes these sad events in the margin next to the date. The most recent English translation, *Tackling Life's Tasks* (2010), refers to the murder of Rebbetzin Sheina in the introduction.

8. Rabbi Chaim Miller, *Turning Judaism Outward: A Biography of the Rebbe, Menachem Mendel Schneersohn* (New York: Kol Menachem, 2014), p. 377.

9. One of Rabbi Menachem's two brothers, Dov Ber, lived in Yekatrinoslav, and—notes current editions of *Hayom yom* in the section "Genealogy and Brief Notes"—"was murdered during the Holocaust by the Nazi rulers of the town of Igren near Yekatrinoslav." More generally, the Rebbe spoke of losing "very close and dear relatives such as a grandmother, brother, cousins and others in the Holocaust, *haichi dami.*" These words appear in the postscript to the Rebbe's 5744 (1984) letter to a child of Holocaust survivors. My thanks to Rabbi Dovid Ziklikowski, chabad.org archivist, for sending a copy of the letter, "archived in the secretary's file."

10. "Over the last nine months we have warned the Jewish world in our monthly journal HK [*Hakriya v'hakedusha*] that we were experiencing the Hevlei mashiah [birth pangs of the Messiah]." Yosef Yitshak Schneersohn, "Kol kore fun'm lubavitsher rabin," *Hakriya y'hakedusha*, vol. 1, no. 9 (1941), pp. 15–16.

11. *Days in Chabad*, Iyar 2. For further contemporary pronouncements, see ed., "Ah spetsieler sefer torah mit velkhen tsu mekabel panim zayn mashiah tsidkenu," *Hakriya y'hakedusha*, vol. 1, no. 14 (1941), p. 12; and "Va'ad sefer ha'torah le'kabbalat penei mashiah," *Hakriya y'hakedusha*, vol. 3, no. 25 (1942), p. 8.

12. Aimed at a wartime deadline, the Torah scroll came to be finished over twenty-five years later, in 1970 (Shevat 9, 5740). Rabbi Menachem, having succeeded his father-in-law as the leader of the movement, celebrated its completion with great joy and fanfare. See *Days in Chabad*, Shevat 9.

13. Republished under the title *From Day to Day: Young Scholar's Daily Calendar and Encyclopedia*, ed. Shalom Ber Schapiro (Brooklyn: Nissan Mindel Publications, 2013). For background on its publication, see Rabbi Levine, *Toldos*, pp. 316–18. There were at least two earlier reprints, including one as late as 5733/1973. A recent overview of the *Young Scholar's Pocket Calendar* project includes a page from the holograph. "U'Moshe haya royeh," *Tichayainu* 7 (Nisan 11, 5777 [2017]), pp. 32–40.

14. Schapiro, p. 4.

15. Schapiro, p. 79.

16. To be sure, a regimen of daily Talmud learning linked to the Jewish calendar—the Daf Yomi—had been launched by Rabbi Meir Shapiro almost twenty years earlier, in 1923. But this program, while making use of the Jewish calendar, did not, as far as I am aware, orchestrate a calendar of its own.

17. Cecil Roth, *A Jewish Book of Days* (London: E. Goldston ltd., 1931).

18. Roth, "Introduction."

19. Letter, *Igros Kodesh*, vol. 7, p. 231.

20. Simchas Torah, 5697, *Sichos HaShavuah*, 5696–5705, p. 199.

21. It is not only casual readers that miss the fact that "Today is the Day" is a calculated response to the wartime ordeal of European Jewry. Recent biographers of Rabbi Menachem Schneersohn (aka the Lubavitcher Rebbe) also overlook this crucial aspect. For example, in *Turning Judaism Outward*, Rabbi Chaim Miller generally downplays the context of the Holocaust, and does so completely in his brief discussion of *Hayom yom*. Instead, he views the move of the Chabad leaders to America as the catalyst for what he perceives to be the calendar's "sound bite" format, since in America, "there was a need for information that was more accessible." See Rabbi Chaim Miller, *Turning Judaism Outward: A Biography of the Rebbe, Menachem Mendel Schneersohn* (New York: Kol Menachem, 2014), p. 159. Rabbi Adin Steinsaltz refers to a changing world and threatening situation but does not associate the calendar with the Holocaust. See Rabbi Adin Even-Israel Steinsaltz, *My Rebbe* (Jerusalem: Maggid, 2014), pp. 54–55. In his recent Hebrew biography, Rabbi Schneur Zalman Ruderman acknowledges the importance of *Hayom yom* but again does not link it to the Holocaust. See *Had Bidra: Biography and Chapters from the Life of the Lubavitcher Rebbe* (Hebrew) (Jerusalem: Toratchabad, 5776), p. 245. Chronicling Rabbi Menachem's daunting schedule of tasks in 1943, Joseph Telushkin indicates that *Hayom yom* was Rabbi Menachem's "first book" and offers a short characterization of its contents. But Telushkin does not draw a connection to its fraught time of publication. Joseph Telushkin, *Rebbe: The Life and Teachings of Rabbi Menachem M. Schneersohn* (New York: Harper Collins, 2014), p. 475.

22. For the Piaseczner Rebbe—Rabbi Kalonymous Kalman Shapira—see his collection of derashot given during the war, entitled *Esh Kodesh* (Jerusalem: Vaad Chasidei Piaseczno, 1960). On his strategy of not explicitly referring to the enemy or other aspects of the war by name, see Nehemia Polen, *The Holy Fire: The Teachings of Rabbi Kalonymus Shapira, the Rebbe of the Warsaw Ghetto* (Lanham, MD: Jason Aronson, 1994). For the wartime discourses of the Rebbe Raya"tz, see *Sefer Hama'amarim*. They have been translated into English under the title *Chassidic Discourses* and can be found online at http://www.chabad.org/library /article_cdo/aid/82895/jewish/Chassidic-Discourses.htm.

23. The larger type in the original Yiddish is reproduced in the English translation by the use of capital letters. From an address given to Young Israel, Tammuz 11, 5702. *Igros Kodesh*, vol. 6, p. 372.

24. Letter to Rabbi Benyaminson, Iyar 26, 5702 (May 13, 1942), *Igros Kodesh*, vol. 6, p. 340.

25. Letter, Elul 3, 5702 (August 16, 1942).

26. Letter to Rabbi Cooper, Sivan 18, 5701 (summer 1941). See Igros Kodesh, vol. 5, p. 388.

27. Letter, Tammuz 18, 5699 (summer 1939), *Igros Kodesh*, vol. 4, pp. 540–41.

28. One detail is perhaps in need of explanation: Why did Rabbi Menachem choose as the day of this teaching the eighteenth of Tammuz rather than the seventeenth, which officially ushers in the period of *Be"en hamitzarim*? What is the special merit of the eighteenth? It is because on this day the Jews began the process of making amends. The seventeenth of Tammuz marks the breaking of the first set of tablets. On the eighteenth, according to Rashi's commentary, Moses ascended the mountain to pray for God's forgiveness. The eighteenth, in other words, launched the actual effort of Moses and the Jews to make amends for the sin of idol worship. This effort resulted in God's reconciliation with the Jews and climaxed—after the ten weeks and the ten Days of Repentance—with the giving of the second set of tablets on Yom Kippur.. Hence it was on the eighteenth of Tammuz that the effort to draw close to God with a new level of intimacy actually commenced.

29. Hence the calendar's methodical listing of each day's quota of Torah study, psalm recital, and Chasidic learning, setting out a regimen that would help enable one to do one's share.

Epilogue

Eᴀᴄʜ ᴏғ ᴛʜᴇ calendars (or diaries) embodies a story, with a distinctive origin, mode of expression, and saga of wartime and postwar survival. Yet, taken together, the phenomenon of wartime Jewish calendars, the significance of which has been overlooked by virtually every stripe of Holocaust researcher, also leads to several observations. The fact that women crafted a number of calendars carries its own significance. Lest one think that tracking time with fidelity fell to men more than women, the Auschwitz calendars, together with those produced by women in hiding or in other camps, lay the idea to rest.[1] The supposition that fashioning a calendar may be more of a man's domain has a certain persuasiveness, since the skill required to calculate the basic features of a Jewish calendar usually demands a high level of yeshiva-acquired knowledge. But the calendar is not a tool of the elite.[2] All adult Jews have the same obligation to observe the Sabbath and festive days and to distinguish them from the ordinary weekdays. Hence the experience of women in this regard was equal to that of men.[3] As we have seen, the education of girls, at least in some instances, followed from this belief. Such an educational premise shaped the Munich-based lessons given by Julius Kissinger that provided Sophie Sohlberg with the equipment to fashion a calendar and with a deep enough sense of responsibility toward it that she would, even or especially in Auschwitz, undertake the task. As we have seen, she was not the only one.

Most wartime calendars chronicle the same year, 5705 (1944–45)—the year that turned out to be the last one of the war. Such a finding makes a kind of artifactual sense. There may have been more calendars for earlier years, but they were likely destroyed, together with the individuals who fashioned them. Even for those Jews able to survive, the likelihood of preserving an artifact such as a calendar was not good (Sophie Sohlberg's first Auschwitz calendar, crafted for the year 5704 and stolen after the year had run its course, is a case in point; so are Rabbi Avigdor's repeatedly made and repeatedly destroyed calendrical productions). Moreover, most calendars have a built-in obsolescence. Once they have fulfilled their purpose of tracking time for the designated year, they have little practical value. It would make more sense than not to discard it, as one does in normal times, at least with most calendars. In contrast, the calendars for 5705 were still operative when the war ended; May 8, 1945, the official end of hostilities, was the twenty-fifth day of the month of Iyar, so just over four months remained in the Jewish calendar for 5705. There would be every reason to hold on to such a calendar for at least the rest of the year.[4]

Richly complex artifacts in their own right, the three dozen or so wartime calendars establish Jewish time and culture as an important facet of the Jewish Holocaust victim's wartime experience, even in a setting where one might have least expected to find it. This significantly alters the paradigm of research as it currently stands, whereby the Jewish calendar most often comes into view, if at all, through the perverse use made of it by the perpetrators. Further, the fact that Joseph Czarnecki omits Jewish calendars from his catalog of efforts to mark time in Auschwitz is arguably a symptom of a more generally skewed perception. This perspective views the Holocaust's Jewish victims as having been stripped of their Jewish world at the same time as they were stripped of their clothing or other possessions. These losses were surely grievous, causing the Jews who suffered them anguish and hardship. But the victims' Jewish world did not simply go the way of the items that were plundered. It remained more or less steadfast, in some cases in fragments or snatches, in other cases whole cloth.[5] In literary and cultural studies especially, the mistaken scholarly focus on the "muselman," the so-called walking dead, as representative of Jewish victims, likely reinforces this error. Such a misguided emphasis puts into the foreground the image of prisoners who could do nothing more than attend to basic needs—if even that.[6] But for many prisoners, basic needs also included Jewish cultural and religious practices, in whatever modified or abridged form they could be observed.

To reinstate the victims' Jewish world also leads to a more general reevaluation of scholarship on time and the Holocaust. The presumptions that have guided approaches to the topic may be based on the value placed on "rupture" over that of "continuity."[7] In this light, the more the events or episodes of the Holocaust are viewed as having created a rupture with the past, the greater their significance. In contrast, continuity simply brings more of the same. If this is indeed the case, then Jewish culture and religious observance, including the fashioning of calendars designed to inspire and guide such observance, would be unlikely to receive much attention, since they point to continuity with previous life.

The Jewish calendar, moreover, may be the symbol of continuity par excellence, as weekday follows weekday, one Sabbath follows another, the festivals of the spring follow those of the previous fall. The Jewish calendar maintained a continuity with both the near and distant past and, more audaciously, projected a seamless future wherein Sabbaths and festivals would predictably arrive at their appointed times. This familiar interlocking grid of weekday and sacred days was envisioned by the Jewish calendars, even when death and destruction were the order of the day. By way of wartime calendars created, circulated, and preserved, *continuity* in the midst of the Holocaust also receives its due.

According to tradition, the commandment for the Jewish nation to make a calendar came at a pivotal moment in history. The Jews had been enslaved in Egypt for several hundred years. The oppressor's grip had been steadily loosened and the people were told how to prepare for their departure. The first step was to fashion a calendar.

Why was such a step necessary? A sixteenth-century sage, Rabbi Ovadia Sforno, has given one of the most compelling explanations. As slaves, the Jews were forced to do the bidding of others. Carrying out the will of "others," the Egyptian slave owners, meant that time was lived as the overseers dictated. In Sforno's words, time "did not belong to you [the Jewish people] but you rather had to work for others and fulfill their will." To be a slave was to live without a calendar of one's own, to live without a way to mark time in one's own idiom. For Sforno, the fact that time "did not belong to you" defined Jewish slavery in Egypt.

The first nod toward freedom, the making of a calendar, changed the equation. From that moment forward, time belonged to the Jewish people. In Sforno's striking formulation, "Henceforth the months [of the year] shall be yours, to do with them as you wish." Calendar making was thus both a foundation and reflection of the Jews' new reality as a redeemed people. To plot time's sacred course gave the Jews a key to freedom, destiny, and identity.

During the Holocaust, the desire to track Jewish time may well have issued forth because making a Jewish calendar demonstrated that time belonged—continued to belong—to the Jews. Hence, they crafted Jewish calendars knowing that such calendars, no matter how rudimentary they might be, bore within them the secret of freedom, the pitched determination to refuse enslavement of the Jews' innermost selves. Every calendar recapitulated the original impulse to measure time to a Jewish standard, to make graphic the fact that time continued to belong to the Jews. Admittedly, calendars convey this in an understated, implicit way. Columns and boxes, numbers and names of months, seem all too commonplace to be weighted with such meaning. Yet in these years of terror and oppression, the calendar showed itself for what it really was: a blueprint of irrefutable freedom.

Notes

1. Other women who composed wartime Jewish calendars include Adela Levisson (née De Beer), wife of Rabbi Avraham Salomon Levisson, who, we recall, fashioned a calendar for the year 5705 (1944–45) while in hiding in the north of Holland with her oldest child; Golda Finkler, the daughter of the Radoschitz rebbe, who, imprisoned at a labor camp in Leipzig, composed a calendar to help her fellow prisoners observe the Jewish holidays. See Kaja Finkler and Golda Finkler, *Lives Lived and Lost: East European History before, during, and after World War II as Experienced by an Anthropologist and Her Mother*, foreword by Michael Berenbaum (Boston: Academic Studies Press, 2012); and Yechiel Granatstein, *One Jew's Power, One Jew's Glory: The Life of Rav Yitzchak Shumuel Eliyahu Finkler the Rebbe*

of Radoschitz in the Ghetto and Concentration Camp (Jerusalem: Feldheim, 1991). Though Finkler's calendar is likely as interesting as any of its counterparts I have commented on at greater length, I felt constrained by the fact that only a portion of the calendar is available for viewing. In the Parschnitz labor camp, "a Rabbi's daughter" made a Jewish calendar in January 1944, and so, reports Laura Hollander, "we kept the *Shabbes* and holidays for all [with all? for the sake of all?] the neighboring camps." From the oral testimony of Laura Hollander (née Jacobowicz), *Amcha: An Oral Testament of the Holocaust,* ed. Saul Friedman (University Press of America, 1979), p. 415. And as we mentioned earlier, Bertha Ferdiger-Salz reports her extraordinary meeting in Bergen-Belsen with an old dying women reciting "Gott fun Avraham" who had each day made a knot in her dress, thereby creating a remarkable improvised calendar. And because the "dress" that served as the medium for the calendar was, after all, a specifically women's garment, this humble calendar, used far too briefly, could be said to be a women's calendar through and through.

2. In this light, one might take note of Elisheva Carlebach's thoughtful comments on a "two-tiered system"—an elite in contrast to a general public—"to disseminate knowledge" concerning calendars. It is not clear to me, however, how this model applies to periods of crisis such as I have been dealing with in my study. See Elisheva Carlebach, *Palaces of Time*, pp. 6–7.

3. Indeed, cultural and physiological factors may have heightened women's sensitivity to issues of tracking time. See Jane Caplan, "Gender and the Concentration Camp," in *Concentration Camps in Nazi Germany: The New Histories*, eds. Nikolaus Wachsmann and Jane Caplan (New York: Routledge, 2010), pp. 86–87.

4. Sophie Sohlberg says that there were three reasons she held on to the first calendar she fashioned even after it became obsolete: (1) possessions were so few that every one was precious, (2) she had received as a birthday present the notebook in which the calendar was made, and (3) she herself had written it.

5. See my discussion above of Auschwitz, the Auschwitz calendars, and the references to primary and secondary sources on Jewish religious observance in the camp.

6. For one of the most influential formulations of this skewed perception, see Giorgio Agamben, *Remnants of Auschwitz: The Witness and the Archive*, trans. Daniel Heller-Roazen (New York: Zone Books, 2008), p. 164. "Let us, indeed, posit Auschwitz, that to which it is not possible to bear witness; and let us also posit the *Muselmann* [sic] as the absolute impossibility of bearing witness . . ." Primo Levi's troubling comments on the Muselmanner—"'Muslims,' the submerged, the complete witnesses, the ones whose deposition would have a general significance" (i 'mussulmanni,' i sommersi, i testimony integrali, coloro la cui deposizione avrebbe avuto significato generale)—serve as the basis for Agamben's thesis. See Primo Levi, *The Drowned and the Saved*, trans. Raymond Rosenthal (New York: Vintage, 1989), pp. 83–84. Joseph Farrell examines Levi's "strange" preoccupation with the phenomenon in "The Strange Case of the Muselmänner in Auschwitz," in *New Perspectives on Primo Levi*, eds. Riso Sodi and Millicent Marcus (New York: Palgrave Macmillan, 2011). Historians have been far less prone to see the so-called "musselmanner" as a pivotal dimension of the Holocaust, likely because unfortunate prisoners of this sort made up such a small minority of the victims overall—and most were murdered within a short time of capture or imprisonment. For a more general formulation of rupture being at the essence of the Holocaust, see Alon Confino, *Germany as a Culture of Remembrance* (Chapel Hill: University of North Carolina Press, 2017), p. 233.

7. I am grateful to Rakhmiel Pelz for ongoing discussions on this point.

Appendix 1: Inventory of Wartime Jewish Calendars

Copies of calendars highlighted in bold survived the war and are in my possession; those listed in regular script indicate calendars brought to my attention but that I have not seen a copy of.

Ghettos

Rabbi Tzvi Elimelekh Talmud (Lublin) 5703
Zvi Liberman (Zurawno, Poland) 5702–3
Lodz 5701–5704
Lvov (Lemberg) 1942a
Lvov (Lemberg) 1942b
Shimon Pinkesfeld (Lvov) 5702
Warsaw ("tiny flawed calendars"; Rabbi Huberband) 5702
Kovno Jewish Police 1943

Labor Camps

Rabbi David Kahane (Janowska)
Golda Finkler (Hasag-Leipzig) 5705
"Rabbi's Daughter" (Parschnitz)
Yosef Meir Wenrov / Shalom Weinrov (Vologda) Adar 5701–Tishrei 5702
Moshe Mendel Herstik (Aninoasa, Romania)
Shifra Yudasin (Leipzig)

Theresienstadt

Rabbi Asher Berlinger 5704, 5705
***Luach Katan* 5703**
Hilde Zadikow 1943

Concentration Camps

Sophie Lowenstein Sohlberg (Auschwitz) 5704, **5705**
Anneliese Borinski (Auschwitz) 5705
Rabbi Tzvi Elimelekh Talmud (Maidanek) 5704
Rabbi Yitzchak Avigdor (Buchenwald) 5705
Emil Neumann (Bergen-Belsen) 5705
Anonymous (Bergen-Belsen) 5705
Rabbi Yisrael Simcha Zelmann (Westerbork) 5704
Simon Azaria Colthof (Bergen-Belsen) 5705

Holland

Rabbi Yehoshua Neuwirth 5703, 5704
Rabbi Shimon Hammelburg 5703
Rabbi Avrohom Prins 5704
Tsewie Herschel 1942
Adela Levisson 5705

Belgium

Rabbi Menachem Mendel Kirschboim 5702
Jacqui Israel Offen 5704

France

Nephtali Grunewald (with prefaces by Rabbis Hirschler and Deutsch) 5702, 5703, 5704, 5705
A. Jacobsen (Gurs) 5702

Poland

Rabbi Shlomo Yosef Scheiner 5703, 5704
"Kodak" 5704
Leyb Rochman

Appendix 2: Months of the Jewish Calendar Year, with Their Holidays and Fast Days

Regular year (353–55 days)

Jewish Months	Gregorian Month(s)	Number of Days	Holidays and Fast Days
Tishrei	Sept/Oct	30	Rosh Hashana, Fast of Gedalia, Yom Kippur, Sukkoth, Shemini Atzereth, Simchat Torah
Marcheshvan	Oct/Nov	29 or 30	Beha"b series of three fasts (Mon/Thurs/Mon)
Kislev	Nov/Dec	29 or 30	Chasidic celebration of the nineteenth of Kislev Chanukah
Tevet	Dec/Jan	29	Chanukah Asera b'Tevet (fast of the tenth)
Shevat	Jan/Feb	30	Tu b'Shevat (fifteenth day of Shevat)
Adar	Feb/March	29	Fast of Esther Purim
Nisan	March/April	30	Passover, Omer count
Iyar	April/May	29	Omer count, Lag b'Omer (thirty-third day of the count) Beha"b series of three fasts (Mon/Thurs/Mon)
Sivan	May/June	30	Shavuot
Tammuz	June/July	29	Fast of the seventeenth
Menachem Av	July/August	30	Tisha b'Av (fast of the ninth) Tu b'Av (celebration of the fifteenth)
Elul	August/Sept	29	Selichot

Leap Year with an Added Month of Adar II (383–85 days)

Jewish Month	Gregorian Month(s)	Number of Days	Holidays and Fast Days
Tishrei	Sept/Oct	30	Rosh Hashana, Fast of Gedalia, Yom Kippur, Sukkoth, Shemini Atzereth, Simchat Torah
Marcheshvan	Oct/Nov	29 or 30	Beha"b series of three fasts (Mon/Thurs/Mon)
Kislev	Nov/Dec	29 or 30	Chasidic celebration of the nineteenth of Kislev Chanukah
Tevet	Dec/Jan	29	Chanukah Asera b'Tevet (fast of the tenth)
Shevat	Jan/Feb	30	Tu b'Shevat (fifteenth day of Shevat)
Adar I	Feb/March	30	Purim Katan (the "small" Purim)
Adar II	March/April	29	Fast of Esther Purim
Nisan	April/May	30	Passover, Omer count
Iyar	May/June	29	Omer count, Lag b'Omer (thirty-third day of the count) Beha"b series of three fasts (Mon/Thurs/Mon)
Sivan	June/July	30	Shavuot
Tammuz	July/August	29	Fast of the seventeenth
Menachem Av	August/Sept	30	Tisha b'Av (fast of the ninth) Tu b'Av (celebration of the fifteenth)
Elul	Sept/Oct	29	Selichot

Appendix 3: English-Language Rendering of Rabbi Scheiner Calendar

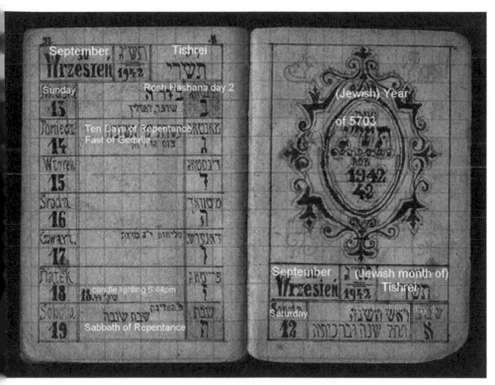

Fig. A3.1: The first page of Rabbi Shlomo Yosef Scheiner's calendar for 5703 (1942–43; see fig. 4.1), composed in hiding in Debowka, Poland, is here glossed with English translation.

Glossary

Beha"b A series of three optional fast days (Monday, Thursday, Monday) following Passover and Sukkoth.

Candle-lighting time The hour and minute at which Shabbat or holidays begin. The entry of the holy day is marked by lighting candles.

Chanukah Eight-day holiday that begins on Kislev 25 and celebrates the rededication of the ancient Jerusalem Temple.

Chasidim Orthodox Jews spiritually bound to a master or rebbe and guided in practice by the mystical precepts of Chasidic teaching.

Chasidism A movement of joyous piety initiated in eastern Europe in the eighteenth century. Decimated in the Holocaust, the movement has been rebuilt throughout the world.

Chasidei Ger The largest group of prewar Polish Chasidim. The postwar center was established in Jerusalem.

Chumash A volume containing the Five Books of Moses (the Pentatuch), usually accompanied by an Aramaic translation and glossed with classical rabbinic commentaries.

Erev Generally, the day leading up to Shabbat or a holiday; occasionally the actual nighttime thereof.

Fast days Dawn to dusk: Tishrei 3 (Fast of Gedalia); Tevet 10; Adar 13 (Fast of Esther); Tammuz 17. Dusk to dusk: Av 9; Tishrei 10 (Yom Kippur). See also *BeH"ab*.

Gregorian calendar The Christian/civil (solar-based) calendar in use throughout much of the world today, first issued by Pope Gregory in 1582.

Julian calendar The version of the Christian/civil calendar that preceded the Gregorian and that continued to hold sway in some eastern European countries during the Holocaust.

Kiddush levana A monthly blessing of the moon.

Lag b'Omer Iyar 18, the thirty-third day of the Omer count, a day of rejoicing

Leap year In Hebrew referred to as *shana miuberet*; seven out of nineteen years add an extra month, called Adar II, in order to align the lunar calendar with the solar year.

Luach A calendar.

Lubavitch Chasidim Also known as Chabad, the group's original base in White Russia was shifted to Brooklyn during World War II.

Matzah Unleavened bread ritually eaten on Passover.

Menorah A ritual candelabra lit in the ancient temples; a personal candelabra lit to celebrate the festival of Chanukah.

Megilah/Megiloth The five biblical books of Song of Songs, Ruth, Lamentations, Kohelet, and Esther; on specific sacred days, these are read from parchment scrolls.

Messiah The redeemer who, according to Jewish teaching, will announce a new era of peace and will serve as Israel's king and foremost teacher.

Molad "Birth" of the new moon, which signals the onset of the new month.

Omer count A special ritual of counting the forty-nine days and seven weeks from Passover to Shavuot.

Parsha hashavuah The weekly Torah reading drawn from the Five Books of Moses.

Passover Eight-day spring pilgrimage festival observed from the fifteenth to the twenty-second of Nisan celebrating the exodus of the Jews from slavery in ancient Egypt.

Purim One-day spring holiday celebrated on the fourteenth (or in Jerusalem, the fifteenth) of Adar to commemorate the thwarting of an edict of annihilation in ancient Persia.

Rebbe Chasidic master, also known as Admor or Tzadik.

Rosh Hashana The onset of the new Jewish year.

Rosh Chodesh The onset of the new Jewish month.

Shabbat/Shabes The Jewish Sabbath, a weekly celebration observed from Friday at dusk to Saturday at dusk.

Shavuot Pilgrimage festival observed on the sixth and seventh of Sivan, to celebrate the giving of the Torah on Mount Sinai, fifty days after the exodus from ancient Egypt.

Shimini Atzeret Eighth day of Sukkoth, and also an independent holiday that features a prayer for abundant rainfall.

Shofar Ram's horn obligatorily blown on Rosh Hashana and customarily blown during the preceding month of Elul.

Siddur Prayer book.

Shema Yisrael (Hear Israel) A central prayer affirming God's oneness and supreme authority.

Simchas Torah "The Rejoicing of the Torah"; one-day festival immediately following Sukkoth, on which the weekly ritual reading of the Torah is annually concluded and begun anew; observed with dancing and processions with the Torah scrolls.

Sukkah Booth erected to dwell in during the holiday of Sukkoth.

Sukkoth A fall pilgrimage holiday observed for eight days from the fifteenth through twenty-second of Tishrei.

Tallit Fringed garment worn by Jewish men under or over a shirt; or, fringed prayer shawl worn by men during morning prayers.

Tanach The twenty-four books in the Jewish Bible.

Tehillim Psalms.

Tekufah/Tekufoth Seasons.

Torah Traditional Jewish sacred teachings.

Tzizit Fringes worn on a tallit.

Yahrzeit Anniversary of a Jewish person's passing, observed according to the Jewish calendar date.

Yom Kippur Day of Atonement; final day of the ten days of repentance that begin with Rosh Hashana.

Selective Bibliography

Calendar: History, Sociology, Anthropology

Allen, Thomas M. *A Republic in Time: Temporality and Social Imagination in Nineteenth-Century America*. Chapel Hill: University of North Carolina Press, 2008.

Blackburn, Bonnie, and Leofranc Holford-Strevens. *The Oxford Companion to the Year*. Oxford: Oxford University Press, 1999.

Brown, Alyson. "'Doing Time': The Extended Present of the Long-Term Prisoner." *Time and Society* 7 (1998).

Dohrn-van Rossem, Gerhard. *History of the Hour: Clocks and Modern Temporal Orders*. Chicago: University of Chicago Press, 1996.

Dudziak, Mary. "Law, War, and the History of Time." *California Law Review* 98 (2010): 1669–1710.

———. *War Time: An Idea, Its History, Its Consequences*. New York: Oxford University Press, 2012.

Greenhouse, Carol. *A Moment's Notice: Time Politics across Cultures*. Ithaca: Cornell University Press, 1996.

Hughes, Diane Owen, and Thomas Trautmann, eds. *Time: Histories and Ethnologies*. Ann Arbor: University of Michigan Press, 1995.

Hunt, Lynn. *Measuring Time, Making History*. Budapest: Central European University Press, 2008.

Kern, Stephen. *The Culture of Time and Space, 1880–1918*. Cambridge, MA: Harvard University Press, 2003

McCarthy, Molly. *The Accidental Diarist*. Chicago: University of Chicago Press, 2013.

McCrossen, Alexis. *Holy Day, Holiday: The American Sunday*. Ithaca: Cornell University Press, 2000.

Ogle, Vanessa. *The Global Transformation of Time: 1870–1950*. Cambridge, MA: Harvard University Press, 2015.

Richards, E. G. *Mapping Time: The Calendar and Its History*. Oxford: Oxford University Press, 1998.

Rosenberg, Emily. *A Date Which Will Live: Pearl Harbor in American Memory*. Durham: Duke University Press, 2003

Schleifer, Ronald. *Modernism and Time: The Logic of Abundance in Literature, Science and Culture 1880–1930*. Cambridge: Cambridge University Press, 2000.

Smith, Mark M. *Mastered by the Clock: Time, Slavery, and Freedom in the American South*. Chapel Hill: University of North Carolina Press, 1997.

Wells, Cheryl A. *Civil War Time: Temporality and Identity in America, 1861–1865*, Athens, GA: University of Georgia Press, 2005.

Zerubavel, Evitar. *Hidden Rhythms: Schedules and Memory in Social Life*. Chicago: University of Chicago Press, 1981.

———. *Time Maps: Collective Memory and the Social Shape of the Past.* Chicago: University of Chicago Press, 2003.
———. *The Seven Day Circle: The History and Meaning of the Week.* Chicago: University of Chicago Press, 1985.

Jewish Calendar: Conception, Evolution, Persecution

Classic Sources

Babylonian Talmud:
Tractate Rosh Hashana
Tractate Sandhedrin
Rambam, Hilchot Kiddush Hachodesh, Mishnah Torah
Tur Orach Chaim, section 427–28

Contemporary Commentary

Bloch, Abraham. *Day by Day in Jewish History: Chronology and Calendar of Historic Events.* New York: Ktav, 1983.
Bushwick, Rabbi Nathan. *Understanding the Jewish Calendar.* New York: Moznaim, 1989.
Carlebach, Elisheva. *Palaces of Time: Jewish Calendar and Culture in Early Modern Europe.* Cambridge, MA: Harvard University Press, 2011.
Feinstein, Rabbi David. *The Jewish Calendar : Its Structure and Laws.* Brooklyn: Mesorah, 2003.
Finkin, Jordan D. *An Inch or Two of Time: Time and Space in Jewish Modernisms.* College Park, PA: Penn State University Press, 2015.
Goldberg, Sylvie Anne. *Clepsydra: Essay on the Plurality of Time in Judaism.* Stanford, CA: Stanford University Press, 2016.
Greenberg, Irving. *The Jewish Way: Living the Holidays.* New York: Touchstone, 1988.
Handelman, Don. *Models and Mirrors: Toward an Anthropology of Public Events.* Cambridge, Cambridge University Press, 1990.
"HaLuach HaShana." *Encyclopedia Talmudit.* Vol. 36. Jerusalem, Yad Herzog, 2016.
Kaye, Lynn, *Time in the Babylonian Talmud*, Cambridge: Cambridge University Press, 2018
Roskies, David. *Against the Apocalypse: Responses to Catastrophe in Modern Jewish Culture.* Cambridge, MA: Harvard University Press, 1984.
Roth, Cecil. *A Jewish Book of Days.* London: Edward Goldston, 1931.
Stern, Sacha. *Calendar and Community: A History of the Jewish Calendar, 2nd Century BCE–10th Century CE.* Oxford: Oxford University Press, 2001

Holocaust, Time and the Calendar

Avigdor, Rabbi Isaac. "The Camp Calendar of Buchenwald." In *Faith After the Flames.* 95–106. New Haven, Rodgiva, 2005.
Czarnecki, Joseph. *Last Traces: The Lost Art of Auschwitz.* New York: Macmillan, 1989.
Eliach, Yaffa. *Hasidic Tales of the Holocaust.* New York; Vintage, 1982.
———. "Jewish Tradition in the Life of the Concentration-Camp Inmate." In *The Nazi Concentration Camps,*" edited by Y. Guttman and A. Saf. Jerusalem, Yad Vashem, 1984.
———. "Popular Jewish Religious Responses during the Holocaust and Its Aftermath." In *Jewish Perspectives on the Experience of Suffering,* edited by Shalom Carmy, 297–329. Northvale, NJ: Jason Aronson, , 1999.

————. "Primo Levi and His Concept of Time: Time of the Gun, Time of the Spirit." In *Memory and Mastery: Primo Levi as Writer and Witness*, edited by Roberta Kremer, 21–34. Albany: SUNY Press, 2001.

Eliav, Mordechai, *Ani Maamim*. Jerusalem: Mosad Ha Rav Kook, 1965.

Engel, David. "Resisting in Jewish Time." In *Daring to Resist: Jewish Defiance in the Holocaust*, edited by Yitzchak Mais. New York: Museum of Jewish Heritage, 2007.

Engelking, Barbara. *Holocaust and Memory*. Trans. Emma Harris. New York: Continuum, 2001.

Farbstein, Ester. *Hidden in Thunder: Law, Reflections, and Customs in the Time of the Holocaust*. Jerusalem: Mosad HaRav Kook, 2002 [Hebrew].

Garbarini, Alexandra. *Numbered Days: Diaries and the Holocaust*. New Haven: Yale University Press, 2006.

Grunewald, Jacquot. "Calendriers de la Resistance." *l'Arche* 498–99 (Sept. 1999).

Marrus, Michael. "Killing Time: Jewish Perceptions During the Holocaust." In *The Holocaust: History and Memory*, edited by S. Almog et al. Jerusalem: Yad Vashem, 2001.

Herzog, Pearl, "Purim Vinz," *Mishpacha* (Kolmus) (March 16, 2011).

Michman, Dan. *Holocaust Historiography: A Jewish Perspective*. London/Portland: Valentine Mitchell, 2003.

Miron, Guy, ed., "Jewish Time during the Shoah," *Bishveel HaZicharon* 28 (Kislev 5778/2017)

Patterson, David. *Along the Edge of Annihilation: The Collapse and Recovery of Life in the Holocaust Diary*. Seattle, University of Washington Press, 1999.

Preschel, Rabbi Tovia. "Calendars in the Theresienstadt Ghetto." *HaDoar* (5726/1966) [Hebrew].

————. "The French Jewish Calendar during the Shoah." *HaDoar* (5723/1962) [Hebrew].

————. "The Jewish Calendar in Belgium during the Shoah." *HaDoar* (5724/1963) [Hebrew].

Rachmani, Moriya. "Ritual Existence and the Preservation of Self-Identity in the Concentration Camps: Time, Body, and Objects." *American Imago* 73 (2016): 25–49.

Rosen, A. "Hidden Time: Calendar Consciousness on the Edge of Destruction." In *Hiding, Sheltering and Borrowing Identities: Avenues of Rescue During the Holocaust*, edited by Dan Michman. Jerusalem: Yad Vashem, 2018.

————. "The Languages of Time: Translating Calendar Dates in Holocaust Diaries." *Holocaust and Genocide Studies* 26 (2012).

————. "On Calendars and the Holocaust." *Jewish Action* 72:1 (2011).

————. "Today Is the Day: Reading between the Lines of the Lubavitcher Rebbe's Holocaust Era Calendar." *Hasidology*/Chabad.org (2012).

————. "Tracking Jewish Time in Auschwitz." *Yad Vashem Studies* 42.2 (2014).

Roskies, David. "Landkentenish: Yiddish Belles Lettres in the Warsaw Ghetto." In *Holocaust Chronicles*, edited by Robert Moses Shapiro. Hoboken, Ktav: NJ, 1999.

————. "1943: The Jewish World at Ground Zero." Unpublished Lecture, 2005.

Sofsky, Wolfgang. *The Order of Terror: The Concentration Camp*. Trans. William Templer. Princeton, NJ: Princeton University Press, 1996.

Wieviorka, Annette. "Deportation and Memory: Official History and the Rewriting of World War II." In *Thinking about the Holocaust*, edited by Alvin Rosenfeld. Bloomington: Indiana University Press, 1997.

Young, James. "When a Day Remembers." *History and Memory* 2 (1990): 54–75.

Index

ALAN ROSEN is the author or editor of twelve books on Holocaust literature, testimony, and history. Most recently he is author of *The Wonder of Their Voices: The 1946 Holocaust Interviews of David Boder*, editor of *Literature of the Holocaust*, and editor (with Steven T. Katz) of *Elie Wiesel: Jewish, Literary, and Moral Perspectives*. He lectures regularly at the International School for Holocaust Studies at Yad Vashem and other Holocaust study centers. His current writing focuses largely on the legacy of his teacher and mentor, Elie Wiesel. He is privileged to live in Jerusalem with his wife and children.

CPSIA information can be obtained
at www.ICGtesting.com
Printed in the USA
BVHW020902010319
541542BV00019B/153/P